T H E
ORTHODOX
UNION STORY

T H E
ORTHODOX
UNION STORY

A CENTENARY PORTRAYAL

SAUL BERNSTEIN

JASON ARONSON INC.
Northvale, New Jersey
Jerusalem

This book was set in 11 pt. Stempel Schneidler by Alabama Book Composition of Deatsville, Alabama.

10 9 8 7 6 5 4 3 2 1

Library of Congress Cataloging-in-Publication Data

Bernstein, Saul,
    The Orthodox Union story : a centenary portrayal / by Saul Bernstein.
       p.   cm.
    Includes bibliographical references and index.
    ISBN 0-7657-9953-7 (alk. paper). — ISBN 0-7657-9953-7 (pbk.)
    1. Union of Orthodox Jewish Congregations of America—History.
    2. Orthodox Judaism—United States—History. I. Title.
    BM205.U55B47   1997
    296.8′32′0973—dc21   97-14593

Manufactured in the United States of America. Jason Aronson Inc. offers books and cassettes. For information and catalog write to Jason Aronson Inc., 230 Livingston Street, Northvale, NJ 07647.

Contents

PART III: THE GROWING-UP YEARS

PART IV: ON A NEW PLATEAU

PART V: IN GREATER DIMENSION

Acknowledgments

Thanks are hereby accorded to the following publishers and other sources, all of whom kindly gave permission for the use of excerpted material appearing in this volume.

American Jewish Archives, for excerpts from *Unwritten History* by Captain N. Taylor Phillips, and from *A Jewish Peddler's Diary, 1842–43*, by Abraham Kohn, translated from the original German by Abram Vossen Goodman, appearing respectively in the Vol. I, No. 2 and Vol. 1, No. 3 issues of *American Jewish Archives.*

American Jewish Historical Society, for excerpts from *New York Chooses a Chief Rabbi*, by Abraham Jay Karp, published in *American Jewish Historical Society Publications*, Vol. XLIV, September 1954.

University Press of New England, for excerpts from *The Americanization of the Synagogue, 1820–1870*, by Abraham Jay Karp, copyright 1976 by Trustees of Brandeis University.

Columbia University Press, for excerpts from *An Old Faith in a New World*, by David and Tamar deSola Pool, copyright 1955 by Columbia University Press.

Holmes & Meir Publishers, Inc. for excerpts from *People Walk on Their Heads; Moses Weinberg's "Jews and Judaism in New York,"* edited and translated by Jonathan D. Sarna (New York: Holmes & Meir, 1982). Copyright by Jonathan D. Sarna.

The Jewish Publication Society of America, for excerpts from *Three Years in America*, translated by Charles Reznicoff from the original German by Israel Joseph Benjamin ("Benjamin II"), copyright 1956 by the Jewish Publication Society of America.

I hereby express my gratitude to Shulamith Z. Berger, Archivist of Yeshiva University Archives, for her ready cooperation in making available various items relevant to this book. Particularly valuable were the Central

Relief Committee Collection and the Benjamin and Pearl Koenigsberg Collection.

My warm thanks go to the following, whose readings of, and comments on, much of the manuscript of *The Orthodox Union Story* were of particular value: Moses I. Feuerstein, Rabbi Joseph Karasick, Rabbi Julius Berman, Professor Shimon Kwestel, Dr. Mandell I. Ganchrow, Donald Butler, Gerald Feldhamer, Michael Wimpfheimer (all officers of UOJCA), Rabbi Hyman Arbesfeld, Dr. Jacob Rothschild, Fred Friedman, Rabbi Bernard Rosenweig, Paul Schiller, and Dr. Elliot Bondi.

The word-processing of the manuscript of this book underwent successive stages by several hands. Tribute and deeply felt thanks are due to Sylvia Bordzuk, and Caroline Torge of Resumes, Etc. . . . Their expertise and ever-ready cooperation contributed much to the progress of the work. Sincere thanks, also, go to Adrianne Lefkowitz, Edith E. Krohn, Eva Holczer, and Patricia Kupecki.

I take this opportunity to express much appreciation to Rabbi Pinchas Stolper for his interest in the launching of this book. Rabbi Raphael Butler, executive vice-president of the Orthodox Union, too has given continued cooperation which has meant much to me.

Dedicated to the memories of SAMUEL C. AND MITZI FEUERSTEIN Exemplars of the Torah way in American Jewish Life.

The endeavors they led and the courses they sustained brought vigor and regeneration to America's Orthodox Jewish community.

Among the prime movers in the apochal rersurgence of Torah, Samuel C. and Mitzi Feuerstein left an imperishable heritage of courage and vision.

Saul Bernstein
2 Cheshvan 5757/October 15, 1996

Preface

The idea for this book came with the nearing one hundredth anniversary of the establishment of the Union of Orthodox Jewish Congregations of America. The approaching milestone could be seen as bearing promise of bringing a fresh perspective, among Jews in North America and beyond, on what has transpired throughout this era in the life and world of the Jewish people.

The upcoming anniversary, I felt, patently warranted the composition of a comprehensive presentation of the century-long course of the Union of Orthodox Jewish Congregations of America, never before undertaken. Through Rabbi Pinchas Stolper, then executive vice president and now senior executive of UOJCA, I suggested to the Union's officers that a qualified historical scholar or historian-writer be engaged to undertake the preparation of such work. The officers collectively approved the idea, but mindful of my long immersion in the life of the Orthodox Union passed the ball back to me with the charge: "No one could handle this project so knowledgeably as yourself." Being much engaged with other commitments, I was hesitant. The work involved, I knew, would be formidable; finally, however, I agreed to undertake the project.

Once proceeding with the task, I found that the original intent—to compose a more limited treatment of the topic—was impractical. It was impossible to adequately treat the subject without the most painstaking thoroughness, depth, and scope.

The preparation of *The Orthodox Union Story: A Centenary Portrayal* has presented difficulties beyond the purely literary. Throughout its existence, the Orthodox Union has been too busy with its many activities to concern itself with archives or the systematized retention of records. The research entailed, in the absence of a reference base, much pursuing of obscure trails and remote possibilities. And because the Union's work has been so wide and diverse in scope, much perplexity attended the selection of what, in view of an integrated presentation, should be included and what developments warranted particular emphasis.

The product of this process is now before you. I trust that the book's merits outweigh its shortcomings.

Introduction

For the American Torah community—adherents to the Jewish faith as handed down through the ages—the founding of the Union of Orthodox Jewish Congregations of America was a watershed event. From that time, Sivan 17, 5658 of the Jewish calendar (June 8, 1898) to now, that Union has been central to American Orthodox Jewry's response to the challenges of the times.

The centenary soon to be marked prompts focused awareness of historic forces at play. Too, there comes fresh realization that the launching of the Orthodox Union was itself an outgrowth of prior chapters of North American Jewish history—and that the Orthodox Torah-observant Jew in America of today is heir to what was striven for by their predecessors through a century—indeed, more than a century—of New-World, new-age life.

New World, new age—it is within the epochal sweep of what these terms signify that the story of the Union of Orthodox Jewish Congregations of America is framed. Seen in relation to the phenomenon that is America and the stupendous new-age refashioning of man and his world, the significance of this instrumentality is impressive. The labors of the organizational process, the continuous sequence of involved personalities, the ups and downs of effort and accomplishment, the varying levels of public impact and impress on daily life—all stand out as pregnant with meaning when recognized as addressed to a time and place so new to the experience of humanity, and so mighty in the shaping of human affairs.

For those loyal to the covenant made at Sinai to have ventured to rally in this setting, to have made place in this clime and time for the heritage of timeless Purpose—therein is to be seen an endeavor whose every detail, however seemingly prosaic, takes on deep consequence.

The world that presents itself at the eve of the centennial of the Union of Orthodox Jewish Congregations of America is far different a place from that of a century before. So, too, did that world differ from what had preceded it in turn, from whence emerged the experiences that, in the course of time, led to the birth of American Torah Jewry's banner-bearing force. Within a transformed global scene stands a transformed Jewish world. Of yesterday's Jewish world, nothing of its physical composition remains; what exists now is new-built. But the domain of the Jewish spirit—that, thank God, has endured: vital, fruitful, as living a force as ever.

The Torah of today is the Torah everlasting of all our yesterdays. The Torah way—the daily and seasonal observances, the code of living, the Siddur, the stored treasures of Torah learning—is, as in all the preceding generations, alive and well in the life of every Torah-loyal Jew.

In setting forth the course of the Union of Orthodox Jewish Congregations of America, varied aspects of its history and development will be considered. It is a panorama of continuous change, yet there is no need to treat theological change, as might be the case with accounts of other religious groups. Reflected in this book's pages are constant vast changes—in events, idea patterns, molding of new life circumstances to the Torah way, in application of tenets and principles to new situations, policy stance, mode of action, and expression. Withal, the basis of Jewish life (belief, practice, heritage)—this is unchanged and unchangeable.

Exploration of many sources and deep delving into records written and unwritten have gone into the preparation of this book. It is not, however, intended as a formal history. The aim, rather, has been to bring to the reader a sense of what transpired over the years as manifest in the career of the Orthodox Union—with preceding glimpses of the earlier experience of Jews on the New-World scene—and an idea of the meaning of this story to Jews (and others) of today. It is hoped that what follows in the course of this book brings the reader a strengthened sense of being personally an integral part of a profoundly significant historical process.

I
THE PREHISTORY

1

The Pioneers

For many American Jews, the world began, so to speak, when their parents, grandparents, or great-grandparents came to America. The sense of personal and family "place" is in a home-in-America frame. Correspondingly, except for those who have delved into American Jewish history, the Jewish presence in America is thought of in relation to one's own family beginnings in the land. The great majority of American Jews, being products of one to four generations of American settlement, relate as Jews of American Jewishness to their family timelines.

So it seems to be the case that for most of this country's Jews, there is no real sense of personal ties to Jewish life in America throughout the years of this nation's history. Today's American Jews, by and large, do not see themselves as part of a community rooted in the very origins of the United States—indeed, rooted even in the colonial seedbeds of the American people. A change may well be anticipated, however. With the continuing succession of American-born generations, the current family-experience vista of the Jewish presence in America must fade. The year 1948 or 1933 or 1921 or 1898 or 1871, or, for fewer, 1848 or 1821—all such time boundaries, respective tidemarks of family beginnings, will doubtless fade from personal consciousness as the sense of identity as American Jew attaches itself to the foundations of American Jewish life, as part of a community whose history is entwined with the story of America, going back as far as the year 1654.

THE FOUNDING FATHERS

For the Jew of America, the year 1654 holds the same meaning as does the arrival of the Mayflower for his fellow American of British origin or

3

Anglo-Saxon Protestant tradition. As told by Dr. David and Tamar deSola Pool in their epic work, *An Old Faith in the New World*:[1]

> Early in September, 1654, a small group of Jews, twenty-three in all, providentially reached the port of Niew Amsterdam. They were the founding fathers of Congregation Shearith Israel in the City of New York and of the Jewish community in the United States of America, a community destined to become the largest Jewish [Diaspora] settlement in all the long history of the Children of Israel. The story of their momentous journey has been transmitted through the generations as a proud and precious tradition.
>
> Perilous adventures had beset the Founding Fathers, beyond the measure common to pioneers in those days. Early in 1654, they sailed from Recife,[2] Brazil when the Portuguese conquered the Dutch. Hither and yon went the defeated, and many reached the safety of Holland. Others who clung to the New World were storm-driven to a Caribbean port and held by the very Inquisition they had fled. A ship of that convoy was captured by pirates.

Here the authors quote from an eighteenth-century source[3] wherein it is recounted:

> "But God caused a savior to arise unto them, the captain of a French ship arrayed for battle, and he rescued them from out of the hands of the outlaws who had done them violence and oppressed them, and he conducted them until they reached the end of the inhabited earth called New Holland, and then (the ship) also came to our encampment here. And so no man was missing, thanks be to God."

The authors then note that:

> The time of their arrival [in Niew Amsterdam, later to become New York] preceded by but a few days the Jewish New Year. . . . In the soul-searching communion of those Holy Days they must have found strength to face their still uncertain future, and courage to believe with the prophet of old that "a remnant of Israel"—for that is what Shearith Israel means in Hebrew—was to be a new fount of life.

Adding to the dire straits of the newcomers was the hostility of the governor of the Dutch colony, Peter Stuyvesant. All hardships were endured, however. Standing their ground in the face of want and efforts to

---

1. David and Tamar deSola Pool, *An Old Faith in the New World*, Columbia University Press, New York, 1955.
2. Also known as Pernambuco.
3. *Hameassef*, 1784.

eject them, the pioneers—joined by other arrivals from Amsterdam, and with the intercession of the Amsterdam Jewish community—were accorded the right of residence and the means of livelihood.

While religious life was devoutly maintained by these stalwarts, it was not until the end of the eighteenth century—by which time Niew Amsterdam had long since come, as New York, under British rule—that "the synagogue of New York's Jewish community was given [official] recognition and the right of the Jews to conduct worship in a publicly recognized synagogue was never again questioned."

Well do David and Tamar deSola Pool declare, in the quoted work:

> The Jews who came to Niew Amsterdam did not *find* freedom, they *fought* for it. Their unrelenting struggle to secure freedom of worship in no small measure enlarged the very conception of religious liberty and helped lay the foundations for its achievement. What they did with simplicity and assurance, assumes an importance far beyond what might have been expected of their small numbers. It helped open the road to the American credo of full, free, and equal right for all. For what the Jews secured for themselves, they furthered for others . . . men of all faiths. . . . Those who battled for freedom molded the face of the future.

For several decades, the congregation's services were held in rented quarters on Mill Street (which had become known as "Jews' Alley"), until 1728, when a piece of land on that street was purchased for the construction of a synagogue, "at the price of £100, one loaf of sugar, and a pound of bohea tea." Thus was erected the first synagogue built by Jews in North America.

The Mill Street Synagogue was consecrated on the seventh day of Pesah—April 9, 1730. It was a brick building, 35 feet square and 21 feet in height, including the women's gallery. Six months later, the congregation's *cabana* (sukkah) was built in the yard behind the synagogue. A *mikveh* (ritual bath), early on, drew water from the spring that powered the mill for which the street was named.

As great an object of fascination as this first synagogue was to others, the ner tamid excited particular interest in Christian neighbors and visitors.

The quoted work states:

> Gabriel P. Disoway, who remembered the first Mill Street Synagogue, tells that as a boy "very often have I looked in at the window to see if the 'Holy Light' was burning before the altar. This ever burning Jewish light was the wonder and mystery of the First Ward."

The de Sola Pools point out that the pioneering Shearith Israel, composed as yet of but a few dozen families, was still the only Jewish community in North America, and that:

It was still early in the history of even the Atlantic coast states of colonial America. Plans were being laid out for a city to be called Baltimore. Three years later, 1733, Jews arrived with the earliest settlers in Savannah, Georgia. It was not until two decades later that there were the beginnings of organized Jewish settlement in Philadelphia, Lancaster, and Charleston.

~

Intriguing glimpses of the life of the community in early generations were presented in a talk given in 1927 to the Shearith Israel membership by Captain N. Taylor Phillips,[4] of a family that had belonged to the Spanish and Portuguese Synagogue since 1700. In his address, Captain Phillips (who had participated in the founding of the Union of Orthodox Jewish Congregations of America in 1898 and served on its executive board for many years thereafter) drew upon his own family's store of reminiscence, including an account of:

> . . . the manner in which Dr. Samuel Nuñez, my grandfather's great-grandfather, came here about 1733. He was a Marrano from Portugal and his family had lived there as secret Jews for many years, two or three hundred years. They finally were discovered by the Inquisitors and they were, in the parlance of New York, 'tipped off' by somebody that the Inquisitors were 'on to them.' Dr. Nuñez gave a great banquet on his estate, which was on the banks of the Tagus. He had previously arranged with the captain of an English brig to stand out in the bay, and at the proper time to take them away. So he invited all the highbrows to come there and enjoy themselves, and in the midst of the fiesta, the drinking and eating and merrymaking, the family slipped out, gathering as much silver and jewelry and other things as they could easily carry, and went on the brig. The brig shot out and they were carried to London.

One member of that family who had survived Inquisition torture, Captain Phillips related, was released, and, after fleeing to New York, was observed to have marks of the Inquisition torture on his hands.

The compact orderliness of the trail-blazing community came to an abrupt halt with the onset of the American Revolution and war for independence. Most of the congregation's leaders and members were ardent patriots of the Continental cause, and, upon the occupation of New York by British troops, left the city for parts held by the American forces. After the war, congregational life was pieced together again, but the environment of American life had changed—a change fully shared by the

---

4. Published under the title "Unwritten History" in the Vol. V, No. 2 issue of *American Jewish Archives*, June 1954.

Jewish populace of the land, now increasing beyond the estimated two thousand of pre-Revolutionary days.

NEWPORT

The sole surviving structure of colonial-era Jewish Americans is in Newport, Rhode Island. There, a small but historically significant Jewish community with close ties to the New York congregation took shape in the mid-seventeenth century. By the mid-eighteenth century it was flourishing sufficiently that a synagogue was built, but in the aftermath of the Revolutionary War, economic changes caused the congregation's decline. After a long lapse, a new congregation formed in Newport, now occupying, by due arrangement, the site of the original group. This is the famed Newport Synagogue,[5] an architectural jewel built in 1763 and now a national historic landmark.

It was in the Newport Synagogue that a notable visitor of the pre-Revolutionary years, Rabbi Yitzhak Hai Carigal, delivered a discourse on Shavuoth in 5733 (May 28, 1773). Those present included, in addition to the congregants, non-Jewish government officials and the Reverend Ezra Stiles, prominent clergyman and distinguished scholar, later to become the third president of Yale College. Rabbi Carigal, the first rabbi to appear in what was soon to be the United States, had been born and educated in the land of Israel, and had traveled throughout Asia, North Africa, and Europe before journeying to America. There, his personal qualities, as well as his status as a Holy-Land emissary and his rabbinic stature, won him high regard.

At Newport, Dr. Stiles, who had taught himself some Hebrew, pursued opportunities to meet and converse with Rabbi Carigal, and they became friendly. Extracts from Dr. Stiles's diary and other records of Rabbi Carigal's visit were compiled by the historian Lee M. Friedman and published in a privately printed volume (*Rabbi Haim Isaac Carigal*, 1940). We learn from this account that Dr. Stiles attended services at the synagogue numerous times to observe the distinguished visitor. Of the Shavuoth occasion, Dr. Stiles's diary states:

> Went to the Synagogue at six A.M. At reading of Law the Rabbi was desired and read the Ten Commandments. But before reading the Law and the Prophets the Rabbi went to the Desk or Taubah and preached a sermon about

---

5. Also known as the Touro Synagogue, named after the famed philanthropist whose beneficence aided many Jewish and public institutions, including the Newport Synagogue.

47 minutes long in Spanish. It was interspersed with Hebrew. His Oratory, Eloquence and Gestures were fine and Oriental. . . . He exhorted them not to perplex themselves with Traditions and Criticisms, but to attend to certain capital points and principal points of Religion—he expatiated upon the Miseries and Calamities of their Nation in their present Captivity and Dispersion and comforted them . . . by the assured Prospect of the Messiah's Kingdom.

Of all the treasures of the early American Jewish heritage, one stands in a place all its own: George Washington's letter addressing America's Jews through the Jewish community of Newport. In this letter are the immortal words:

It is now no more that toleration is spoken of as if it were by the indulgence of one class of people that another enjoyed the exercise of their inherent natural rights, for, happily, the Government of the United States, which gives to bigotry no sanction, to persecution no assistance, requires only that they who live under its protection should demean themselves as good citizens in giving it on all occasions their effectual support.

$\sim$

Well may all generations of America's Jews take pride and inspiration from the role of their pioneering forbears. The qualities of these early American Jews have been summarized elsewhere[6] in these words:

Although the members of the pioneer community, and of the others to which it gave birth in the later colonial period, became fused into the life and lifestyle of colonial America, religious integrity in the corporate capacity, and to a lesser extent on the personal level, remained strong. There was no condoning of disregard, not to speak of discard, of traditional tenets. . . . Few as they were, the early American Jews accomplished several of the purposes necessary to Jewish continuity in the Modern Age situation: They absorbed the demands of the environment without commutation of religious belief; they developed a functioning inner environment; and they won recognition of Judaism, authentic Judaism, as a rightful facet of American life on a par with other religions.

---

6. Saul Bernstein, KTAV, Hoboken, NJ 1985. *The Renaissance of the Torah Jew.*

2

America: The Magnet

With the attainment of independence as a self-proclaimed, self-sovereign republic, the dynamism unleashed had charged the very air of the land with a new quality. As has been expressed in the above-quoted source:

> There emerged . . . a heavy challenge; to be woven into the fabric of the American nation and yet to persist in Jewish identity and goal, to sustain the integral Jewish self.
> This was the challenge that confronted post-Revolution American Jewry, as it has confronted their successors ever since.

As the message of an unshackled America began to penetrate Old-World lands, it touched Jewish communities baffled by a multitude of problems spawned by the onset of a new time. Although America was still seen as a remote wilderness, some began to respond to its allure of freedom and fresh opportunity. What had been a slow trickle of new arrivals throughout the colonial era became a rivulet of migration in the first decades of the nineteenth century, and then became a rising stream. The Jewish newcomers, mostly western and central Europeans, of Ashkenazic identity, settled alongside the older, established families in the existing communities and formed groups in the new cities and settlements that were springing up in the widening reaches of a pulsating nation. An undirected, spontaneous migration, it was born by an adventurous spirit that made for an indivualistic rather than a cohesive development.

MAKING THEIR OWN WAY

The new Jewish settlers, no less than their forerunners, had been reared in the traditional faith of Israel that was still the universal spiritual currency of the Jewish world. But while some were scrupulous in their observance, among others the tenets of religious practice were apt to be honored more in the breach than in the observance as the newcomers plunged into the flux of American life and shared in the movement to the far reaches of the ever-widening frontier. The tight-knit cohesion of colonial days gave way before the new promptings, not to be replaced.

From the previously quoted historical review given in 1927 by Captain N. Taylor Phillips, it appears, however, that among the original group, religious standards continued to be carefully maintained as the generations passed. He narrated that:

> Quite as late as 1813, the Common Council of the City of New York passed an ordinance giving the Board of Trustees of the congregation the absolute power over the matter of *kashruth*. They were the controlling body by law, and they decided who could be shochetim, who could kill [cattle and poultry] and who should not kill, what is *kasher* and what is *treifa*. . . . Most people kept in line . . . the things that were of their religion were absolutely part of their lives. . . . For the first century and a half and more, the women of the congregation were real actors in the kitchen business. No matter how well off they were, how rich they were, or who they were, the women either did the cooking themselves or superintended. The house that permitted the servants exclusively to run the kitchen was [considered] a *treifa* house. People would not eat there. . . .

Also, in regard to Pesach observance, Captain Phillips related that while prior to the Revolution "the cow would be brought to the house" of each family during an eight-day period and milked into the householder's can, therefore, "[t]he children would be sent up to the farms, up around what is now Greenwich Village. . . . I have heard my father say that in his boyhood at Passover time, he would carry the can to a farm on Greenwich Street at what is now Thirteenth Street."

~

THE BECKONING FRONTIER:
"WITH A PACK ON HIS BACK"

Those newly arrived, whether in the earlier or in the later nineteenth-century decades, struggled hard for the barest livelihood. Some found their place as craftsmen or employees of business enterprises, some opened small retail stores; many others, however, took packs and roamed far-flung towns and distant rural byways as peddlers of assorted merchandise. The hardships exacted a harsh toll—physically, emotionally, and, not least of all, religiously.

From the diary[1] of one of the newcomers of the time, Abraham Kohn, who, at age 23 in 1842, journeyed from the little town of Monschroth in Bavaria to New York, a sense of this experience is conveyed. Arriving in New York after a long, trying voyage on a sailing ship, Kohn found the city bewildering:

> The frantic hurry of the people, the hundreds of cabs, wagons, and carts—the noise is indescribable. Even one who has seen Germany's largest cities can hardly believe his eyes and ears. Feeling quite dizzy, I passed through Grand Street. . . . Sunday, New Year's Day. On the eve of Rosh Hashanah I found myself with a new career before me. What kind of career? . . . At night, in the Attorney St. Synagogue, I prayed to the Almighty. . . .
>
> During this period I was in New York, trying in vain to find a job as a clerk in a store. But I had to do as all the others, go out into the country with a bundle on my back, peddling various articles. This then is the vaunted luck of the immigrant from Bavaria: O misguided fools . . . you have left your friends, your relatives and your parents, your home and your fatherland and your religion—only to sell your wares in the wild places of America, in isolated farmhouses and tiny hamlets.
>
> Is this fate worth the losses you have suffered . . . is this the celebrated freedom of America's soil, when in order to do business one must profane the holy Sabbath. . . .
>
> Such as are married not only suffer themselves but bring suffering to their women. How must a woman feel when, after a brief stay at home, her supporter and shelterer leaves with a pack on his back, not knowing where he will find lodging the next night? On how many winter nights must such a woman sit forlornly with her children, wondering where this night finds the head of the family, which homestead in the forests of Ohio will offer him a poor night's shelter?
>
> O son of Israel, to follow God sincerely one must follow the holy Torah—but leading such a life none of us is able to observe the commandments.

---

1. As presented, in translation from the original German, in "A Jewish Peddler's Diary, 1842–1843" in *American Jewish Archives*, Vol. 3, No. 1, June 1951. Although Kohn's diary was written in German, much of the surviving correspondence and records of German Jewish settlers up to and after the mid-nineteenth century were in Yiddish. The "Germanization" of German Jewry—linguistic, cultural, and ideological—was a post-mid-nineteenth-century process.

From sources such as the preceding and studies of surviving records such as Leon Jickes's *The Americanization of the Synagogue 1820–1870*,[2] it appears that in the early- to middle-nineteenth-century decades America attracted from Europe Jews largely of humble, small-town background:

> They were primarily villagers who came from poor but devout homes. Their education in both secular and Jewish learning was minimal. The Yiddish vernacular in which they frequently wrote was full of errors in grammar and spelling. Lacking authoritative leadership . . . groups of immigrants gathered wherever they were and organized congregations, each governing their own affairs. . . .

Yet, Jickes points out,

> All of the thirteen congregations established between 1800 and 1840 followed the North European ritual, and all sought to recreate the traditional synagogues of their European villages. Because minor variations in ritual had existed in various European localities, they sometimes distinguished between [the German and the Polish versions of the *nusach ashkenaz*].

There was as yet no inclination to allow or condone deviant or heterodox encroachments on synagogue practice, irrespective of the observance standards of the congregants. An example cited in *The Americanization of the Synagogue* concerns the first congregation to have been established as far west as the Mississippi River—the United Hebrew Congregation of St. Louis, Missouri, founded in 1838:

> Its constitution states that "the prayers shall never be performed otherwise than among the Polish Jews [the words Minhag Polin appear in Hebrew script]. This section shall never be altered or amended whatsoever. We will be guided only by the laws of the Shulchan Aruch [the name is written in Hebrew characters]."

Jickes observes matter-of-factly: "The time eventually came, in this as in all other congregations, when strictures designed to prevent changes proved futile." Today, however, with an awareness driven home by the all-too-painful evidence of the cumulative cost of the "changes" that subsequently occurred, one stands aghast at the sequences of brazen captures of congregations and their houses of worship irrevocably established for and committed to a specific faith and practice, for the purposes of an altogether different, fundamentally incompatible, creed. Many years were to pass

---

2. Brandeis University Press, 1976.

before such outrages upon elementary morality and religious rights were effectively checked, as will be discussed elsewhere in this volume.

GROPING AND FRAGMENTATION

By the time of the Civil War, the number of Jews in the United States had grown to a total of about 250,000. Now, shaken by the cataclysm that had erupted, America's Jews were prompted to a new awareness of their collective selves. There came a groping for a defined course for American Jewish life.

A potpourri of notions and urges was astir, a viscous mix of ill-formed ideas crudely garnered from the turbulent American scene and the uncertainties of personal experience. In, too, swept an alluring attitude brought from an Old-World source shaken by epochal change. It was an ideology of sorts, engendered among Jews of Germany swept by the desire to share in the attractions of the new age of enlightenment and industrial progress.

Of the German Jewish immigrants coming to the United States after the revolutionary ferment of the mid-century period, some were touched by these notions of an about-face for Jewry. The conditions of the time lent themselves to teachings calling for the abandonment of cherished fundaments of Jewish belief and practice and the adoption of a pattern of life and religious criteria closely assimilated to those of the Christian world. Bearers of these ideas navigated shrewdly amid the volatile promptings and undirected confusions of the American Jewish communities of the time.

Now, in the post–Civil War decades especially, amid the continuing void of valid, resident rabbinic authority, one after another of the congregations established as vessels of the historical Jewish faith fell under the sway of the "Reform" advocates.

The parent congregation, the Spanish and Portuguese Synagogue, also encountered the onrush of the rising trend, but, ever staunch, it did not succumb. In 1841, the president of Congregation Shearith Israel, Moses L. Moses, responded reassuringly to a communication from the leadership of London's venerable Sephardic synagogue, including Moses Montefiore, that warned against threats to religious integrity. An organized attempt at a takeover of that synagogue, Britain's oldest, had been routed by the London congregation, and secession of the Reform protagonists had followed. The New York synagogue president wrote to the London leaders:

> The authorities of our congregation fully participate with you in decided disapprobation of the alteration made by a portion of your congregation. To this time we have steered clear of the rock of innovation, the most trifling or

immaterial has not been permitted in public worship, fearful that it might afford argument for farther, and more important, alteration. What has kept us together as brethren under the influence of the Divine Presence for so long a period, but a strict and uniform adherence to our ceremonial law and customs? And what assurance can any set of men of the present day have, that their new-fangled notions will continue for any length of time as they may have formed them? . . . until nothing remains of the beautiful consistency of our ritual as established by the sages of our nation and has stood the test of so many ages.

LEESER: TEACHER AND DOER

Other leaders strove to check the sweeping assimilationist trend. Especially notable was the labor carried on over many years by a unique figure of the time—Isaac Leeser. Signal appraisal of Isaac Leeser's role in a doctoral dissertation by Maxine Schwartz Seller[3] may be aptly quoted here:

Can a minority group maintain its identity while integrating itself into American society as a whole? Can the individual members of such a group participate simultaneously in his own culture and in that of the majority? This was the problem that challenged Isaac Leeser, immigrant from Westphalia, from his arrival in the United States in 1824 until his death in 1868. For four decades Leeser waged a heroic battle. Through constant traveling, lecturing, and publishing he stimulated the self-consciousness of the American Jew on the frontier as well as in the city, and helped him to preserve his Jewish identity. He organized synagogues . . . started schools . . . and wrote books . . . [led campaigns] everywhere . . . for the defense of Jewish rights in the United States and overseas. . . . Leeser's primary religious task was to strengthen [among America's Jews] their basic commitment to Judaism itself . . . by taking measures to combat the basic reasons that led Jews to fall away from their faith and by making adjustments, within the frame of religious orthodoxy, [for] the new American environment. His second task was to preserve American Judaism from the growing tendency to fragmentation or sectarianism which came with the rise of the Reform movement.

While battling the inroads made by the Reform forces, Leeser brought his homiletic gifts to bear in elevating the spiritual vistas and moral purpose of

---

3. *Isaac Leeser, Architect of the American Jewish Community,* University of Pennsylvania, Graduate School of Arts and Sciences, 1965.

his contemporaries of all persuasions, as per the following extract from an address on "The Spirit of the Ages."[4]

> But in the very pursuit of wealth there is at times something so heartless, that the man of feeling, even if we leave religion totally out of view, ought to shrink from it as he would from destruction.

Quite remarkably for his mid-19th century time, Isaac Leeser sought fervently the restoration of the Jewish people in their homeland. He stressed that the Torah, the House of Israel, and the Land of Israel were made for each other[5]:

> The whole Torah was precisely adapted to the character of the country they inhabited . . . our religion is in its nature permanent and requires at the same time a certain location for its perfect execution; it follows that a time will come when the people . . . shall be enabled to fulfill to the letter all the duties enjoined on them . . . it likewise follows that our redemption . . . cannot be accomplished by a mere civic emancipation. . . . We do not ask merely to be freed from tyrannical rule, but to see the supremacy of our code restored.

In furtherance of his far-seeing purposes, Isaac Leeser projected moves to bring some unity to America's Jews and to link them with endeavors for the building up of Jewish life in the Holy Land. Not surprisingly, these attempts were foiled by leaders of the Reform forces. "The stupid cry [by the Reformists] for changes in our religion has estranged brother from brother and has endangered almost any united effort," was Isaac Leeser's saddened message, but on he went nevertheless, carrying on his consecrated work to the end of his days.

The struggle for loyalty to the historic faith in that time of spiritual muddle was engaged in many Jewish communities, Cincinnati among them. In that "bed of Reform," the loyalist cause was led by the noted Isaacs family, established there since the early nineteenth century—a family whose successive members, to the present day, have been marked by undeviating fidelity to Orthodox Judaism. The pillar of this family, the "Reb Schachne" of proud memory, at a time in the 1850s moved to "a tiny crossroads village more than 30 miles away from Cincinnati." In this

4. In *Discourses on the Subject of the Jewish Religion* delivered at the Synagogue Mikveh Israel, Philadelphia, in the years 5590–5597, by Isaac Leeser.

5. The following excerpts from *The Occident* and Leeser's published *Discourses* are also those cited by Maxine S. Seller in "Isaac Leeser's Views on the Restoration of a Jewish Palestine," *American Jewish Historical Quarterly*, Vol. LVIII, No. 1, September 1968.

outlying farming community, as recorded by a grandson,[6] "where the only shopping day was Saturday," Reb Schachne boldly set up his general store—on undeviatingly shomer-Shabbath basis.

> On the first Saturdays, the farmers learned they could get nothing by pounding the locked door, but little by little they learned that it was worthwhile to drive in some other day for what they wanted. . . . The admiration for a person to whom his religion came first, together with appreciation for his honest merchandise, led to a complete change in the buying habits of the community.

THROUGH CONCERNED EYES

The onset of a new flow of immigration in the years before and especially after the Civil War brought marked changes to American life as a whole and to the American Jewish scene. As the era bringing ideas of "Enlightenment," scientific progress, industrial development, and social stirrings moved across Europe from west to east, its currents collided with prevailing mentalities and social and political compositions. Especially in the domains of Czarist Russia, which then included most of Poland and Lithuania and the Baltic lands, as well as the Ukraine and White Russia, Jewish life was enduring crushing pressures. Difficult, too, was the situation of the Jewish communities in the Austro-Hungarian Empire—whose multinational domains included Galicia, and the lands of the Czechs and Slovaks. And so too, in other areas with deep-rooted Jewish communities, including Rumania, now no longer under Turkish rule. Jews from these parts had been finding their way to the United States and lands of western Europe since the early eighteenth century, but this had been a migration of adventuresome individuals. By the 1870s, the flow of Jews from eastern Europe seeking a better life had taken on more substantial proportions, vanguard of the mass influx to come. Most came with little, if any, means, and were perhaps even worse equipped for the radical unfamiliarities of American life than the previous arrivals had been. Coming from lands with a nationality-conscious Jewish populace and a richer Jewish life, these newcomers brought with them a more pronounced Jewishness. Yet the challenge of the American environment attained much the same spiritual attrition as it had with the prior arrivals.

---

6. Dr. Moses Legis Isaacs, "Ad Meah Shanah," *Jewish Life*, Sivan 5713/May–June 1953.

BENJAMIN II IN AMERICA

Among the visitors who came to observe the American scene in that period was "Benjamin II," the cognomen of the extraordinary traveler I.J. Benjamin. Inspired by the examples of the famed world travelers of centuries before, Benjamin of Tudela and Petachia of Ratisbon, this latter-day Benjamin wandered from his native Moldavia to remote lands to see and meet his fellow Jews. After journeying through Asia and Africa from 1846 to 1855, Benjamin's world-roaming itinerary brought him to America, where he spent the years 1859 to 1862 in coast-to-coast travels.[7]

Benjamin's encounter with New-World life prompted severe judgment on what he saw as the materialistic conditioning of American society in general. He saw—to a degree perhaps sharpened by his visits to California settlements born of Gold-Rush impetus and its continued urgings—the drive for wealth and "gold" as permeating the ranks of Americans of all backgrounds. Insofar as this attitude was shared by Jews, he maintained, its effects on Jewish life were pernicious:

> The principal cause for the decline of Judaism [in the U.S. as then found] is due to two sources: One is materialism. The grubbing and hunting for money and gold, which is hardly interrupted by night, almost buries the soul; it permits no higher thoughts to spring up and kills . . . all nobler and sacred feelings. . . . The second source . . . is the mentality of many spiritual leaders and teachers, who have knowledge neither of the Talmud nor of the literature of Judaism.

Like others before him and many since, Benjamin voiced his deep concern at the educational gap. He was particularly pained at the failure to provide girls with meaningful Jewish education:

> The Jewish boys attend some Hebrew school or other, or are instructed privately, but in this respect, what does the situation look like for the daughters of [the House of] Israel? How sad is the provision for the religious education of these Jewish mothers and housewives of the future!; how little do they learn of their duties to God and man!. . . . All who are members of the religious community are to blame, as a body. They should have established Jewish schools for girls as well as for boys.

---

7. Recorded in his *Drei Jahre in Amerika, 1859–1862*, "J.J. Benjamin II," Hannover, 1862. The following quotations are from *Three Years in America 1859–1862*, by Israel Joseph Benjamin, translated from German by Charles Reznikoff, Philadelphia: Jewish Publication Society of America, 1956–1957 (2 vols.).

LOYALTIES NEAR AND FAR

At each place he visited, Benjamin II took careful note of the synagogues and their origins, rituals, and accomplishments. He took satisfaction in noting the Orthodoxy of various synagogues. Among these were some that were later proved, by their abandonment of their original commitment, to have been less well safeguarded in their religious integrity than Benjamin had supposed. Here are some examples from among his citations:

> The place now occupied by Chicago was still in the possession of Indians as recently as thirty years ago. . . . There are three congregations in Chicago, [including] Anshe Ma'ariv ("Men of the West") founded in 1847 (5607); in 1851 (5611) the congregation built a very beautiful synagogue. . . . This congregation consists mostly of Germans, its ritual likewise and consequently still truly orthodox. . . . B'nai Sholom, founded somewhat later than the former, has no teacher; it follows the Polish rite.
>
> There are two congregations in St. Louis (Missouri). One is Achduth Israel; it has eighty members and its rite is Polish. It was organized in 1842 (5602). Two years ago, the congregation erected a very beautiful synagogue on Sixth Street; it cost about $130,000 to build. The money was borrowed and interest had to be paid for it. It had been announced twice that the synagogue would be sold to the highest bidder, for the congregation could not or would not pay the interest. . . . I visited the synagogue on a Shabbos but must report to my regret that the *minyan* necessary for public services were hardly present.

In his roamings in the far West, Benjamin viewed congregations such as the following:

> Congregation Shearith Israel was organized in San Francisco in 1849. It held services in various places which, from time to time, were destroyed by fire. Finally, the congregation in 1850 bought a place on Stockton Street. . . . The congregation has about 110 members. They all come from northern Europe or England. The service follows the correct Polish Minhag and is strictly orthodox. From the very beginning the congregation was founded on these principles and they are embodied in its constitution so that they remain in force to this day and, according to all appearances, it is very unlikely that innovations will be made.

~

While Benjamin II found much in the life of America's Jews to deplore, he also found occasion for praise, particularly in the area of charitable giving. He summarizes:

Perhaps in a short time Judaism in America will recover; for the many charitable institutions there, without equal in any other land, show that the Jewish spirit still lives, and we may hope that the other two pillars of Judaism, *Torah* and *Avodah*, Torah learning and religious service, which along with charity, Chesed, have been declared by our Sages to be the foundation of our religion, will soon rise up again in full splendor.

Today, after the passage of long years of endeavor, years of much trial and error, we can see that the hope of this traveler across the Jewish world has found a growing measure of fulfillment among Jews in America.

3

Onset of the Great Migration

In the 1880s, with the Jews under Russian rule locked in a Pale of Settlement that was a tightening noose, there ensued a tidal wave of movement that in the course of a few decades was to bring millions of Jews to the United States. Most came with but a trifle of funds, or were all but penniless.

Coming from lands backward in social and economic development, the immigrants were at a loss to find themselves in the totally alien surroundings of American life. While grasping with might and main for livelihood— for most, via the sweatshop route in the burgeoning garment industry— they had to piece together as best they could some provision for religious needs and some format for the Jewish life. Among the oncoming thousands were some few imbued with the radical notions of a new order of life and society that had begun to find a following among the hard-pressed Jews of eastern Europe. Others came with spiritual ties weakened by new-day influences, and were disposed to make getting ahead in their new land the governing code of life. Most immigrants, however, were well entrenched in the traditional religious life-pattern that had been absorbed from birth on amid an intensely Jewish, Torah-oriented environment.

Many of these newcomers felt ill at ease in the unfamiliar atmosphere of the established congregations. The greater tendency was to unite for provision of shared religious needs with others from the same hometown or region. The little storefront or back-of-the-workshop *chevrah* or *shtibel* that arose wherever the immigrant wave found dwellings multiplied, some achieving sturdy permanence, others disappearing to be replaced by newer groups, some evolving into large, fairly stable congregations, each with its own cherished *shul*. Also taking shape were *lantsmanshaften*—hometown fraternities and mutual aid societies, to buffer exigencies of illness or

20

distress, and chevroth kadisha, sacred societies to provide for care of the dying and interment.

Around these improvisations evolved a heterogeneity of further facilities for observance of Jewish life: the inimitable cheder schools for the instruction of children in the basics of Judaic knowledge; mikvaoth for family purity ritual ablutions; provisions for kosher slaughter and purveying of meat and poultry; officiants for marriages and for b'rith milah, circumcision pursuant to the Divine covenant with Abrahām; sacred study groups for the daily learning of Torah—the scriptural Torah with the favored commentaries, the oral Torah embodied in the Talmud with its Mishnah and Gemara, and other cherished treasures of Jewish heritage.

The aggregate whole was composed of diversities. Each of its many parts was a spontaneous creation by the mitzvah-directed; each was an achievement by self-sacrificing, deeply dedicated, self-prompted individuals and small groups. It was a many-handed work, essentially a single-spirited work, a life-generating commitment to the renewal of the Jewish people and its Torah faith.

For all its greatness of spirit, however, it was an endeavor completely devoid of central direction or collective planning; of any kind of broadly inclusive concerted effort or group-to-group cooperation; of clear-voiced coherence. It was a phenomenon of unsparing endeavor, of noble purpose. It was also a phenomenon of structural crudity and communal chaos.

WITH A CRITICAL EYE

A graphic portrayal of conditions among Jews in America at the onset of mass immigration from eastern Europe was penned in the 1880s by one of the participants, Moses Weinberger, who came from Hungary. His book, *Jews and Judaism in New York*, first written and published in Hebrew, now appears in English as translated and edited by Jonathan D. Sarna.[1] Weinberger's observations, often sharp-edged and frequently heavily sarcastic, like those of Benjamin II before him, are made with a critical but concerned eye.

Weinberger notes, in the Sarna translation, that while "the number of organized and settled" Orthodox congregations in New York then numbered 130, there were actually many more—"small *minyanim* in private

---

1. *People Walk on Their Heads—Moses Weinberger's Jews and Judaism in New York*, translated from the Hebrew and edited by Jonathan D. Sarna, ———: Holmes & Meier Publishers, Inc., New York 1982. Sarna gives the date of Weinberger's New York stay as 1887.

homes and houses of study, in lofts and courtyards," bringing the total to about 300. In typical vein, he says that beyond serving to provide twice-daily worship services and to meet members' needs, "the more exalted aim of the congregations is to build beautifully adorned synagogues." With more satisfaction, he tells that "the synagogues of our Orthodox brethren follow the Torah and do not differ in any way from those of their fellow God-fearing Jews wherever they might live." Only a few exceptions among them, he says, have undertaken such changes as "slightly altering the place of the *bimah*" (from its normative location in the center of the shul).

In the opening chapter of *Jews and Judaism in New York*, Weinberger asserts in caustic vein:

> Many synagogues have a *beth hamidrash*, a room for sacred studies . . . occasionally this is opened by a few old men, who learn, so to speak, on one foot—a chapter of Mishnah or a page of Gemara. . . . [In a few places] people regularly study Talmud in groups, but their sessions . . . are without depth and penetration.

Quite a different assessment is indicated, however, elsewhere in Weinberger's book. In the Sarna translation, in a letter to a friend in Hungary that appears as an appendix at the end of the book, he writes in part:

> Congregation Beth Hamedrash Hagodol in this city is old and wealthy, its *beth hamidrash* is large—five hundred students could find a place there—its synagogue is a huge, magnificent building . . . and most of its members are prosperous and prominent. Even those who know Torah are great merchants.
>
> The Hungarian Congregation Beth Hamedrash Hagodol, however, is poor and young. Its *beth hamidrash* is small. Its members are mostly all people who support themselves with difficulty with the work of their own hands.
>
> Although things have not gone exactly as the founders [of the Hungarian Beth Hamedrash Hagodol] wanted, . . . *most of its members are acquainted with God's Torah and many are excellent scholars who set special times aside for Torah study. This, to be sure, is not a rare phenomenon in this city. Among our Russian and Polish brothers, we see this in almost every large congregation, especially in [large] Congregation Beth Hamedrash Hagodol mentioned above. Even uptown there is a congregation named Orach Chayim, whose members are wealthy and completely German and who gather daily after Minchah [the afternoon prayers] to enjoy Torah study.* (italicization added)

But here Weinberger, returning to his more customary tone, adds: "But will their children follow in their ways? I doubt it very much; at this time we have no hope at all. Only time will tell."

With all too evident reasons, a bleak vista is offered by this 1880s settler of the state of affairs in regard to authoritative determination of matters of Jewish law and the exposition of Torah teachings.

> In this great city [New York] of 100,000 Jews and 130 [established Orthodox] congregations, there are no more than three or four superior court [Beth Din] rabbis, rabbis who decide what is prohibited and permitted. They located their positions only after a great deal of trouble and effort. . . . Their regular salaries are so small it would be shameful to record the amount in print . . . a small communal stipend combined with a few isolated gifts barely cover their basic human needs.

Among the incoming thousands were many who in their former homes had served religious functions held in high esteem. Now, in their New-World haven, "*Musar magidim, ba'aley agadah,* and *darshanim* [expounders, respectively, of ethical teachings, homiletic lore, and biblical direction] are found here by the hundreds, but only a few succeed in acquiring positions."

STRUGGLING WITH SHOCK AND SHAME

Although lightened at a few points by more encouraging indications, Moses Weinberger's contemporary 1800s portrayal of what was becoming the most populous urban center of Jewry in the world presented a panorama of shaken standards, misplaced priorities, vain values, and general disorder. Above all, the state of kashruth, observance of the laws pertaining to food and particularly to Shechitah, had sunk to a disastrous level.

All other records of this time and of the years following reveal much the same shocking picture of conditions in the slaughter, distribution, and vending of supposedly kosher meat and poultry. The following few passages from Weinberger's work are illustrative:

> Shochatim and butchers are perfectly independent here; neither they nor their work is inspected. Congregations do not hire their own Shochatim, and Shechitah here can be undertaken by anybody who finds an opening. . . . The upshot is that in our slaughterhouses each man takes what he can get. . . . [But] in our community there are, thank God, also outstanding shochatim. They have certificates from leading rabbis in Europe attesting to their skills, their good conduct, and their piety. Since the city government ordained that it was henceforth illegal to keep live poultry for sale in the stores, and that all poultry must be slaughtered in a specified spot outside the city, we now face a whole new series of terrible obstacles.
> It is very narrow and forever filled with rivers of mud, mire, and blood.

Throngs of frightened, impetuous people stand crowded together, pushing each other. The shochatim lack room to turn, hardly able to even move their hands. Since most of the poultry is slaughtered on Sabbath eve or on Thursday, every slaughterhouse boss wants to get a headstart to get to market as early as possible. The shochet therefore must sometimes slay as many as 200 birds "in one breath." Woe to the pious and God-fearing, but the commands of the boss standing over him take precedence. So the shochet, though his soul troubles him, continues so long as he has strength within him. The shochet knows that he did not properly sharpen the knife, inspect it more than once, and even then in a great hurry. But what can the wretchedly poor shochet do? He has to maintain his wife and children, and this is his one source of support. . . . The salesman-butchers: As far as many of them are concerned, any slaughtered fowl with blood removed is marketable, even if the shochet admits that he slaughtered impermissibly.

We see sometimes shochatim who look as if they learned their art a month before they left their native lands. [Others had] served in this profession but became corrupted and were removed from office by the rabbis. Now they have come here to try their hand again. Finally there are those who . . . after years in other fields became poultry slaughterers overnight. The newcomer here does not realize how different the situation is here from that which existed in his old small town. . . . Who could force the butcher here to show what is back in the ice house, or what was hidden in holes and crevices? So great is the scandal in this great city that thousands of honest families who fear and tremble at the thought of straying into one tiny prohibition or sin never suspect that they are eating all kinds of unkosher meat.

CHEDER: TEN CENTS A WEEK

Weinberger was aghast, too, at the educational failings in those days of inpouring immigration: "Our faithful Orthodox brethren, who revel in their own piety and righteousness . . . allow their sons to grow up without Torah and faith." Of the innumerable private cheder classes where sorely pressed, self-appointed instructors struggled to impart to clusters of unruly youngsters the rudiments of Jewish knowledge, he writes:

Chadarim, where teachers give instruction in Aleph-Beth and Hebrew reading, are found here in abundance. Many teachers have issued a handbill in which they agree to teach any Jewish child, however he may be—rich or poor, bright or dull—for only ten cents a week, or forty cents a month. Obstinate householders tell themselves that just as the price has fallen, it will fall again. . . . We have already heard *melamdim* whispering that if they cannot improve their lot they will abandon teaching completely and return to sewing clothes, tanning leather, or making shoes—each to the type of job he performed in his native land.

The author of *Jews and Judaism in New York* adds that:

More advanced teachers with wisdom and learning are also to be found here in abundance. But they find it impossible to use their knowledge. During the time when the Hungarian or Polish Jewish youngster was brought to a level where he could understand the Prophets and listen to rigorous Biblical and legal [Halachic] studies, the American youngster is merely able to stammer a few words of English-style Hebrew, to pronounce the blessing over the Torah, and to chant half the *Maftir* on the day he turns thirteen—a day that is celebrated here as the greatest of holidays among our Jewish brethren. From that day onward a youngster considers his teacher to be an unwanted article . . . he forgets all he has learned.

Better promise is also to be found, however. Weinberger tells us:

There are two Talmud Torah schools for children of the poor. One of them is about to collapse for lack of support. The second (Machzike Talmud Torah) still stands strong at Number 83 East Broadway. Some 400 students study there. This house of study was set up four years ago [1883] through the efforts of lovers of their people and religion whose spirits never darkened, no matter how they toiled. They let money flow from their own pockets, knocked on the doors of large donors. . . . Finally they succeeded: a miracle, a true wonder: The teachers, all men of wisdom and learning, perform their work with perfect integrity. According to many who understand the field of education, this school can compete successfully with any school of its kind in our native lands.

AT LAST—A YESHIVAH

With special—and, to him, unexpected—cause for rejoicing, Weinberger reports of a new development:

We just heard the pleasant news that in recent days, a new school has been established here called Yeshivath Etz Chaim for the study of Mishnah and Talmud, that is, Gemara, Rashi, and Tosafoth. Fifteen hundred people are supposed to be standing ready to finance the building and appoint eminent teachers who will receive their salaries in honorable fashion from a large community fund. All is said to be prepared. . . . Hurrah! How lovely, how dear! A yeshivah for Mishnah and Gemara! How much good is hidden in those words. I can hardly believe my own ears; is this possible, can it be? Here in New York? In America?

Yes, events soon proved that it was, indeed, not only possible, but a fulfilled reality. Yeshivath Etz Chaim was duly established, functioned steadily, and presently merged with a kindred institution that had soon come into being, Yeshivath Rabbi Yitzchak Elchanan, the Rabbi Isaac Elchanan Theological Seminary. Long serving as the only postelementary yeshivah on the American continent, the Rabbi Isaac Elchanan Yeshivah is the core institution from which sprang Yeshiva College and, then, the Yeshiva University of today.

Among several other areas of the 1880s New York Jewish scene dealt with in the cited source, Weinberger brings home the grim hardships of the immigrant life of that time:

> Those expertly learned in the Torah, the Talmud, and the wisdom of our blessed rabbis are, thank God, numerous in this city. Some of them settled in this land years ago, and have been blessed with wealth, honor, and property. The bulk of the learned, however, are wretchedly poor immigrants who have come here only in the last few years. They have abandoned their Torah [learning] only from necessity—much against their will. They spend all their time toiling.
>
> These impoverished ones share occupations well known [as those of Jews coming from eastern Europe]: tailoring, sewing, and ironing—all in the garment trade; portering: pack-carrying [peddling]; and begging. But what else can the unfortunate refugees do? For if they do not save themselves on the strength of their own blood, sweat, and tears, they'll be lost forever. So much of their time do these people spend on burdensome labors that all their days are used up. When they return home in the evening or dead of night exhausted, all their cravings have left them; they are happy just to find a place to rest from toil, sadness, and rage. They work entirely in order to eat; daily bread is their reward and portion.

We know now that, whether or not Moses Weinberger's words, "To our brothers in Russia, Poland, and Hungary . . . listen to us: tough it out and stay home," reached their target, two million more Jews came from those parts to the New World in the few decades following. Others migrated elsewhere, some found their way to the land of Israel—and some six million remained.

OBSERVANCE IN BETTER VIEW

As was noted earlier, in his letter to his friend in Hungary that appeared in an appendix, Moses Weinberger's passing comments on aspects of the New

York scene are in different vein from that found in the book proper. Thus, in the course of the letter, we find:

> With regard to Sabbath observance—the stopping of manual labor and other work in factories, stores, and businesses—hundreds and even thousands of people are careful. In many New York streets and markets you won't find even one open store. The Shabbath tranquility compares favorably to that found in most Jewish areas [in the old country]. On the other hand, there is a great deal of laxity with regard to the prohibitions against carrying, handling forbidden articles, and doing indirect business.
>
> With regard to the mitzvah of Sukkoth, people are now far more scrupulous than in previous years. When I arrived here, I found not more than one or two sukkahs in the entire neighborhood where I live. Now, just on the street where I have my business, there are more than twenty—though most people honor their obligation simply by making Kiddush in the sukkah and then return home for the Festival meals.

The closing recommendations of the author of *Jews and Judaism in New York* call for the uniting of the congregations into one central force "for all matters that relate to the community as a whole"; each congregation to have at its head a Rav, a rabbi "of stature and greatness in Torah, wisdom, and piety to guide them, instruct them, and tell them how to act"; and the creation of "a Chief Rabbinate or Jewish Supreme Court," and the raising of "the dignity of and concern with Torah, its investigation, and its study."

Unknown, probably, to Moses Weinberger, others who also had pondered the same problems with no less concern had reached similar conclusions. With spiritual chaos worsening as the mass influx continued to mount, action became imperative.

4

On the Sidewalks of New York

In hearing the voices of Jews of times past, we must be mindful of the great differences between the pre-automobile world of a bygone century and the super-computer world of the late twentieth century. In his ways of living and working, in his language and his ideas, the Jew of the 1990s North American cities is, collectively speaking, a very different person from his 1890s forebear. All is different—the world about him, the world within him.

The American Jew's locale itself is much different. Once crowded into close "downtown" quarters of the larger cities, many Jews are now settled in outspreading suburbs. This is especially true of the so-called "New York" Jews, now spread over a dozen counties in three states, besides what are now the five boroughs of the City of New York—although they may still be among those relative few still contentedly living amid transformed surroundings on Grand Street on the Lower East Side of what was once all there was of New York City and is now New York's Borough of Manhattan.

The island of Manhattan is where, as the nineteenth century neared its close, the city's Jewish population, having passed the half-million mark, was daily multiplying to reach its eventual two million. It is where nine of every ten Jewish New Yorkers then dwelt. And so it was with the immigrant settlers in Philadelphia, Chicago, Boston, Pittsburgh, Cleveland, St. Louis, Denver, San Francisco, and so on, and across the border in Montreal, Toronto, and Winnipeg, and any number of larger and smaller cities and towns across the continental span.

New York was, for those of the immigrant generations, a Jewish community tightly packed into a few score city blocks composed largely of five- and six-story tenement buildings. Each such building on each such block was jammed roof to cellar, wall to wall, room to tiny, boxlike room, with growing families. Blocks of streets pulsated with the noise and uninhibited motion of vibrant human life. New York meant blocks lined with push-carts of goods for poor people's everyday needs; blocks punctuated with fetid workshops and hole-in-the-wall stores; blocks of synagogues large and small, shul after vibrant shul, shtibel after backroom shtibel, squeezed in here, there, and everywhere rooms for Torah study—chevroth shas, chevroth mishnayoth. New York was blocks of heartbreaking struggle and want, blocks of indestructible hope, purpose, will to live, will to live Jewishly. Moving, stirring, shocking, exhilarating, saddening, bewildering, inspiring—Jewish New York was a world drawing to and from itself every sense, every emotion except only that of dullness.

In this New-World portal, each entered on a new life in a new age, each starting afresh, each fending for himself in new scenes of bewildering strangeness. Here was America, there was the Old Country. What pertained to the one was out of place in the other. In the United States, one was to think and act and live differently than in the life of before; one must, perforce, be a different person than the person of before.

So, for all coming to its shores, America proffered its new day and, with magnetic force, engaged each in the process of absorption into American life. For many, the process of self-translation, from Old-World self to New-World self, was strewn with perplexity. For the Jew, it was more than a matter of "American self" versus "Old Country self"—it was a matter of implanting in the new self the self of Jewish being, the self of the Jewish ages and Jewish eternity. This problem has ever been at the heart of the Jewish situation in America; it still exists today.

In the unstructured, high-tempo froth of Jewish life in the United States during the mounting tide of immigration, this problem confronted one and all in harsh terms. Some, interested only in their personal material betterment, cared little; others were in conscious rebellion against the beliefs and the life of before. Most, however, strove amid the struggle for existence to maintain their Jewish selves.

There ensued the makeshift improvisation that was the hallmark of immigrant days: a bit here, a bit there. Who in that harried pressure-cooker situation could be expected to view broadly the scope of American realities in relation to Jewish needs? Yet, fortunately, those of stronger purpose emerged from among the ranks, those who could think and act for the group interest. Thanks to this spontaneous leadership, there came about in hand-to-mouth fashion the varied complex of institutional development that was the product of eastern European Jewry in the cities of the United States and Canada, and in many smaller communities, too. By far the greatest concentration of all, the most massive and most vibrant, was that to be found in the New York of the end of the nineteenth century and the beginning of the twentieth century.

Unfortunately, there were also those who exploited Jewish need. There were charlatans pretending to be rabbis, and even rabbis turned charlatans; there were self-appointed "reverends," self-designated *mohalim*, self-certified shochatim, respectively—and, on occasion, in two or all three capacities—exploiting needs in the performance of marriage, b'rith milah, and shechitah. In these areas and in such as the granting of *hechsherim*, in the issuance of divorces, in the manufacture of religious requisites—in every function of Jewish religious practice that lent itself to exploitation and manipulation, there was a range of wrongdoing from gross incompetence to gross fraud. Fattening on the abuses, distinguishable from the less culpable driven by desperate need, were men who, prior to debarking on American shores, had dropped overboard, with or without their tephillin, their consciences.

There can be no doubt that the weedlike spread of such abuses was a potent factor in the alienation of many from religious adherence. These abuses festered in the anarchic confusion of the hard-pressed immigrant world.

By the later decades of the nineteenth century, the state of fragmentation was recognized by the percipient as the key problem. By that stage, however, the complexity and sheer mass of the problem seemed to defy resolution. After a succession of efforts at unity among Orthodox groups had collapsed in turn, better promise appeared with the launching in 1887 of the Association of American Orthodox Hebrew Congregations. At the initiative of Beth Hamidrash Hagodol, the leading synagogue of New York's Lower-East-Side community, representatives of eighteen congregations joined in forming the association. Out of it was to come an undertaking with potential for reshaping the character of Jewish life in America: the establishment, within an organized Torah community frame, of a Chief Rabbinate.

The story of this hopeful but, as it proved, ill-fated project may be traced through various sources. Among those cited or drawn upon in the following pages, especially comprehensive and thorough was the study by Abraham J. Karp.[1] Quoted in the following section are some excerpts from Karp's work.

NEW YORK CHOOSES A CHIEF RABBI

The participants in the new Association were convinced that only the effectuation of the office of Chief Rabbi could move the diversity of

1. Abraham J. Karp, "New York Chooses a Chief Rabbi," *Publications of the American Jewish Historical Society*, Volume XLIV, September 1954–June 1955.

congregations and groups to function together and to address pressing needs in the common interest.

Announcements of the undertaking were placed in European Hebrew periodicals, and letters inviting candidacy recommendations were addressed to the following eminent rabbinic leaders[2]: Rabbis Yitzchak Elchanan Spektor of Kovno; Hillel Lifshitz of Suwalki; Eliyahu Chayyim Weisels of Lodz; Ya'akov Yoseph of Vilna; Azriel Hildesheimer of Berlin; Eliyahu Levinson of Krittingen; Yoseph Duber Diskin of Brest Litovsk; and Chayyim Berlin of Moscow.

The letters to the aforementioned rabbis, as cited in Karp's study, stated in part:

> Many improvements must be undertaken to raise the standard of Judaism in our country, and if the Orthodox congregations do not unite, then there is no hope for the preservation and upbuilding of Judaism in our city.
>
> For this purpose . . . we unanimously decided to invite as our spiritual leader a Rav noted for his scholarship and piety. His mission would be to remove the stumbling blocks before our people, to unite the hearts of our brethren, the House of Israel, to serve God with one heart and soul, and to supervise with an open eye the shochatim and all other matters of the House of Israel, which to our sorrow are neither observed nor respected, because there is no authority nor guide revered and accepted by the whole community, and each one is an authority unto himself. The congregations already participating have pledged to [share the salary expense], and many other congregations stand ready to join the Association, and thus make it possible to offer the rabbi a generous salary as would befit the Chief Rabbi of so important a community as New York.
>
> We are not unaware that the person we would invite is one respected in his community, and there is no reason that would urge him to leave his home and travel across the seas. Yet our faith is in God, and there has not ceased among our people those who are deeply concerned with the preservation of our holy faith. The rabbi who heeds our call will do so for the sake of the Jewish community across the sea, to save many souls of our brethren who have emigrated and wandered to this land, and infuse in them the spirit of knowledge and the fear of God.

Most of the rabbinic leaders addressed responded in one form or another, saluting the establishment of the Association and requesting more information. Hesitation came with the realization that, unlike elsewhere, the

---

2. From J.D. Eisenstein, *History of the Association of American Orthodox Hebrew Congregations.*

American context with its separation of religion and state could not provide a basis of civil authority for a Chief Rabbinate. Shortly, however, some serious candidates emerged. After pursuing various possibilities, the Association then turned with its proffering of the office of Rav Ha-Kollel, Chief Rabbinate of New York, to the illustrious Rav Ya'akov Yoseph (Jacob Joseph in English usage). This personage, famed as *Reb Yankele Ha-charif* ("the acute-minded"), served as both *moreh tzedels* (law decisor) and *maggid yesharim* (community preacher) of Vilna, "the Jerusalem of Lithuania." Negotiations proceeded, terms were agreed on, and preparations were made for Rabbi Jacob Joseph's departure for America.

In view of the fact that the Association of American Hebrew Orthodox Congregations was the product of the "downtown" congregations of eastern European immigrant origin, it is notable that, as reported in the *American Israelite* of March 30, 1888, the assemblage convened to resolve the funding of the undertaking was addressed by the spiritual leaders of the two foremost "uptown" Orthodox congregations. One was Dr. Henry Pereira Mendes, Minister of the patrician Congregation Shearith Israel, the Spanish and Portuguese Synagogue, parent congregation of American Jewry. Already a rising voice in American Jewish affairs, Dr. Mendes was later to become the founding president of the Union of Orthodox Jewish Congregations of America. The other leader was Dr. Bernard Drachman, then the Rabbi of the long-established prominent Congregation Orach Chayim, who in due course succeeded Dr. Mendes as Orthodox Union president.

While both the foregoing had initially feared that any incumbent to the Chief Rabbinate lacking familiarity with American minds and conditions and without a command of English would be fatally handicapped in coping with the onerous difficulties of the projected office, once the matter had been determined, they gave the undertaking, and the Chief Rabbi himself, when in office, their full support.

A SADDENED FAREWELL,
A JOYOUS WELCOME

While Rabbi Jacob Joseph's arrival was awaited with great anticipation in America, his departure evoked deep sorrow in the community he was leaving. A letter from one Michael Bairack of Vilna to his nephew in New York, Abraham Cahan—who was to achieve fame as Abe Cahan, editor of the Yiddish, socialist-oriented Jewish *Daily Forward* (*Forverts*)—which appeared in Cahan's 1926 autobiography[3] is illustrative:

> Rabbi Ya'akov Yoseph is very dear to us. A great *charif* [keen mind], he is of a rare devoutness. Our hears ache that we had to part with him. It is hard to lose such a precious treasure. See to it that he is well appreciated. Tell everyone that Vilna gloried in him. See to it that New York Jews know what a gem they have taken from us, and that New York must recognize what a precious crown it bears.

The recipient of the letter was also adjured by his uncle to advance his message, "even though I know that you do not go to school, but I know that you have a Jewish heart." Although in his autobiography Cahan speaks of Rabbi Jacob Joseph with distinct respect and with feeling for his ultimate fate, there is nothing otherwise to indicate that his uncle's adjuration bore the hoped-for effect.[4] There was surely no mitigation of the vicious attitude of the radical circles in which Cahan found his place. From the first, the varied elements of these circles vied with each other in venomous hostility to the Chief-Rabbinate undertaking and to Rabbi Jacob Joseph himself.

Among the masses of East-Side Jews, and among their counterparts elsewhere throughout the United States, the arrival of the awaited figure in New York after the conclusion of Shabbath on July 7, 1888, was greeted with rapturous enthusiasm. Karp, drawing on reports in *The American Hebrew*, the *Jewish Messenger*, and other contemporary sources, writes:

> When the reception procession reached the house chosen for the Chief Rabbi's residence at Henry and Jefferson Streets, thousands upon thousands milled about. Police had been called earlier. The crowd consisted almost entirely of East European immigrant Jews, who felt that the arrival of Rabbi Jacob Joseph marked the beginning of a spiritual revival for American Jewry and a new deal for the disregarded and despised Russian Jews.

(At the time, the term "Russian Jews" was the general identifying term for all Jews from eastern Europe.)

The arrival of the religious leader was widely reported in the leading daily newspapers as well as in Jewish media. The foremost New York daily

---

3. *Bletter Fun Mein Leyben*, Vol. 2, New York: Forward Association, 1926.

4. Cahan writes: "I was interested in the Chief Rabbi's role simply as an observer. I had no thought of writing about him in the English-language press, and I didn't want to write about him in the Yiddish press. For a Socialist to write in a friendly way about a religious matter was impossible."

of the time, the *New York Herald*, referred to the Chief Rabbi as "the only such dignitary in this country," and gave continuing coverage to the development.

Needless to say, the enthusiasm of the traditional loyalists was not shared by those of opposing outlook. The channels of the Reform movement voiced acid sentiments about the Chief Rabbinate undertaking and the advent of the luminary from Vilna. One Reform periodical, *Jewish Tidings,* editorialized on August 17, 1888: "What do we need of an ignorant and prejudiced rabbi? He should go back to the land that gave him birth."

Apparently, similar sentiments were voiced by others of assimilationist circles who were interviewed in this connection by a *New York Herald* reporter who, in his news story—published on July 21, 1888 under the headline, "Will He Be an Autocrat?"—quoted the hostile expressions of several of this type. This same reporter, however, also interviewed to very different effect Dr. Henry Pereira Mendes, who, as spokesman for a heritage of over two centuries of Torah loyalty on American soil, said: "The introduction of the office of Chief Rabbi is a very good move in the right direction." In awareness of the slurs that had been cast, Dr. Mendes added: "Most of the uptown Jews themselves who may object to it are themselves a bad lot [Jewishly] except in the charitable way, and are hardly Jews at all."

When the Chief Rabbi appeared at the Beth Hamidrash Hagodol to deliver his first discourse, the pressure of the thousands surrounding the synagogue, itself packed to the last inch, made it necessary for the police in attendance to call for reinforcements.

Rabbi Jacob Joseph's discourse at this occasion, which was Shabbath Nachamu, was quoted by several of the New York dailies (copies of an English translation of the Yiddish text having been prepared for the press), the *Sun*[5] and the *New York Herald* giving lengthy excerpts as well as detailed reports of the event. Particularly welcomed by many of the Jewish publications was the Chief Rabbi's temperate, nonpolemical tone.

Calling for "loving kindness and understanding" on the part of all, Rabbi Jacob Joseph said, in part:

> Our principal efforts shall be to gain recognition and to attract the adherence of others to laws of grace and truth, by virtue . . . of our moral living and our deeds of liberality and kindness.

The happy aura of the "honeymoon days" continued to pervade the scene until the point where Rabbi Jacob Joseph came to grips with his formidable tasks.

---

5. Excerpt in the [New York] *Sun*, July 22, 1888.

In view of the overwhelming urgency of the need to eradicate the flagrant evils in the slaughter and the handling and sale of meat and poultry, it was decided that the Chief Rabbi's efforts should at once be focused on that problem. So forthwith plunged both the Association and the Chief Rabbi into what promptly proved to be an utter morass.

THE KEY POLICY QUESTION

A sharp difference of opinion had arisen as to the respective primacies of jurisdiction between the Chief Rabbinate and the Association itself. As quoted from Karp:

> Those who looked to the Chief Rabbinate and to the person of the rabbi as a source of prestige and acceptance, spent their efforts in exalting the office. Others who saw the election as a means toward the consolidation of Orthodoxy and the office of the Chief Rabbi as an effective way to deal with the abuses that plagued the Orthodox Jewish community, contended that greater concern and labor be devoted to strengthening the organization and establishing its effectiveness through committees and boards.
>
> The leaders, Henry Chuck and Dramin Jones, chose to concentrate on the rabbi. But . . . the group which placed emphasis on organization began to exert greater influence. . . .
>
> The Board of Trustees had the power to charge fixed fees for such hashkamoth and hechsherim as the Chief Rabbi may issue. All funds derived from the supervision of Kashruth [were to] be added to the funds of the Association. . . .

Karp observes the fact that "this income [from kashruth supervision] was to be utilized for maintenance of the Chief Rabbinate via the Association was not sufficient to rebut the criticism that the Association would compel buyers of kosher meat to foot the bill for the Chief Rabbi."

However well-conceived in principle, the policy manifest was all too subject to detraction in the conditions of the time, as events were to show. Few could appreciate that fiscal viability was necessary for Association and Chief Rabbinate alike, and the alternative of dependence on allocations from the meager means and fluctuating interest of the mostly small, hard-pressed, struggling congregations was at best an uncertain and inadequate resource. In view of the dismaying experience of rabbis on income from hechsherim, it was obviously preferable to free the Chief Rabbi from the financial and business aspects of this service, with full jurisdiction for him in rabbinic areas proper.

In one way or another, the purchaser is "compelled to foot the bill" for what is involved in meat and poultry production from the point of slaughter to the point of sale and for the indispensable supervision thereof. The provision of means to *authoritatively* assure that what was offered as kosher was truly kosher was necessarily to be funded somehow. And surely the redeeming of the kosher meat and poultry process from the demeaning, demoralizing, and corrupting subjection to the financial rule of the slaughterhouse operators, wholesalers, or butchers was well in order.

Hence the Association provided that the costs involved in the administration and functioning of the reorganized kashruth apparatus and the requisite Beth Din was to be met by a fee levied through the purveyors of the supervised products on the consumers. But—and this proved to be a very big *but*—such a concept could be effective only if prevailing conditions could be adapted to it, if the minds of the people could respond to it, and, especially, if those with personal interests at stake would yield to it. The answer was revealed in the course of events.

THE PITFALL

From the first, Rabbi Jacob Joseph and an influential group in the Association of American Hebrew Orthodox Congregations had differed as to the advisability of its constitutionally adopted supervisory fee policy. Under the existing conditions, the policy was actually a pitfall: A public unversed in the principles involved and the procedures required, and mostly struggling for a bare livelihood, could too easily be led to see the fee as an unwonted, exploitive imposition. Better, Rabbi Jacob Joseph urged, in light of the critical need for an atmosphere of order and harmony, for the Association to bear the costs directly, raising the necessary funds from other channels.

The dominant group in the Association, however, looking for long-term viability, insisted on application of its policy. It compromised only to the extent of limiting application of the fee to poultry and not levying it on meat, then the staple of the poor.

Then was circulated in Yiddish and English, in New York's populous Jewish neighborhoods, the following announcement:[6]

ANNOUNCEMENT FROM THE CHIEF RABBI

Herewith I make known to all our brethren, the Children of Israel, who tremble at the word of the Lord, that inspectors have already been appointed

---

6. English text in *American Hebrew*, October 5, 1988; Yiddish text in *Der Volksadvokat*, Vol. 2, No. 9, Sept. 19, 1888, accompanied by pages of lampoon, ridicule, and distortion.

in the poultry slaughter houses to test the knives and to have supervision of everything in their care. From this day forward every bird slaughtered in the abbattoir under our supervision will be stamped with a plumba [lead seal]. On the pluma will be the words:

הרב הכולל ר״יעקב יוזפא

Rav ha-Kollel R. Jacob Joseph

and we make it known to you that if you find any butcher's chicken not so stamped, that it was not killed under our supervision and we cannot guarantee it to be kosher. May those who hearken [to our words] prosper and share in the heavenly blessing. On the third day of the *Sidra Zoth Ha-Berachah*, 5649 [September 18, 1888].

Saith: JACOB JOSEPH, Chief Rabbi of New York

One cent was to be charged for the metal tag attached to the leg of the chicken to certify its kashruth. In the English announcement, the footnote was added: "The fowl bearing seals should not be sold for any higher price than others, except one cent on each fowl for the seal."

No sooner did the announcement appear than there broke upon Jewish New York a storm that darkened its skies as never before, bringing poisoned air that was to linger for a long time to come. It was precipitated by an assortment of people whose interests had been touched by the emergence of the Association of American Orthodox Hebrew Congregations and the Chief Rabbinate, with their joint capacity for decisive, abuse-purging religious authority. Now the announcement of the plumba and the cent charge offered them a weapon to their purpose. They seized it instantly, with avidity.

UNDER FIRE: THE ONE-CENT PLUMBA

The opposition now unleashed came from certain local rabbis, shochatim, poultry and meat wholesalers, butchers, and an assortment of "reverends" and others feeding, barnacle-like, on the vessels of religious life. Allied with these for the nonce—and, as experts in vilification of the faith of their fathers, well-tooled allies—were the clusters of anarchists, socialists, and others of the radical forces that had bestowed their edifying presence on the Lower East Side. To again quote Abraham J. Karp:

It was a heaven-sent opportunity. . . . *Karobka* became the battle cry. Karobka was a tax imposed by the Russian government on kosher meat. The Russian Jew knew its meaning well, and the very mention of the word conjured up all the disabilities and persecutions he had suffered in the land of the Czars. They knew too, that income from the tax was used for anti-Jewish purposes. "Karobka" represented everything evil in Czarist Russia. What was the Chief Rabbi's poultry tax but "karobka"? Were the heads of the Association any better than the Jewish tax farmers who were lackeys to the Czar and enemies of their people? A successful catch-phrase is often far more effective than the most reasoned argument. "Karobka" was such a word. It evoked deep emotion; there was no arguing its evil and it could so aptly describe the newly imposed tax.

The barrage of propaganda that ensued had a dire effect. Ridicule was joined to falsification, distortion to condemnation. Housewives struggling hard to make ends meet, faced with the declaration that an outrageous exploitation was afoot, were stirred to bitter protest. Among all ranks there was puzzlement and doubt.

Daily the organs of the antireligious forces poured forth, with every ingenuity of ridicule and calumny, their portrayal of the Chief Rabbi as the willing instrument of schemers inflicting price-gouging on poor families. Those butchers who, doubtless for reasons of their own, were opposed to real supervision, attacked in concert. In collusion with these strange allies were several rabbis who, seeing their standing and jealously guarded prerogatives subject to scrutiny, were jealous of the Chief Rabbi and were no longer hesitant to act. So, too, it was the shochatim and other functionaries, such as one impassioned "marriage performer, mohel, and preacher," who, as spokesman at a public meeting for the opposing parties, declared that Rabbi Jacob Joseph, the charif, moreh tzedek, and maggid yesharim of Vilna, had no right to the title of "Chief Rabbi of New York."

Thus armed, a group of butchers and the rest of the assortment projected a rival setup. The supporting rabbis thereupon constituted themselves as the "Beth Din Tzedek, the Great Court," and announced their appointment of "qualified ritual slaughterers in the slaughterhouse" and of two supervisors who, they pointedly stated, "serve without pay."

Issued with the rival announcement was a list of the thirty-one butchers constituting the Butchers Association and under the jurisdiction of the anti-Chief-Rabbinate rabbis. An accompanying resolution read[7]:

> The karobka plumba on chickens which evil men wish to import from the Old Country to the New World is an insult to Judaism and an affront to Mosaic law, because these men mean only to flay the skin off our backs through this despicable tax and put us to shame in our city, New York. Therefore at this assemblage in the presence of three rabbis we declare as *terefah* all meats sold by the butchers who have made common cause with the charlatans who impose the karobka. All this we do and ordain the permission

---

7. *Der Volksadvokat*, September 26, 1888.

and under the supervision of the Beth Din Zedek [Righteous Court] which consists of three rabbis. Down with the shameful karobka.

Rabbi Jacob Joseph responded to the attacks with words free of rancor. Undeterred, he proceeded with the work of eradicating abuses and wrongdoing in the conduct of religious requirements. The kashruth problems in meat and poultry were addressed at all levels, from the point of slaughter to the point of retail sale. In a letter to the Association of American Hebrew Congregations that responded to attacks on his shechitah regulations, published in the *American Israelite* of October 19, 1888, the Chief Rabbi said:

> Those who oppose my regulations are nonetheless to be treated with humane consideration. It is a question of business with them. . . . Believe me, I have not the least sense of resentment in my heart for all the evil they speak and publish about me.

It is not to be supposed, however, that he could remain altogether impervious to the barrage of attacks heaped upon him. He was impelled at one point to voice reproaches:

> If they choose, they can demand truly kosher meat or poultry or if they choose they can buy whatever is offered them, little concerned whether it is really kosher or not. . . .

With unconcealed sadness, he said of the many whose sole concern was the added penny charge:

> May the Ribono Shel Olam make them all rich. Then they will return to the observance of kashruth. The penny for which they now eat terefah [non-kosher] meat will then not be a factor, so they will not only attain wealth but religious observance as well.[8]

Despite the furor of the attacks, the more conscientious butchers bore on the windows of their shops the sign of the official Chief Rabbinate *hashgachah.* But as the vilification and disruptive moves took their cumulative toll, proponents of the Chief Rabbi, among them those most noted for Torah learning, drifted away, weary of the ugly dispute. The Association itself became enfeebled as "downtown" support diminished. Rabbi Jacob

---

8. From a sermon published in pamphlet, *Sefer Toldoth Ya'akov Yoseph B'New York* (The History of Jacob Joseph in New York), dated Kislev–Teveth 5649, 1889.

Joseph then turned for aid to his "uptown" well-wishers, Dr. Henry Pereira Mendes and Dr. Bernard Drachman.

These two supporters, young but already marked out for fervent devotion to the Torah cause at large, responded readily, bringing their prestige and influence to the embattled Chief Rabbi's aid. The public support of the two uptown leaders proved, however, to be but a transient shelter from the unceasing war waged against the Chief Rabbi.

Not least of the mounting fray was rising friction between the "Litvaks" and the "Galitziener," those originating, respectively, from Lithuania and from Galicia, the parts of Poland which, upon the eighteenth- and nineteenth-century dismemberments of Poland, had been absorbed by the Russian Empire and the Austro-Hungarian Empire. Now the bitterness of the communal fray in New York had sharpened differences that were due to differing temperaments.

From the discussion appearing in the *American Israelite* of July 28, 1888, it seems that among the Galitziener particularly, including their spiritual leaders, a feeling had already arisen that the illustrious scholar from Vilna and the Litvak-led Association of Congregations were not really attuned to their views and concerns. The downtown Hungarian congregations, of similar inclination, also began to look askance at the Association and the Chief Rabbi.

THE CHIEF RABBI IMPERILED

With so prejudicial an attitude taking hold among such important constituencies, the Association of American Orthodox Hebrew Congregations began to crumble. The Chief Rabbi became increasingly more isolated as the months passed. His entire situation became ominously insecure.

There came forth diverse new claimants to the title "Chief Rabbi." Karp's report tells of one of these:

> In 1893, Rabbi Chayyim Ya'akov Vidrowitz came to New York from Moscow, gathered a few small Chassidic *shtibalech* under his control, and hung out a shingle which bore the legend "Chief Rabbi of America." When asked: "Who made you Chief Rabbi?" he replied with a twinkle in his eye: "The sign painter."

In a final attempt to stop the unremitting slander campaign against the Chief Rabbi, Association figures wrote to the foremost rabbinic figures of eastern Europe, sending copies of the printed vilifications. The shocked recipients responded with statements denouncing the authors of the attacks and pledging their support of Rabbi Jacob Joseph. Rabbi Simon Strashun of Vilna is quoted in J.D. Eisenstein's *Ner Ha-Ma'aravi*[9] as writing:

> It is not possible for me to set on paper the depth of my grief on the suffering of this great rabbi, renowned for his learning and piety. We never would have believed this could happen to Rav Ya'akov Yoseph after the honor and glory which was his in this community.

Defying even these outraged luminaries of the Torah world, the wreckers of the Chief Rabbinate continued undeterred. Support for the Association was steadily whittled away as congregation after congregation tired of the battle, and individual backers such as Henry Chuck became unwilling or unable to continue subsidizing the budgetary deficit. After a few months of feeble existence, the Association of American Orthodox Hebrew Congregations finally ceased to function.

Throughout these bitter years, Rabbi Jacob Joseph had maintained his activities as Chief Rabbi in the wider frame of communal service and guidance as well as in the mired kashruth field. Not even now, with his very livelihood without foundation, his financial plight become desperate, did he diminish his endeavors.

In the spring of 1895, the butcher group that had rallied to the Chief Rabbi's side terminated the arrangement and the Chief Rabbi was left stranded.[10]

Sickness now crowned Rabbi Jacob Joseph's suffering. He remained an invalid for the rest of his sadly shortened life, paralyzed for the last five years. Neglected by all but a few, all but forgotten by the community to which he had brought such new hope and to which he had consecrated his endeavors, Rabbi Jacob Joseph, the one and only Chief Rabbi of New York, died on July 28, 1902, 23 Tammuz 5662, aged 59.

With the passing of this noble figure, a tragic victim of scurrilous mendacity, there ended the dream of New York Jewry as a consolidated Torah community . . . the dream of the largest metropolitan center of Jewry in the world mobilized for mutual weal, structured for integrity, for strength in the fruition of authentic Judaism in the New World.

POSTSCRIPT

In a final irony, trouble attended Jacob Joseph's death, even as it had shadowed his life. As his funeral procession, with a hundred thousand

---

9. Vol. 1, No. 12.

10. Letter from Rabbi O.N. Rapeport, the Chief Rabbi's Dayyan, to the Reverend Judah Berman and his son-in-law Dr. Simon P. Bornstein, quoted by Karp.

remorse-stricken mourners following his bier, passed the printing plant of R. Hoe and Company, plant workmen hurled volleys of stones, pieces of metal, and garbage on the cortege of mourners below. In the ensuing riot, the police—among whose ranks hostility to Jews was notoriously rife— wielded their riot sticks more against the attacked than the attackers. Astounded and shocked by the attack on the funeral, and no less shocked by the conduct of the police, all elements of the country's public, officialdom, and press joined in a storm of denunciation, to subsequent good effect. Also bearing continuing moral benefit, the sturdy resistance mounted by the cortege participants won wide commendation.

The purpose as well as the memory of New York's only Chief Rabbi live on in meaningful ways. Since the demise of the short-lived Chief Rabbin- ate, the battle for integrity in the production and provision of kosher meat and poultry, and in kashruth generally, the fulfillment of the laws of the Jewish religion in the food supply as a whole has gone forward through many phases. Of various studies of this vital problem, that by Harold P. Gastwirt, *Fraud, Corruption, and Holiness*,[11] covering the period 1881 to 1940, is notably comprehensive.

The wider public ramifications of the abuses in the provision and representation as kosher of foods and products have prompted governmen- tal intervention at times, on federal, state, and local levels. Of singular interest in this connection is the report of the Fact Finding Commission appointed in 1939 by New York City's Mayor Fiorello LaGuardia, desig- nated, "An Investigation into the Kosher Poultry Industry." While the Committee's report offered a revealing factual survey of the problems studied, the effects may have been moral rather than specifically corrective.

Since 1915, legislative enactments have provided a measure of protection against outright fraud. While these measures adopted by several states have served to curb the grossest abuses, of themselves governmental means cannot do what only the instrumentalities of a religious fold can and must needs do in a religious matter.

Over the years, and especially in the past fifty years, conditions in this connection have markedly improved. Puzzling questions remain, but the advance toward Torah community coherence offers better promise.

---

11. Kennikat Press, National University Publications, 1974.

Having culled a selection of voices of the New World from the mid-seventeenth-century birth of the American Jewish community to the close of the nineteenth century, this section of the book concludes with the voice of a great figure whose unique contribution to American Jewish life and the Torah cause in the late nineteenth century lives on to this very day—Dr. Henry Pereira Mendes.

From his arrival in New York from Manchester, England, in 1877, to his death in 1935, Dr. Mendes[12] strove to rally Orthodox Jewry, the settled and the immigrant alike, to sustain amid the realities of the American environment the eternal validities of Torah belief and the Torah way. Undeterred by a succession of difficulties and mindful of the pitfalls that led to the tragedy of Chief Rabbi Jacob Joseph, Dr. Mendes issued a call to Orthodox congregations throughout North America to join in a strong union. His call was heeded. On 18 Iyyar 5658/June 8, 1898, the representatives of an array of congregations joined in establishing under Dr. Mendes's leadership the Union of Orthodox Jewish Congregations of America. It was "to speak with authority in the name of Orthodox Jews, and to defend the rights of Orthodox Jews." Now, with its centenary nearing, this product of Dr. Mendes's endeavors testifies to the force of his vision.

With the launching then of a new force for Torah, marking the transition from one era in American Jewish life to another, the words of its creator, spoken at a subsequent assembly, speak well to our own times:

> Watchman, what of the night? I pray that I may not have to answer: Morning comes and also the night, another night with its dreams, phantoms, and nightmares, that mean suffering for the House of Israel. I pray that the dawn of hope is here and that the day of better things has begun for all of us. I pray you, my brothers, let us all work together. We are all working in sincerity, let us work with charity and forbearance. Whatever we do is not for our glory, but for the glory of God. And may the blessing of God rest upon us all.

---

12. Mendes pursued medical studies at Columbia University during his first years in the United States, gaining his M.D. degree, while also serving as the religious mentor of the Spanish and Portuguese Synagogue.

II
THE FIRST YEARS

5

The Legacy of Dr. Mendes

The unfolding story of the Union of Orthodox Jewish Congregations of America bears, in its varied facets, a potent message: the strength of Torah-committed purpose. When, on 18 Iyyar 5658/June 8, 1898, the establishment of this "strong union" took place, it was because the participants were moved by that purpose. They were the delegated representatives of forty-seven[1] congregations in eleven states, Washington, D.C., and Canada's Montreal. Actually, they spoke and acted for many times their number, for, in essence, and, to an extent, in practical fact, they represented the broad ranks of the Torah-loyal as a collectivity, the American Torah community. The spirit of that historic occasion, the resolve to advance in common endeavor, has endured. It has persisted amid unceasing challenge through the near-century since.

Such a century! A century of utmost testing of the Jew and of Jewish meaning. A century of confusion, agony, searching, and rebirth for the Jewish people . . . a century of epochal world change and transformation of human life . . . a century of universal conflict . . . a century of undeviating devotion to the task for which this Union was brought into being.

In itself, the birth of the Orthodox Union, as it is popularly called, bears historical significance. Considering the circumstances of the time of its birth, however, the fact of its launching is the more remarkable. And, considering all the circumstances since, the Union's persistence in its living course and the rise to its present status are even more extraordinary.

Up to the new beginning, cohesive endeavor in the common interest had

---

1. Contemporary sources refer to "over fifty" congregations represented, but the number cited by name totals forty-seven.

been an elusive goal among the formless ranks of the traditional among America's Jews. Each year, thousands more hard-pressed immigrants added a new stratum of uncertainty and bewilderment to the spiritual confusion besetting new and preceding arrivals and their established fellow Jews alike. The transition from Old World to New World exacted a heavy toll from all.

Each wave of newcomers, coming from lands where the Torah-rooted life of old was shaken by oppression and the inroads of New-Age influence, strained for a toehold on the strangeness of America. The sweatshop or the pushcart was the route to a better life. As the Prehistory to this book has shown, the urge to provide for religious basics had borne fruit in innumerable sites of places to *davven* and to *leven*, and of lantsmanshaften fellowship and mutual aid. But there was a tragic void of coordination or overarching organization. In the absence of qualified guidance, central direction, or established authority, the traditional religious scene was one of fragmented chaos. The channels of religious need were open to exploitation by anyone, with or without ecclesiastical qualification.

Thus, as the contemporary accounts quoted in the Prehistory so graphically show, private interest held sway in means of observance of religious sanctities in everyday living, a hodgepodge of self-determined personal vestment. Shechitah and kashruth, the laws pertaining to animal slaughter and food requirements generally, were particularly exposed, the most conspicuous stains on a much-blotted picture. The conscienceless depredations of charlatans and scoundrels befouled these crucial facets of the religious heritage.

Surely not the least of the unmet dangers was the devastation among the young generation. Not only literally but in outlook, parents and children thought and spoke in different languages. Between the Old-Country-reared parents and their offspring born or reared in the new land lay a gap that, for some, was an unbridged chasm. Jewish education was on the crudest level; means of transmission of the Jewish heritage geared to American conditions were thought of by few. Calamitous losses loomed.

Together with critical internal problems was the collective defenselessness and voicelessness of the religious faithful. The bearer of authentic Jewish belief was inarticulate amid the spiritual confusion of the Jews spread across America; lacking a channel of joint expression, his Torah-derived message was neither formed nor heard. The spurious and the misbegotten flourished weedlike in the environs of Jewish America; pseudo-Judaism and flight from Jewishness alike siphoned away faith and heritage.

One after another, attempts to get to the root of the problem by concerned group-to-group effort among Torah-loyal circles had been projected. Each in its turn, climaxed by the memorable debacle of the Chief

Rabbinate undertaking, had foundered. To put forth yet another such attempt in the face of all that had transpired took more than good intentions; if this venture was not to be battered down by seemingly intractable realities as previous carefully framed plans had been, some special element had to be brought to bear. In this case, a special factor was at the heart of the enterprise. It was the person and personality of Henry Pereira Mendes.

Remarkable, then, was the fact that through this key figure in the American Jewish story, Orthodox Jewry in America gained a unifying instrument that came into firm being—firm, because the guiding hand of the convenor, Mendes, weighed in the balance against all that might have caused it to be stillborn or short-lived. The same was true in succeeding years. Remarkable always was the persistence in the organization's course, despite the tenuousness of its relationship to its constituency, and despite the attrition of addressing great needs with small means. Year after year, decade after decade, through a century-long epoch of climactic challenge to Jewish life, the work set in motion by Dr. Mendes, lastingly permeated by his spirit, had proven vital.

~

THE MENDES PERSONALITY AND PURPOSE

In the November–December 1937 issue of a former publication, *The Orthodox Union,* an article by Dr. David deSola Pool, "The Influence of Dr. Mendes on Orthodox Judaism in America," read, in part:

> To measure the significance of the life, work, and character of Henry Pereira Mendes one must look back in history. In 1877, when Dr. Mendes arrived in the United States from England, the burning issue in American Jewish life was the violently waged struggle between Reform and Orthodoxy. Reform seemed to be sweeping everything before it. More and more the rich and socially prominent Jews were flocking into Reform. Synagogues that had been in existence for some time were becoming Reform in order to proclaim their American character. Orthodoxy was being labelled as foreign and un-American, and "American Judaism" was to be the title by which Reform designated itself.
>
> Dr. Mendes came from an English background. He spoke English with a vigor and chasteness that were altogether beyond the German English of the

leaders of Reform at that time. In his personality he exemplified the complete congruity of Orthodox Judaism and the Anglo-American cultural tradition. As the religious head of the oldest Jewish congregation in the country, with its American tradition going back through Revolutionary and Colonial days to the Dutch period in New York, he symbolized historical American Judaism as could no other man in the United States. In his person he took away all support from the clamorous assertion that Orthodox Judaism was un-American and that Reform was American Judaism. He made it clear that the term "American Judaism" had only one correct meaning, and that was Orthodox Judaism.

But not only polemically was Dr. Mendes a unique influence in this respect. In a more positive way his influence and example slowly filtered through to raise the standard of dignity in many an Orthodox congregation in the United States. His personal dignity and deep sense of reverence for the synagogue as the House of God were messages which carried silently through his person-ality as well as eloquently through his words into Orthodox synagogues which were making standards for American Jewish Orthodoxy.

One of the lines of attack which Reform used to make on Orthodoxy with monotonous iteration was an echoing of the ancient attack by Paul on Judaism. Reform would assert that Orthodoxy was a mechanical observance of ritual forms, and a formal carrying out of commands in which the spirit of religion was sacrificed to the letter of the law. To denounce Orthodox Judaism as being a spiritless legalism became an absurdity when faced by Dr. Mendes. In him the letter of the law and its spirit were fused in perfect harmony. In him a faithful adherence to Jewish ritual proscriptions engen-dered a profound religiosity. He was an exemplar of the spiritual beauty of Orthodox Judaism.

Had Dr. Mendes been merely an individual, these qualities, beautiful as they are, would have had limited value as an influence. But Dr. Mendes was the principal organizer of the Union of Orthodox Jewish Congregations of America, and its president during the first sixteen years of the Union's existence. As president of the Union, these qualities became in a measure symbolical of American Jewish Orthodoxy as a whole. It was Dr. Mendes, representing and speaking in the name of Orthodox Jewry, who vindicated for Orthodox Judaism its complete concinnity in American Life.

Demonstration of the concinnity of authentic Judaism in American life was, however, but one of the tasks undertaken by Henry Pereira Mendes. The overriding urgency, to him, was to enable the Jew in America to find himself as a true Jew in spirit and mind, in belief and practice, and to give voice and arm to that Jew. This need had engaged the profound concern of Mendes from the beginning of his American career, continuing through the rest of his life. Well might Dr. Mendes have confined his ministrations to the concerns of his congregants at Shearith Israel, but, while fully attentive to his official duties, he saw these within an encompassing frame. As has been expressed elsewhere[2]:

> From the first, Mendes had seen the calamitous threat to American life in the anarchic conditions he found. Among the established communities, uncurbed assimilation and rampant heterodoxy threatened to submerge every loyalty to the ancestral faith and way of life. Among the increasing masses of new immigrants arriving destitute and demoralized, religious life was in chaos. As spiritual leader of the patrician Shearith Israel, the rock on which American Jewish life was founded, the young Mendes was placed in a focal position. The direction he set, the note he struck, would have crucial influence.
>
> Mendes rose to the test. In word and action, he called forth fidelity to the Torah way, rallied spirits, turned the light of authentic Jewish teaching on the dilemmas of the time, strove to guide the Jew in America toward the Modern Age and New World challenges while holding fast to his heritage. He reached out to the established and the newly arrived ranks alike. Devoted as Henry Pereira Mendes was to his own congregation, his concern embraced the American Jewish totality.
>
> With clarity, Mendes perceived core needs and set them forth: communal order; recognition of the binding authority of the Halachah, Jewish law, and proper provision for its implementation; the training of a religious leadership attuned to American conditions and equipped to make historical Judaism intelligible to all; a concerted approach to the educational and social needs of the young generation; solidarity within loyalist ranks. He addressed himself to these needs with a determination that disappointments and frustrations could not undo.

Within a few years of Mendes's advent, there transpired that somber page of American Jewish history, the Chief Rabbinate debacle. Within a few years, what many had envisioned as a golden new hope turned out to be a shattering tragedy. Dr. Mendes brought whatever aid he could to the sorely embattled Chief Rabbi Joseph Jacob, standing by him through crushing trials. Nought had availed, however.

Disappointments came, too, with plans Dr. Mendes himself had made. One plan, for a "synod," a Beth Din tribunal of recognized authorities in halachah, to have countrywide jurisdiction on all religious questions, was promptly shot down by the Reform forces. Another of his dreams, the original Jewish Theological Seminary established as an Orthodox institution for the training of religious leaders and teachers, had been captured after a decade of financial struggle by wealthy magnates, who reestablished it in new character and changed location as the training school of Conservative Judaism. Severing his connection with the converted institu-

---

2. Saul Bernstein, *The Renaissance of the Torah Jew*, KTAV, Hoboken, NJ 1985.

tion, Dr. Mendes gave no countenance to the Conservative movement. As cited in a report to the 1913 convention of the organization of which he was to be founder, Dr. Mendes categorized the Conservative movement as following in the footsteps of the abhorred Reform: "The word 'Conservative' . . . in its meaning as demonstrated in the history of American Jewry, means gradual but sure alienation from traditional, Orthodox Judaism."

6

Call and Response

Refusing to bow to adversity, Dr. Mendes issued, in 1896, a call to Orthodox congregations throughout the United States and Canada to join in organizing a representative common body. His call, mindful of the lessons of hard experience, proffered a limited frame of competence. His letter states:

> [The planned organization] does not affect the autonomy of the congregations at all but leaves them free and independent in internal matters—being only intended for matters of public and general action. . . . There will be no expense to individual congregations.

The call was heeded. Two years later, the founding assemblage was convened. It took place in New York at the Spanish and Portuguese Synagogue, Congregation Shearith Israel, "which had first planted the Torah banner on American shores, and whose roots, centuries deep in American soil, now nourished the collective purpose of the Torah fold."

The *Jewish Gazette*, a prominent Yiddish weekly of the time, on 26 Sivan 5658/June 17, 1898, hailed the event in its English-language section, under the heading "The Orthodox Congregational Union," with a subhead reading: "The first Conference of 'Jewish Jews', who want 'The Thorah [sic], the whole Thorah, and nothing but the Thorah.'" It said:

> The first Orthodox Congregational Conference has been held. It was a splendid success, the meeting of true Jews, gathered for the purpose of giving life to the age-old faith, and to rebuke and repudiate the Reformers who have been foisting some strange devices upon us, and calling that Judaism. From every Jewish community came prayers of God-speed. The voice of all Orthodoxy was heard, demanding that this step be taken. It now remains for Orthodoxy to sustain the work of its representatives.

A more serious, solemn, and holy conclave never met in America before. It was the initial step . . . [it may lead to] a grand union which will gather all Orthodoxy within its folds. . . . To the younger generation, this element is an especially gratifying one. . . . The cry of the thousands who were wandering aimlessly without spiritual guidance has been heard.

The *Jewish Gazette*'s article listed the names of the delegates and of their congregations and communities. Eighteen of the congregations listed as being of New York City were all in what is now the Borough of Manhattan, both "downtown" and "uptown." One congregation is listed as being of Brooklyn (B'nai Jacob); as yet the move of Jewish population across the East River was sparse. Montreal, with five congregations represented, was second only to New York City in communal representation. Three Baltimore congregations sent delegates. Louisville, Kentucky, and New Haven and Hartford, Connecticut, each had two congregations represented. Each of the following communities had one congregation represented: Syracuse and Buffalo, New York; Cleveland and Dayton, Ohio; Newark and Trenton, New Jersey; Lancaster, Pittsburgh, and Philadelphia, Pennsylvania; Charleston, South Carolina; Chicago, Illinois; San Antonio, Texas; Newport, Rhode Island; and Washington, D.C.

Elsewhere, the *Jewish Gazette* report refers to "over fifty" delegations but the participating congregations listed by name total forty-seven. It can be understood from the same source, however, that many other congregations, though for one reason or another without delegates at the founding conference, had voiced support of the projected Union.

The assemblage adopted a constitution with a Declaration of Principles that declared:

> This Conference of Delegates from Jewish congregations in the United States of America and the Dominion of Canada is convened to advance the interests of positive Biblical, rabbinical, traditional, and historical Judaism, and we affirm our adherence to the authoritative interpretation of our Rabbis as contained in the Talmud and Codes (Shulchan Aruch, etc.).
>
> We are assembled not as a synod and therefore we have no legislative authority to decide religious questions, but as a representative body which by organization and cooperation will endeavor to advance the interests of Judaism in America. . . .
>
> We affirm our belief in the existence of God, His Revelation to Israel, the coming of a personal Messiah, and the Thirteen Principles of Maimonides.

At a later occasion,[1] the guiding purposes of the Orthodox Union's founding were retrospectively summarized by one of the founding group as:

---

1. In *Reports . . . of the Sixth Convention* (24 Sivan 5673/June 29, 1913), Foreword.

To speak with authority in the name of [the fold of] Orthodox Judaism, and to defend the rights of Orthodox Jews as citizens. . . . It was also established to protest whenever necessary against "Reform" Judaism.

Dr. Mendes was elected as president of the newborn Union of Orthodox Jewish Congregations of America. He was to be reelected again and again, though against his own wishes, at the call of all, until the 1913 convention of the organization, when, worn and ill, Mendes insisted upon being replaced.[2]

The tasks at once engaged in were of notable scope, as can be seen from reports by Dr. Mendes and his fellow officers at the Union's early periodic conventions. Jewish religious interests and general welfare on the foreign as well as the domestic scene were acted on, with pioneering spokesmanship in public affairs.

The Torah Jew in America was voiceless no longer.

---

2. Apparently, however, Dr. Mendes continued to serve until another Convention held in June 1914. A letter appearing in the Henry S. Morais Papers collection of Yeshiva University's Archives department, from Albert Lucas, then (Honorary) Secretary of UOJCA, to Dr. Morais, dated June 30, 1914, making references to a recently concluded Orthodox Union convention, says in passing, "Through the retirement of Dr. Mendes from the Presidency due to ill health, Dr. Drachman became the only logical candidate." And in the same repository, a form letter notifying the recipient of a meeting of the UOJCA Executive body to take place on April 29 lists as item 5 of the Agenda: "The next convention, and the resignation of Dr. Mendes as President."

7

Broad Vision, Bold Moves

Information about the Union's early activities can be gleaned primarily from recorded proceedings of convention assemblages of those years.[1] From 1901 to 1915, the national (or more correctly, binational) conventions were held at mostly yearly intervals, in the New York area. Thereafter, for many years, these major assemblages were to convene with irregular frequency. From the Fiftieth Anniversary Convention (in 1948) on, the binational convocations, North American Orthodox Jewry's premier forums, have taken place with unfailing regularity on a biennial schedule, in late November of each even-numbered year, at varying locations.

From the first, efforts were made to address the needs of the young generation and to counter adverse influences. Dr. Mendes waged an untiring campaign against the flagrant imposition of Christianizing teachings on the Jewish children who, in those yeshivah-less years,[2] all attended public schools. Likewise, he fought missionary snares aimed at Jewish children left to their own devices while their parents toiled day and night to eke out a livelihood. He carried the campaign to the public arena as Jews

---

1. Some copies of the printed June 20–21, 1914 *Proceedings of the Sixth* (24 Sivan 5673/June 29, 1913), *Seventh* (26–27 Sivan 5674/June 20–21, 1914), and *Eighth* (Sivan 17–18, 5675/May 30–31, 1915) Conventions survive in UOJCA headquarters archives. Records of preceding conventions have not been found; their deliberations probably were not printed. Information about these assemblages is gleaned from various references.

2. The only yeshivah (of either primary or advanced level) to have achieved sustained existence at that time was Yeshivath Rabbenu Yitzchak Elchanan, which had absorbed the earlier-established Yeshivath Etz Chaim, and which was to eventually become, as the Rabbi Isaac Elchanan Theological Seminary, the basis of today's Yeshiva University.

had never dared to do before. His public statements were reported frequently in leading daily newspapers.[3]

From the start, too, action was taken against the menace—unprecedented on such a scale in Diaspora history—to Sabbath observance. In a mounting tide, thousands upon thousands of the immigrant masses, although typically deep-rooted in traditional observance, were swept from their moorings. Driven by the struggle for bread and exploited in their desperate need by those offering means of livelihood at cost of conscience, more and more succumbed to transgression of the most pivotal and most universally cherished of all Jewish sanctities.

A special unit of the Union, designated the Jewish Sabbath Association, was instituted to focus on this area. Besides educational work to rally loyalty to Sabbath observance and prevailing upon business establishments to remain closed on Shabbath, employment opportunities were sought for the Shomrey Shabbath. In 1907, Dr. Bernard Drachman, as chairman of that committee (which subsequently became an autonomous organization, the Jewish Sabbath Alliance), reported that within the preceding years jobs had been obtained for 1,500 Sabbath observers.

Another officer, Albert Lucas, reported on religious classes conducted under his direction at several downtown New York synagogues. These, he said, drew upon

> . . . volunteer teachers whose influence over the children is distinctly Jewish, I mean religiously Jewish. . . . The classes not only teach the children how to read Hebrew and how to translate it, they not only teach the history of our people, they teach "Thou shalt" and "Thou shalt not" because it is or is not right or wrong for a Jew.

Clubs and study circles were also part of the project, and Mr. Lucas pleaded for the provision of

> . . . Small centers . . . places spread through the districts where the children, and not less the young men and the young women, can go during their leisure hours and find their recreation in an atmosphere that is truly Jewish, rather than be drawn to the [de-Judaizing, assimilationist-sponsored] centers and settlement houses as sole alternatives to the pool rooms, dance halls or the streets.

---

3. In the early days of the writer's own tenure, I unearthed a collection of press clippings from the Union's first years, quoting the founding president on these and other issues. Lamentably, however, this collection and other archived material were lost in the process of moving UOJCA headquarters to a new location.

Presently a few of the proposed neighborhood centers were set up, but the means to do so on the scale and permanence required were altogether beyond the young Union's possibilities.

Also reported at the trail-blazing assemblages were:

> Obtaining Sabbath-observance privileges for college students, transfer of Bar examinations from the Sabbath, and leaves of absence for Jewish municipal employees on Yom Tov days. Also, promotion of enactment of provisions for exemption of Sabbath-observing businesses from Sunday Closing Laws restrictions; fighting attempts to enact anti-Shechitah legislation in several states; and representation to Washington "concerning the proposed immigration bill and its supposed exclusion of Hebrews able to speak [only] in Yiddish, on the theory that Yiddish was not a recognized language."

Dr. Mendes also called upon the United States government to provide "an emblem other than the Red Cross for Jewish physicians, surgeons, and nurses who had conscientious scruples against wearing an emblem associated with a religion whose doctrines are antagonistic to their own."

A notable early success on behalf of Jewish interests was the assent by the War Department, at the time of the Spanish-American War, to the Orthodox Union's request that Jewish soldiers and officers be given furloughs for observance of Jewish holy days. This was followed, in 1904, by an order from President Theodore Roosevelt himself, in response to a letter from Dr. Mendes, that "commanding officers be authorized to permit Jewish soldiers to be absent for services on Jewish holy days."[4]

Thereupon, the War Department issued an official regulation that the requisite leave be granted to:

> . . . such enlisted men of the Jewish faith as may desire to avail themselves of the privilege to be absent from their duties for such length of time as may be necessary to enable them to attend Divine Service.

In addition to such moves were the mobilization of aid to victims of the Galveston Flood and on behalf of overseas communities suffering outrage, including the murderous Kishineff Pogrom and outbreaks in Rumania and Morocco, and also in protest of discriminatory acts in some Latin American countries.

A summation of the activities range to that date, appearing in the foreword of the printed *Reports* of the 1913 convention, said:

> During the fifteen years [the Union] has been in existence it has been occupied with the following subjects:

---

4. David and Tamar de Sola Pool, *An Old Faith in the New World.*

Russian persecutions; immigration laws that hinder Jews coming to America; the passport question; International and Labor arbitration; kashruth, Shechitah, Milah, Get, etc.; Organization of a Sabbath Society.

The establishment of Orthodox Jewish religious schools; schools for crippled and deaf and dumb Jewish children; Jewish school-books.

The defense of Judaism against misrepresentation by Reform Jews or Christians; Jewish rights in public schools; Conversionists' activity; College examinations on our Holy Days; Government employees and Holy Days observance.

Our co-religionists in Russia, Rumania, Turkey, Cuba, Haiti, Central America, etc.

Yet, for all the astonishing range and quantity of activities enumerated, it appears that the listing was by no means all-inclusive. This is indicated by numerous references in various sources, one of which is an agenda item in the previously cited notice of an April 29, 1914, Executive meeting: "Shall we head a proposed Federation of Orthodox Synagogues of New York, to take up Orthodox Jewish requirements not met by existing organizations?" This probably related to the ambitiously conceived but short-lived "New York Kehillah" project initiated by Dr. Judah Magnes.

Item 2 of the same meeting notice agenda pertains to an ugly development of the time: "The disclosures of gangster-life and our duty to do something to remedy conditions affecting Jews."

MATCHING AIMS AND MEANS

The pattern thus set in the Mendes era was to continue through the years. In the course of time, new services were added in irregular, mostly unplanned sequence under the constant pressure of ever-unfolding areas of need. Under the financial constraints of the organizations' situation, the means to carry out the work were chronically dwarfed by what was required, so that, especially after the end of the Mendes presidency, much was done in sketchy fashion rather than with the necessary thoroughness.

Once the instrument of cohesion was launched, many more congregations registered their affiliation, with the original enrollment multiplied manyfold. In the Torah-loyal sphere as a whole, among congregations that did not bother to undertake UOJCA affiliation as well as those that did, the Union was looked upon as their central force.

From the beginning, however, a less advantageous feature of the Orthodox Union's situation became apparent, to persist through the years. On the one hand, the feeling prevailed—with little distinction between those with or without formal affiliation—that the Union was bound to provide such services as Orthodoxy's needs might require and was the address to which any traditional synagogue or community might freely apply with its special concerns, or to which Jews of traditional loyalty at large might turn with their problems. On the other hand, lacking from the beginning was a sense of shared obligation for the maintenance of the organization, or of shared responsibility for its work. A basic impediment to the Union's development, long years were to pass before this disparity was to be remedied to a degree.

Although discussion of the constituency relationship in the early years was not set forth in the recorded proceedings, indications of such concern are to be detected in the background of surviving reports and other references. An example, perhaps, is an agenda item, "Finances and Propaganda," listed for the April 29, 1914 meeting of the Orthodox Union Executive Board—no doubt a rubric for discussion of this matter.

Those at the helm of the organization and in its active circles were bound to be aware that the relationship limitation derived from the lack of organic tie between the central Union and its constituent congregations. They had to reckon with the fact that it was an unavoidable consequence of the restricted frame of competence under which the Union had been launched, as dictated by experience-born practicality.

It is apparent that the leadership circle, from its earliest days, realizing that the Orthodox Union's course must of necessity be steered within the confines of governing conditions, aimed to develop the Union–constituency relationship to the optimum point within those bounds. At the same time, the leaders found effective action on the multiple areas addressed critically hampered by the financial limitations resulting largely from the relationship limitation.

The very coming into existence of the Orthodox Union had loosed upon it a flood of urgent calls for action on a multiplicity of Torah-community needs. As the citation of matters addressed shows, the unstinting response resulted in the Union's becoming engaged in a limitless array of endeavors. Functioning as it did on a hand-to-mouth basis with such sparse funds as could be scraped together, and devoid of professional staff, with its devoted officers and board circle as its volunteer work force, the Union's across-the-map efforts were not equally effective in all cases. It is remarkable, in fact, that under the circumstances so high a degree of practical accomplishment was achieved in so many areas.

The deficiency of resources, at that stage, defied remedy. Each congregation, having come into self-constituted existence independently, from its own more or less spontaneous sources, was its own "boss." In the majority of cases, each was concerned only with its own immediate sphere of affairs. In contrast to movements whose constituent units are branches of the parent tree or arms of the central entity, the Union of Orthodox Jewish Congregations originated as an accessory of its constituency. Thus, while the Union's role in relation to the communities could be seen, in effect, as obligatory, the role of the communities vis-à-vis their common arm was looked upon as voluntary. Membership dues, set at minimal amounts, were seen by some congregations as a token of support—to be paid or not, as a congregation's administration might decide—rather than as a basic budgetary obligation. Affiliation with the national body was often apt to be thought of as a manifestation of religious identity rather than of sharing in a great nationwide (or binational) religious force.

The personal aura of the founding president and the extraordinary volition of his personal direction and conduct of the work served, during his lifetime, at least, to offset the structural limitation. The effects were felt in trends toward stabilization of the synagogue sphere and an improved climate of religious life. Better promise of alleviation of the community's entrenched problems came into view, although the young Union carefully avoided entanglement with the spheres of prior disaster.

The range of actions in these first years is the more impressive in light of the absence of professional staff. (As far as can be seen from the available records, it was not until a good many years had passed that a salaried director was appointed.) It is appropriate to say, however, that while Henry Pereira Mendes was the key to all, supporting him was a group of men who had been at the forefront of practically all efforts for the betterment of authentic Jewish religious life and the perpetuation of Orthodox Judaism on the American scene. Their devotion to the Union of Orthodox Jewish Congregations and what it stood for counted for much. Such figures as Rabbi Philip Klein; Albert Lucas; Rabbi Bernard Drachman; Morris Engelman; Julius Dukas; Charles Shapiro; Captain N. Taylor Philips; Lewis Dembitz; Dr. Solomon Solis-Cohen; Aaron Friedenwald; Kasriel H. Sarasohn; and Jacob Hecht, among others of the founding group and early stalwarts, shared invaluably, through their work for the Orthodox Union and other channels of Torah endeavor, in laying the foundations of America's Orthodox Jewish life of today. We would do well to see that these pioneers are lastingly remembered, and to realize that the hard work done then made possible the accomplishments of more recent decades.

8

The Zion Vista

The permanence of the Mendes impression on the outlook of the national congregational union as manifest through the years is to be seen, among other ways, in his positive attitude toward Zionism. It was expressed forcibly, at a time when the Reform forces then riding so high were in rabid opposition to the Zionist movement. Always, Dr. Mendes made it plain that what he stood for was a "Torah-centered Zionism." As noted by Dr. Eugene Markovitz in his essay, "Henry Pereira Mendes, Architect of the Union of Orthodox Jewish Congregations of America"[1]:

> The Zionist views of Dr. Mendes were close to those of the subsequently organized Mizrachi [movement], that of combining Torah (Jewish faith and observance) with Avodah (pioneer labor) to build the land. In a letter to the American religious Zionist leader Dr. Pinkos Churgin, in 1936, a year before his death, Dr. Mendes wrote that "I am a Mizrachi with all my heart" and restated his credo in religious Zionism which he preached during his entire ministry.

Markovitz also cites, from *American Hebrew*, January 4, 1901, a statement by Henry Pereira Mendes that bears enduring force:

> I consider that the spiritual side of Zionism doesn't mean only the possession of a legalized home in the land of our fathers. It means that, and much more. Our possession is already legalized by Him who gave it to us forever and who gives all lands to whom He pleases.

---

1. In *American Jewish Historical Quarterly*, Vol. LV, No. 3, March 1966; also in Dr. Markovitz's fuller, unpublished study of Dr. Mendes, based on his doctoral dissertation.

The 1914 convention hailed "with great pleasure and approval the various Jewish movements for the resettlement and upbuilding of the ancient fatherland of the Jewish people," and called upon "all Jews to give their support to these movements insofar as they are in keeping with the principles of Orthodox Judaism." At the same time, the convention resolved:

> . . . that we recognize in the organization of the Orthodox Agudath Yisrael a most important step for the strengthening of the traditional faith of Israel and we recommend congregations and individuals to join the same.

The resolution was obviously designed to complement the positive support of religious Zionism—the original, pre-Herzlian Torah Zionism of which the Mizrachi organization was the banner-bearer—with even-handed approval of the newly launched (1912) independent movement of Agudath Israel. In the years that followed, Orthodox Union leaderships sought, unsuccessfully, to bring together the American wings of the two movements.

The gap between the two Orthodox world movements added to divisive rather than cohesive trends within the traditional fold. Since Agudath Israel gained relatively few supporters in the United States up to mid-century, however, the rivalry was more a matter of potential clash than of felt public dispute. A more serious bar to communal cohesion was the separateness between the ranks of the rabbis of eastern European background and the Orthodox Union.

With the organization in 1902 of the Agudath Harabbanim, the Union of Orthodox Rabbis of the United States and Canada, its members—products of the great yeshivoth of Lithuania, Poland, and elsewhere in eastern Europe—had gained an instrument for their collective interests. Their numbers had increased with the continuing influx of immigrants, but the status and vocational conditions of these rabbis had been sadly impaired amid the rampant disorders of the immigrant scene. It was hoped that now, through organization, better standards would be maintained, abuses would be curbed, and the dignity and material welfare of the rabbinate would be upheld. All the leadership and ranks of the congregational Union were in strong accord with these aims, and efforts were repeatedly made to establish a tie between the two organizations. Intermittently, the negotiations showed promise, culminating in acceptance by both organizations of an agreement, drawn up by a joint committee, that (as reported and approved at the Seventh Convention of the UOJCA, held in Arverne, New York, on June 20–21, 1914) read:

Resolved: That it is the sense of this meeting that the religious principles and objects of the Union of Orthodox Rabbis of the United States and Canada and the Union of Orthodox Jewish Congregations of America are identical, and that in order to strengthen Orthodox Judaism in America it is advisable to form a joint standing Committee representing the two bodies.

Quickly thereafter, however, the Agudath Harabbanim retracted its agreement. The negotiations then lapsed and were never renewed, each organization pursuing its separate course ever since.

~

After the close of the Mendes presidential era, the pace of American Jewish Orthodoxy's cohesive movement flagged. Not until a later era was the UOJCA to regain the measure of élan and prestige it had initially acquired. The organization's role had been established, however. Its functioning existence, even within a restricted range, strengthened the morale of those who remained steadfast in Judaic loyalty amid the New-World maelstrom. As never before since the onset, in the 1840s, of the larger Jewish presence in America, Orthodox Jewry in this strange new setting had found itself as an articulate force. Thus buttressed, the institutions of traditional Jewish life gained assurance and became progressively better attuned to American conditions. The collective status of Torah Jewry rose.

9

Pioneer Force for Overseas Aid

The capstone of the Mendes era, in a sense, was the inception by the Orthodox Union of American Jewry's first major organized program of overseas aid. The instrument thus established by the Orthodox Union, the Central Relief Committee (formally, the Central Committee for the Relief of Jews Suffering Through the War), actually was set up in 1914, subsequent to the close of Dr. Mendes's last presidential term, but the undertaking was animated by his guiding spirit. It was advanced by his successor in office, Dr. Bernard Drachman. A key figure in this work from the first was Morris Engelman, who had participated in the founding of the Orthodox Union and served as its honorary secretary for many years. Engelman recorded the Central Relief Committee's activities in his booklets *Four Years of Jewish War Relief Work* (New York, 1938) and *Fifteen Years of Effort on Behalf of World Jewry* (New York, 1929).

Although subsequently obscured in the annals of Jewish history by the unspeakable horrors of Nazi onslaught and World War II, of terrible magnitude was the disaster that, with the onset in 1914 of the First World War, fell upon millions of Jews trapped in the war zones of eastern Europe and the populace of the Yishuv, the Jewish settlement in the then Turkish-ruled Holy Land. Telegraphed pleas for aid from leaders of the stricken communities were received by two eminent leaders, Rabbi Moses Sebulun Margolies (Ramaz) and Rabbi Philip Klein. These leaders turned at once to the Orthodox Union, which immediately proceeded to mobilize a large-scale relief campaign. In this instance, the Orthodox Union succeeded in enlisting the cooperation of the Agudath Harabbanim, together with that of the Mizrachi organization.

Forthwith, telegrams were sent by the Union to all congregations to conduct an appeal for contributions on Yom Kippur night, and a special conference was convened on September 24, 1914 at which the Central

65

Relief Committee was structured. The officers chosen were Leon Kaminsky, publisher of the Yiddish daily *Tageblatt*, and Harry Fischel, Albert Lucas, and Morris Engelman, officers of the Union.

The CRC moved with unsparing impetus and notable flair. A five-week cross-country speaking campaign by Dr. Drachman and Mr. Engelman, followed by another by Albert Lucas and Dr. Masliansky, stirred thousands near and far and brought an outpouring of contributions. From Engelman's inventive mind came a series of ingenious projects: issuance of War Relief stamps in denominations of one, ten, and twenty-five cents, which brought in, through community groups and business firms, hundreds of thousands of dollars; "dime savings banks" placed in homes; a concert tour by famed cantor Yossele Rosenblatt (at the initial concert at the New York Hippodrome, the attendance of four thousand raised $100,000 for the fund); the proclamation by President Wilson, in response to a request from the Orthodox Union, of January 27, 1916 as National Jewish Relief Day. The Central Relief Committee printed 346,000 copies of the presidential proclamation, issued for sale in denominations of amounts from $1 to $100, and copies of the certificates were printed in newspapers across the country. On the designated Jewish Relief Day, $2 million was raised, "making the drive the most successful effort ever conducted by an American Jewish organization." It is to be borne in mind that the 1916 dollar was the equivalent of about fifteen dollars in the 1990's, and that the great majority of Orthodox synagogue congregants were in humble circumstances.

The Orthodox Union's overseas relief initiative prompted like action by non-Orthodox groups. In October 1914, the American Jewish Relief Committee was established. To avoid duplication, this agency and the Central Relief Committee joined in the establishment of the American Jewish Joint Distribution Committee, popularly called JDC or "The Joint." Jewish labor forces also set up a relief undertaking, and this presently participated also in the Joint medium, which has served a vital role in Jewish life ever since.

The Central Relief Committee thenceforward channeled its fund disbursements largely through the JDC, but also continued some direct allocations, especially to yeshivoth. Fund-raising in Orthodox Jewish channels remained exclusively under the UOJCA-sponsored CRC.

The Central Relief Committee pursued its mission throughout the war and into the post-World War I years. Nightmarish conditions continued to prevail from 1918 to 1921 in eastern Europe, with the upsurge of nation-to-nation warfare together with great revolutions. The Jewish lot, amid havoc and mass starvation, was made even more desperate by pogrom after pogrom.

The efforts of the CRC went on, reaching directly and in conjunction with JDC many devastated communities in Poland, the Ukraine, Russia, and elsewhere in Europe, and also in the land of Israel and several near-Eastern communities.

The Great Depression of the 1930s and other historical circumstances took their toll of the Central Relief Committee's funding resources and progressively curtailed its operations, which at that period were focused on aid to the European and Israeli yeshivoth. By the early 1940s, the committee had ceased to function.

In its years of activity, this arm of the Union of Orthodox Jewish Congregations of America rendered a truly historic service. One cannot but think of what might have been had this force continued to function and to achieve its potential as the autonomous fund arm of the American Orthodox Jewish community. Much in the fiscal configuration of American Jewry, and the effects of this on Jewish life in Israel as well as in the United States, might thereby have been very different from what it is today.

WARTIME TASKS

Wartime ravages followed on the heels of pogrom and persecution in eastern Europe, and amid eruptions of a new mode of anti-Semitism in central and western Europe. With such manifestations presenting grim portents for his brethren abroad, the Jewish loyalist in America was beginning to sense his own greater responsibility for Jewish destiny. He was at the same time moved by the dynamics of the American scene—for the America in which the believing Jew was finding himself was now also finding itself anew.

In these first decades of the twentieth century, the last traces of the America of pioneer days were receding before the swift advance of population spread and industrialization. And, events having perforce thrust the United States into the forefront of world powers, it could no longer limit its involvement in international affairs. The entrée of the United States in the First World War marked a decisive change in the American clime. Jewish life, and not least of all its traditional component, was affected accordingly.

At this point, the Union's energies were focused on mobilizing the Orthodox community to wartime tasks. Millions of dollars' worth of war bonds were sold at UOJCA-sponsored rallies. But war demands touched families in a more personal way: With scores of thousands of young Jews entering military service, Orthodox Jewry was confronted by a problem it had never yet encountered on such a scale in America.

An entire generation of Jewish youths, reared in Jewish urban neighborhoods, were now, for the first time in their lives, away from home in a totally non-Jewish environment. Some, put to a new test, cleaved with new purpose to their Jewishness; others were not equipped to resist the strain on already-weakened religious standards. The Union's efforts to bring spiritual aid and practical guidance to the young soldiers and sailors were of small avail in view of the vast scope of the military mobilization and the absence of established channels for the purpose.

Other Jewish groups being in a similar situation, the Union presently joined with several other organizations in convening the National Jewish Welfare Board as a joint agency for aid to Jewish service personnel. As the one body bespeaking historical Judaism in the original composition of the National Jewish Welfare Board,[1] the Orthodox Union was much outnumbered. Its representatives seem, however, to have succeeded in getting their views respected in the preparation of the materials that were distributed and the activities that were undertaken. This work substantially mitigated, but could not undo, the strain on Jewish practice. Capping the long-standing conditions under which religious endeavor had been mired, the wartime upheaval was a watershed in the weakening of observance loyalties among the young American generation of its time.

This experience was to recur a quarter-century later with World War II and the subsequent conflicts in Korea and Vietnam. This time, though, with the institution by the Orthodox Union of its Armed Forces Division, efforts proved to be markedly more significant.

---

1. Later, dropping interorganizational capacity, the NJWB became a self-constituted agency.

10

Transmitting the Torah Heritage

The wartime experience underlined the core problem in the struggle for continuity in the Jewish way: how to transmit the heritage of the House of Israel to the upcoming generation. Practically the only means of Jewish education for the young was the crude, painfully inadequate cheder of the period. Today the term "cheder" has been resuscitated, ironically, as the designation of full-day primary schools of the Charedi (inflexion of piety), in strong contrast to the cheder of old as well as the normative yeshivah day school. For a long time, the cheder in America was the makeshift "room" school—hence its name—for instruction in the rudiments of Judaic knowledge run as a private enterprise by a self-appointed instructor, who might not necessarily have either pedagogic or scholarly qualifications. Often there was little rapport between the sorely tried *melamed* and his often unruly and unwilling pupils.

We have seen how in the early days of the Orthodox Union, projects in elementary education of a more meaningful kind were undertaken, together with other programs to meet the needs of youth. The extent to which these undertakings continued through the successive post-Mendes administrations is unclear. One advance can be clearly noted, however: the establishment by many congregations, at the Orthodox Union's prompting, of their own Hebrew schools. These were on a distinctly better educational level than most of the cheder schools, and in a better setting. On a still better level were Talmud Torah schools established by groups of Orthodox congregations and community groups.

In due course, the realization came that the afternoon Hebrew School and Talmud Torah, adjuncts to the public school, were also not the definitive solution to the problem. Those, in turn, ultimately gave way to the Hebrew day school, or yeshivah ketanah. In the interim, however, the afternoon Hebrew school and Talmud Torah, successors to the older-type cheder and way-clearers for the day school, produced the cadres around which formed the working force of the American Torah community.

Despite its limitations, from this second-stage source came, in its 1920s to 1950s heyday, results that counted for much: the imbuing of many with at least a persisting Jewish awareness and grounding in Jewish basics; and of a lesser number with steadfast loyalty to the Torah way and strong purpose and commitment in forwarding Jewish life. Out of their ranks came communal and synagogal leadership—lay and rabbinic both—and both the builders and the students of the newly rising yeshivoth. It is their children and their children's children who crowd the vast array of yeshivoth today. It is they and their families to whom these institutions have ever looked for support and, yes, for leadership, too.

Educational endeavor strove to keep abreast of advancing Americanization. The acculturation process—given freer rein by the wartime cutting-off of immigration and propelled by the American dynamic—was seen by many as entailing a greater or lesser departure from time-honored Jewish ways. This, for the most part, was as yet tacit rather than ideological, without a sense of break from the ancestral faith. The heterodox and radical social movements that some brought with them from the Old Country found additional followings, but still constituted minor fractions of the Jewish populace. Religious standards so imperiled by the governing circumstances were further shaken by social change, however. This was sharply marked as families with improved means moved from long-established Jewish neighborhoods to newer areas.

Orthodox congregations that moved with their congregants or were newly launched looked to the national Union for guidance in adapting to the changed environment. Responding as best it could, the Union fostered improvements in synagogue techniques and community programming. Now, however, the Union felt more strongly than ever the need for professional staff for field service and administration, for which funds were chronically lacking. Despite repeated moves to reinvigorate the religious scene and gain congregational support for a proper budget for the national arm, more years were to pass before the need could be met.

11

At the Peace Conference:
National Home, Jewish Rights

Standing alone amid the events of that period was the issuance, in 1922, by the League of Nations, of the Mandate for Palestine incorporating the substance of the Balfour Declaration, previously proclaimed by the wartime British government, pledging the establishment in the Holy Land of a "national home for the Jewish people." This vista of fulfillment of a nineteen-centuries-long dream, albeit reduced to the political definitions of the modern age, fired the hearts of Jews everywhere. Notably, active opposition to issuance of the Declaration and Mandate came less from the Arab world than from assimilation-bent elements mobilized by the Reform Judaism movement. Unable, despite their bitter efforts, to block issuance, this source had contrived through influential connections to engineer a contraction of its terms, with eventual costly results.

The acclaim of the Jewish-minded of all outlooks, voiced for its own American tradition-loyal constituency by the Orthodox Union, was recognized universally as the true manifestation of the Jewish people's position.

At this focal point in history, the thousands of North America's Torah-loyal congregations and their congregant families spoke as one through the Union of Orthodox Jewish Congregations of America.

The Orthodox Union, too, shared in mobilizing American Jewish efforts for securing Jewish rights in the postwar reconstruction of the states of eastern and central Europe. These efforts were channeled within a context of rivalry between the American Jewish Committee and the original American Jewish Congress (not to be confused with the present organization bearing the same name). The American Jewish Committee, composed of the wealthiest and most politically influential of the country's Jews and dominated by the assimilation-minded, was opposed to any national consciousness expression. Counter to this, the original American Jewish Congress had been brought together as a roof grouping of established organizations and local communities to work in support of the Jewish commonwealth-in-the-making and for Jewish rights as a national minority in the restored lands of Europe. The Orthodox Union participated in this coalition, and when the American Jewish Committee in its turn sought counter-interorganizational capacity, the Orthodox Union was courted by this entity, also. The relationship with both groups enabled the Union to contribute to the forging between them of a unified approach to Jewish rights issues at the postwar Peace Conference.

Attempts in subsequent years by the UOJCA to exercise meaningful influence on the policies of both the new organization that adopted the name American Jewish Congress and the American Jewish Committee proved futile. Orthodox Union representation in both thus was terminated. In time other organizations also withdrew, leaving the two AJCs as individual membership organizations able to speak only for their own members.

CURRENTS OF NEW MOMENTUM

The ongoing overseas relief work of the traditional community continued to function through UOJCA channels. Emissaries of the great European yeshivoth, coming to garner funds for their institutions, invariably turned to the central organization and found a ready response. The benefits were by no means one-sided. The more personalized tie with the vital centers of the Torah world brought new impetus to American Orthodox Jewry.

These contacts, and the spur of world-shaking events to the sense of historic responsibility, found expression in more broadly conceived developments in elementary education. Bold steps were now made in secondary and advanced Torah learning, as well as in synagogal progress. The current was quickened, too, by the resumption of immigration for a brief few postwar years. In the period from 1920 to 1924, over 250,000 Jews arrived in the United States. Then, a series of discriminatory immigration laws all but closed America's doors to immigration from eastern and southern Europe. Not for many years—not even in the terrible Holocaust days to come—were the doors to be reopened.

Reflecting modern-age effects, the post-World War I influx brought a greater proportion than before of those who had already gravitated away from traditional adherence. Other newcomers, however, had remained steadfast, bringing new strength to American Torah ranks. The influx included an unprecedented number of eminent rabbis and Torah scholars. Their presence was much felt in both congregational and educational realms.

~

The picture of the pioneer Orthodox Union decades that now, in near-century-long perspective, comes into view is one of a diversity of innovative, path-breaking moves consistent in aim, though not emerging from a planned program of organizational function. Like the makeshift melange of Judaic requisites whose deficiencies the Union was instituted to repair, the Union itself was flung into its work along rather makeshift lines. The activities were integrated only in common relation to the Mendes motive power, which persisted long beyond his presidential tenure. Improvisation spurred by the pressures of given areas of urgent need from the first had become the mode. This nurtured the tendency that in later years, with the multiplication of fields of activity, led to the many-faceted, but loosely integrated, directional and operational structure of the present day.

A well-thought-out formulation of organizational mission, structure, and functional program in application to a carefully studied assessment of objective circumstances was hardly to be expected of the busy up-and-at-'em thrust of the early period. When, long after, approaches to broad planning were made, they were crowded out by the pressures of daily demand. A comprehensive blueprint of the why, what, where, when, and how of American Jewish Orthodoxy's central force has yet to be promulgated.

Yet, what emerges in the picture of the Orthodox Jewish Union's beginnings is more than an aggregation of spontaneous actions. Beyond this is to be seen a brave new direction for the Jew of Torah commitment in the New World. We see him in new stance, with a new sense of his place in America and the new-age world.

Not always, in the years and decades to follow, was the purpose to be as clearly grasped, as pointedly directed. That which had been engendered by the founder and his colleagues, however, remained a moving force, bearing the Mendes vision of the American Torah community forward through momentous years to the yet newer age and its yet newer challenges now unfolding.

POINTING THE WAY

For the Orthodox Union, the years were to bring ups and downs rather than continuous progress, spirals of upsurge and decline. But, from the mid-century point on, the course was to remain on the ascendant. Hyperbole is unnecessary to underscore the strength and scope attained by the Orthodox

Union as it now reaches the century mark, a status that must only have been dreamed of before.

Although some of the problems that plagued Jewish religious life in the United States in earlier years have been allayed rather than definitively resolved, others have been more thoroughly excised. Certainly the worst of the evils rampant in the mass immigration years have been uprooted. The atmosphere engendered by the emergence of the Union of Orthodox Jewish Congregations of America, together with practical moves, made possible developments unattainable under prior conditions. In the perspective of the Orthodox Union's present-day capacities, it can be seen that the life force channeled by continuing flow bore the nutrients of Torah-cause progress.

The rise of the UOJCA to its present status is a gauge of the phenomenal upsurge of American Orthodox Jewry in recent decades. The revolutionary change is not only a matter of multiplication of the numbers of the traditionally observant, of elevation of observance standards and facilities, of the numbers and enrollments of yeshivoth and other educational institutions. Beyond all this is the less tangible, but no less real and significant, revolution in presence—in the way Torah-loyal Jewry views itself and is viewed by others; in the way it speaks and is heard; in the way it acts in Jewish and public affairs, exercises its role in the world, and pursues its function in the life of humankind.

Diverse forces have taken effect in the resurgence of Orthodox Jewry. Among them, the role and work of the Orthodox Union have obviously been crucial. Less obviously now, but in the opinion of this writer not less truly, the purpose of Henry Pereira Mendes has been pivotal throughout.

It is the premise here that not only the birth of the Union and its initial duration, but its continuity throughout and the effect of that continuity in the rise of the American Torah community, are to be attributed to the spirit and purpose and personal qualities of Henry Pereira Mendes. It is troubling to find that today so few, even among the more informed, know of the crucial role Dr. Mendes played. It is not to the credit of America's Orthodox Jewish community that awareness of a figure so focal in its development has been permitted to fade.

To strike a personal note, the writer was not privileged to have known Henry Pereira Mendes. He died in 1937, several years before the beginning of my own engagement with the organization he had fathered. In the earlier years of this association, glimpses of Dr. Mendes came to me in the way some of those who had known him spoke of him.[1] Study of the

---

1. Among these was Morris Engelman, then the last survivor of the founding group of the Union of Orthodox Jewish Congregations. He was an officer of the

written record, insofar as fragments have survived, and of the works of historical researchers, have given substance to gleaned impressions. But the sense of his moving presence was something imbibed from the beginning, something distilled from the process of absorption into the work that he had instituted, something felt rather than synthetically formulated. The feeling ripened rather than faded amid the demands of daily realities through the long years when the Union and I were so closely identified with each other. It pervades my thinking in the more detached reflection of these later years.

The same experience that nurtured the sense of a moving presence also brought the realization that none other than a personality of unique qualities could have given life to a vision so seemingly belied by an American Jewish scene that, troubled enough as it was to be perceived in the advancing twentieth-century decades, must have been an altogether hope-defying mess in the late nineteenth-century years. One wondered: Were the Union of Orthodox Jewish Congregations of America not to have come into being in 1898, could it, or some equivalent, have been brought into existence at any time since? Any answer other than "no" would have been idle fancy, and would still be so today. "No," that is, unless another Mendes were to appear. In searching the annals of American Torah Jewry, no such new-day Mendes has been detectable.

It is not a matter of level of greatness, as the believing Jew measures greatness. Orthodox Jewry, in America as in Israel and elsewhere, is blessed with the current or recent presences of figures of exceptional distinction, even of greatness—Torah teachers and leaders of our time, Jews whose contributions are of inestimable worth. But to have the capacity to win people to the standard of Torah-community cohesion, to bring that heaped-up, atomized community a confident sense of itself, to give the Jew of Torah loyalty a coherent identity and an instrument of effectiveness— for that, you need certain very unusual qualities; you need a Henry Pereira Mendes.

Union from its inception until the 1930s, and served on the Executive Board until his death in 1948. Others were Benjamin Koenigsberg and Albert Wald, long-time Executive Board members and officeholders.

III
THE GROWING-UP YEARS

12

From American Roots

What went into the origins of the Union of Orthodox Jewish Congregations of America is reflected in what came out of them. The aims so marked in the formative era can be perceived in the central Union's work through the subsequent changes of circumstances as decades passed. Here, peering beyond the frame of the early periods, we can note some of the milestones further along its way.

One important mark of change was the entrée into American Jewish life of a new species of spiritual mentorship: American-reared, American-yeshivah-nurtured rabbis. The supply of a homegrown complement of *musmachim*, fully ordained American Orthodox rabbis, advocated from the first by Henry Pereira Mendes, was welcomed by UOJCA circles. Congregations were urged by the Torah community force to engage as their spiritual leaders these young bearers of the rigorously attained authentic rabbinic semichah ordination, at once schooled in the Torah lore of the ages and at home in the clime and thoughtways of American life.

The ranks of the American-trained Orthodox rabbis were to grow from year to year. Their collective influence would eventually loom large on the American Jewish scene. This would be especially felt with the establishment in 1935 of the Rabbinical Council of America.

But it was long before the cumulative effect of advance—in religious mentorship, educational progress, ripening maturity in the synagogue realm, the growing articulateness of Torah Jewry—was discernible beyond the circles of the more consistently observant. The broader ranks of America's Jews, exposed with little guidance to the absorptive pull of surrounding society, had at best but a vestige of equipment for the Jewish life. Yet, amid the compelling weight of adverse conditions, new strains of Jewish life were planted and took root, presently to appear above the surface.

Steadily, in these post-World War I decades, the Americanization process was sealing the change from Yiddish to English as the daily language of America's Jews of eastern European birth, while their American-born or American-reared children were largely ignorant of their parents' or grandparents' folk tongue. As yet, however, most rabbis, products of eastern European yeshivoth, nurtured in the Old-World environment, were identified with the Yiddish-speaking world and its ways. Some were successful in developing effective relationships with a congregant populace increasingly more acculturated and English-speaking; others, in many cases, were less able to bridge the gap.

The Orthodox Union, from its beginnings, had sought to bridge the Yiddish-speaking and English-speaking congregations, with some measure of success.[1] By and large, however, the Orthodox Union was identified in the public mind with the language and setting of America, and with a westernized brand of Jewish Orthodoxy rather than that nurtured in the clime of eastern European lands.

The American Jewish populace of the 1920s, by then estimated at over four million, was predominantly of eastern European birth or parentage.[2] Although, as a whole, in better economic circumstances than before and better integrated with American society, this transplanted Jewry was still in the process of collective and individual transition. Each Jew was finding a pattern of occupation, daily mode of life, and social status, and, along with this, a format of outlook and scale of life values. Each was reaching for security and material advancement, and, less consciously, for reconceived identity and life direction.

---

1. In a listing of Greater New York congregations affiliated with UOJCA (appearing in the Benjamin and Pearl Koenigsberg Papers of the Yeshiva University Archives department), undated but apparently from the 1920s, among the thirty-six congregations listed are such apparently Yiddish-speaking ones as Beth Midrash Hagodol, 60 Norfolk Street; First Roumanian Congregation, 89 Rivington Street; Galiciener Bikur Cholim, 65 Prospect Avenue; Gedulath Mordecai Congregation, 489 East 173 Street; and Nusach Hoary Congregation, 1243 Washington Avenue. It is to be noted also that selections from reports and addresses at early conventions were printed and published in Yiddish translation in the early 1900s.

2. Although the immigration up to this time from near-Eastern, North African, and middle-Eastern lands was on a much smaller scale than those from central and eastern Europe, groups of significant number from Ladino-speaking and Arabic-speaking communities had settled among their Ashkenazi brethren in New York, Seattle, Atlanta, and a few other cities. For these Jews, the problems of religious provision and cultural, social, and linguistic transition were compounded, as a minority within a minority and because the disparity between their original environments and that of the New World was even greater than that experienced by the European immigrants.

EMERGING PATTERNS

With this newer, much enlarged layer of settlement, as with those of earlier establishment, the settling-in process resulted in social differentiation according to material circumstances and lifestyle. Social lines, even within families, became distinct. The compartmentalization was not hard-and-fast, with the current of social fluidity always present, but a distinction was felt between the less-skilled and more-skilled wage workers, the self-employed craftsmen and the shopkeepers, the more substantial business people, and the wealthy in fields of large enterprise.

The patterns of religious attitude that were emerging in the postimmigrant sphere reflected, but only partially and irregularly, the socioeconomic trends. Among all classes were to be found some adhering determinedly to Judaic standards, some yielding slowly and reluctantly, others more or less readily jettisoning heritage as an impediment to prosperity or to accommodation to time and place. Each social category, however, showed some tendency toward one or another attitude to religion.

There were the beginnings of gravitation to the Reform temples among the most prosperous of the families rising from the immigrant-origin ranks. They aspired to acceptance in the social circles risen to wealth and public prominence among the offspring of the mid-nineteenth century arrivals from central Europe. Others of the newly prospering element, however, were abashed by the churchlike manner and Germanic-flavored atmosphere of the Reform institutions; they were more apt to find the Conservative institutions to their liking, and this denomination, with its fashionably diluted, whittled-down Jewishness, sought and found its favored resource among them.

Among the mass rank-and-file, bound mostly to a scanty livelihood, the drift from the heritage-governed life was without either ideological or theological rationale, except for the small, vocal minority of adherents of social radicalism. Most clung to some degree of observance—the kosher home, candles and challah loaves and perhaps kiddush at the advent of Shabbath and the major festivals, the Pesach seders, attendance of services on the High Holy Days and perhaps other Yom Tov festivals, particularly for Yizkor memorial occasions. B'rith milah, the circumcision of male babies, continued to be universally observed, and the chuppah v'kedushin rites of Jewish marriage were generally, if not always correctly, respected. Among most, daily attendance (by men) at services to say Kaddish during the period of mourning for deceased parents or others and at the anniversary of death were conscientiously observed.

ECONOMIC AND
IDEOLOGICAL PRESSURES

It is to be noted that certain writers identified with "leftist" associations have pictured the environment of postimmigrant Jewry in America, and particularly that of New York's Lower East Side, as predominantly secular, with social radicalism as its vital force. This is far from the reality. As is well known from memories transmitted and recorded and from many sources of the time, post-mass-immigration Jewish life was basically still traditionally observant, if in lesser degree than previously; it was steeped in the derivative of the Jewish clime.

The social-radical sphere, with its many contending factions, was never more than a peripheral, though aggressive, faction of the postimmigrant world.[3] When the socialists, anarchists, syndicalists, and others of the radical assortment moved, after the turn of the century, from social-revolutionary agitation and its cultural, Torah-decrying expression to a labor-union leadership role, they then began to exercise significant influence, but still as a small numerical and communal minority.

With the grim poverty and brutal sweatshop conditions rampant from the onset of mass immigration modified only to a degree in the post-World War I years, the need remained acute for worker organization to combat gross exploitation and gain improved conditions. It was a need of everyday weight amid the complex of pressing needs of the Jews of traditional background of the time, one of unrelieved concern to the votaries of Orthodox Judaism, ever "the people's Judaism." As with the array of other needs, circumstances and painfully sparse resources permitted but scant effort in this area. The bitter economic conflict between the workers and their employers was sharpened by religious difference. Many of the firms in the "Jewish" trades, especially the larger ones, were owned by assimilation-prone Jews of earlier-settled German extraction. Largely, those of this background in owner circles espoused the then-fashionable Reform

---

3. This is repeatedly indicated as a fact too commonly known to require remark in such a work, among many others, as *Profiles of Eleven*, by the long-time devotee of radical causes Melech Epstein (Wayne State University Press, 1965). For example, in the chapter, "Abraham Cahan," p. 87: "[Cahan], sensing his great chance to ingratiate the *Forward* with the overwhelming number of Jews . . . his reasoning [in change of editorial policy was] that the majority of the Jewish working population was religious," and in the chapter "Joseph Barondess," p. 119: "The [Suit and Cloakmakers] union now had 7,200 members . . . among the machine operators were many *yeshivah bokherim* . . . the bearded pressers were an unruly element. . . ."

creed, in contrast to the traditional, eastern European background of the wage-worker force. Some people, themselves loyal to the Torah faith, had early addressed the need for worker's self-protection. It was then that radical elements, seeing an opportunity for themselves, moved into this endeavor with an agility that, by the 1920s, brought them to key positions—in the apparel trades, especially.

In matters of religious attitude and in social outlook, most of the rank-and-file Jewish union memberships were in different worlds, too. In time, though, the persistent ideological thrust made itself felt among the Jewish unionized thousands. This contributed to the decline of religious practice and to the weakening, among many, of the roots of their faith.

The effects were to be felt, in turn, in the next generation, the offspring of the garment workers of before, now graduating into white-collar, professional, and business-enterprise spheres.

13
The Emerging Leadership Source

In the post-World War I decades, the on-sweeping, ill-guided Americanization process thus had taken varying toll on Jewish loyalties. Yet there were
ever those among the recent-immigrant-background ranks, just as among
their predecessors, who held firmly to the life of mitzvah observance. Even
among the greater number whose grip had slackened, the life pattern bore
in some measure the impression of inward loyalty. In the eyes of the vast
majority, Jewishness and the Torah faith of the Jewish people were
synonymous.

The Jews of accomplishment emerging from the newer-settled ranks
who remained steadfast in faith were now making their mark on, and, in
some cases, beyond, their local scenes. Increasingly, they were prodded by
the problems of imbuing Yiddishkeit in their own children. Stirred by the
urgency of effectively implanting Israel's heritage in American soil, they
perceived the inescapable need to address the realities of the American
situation in doing so. Those of the emerging leadership caliber, spurning
deviation and compromise, sought a mode of Torah-true Orthodoxy fused
with awareness of America and at home in its idiom. They were discov-
ering that there were like-minded Torah stalwarts among the earlier-settled
groups, and that the path they sought had been opened for them by the
Union of Orthodox Jewish Congregations of America.

Men—and women, and youth, too—of this caliber were making
themselves felt in synagogue life. They were coming forward in communal
circles and in various channels of Jewish affairs. The largeness of their
potential was not quickly apparent; time would elapse before their promise
would be recognized. In the meanwhile, the purpose and presence of these
Jews was becoming felt in Orthodox Union circles. This was gradually
becoming reflected in the central Union's active echelons and in the
evolving character of activities.

From the sparse data to be found on the periods of the Orthodox Union's successive third and fourth presidents, Charles H. Shapiro and Julius J. Dukas,[1] it would appear that both, though prominent—especially Mr. Dukas—in the organization's endeavors from the first, tended to a course of stability rather than to new directions. However, the general tenor of activity was sustained, along with moves to reassessment.

At a national convention held in June 1919, there were represented "150 congregations with a membership of 50,000," according to a report given at a subsequent meeting by I.L. Bril, as Organizing Secretary of the convention. Deliberations at the national assemblage apparently had been marked by concern for better definition of the scope and program of the Union, and for enlargement of meaningful membership. It was remarked that while convention participation was sustained, it was not in proportion to the number of Orthodox congregations, then over 2,200, to which the Union addressed itself. Far more congregations looked to the Union to act for them and turned to the central body with their problems than were represented by convention delegations or by dues-paying affiliation. It was felt—perhaps more by the newer participants than by the "old guard"—that while Orthodox Jewry was advancing in acculturation and improving its means for meeting the transition to an America-rooted life, it was still slow to re-envision itself as a collective force on the American scene.

An outcome of convention discussions and the following Executive Board meeting (Hotel Pennsylvania, New York, December 28, 1919, chaired by Charles A. Shapiro as President) was the appointment of a Committee on Program. Rabbi Moses S. Margolis served as Chairman, the other members being Dr. Mendes, Rabbi Drachman, Albert Lucas, Rabbi Herbert S. Goldstein, Morris Engelman, Jacob Hecht, A. Altschul, and I.L. Bril.

A report of a meeting of this committee on December 30, 1919, reads (verbatim):

After a thorough discussion as to the objects and purposes of the Union and their practical application, the following program was adopted.
The activities of the Union are to be three-fold, namely, viz.:—Religious, Educational and General Jewish Affairs. These activities are subdivided in the following mapner.

RELIGION:
Ritual, Kashruth, Mikvaoth, Rabbis, Shochetim, other Ecclesiastical officials and the Sabbath.

---

1. Julius J. Dukas also served for a number of years as president of the Jacob Joseph School, established in 1901 in tribute to the memory of New York's only Chief Rabbi (BK Papers YUA).

In relation to the first six subdivisions, the co-operation of the Recognized Rabbinical Authorities in the United States be sought.

With a view of arriving at an understanding of what is meant by 'Recognized Rabbinical Authorities,' a resolution was adopted calling for an appointment of a con-joint Committee of five representatives of the Union of Orthodox Jewish Congregations, to be appointed by the President, and five representatives of the Union of Orthodox Rabbis, to be appointed by its President.

This resolution is necessary by reason that not all orthodox Rabbis, duly ordained and recognized to pass upon ritual questions, are members of the Union of Orthodox Rabbis of America.

As to questions relating to the Sabbath, not relating to purely ritual matters, the co-operation of all Sabbath Observance Organizations, throughout the country is to be requisitioned.

EDUCATION:
Training of Rabbis, Teachers and other religious workers. The co-operating agencies to be the Rabbi Isaac Elchanan Theological seminary (Yeshiva), and Talmudical Academies. Intensive Education of the young, and the co-operating agencies to be Talmud Torahs, Religion schools, Hebrew Classes.

It would appear from the subsequent course that the formulation of the Committee on Program was observed more as a directional target than as being subject to systematic implementation.

∽

Meanwhile, the Central Relief Committee work continued to function actively. By this time, although a self-contained entity more within the everyday ambit of the Joint Distribution Committee than that of the Orthodox Union, it was still a special UOJCA concern, with its directing group mostly of the Orthodox Union's leadership circle. Especially important were the CRC efforts on behalf of the yeshivoth in the land of Israel and Europe. These great citadels of higher Torah learning were in desperate straits after years of new wars and revolutions that followed, with pogrom, devastation, and mass starvation, the culmination of the global convulsion.

In 1924, the Central Relief Committee and the Orthodox Union sponsored a mission to the United States and Canada by an unprecedented roster of great figures of the Torah world.[2] The group came as a delegation on behalf of restoration of the yeshivoth. It consisted of Rav Yitzchak Hacohen Kook, Chief Rabbi of the Holy Land; Rav Moshe Mordecai

---

2. Account given in Aaron Rothkoff, "The 1924 Rabbinical Delegation Visit," *Jewish Life*, November–December 1963.

Epstein, Rosh Hayeshivah of the Slobodka Yeshivah; Rav Avraham Dov-Ber
Kahane-Shapiro, President of the Agudath Harabbanim of Lithuania and
Chief Rabbi of Kovno; and Rav Ya'akov Lessin, a founder of the Slobodka
Kollel. These luminaries were received with great acclaim as they visited
leading cities. They were given official honors by government and civic
leaders, and were received at the White House by President Calvin
Coolidge. Their visit had a stimulating effect on religious life, besides the
result of raising over $400,000 for the overseas yeshivoth.

NEW ENERGIES, BOLDER MOVES

The Orthodox Union tempo seems to have quickened markedly with the
inception near the end of 1924 of the administration headed by Rabbi Dr.
Herbert S. Goldstein as President. He was one of the few functioning rabbis
to serve as UOJCA president, this office otherwise being held by laymen.
Rabbi Goldstein had early distinguished himself as spiritual leader of the
West Side Institutional Synagogue of New York. This institution, largely
Rabbi Goldstein's own creation, was then a fount of innovative advances in
spiritual regeneration. Leadership regeneration bringing bolder program-
matic vistas was complemented by the addition, to the involved circle, of
both lay and rabbinic figures now coming to the fore. Data of the mid- and
later-1900s record the participation, among many others, of Rabbi Dr. Leo
Jung; Jacob Hecht; C. Joshua Epstein; Albert Wald; Nathan Lamport; Dr.
Henry S. Morais; Benjamin Koenigsberg; Rabbi I.M. Davidson of Wilkes
Barre, Pennsylvania; Rabbi Moshe Shapiro of Atlantic City, New Jersey;
Rabbi S. Neches of Los Angeles; Rabbi Raphael Gold, then of Minneapolis;
Samuel C. Feuerstein of Boston; Israel S. Gomborov of Baltimore; Hersh
Manischewitz of Cincinnati; Rabbi Joseph H. Lookstein; William Weiss;
Hon. Samuel H. Hofstader; Harry Kolko of Rochester, New York; and Max
Herskovits. Also recurring, as Executive Board member and then as
Executive Secretary, was the name of Rabbi I.L. Bril, who apparently
assumed an official capacity for a year or two in the late 1920s.

14

Reaching Out

Throughout the pre-Depression years, the mixed fortunes of attempted new ventures marked the ways in which the Orthodox Union sought wider reaches. At the same time, efforts were made to reinforce the Orthodox Union's capacity in the organizational sense, as the constitutionally functioning representative arm-and-joint force of its congregational constituency. This capacity, the very basis of the Union, had by this point become somewhat blurred in practice. Inadequate involvement by the congregations with the Union's program, inadequate contact by the Union with the lives of the congregations, had distanced relations. Lacking an organic bond, representation at the Union's conventions and nomination of congregant figures for election to the Union's governing board could not of themselves counter the trend to a "we and they" attitude with an attitude of "our Union, our Congregations." Thus came the efforts now to make the Union's evolved aspect as an *organism*, a self-contained instrument of service, to sustain rather than overshadow its primary character as the collective *organization* of the congregations.

The Union-constituency relationship problem, as previously noted, has been chronic. The need for basic organizational reinforcement, perhaps reconstruction, has recurred through the central Union's history.

Activity in this interest was thus undertaken in the mid-1920s together with fieldwork ventures, regional conclaves, and more frequent national assemblages. Much of the work was done on a volunteer basis, with but occasional, temporary engagement of personnel. Under such limitations, the work lacked adequate planning, thrust, and follow-through. While the sense of vitality was undoubtedly stimulating, bringing a current of momentum that stirred congregational life, few of the various undertakings projected proved to be enduring.

It is to be understood that with America's Jews as a whole increasingly more distant in time, culture, and mentality from European origins, what was being done for upholding meaningful Jewishness among American Jewry's millions was far outmatched by the scope of need. But within the realities of its American-geared limits, what was attempted and what was accomplished for the transmission of Judaic essentials was lastingly meaningful. In rallying the strength of traditional religious forces, defending the ramparts, and bearing aloft the Torah banner, a people's innermost life was sustained.

INNOVATIONS

One undertaking sought a new approach to overcoming obstacles to Sabbath observance, in an effort to reclaim many Jews for this basic mitzvah. Under the initial chairmanship of Dr. Samuel Friedman, this project, designated the "Five-Day Week Movement," was carried forward for a number of years, in concert with national organized labor forces. Conducted persistently with little fanfare, the UOJCA-sponsored Five-Day Week movement contributed to the eventual change to a five-day work week in much of American business and industry, with consequent facilitation of Shemirath Shabbath. It has played a little-recognized but not insignificant part in the extraordinary growth in the number of Sabbath-observing households in American Jewish society over the past several decades.

The five-day work week propagation program was additional to the work ongoing since the Union's beginnings for the advance of Sabbath observance. This, since 1905, had been reconstituted as a separate, autonomous organization, the Jewish Sabbath Alliance, with a continuing link to the Union through the UOJCA Sabbath Committee.

A related task, forwarded year after year from the 1920s on, was the combating of internationally propagated moves for a form of universal calendar change. This would have resulted in a "floating" Shabbath that would have occurred on a different day each week. The main instrument to fight this threat, the League for the Fixity of the Sabbath, was led, with Orthodox Union sponsorship, by Rabbi Herbert S. Goldstein. Leaders of communities abroad as well as in the United States joined in this endeavor. The eventual abandonment of the Sabbath-threatening plan in international channels in the 1950s marked the success of the League's campaign.

Sources such as printed copies of the "Message" delivered by Rabbi Herbert S. Goldstein, then the President of the Orthodox Union, to the

Adar 5689/March 1929 National Convention[1] indicate growth in membership and regional development. The document states in part:

> We have regional branches where whole cities are united into Kehillahs or
> local Unions or Councils of congregations, some weak, some strong. I have in
> mind the Kehillah in Chicago, the Councils in Baltimore, Milwaukee, and
> Boston.

Of those cited by Rabbi Goldstein, the only one to have maintained
continuity through the years is the Council of Orthodox Jewish Congregations of Baltimore. It has maintained its role, in varying levels of activity,
to the present day. Another kehillah-inspired intercongregational force, the
St. Louis Vad Hoeir (Jewish Community Council), although not among
those cited in the 1929 Convention message, was also in existence then and
has continued, under a succession of able rabbinic and lay leaders and staff,
to the present.

The 1929 convention also authorized the establishment of a "Greater
New York Branch of the Union." This appears to have been launched with
some vigor under the chairmanship of Benjamin Koenigsberg. The previously mentioned list of "Greater New York Congregations Affiliated with
the Union of Orthodox Jewish Congregations of America," giving the
names and addresses of thirty-six congregations, is one of the few items
pertaining to this project to have survived. Although some correspondence
indicative of a degree of activity has been found, apparently this undertaking, too, was short-lived.

Two attempts in later years to set up a New York City regional unit were
also of transient duration. Lasting success, however, was ultimately gained
with the establishment in 1980 of the present Metropolitan New York
UOJCA region, with continuing innovative and fruitful activity to the
present.

THE WOMEN'S BRANCH

Among the developments of the period that were to prove enduring was
the establishment in 1923 of a new force, designated the Women's Branch
of the Union of Orthodox Jewish Congregations of America.

Emergence of the Women's Branch can be seen as a mark of the
mounting sense among religiously observant Jewish women of a role of
their own in collective Jewish affairs. It is to be noted that this tendency

---

1. BK Papers 9/1.

found practical expression at a time of female assertiveness in public life, manifest in the women's suffrage movement. In this case, new ground was broken, for there was no precedent in the traditional Jewish world for such a women's representative agency, as distinct from the ladies' auxiliaries of many synagogues and philanthropic groups. The idea of forming an autonomous force as the voice of Orthodox Jewish womanhood and the collective arm of the synagogue sisterhoods and other women's groups was an indicator of coming to grips as Torah Jews with the contemporary situation.

While always attuned to the parent Union's program and aims, the Women's Branch from the first conducted its own self-determined activities. A companion organization rather than an auxiliary, the Women's Branch was to finance its work from its own resources throughout its history.

It early became apparent that the Women's Branch would attract and serve as a channel for women of leadership caliber. This was exemplified by those who over the years were to serve as officers and board members, notably by such presidents in the first years as Rebecca Goldstein, Selma Friedman, and Elizabeth K. Isaacs.

In its representative capacity, the Women's Branch of UOJCA was to make its mark in voicing the views of Orthodox Jewish womanhood in the domestic and international channels of the women's organizational sphere, both Jewish and general. Along with this was to go much educational work, giving ideological direction, practical guidance, and programming and lecture service to women's synagogue auxiliaries and sisterhoods.

Numerous special projects were undertaken over the years. An early one was the funding of a dormitory for Yeshiva College students, following the birth of that school in the mid-1920s. Another was the establishment and maintenance of the Hebrew Teachers Training School for Girls, to be further discussed later.

Later, a wide range of undertakings added to the organization's laurels. Among them, under the presidency of Pearl Wadler, was the establishment of the Lyndon B. Johnson Scholarship at Stern College for Women. Lady Bird Johnson, wife of the former president of the United States, addressed the Women's Branch 1983 convention, when the scholarship was instituted.

BIRTH OF THE Ⓤ

It was at the prompting of the Women's Branch that the Orthodox Union took the first step in a process that would eventually touch countless Jewish households in America and beyond. This was the Orthodox Union's initial venture, in 1924, in the field of kashruth supervision and certification.

Until then, mindful of the harsh experiences of the pre-UOJCA times, the Union had avoided getting enmeshed in the tortuous problems of "hechsherim." Efforts to help redeem the kashruth situation from chaos had focused on legislative measures. These had brought passage by the New York State legislature in 1915 (strengthened in 1920) of a law against fraudulent representation as kosher of definitively non-kosher foods. The challenged constitutionality of this law was successfully defended on behalf of New York State by Samuel H. Hofstader, an attorney (and later judge) who was a member of the UOJCA Executive Board. Finally, the case came before the United States Supreme Court, where, "after a masterly brief and delivering a most cogent argument, [attorney Hofstader] succeeded in obtaining a unanimous decision of the eight Justices."[2] Following this, similar legislation was adopted in several other states.

Propelling the Orthodox Union's initial move into kosher validification was both the continued urgency of purging the kashruth field of abuses and the effect on Jewish homes of the rising revolution in the food supply of the industrialized world. This revolution had resulted from agronomical developments and radical advances in the processing, packaging, and marketing of food products. It was hard to know which of the mounting profusion of appealing and convenient new products were kosher.

Perplexities multiplied with the sprouting of a rash of advertised and otherwise professed claims of kosher status. Some bore only the manufacturer's or advertising agency's unsupported assertion; others cited personal endorsement by figures whose rabbinic status and personal qualifications may or may not have been identifiable. Baffled in a maze of doubts, the conscientious Jewish homemaker was at a loss: Which products were legitimately kosher?

In undertaking the first, experimentally conceived *hashgachah*, (supervisory attestation), there was introduced a concept that, after later thorough development of the original inexperienced formulation, was to remain fixed in policy ever since:

> Official *Hashgachah* (supervision and certification) of and by the Union of Orthodox Jewish Congregations of America, as a not-for-profit public service, totally free of the element of personal gain and private vestment.
>
> The personnel engaged in the supervisory process to be appointed by, paid by, and solely responsible to the Orthodox Union.

---

2. *Jewish Forum*, December 1925.

Consideration of the granting of the Orthodox Union's supervision and attestation to be subject to exhaustive prior investigation, through the Union's channels, of the manufacture of the product or products, from the sources of the ingredients through all stages of the processing to the final packaging or readying for distribution.

Thereafter, determination by the Union's Rabbinic authorities of the acceptability under the requirements of Jewish law (*Halachah*) of the product or products, and of the requisite supervisory specifications. Upon affirmative decision as to acceptability and supervisory specification by the Rabbinic authority, decision as a matter of general policy as to acceptance of the firm's application to be made by the Union, through such channel as may be duly designated for the purpose.

The supervision and certification to be granted and effective upon contractual agreement between the applicant firm and the Orthodox Union embodying the Union's Kashruth and procedural requirements, and providing for supervisory fees, the amounts of which to be based on the costs entailed to the Union in performing the service.[3]

Once it became known that American Orthodox Jewry's central arm was providing such official service, companies of high standing seeking acceptance of their products by Jewish consumers began, spontaneously, to turn to the Orthodox Union for that purpose. Since these were mostly major manufacturers of mass-produced and mass-marketed food and kindred products addressed to the American consumer public at large, there was a need for a special form of identification of the official attestation. This was met by introduction of the symbol Ⓤ (i.e., *Orthodox Union*). This symbol of the official kashruth supervision of the Union of Orthodox Jewish Congregations of America became familiar to Jews everywhere in the United States—and eventually in other lands—as the authoritative validation of kosher status.[4]

---

3. Originally, the costs were, in fact, partially absorbed by the Union. For a number of years, the supervised companies were required to reimburse the Union only for the amount paid to the attending supervisory representatives at the plants, without regard to the administrative and general supervisory expenses incurred. In the course of time, as the number of plants and products under supervision multiplied, the costs incurred by the Union soared to the point of crippling its work as a whole. Policy was then more realistically adapted to replace the unwarranted subsidization with the requirement that the supervisory fees be scaled at the full amount of the supervisory and administrative costs entailed in each case.

4. The first reference to the Ⓤ insignia to be found appears in the previously cited convention message (Adar II 5689/March 1929): "A large number of firms are applying to use for supervision and endorsement. . . . We have persuaded Heinz

Looking beyond the period of history now under review, it can be noted in passing that as resorting to the Ⓤ was subsequently to develop, it was necessary for the Union's kashruth service to keep abreast of the extraordinary advances of the food industry. What was to evolve could not have been in any degree envisioned when that providential first step was taken. Not only was it to be a matter of swift increase in the number and diversity of supervised firms and plants—an increase which was to mount remarkably after mid-year and by the 1980s to reach astonishing proportions. Continuously, food technologies and products processing were to become more and more complex, posing unprecedented new problems in halachah and new conditions for the supervisory process. The supervisory operations were to extend to plants and food-processing installations throughout the length and breadth of the United States, and presently to many other lands across the globe, from Israel to Japan, from Pago Pago in the South Sea Islands to Finland's northern reaches.

It was to be a development without parallel in the world, without parallel in history. It was a development that only an instrument of communal force such as the Union of Orthodox Jewish Congregations of America could bring to reality. Not only the functional character and scope of the service was beyond envisionment when that first step was taken in 1924; even more extraordinary, even more significant, would be the impact of the Orthodox Union's Ⓤ service on Jewish life. The Ⓤ was to play an indispensable role in hundreds of thousands of Jewish homes.

This singular phenomenon, so pivotal in the restoration of the repute of kashruth and in facilitating and spreading its observance, was to have a profound effect on the climate of Jewish religious life as a whole. It was to contribute vitally to the resurgent forces in Jewish life.

MOVES IN OTHER KEY FIELDS

Other undertakings of the between-wars years, more within the previously evolved pattern of the UOJCA course, were in education, youth, and student fields.

One aim, but without ultimate success, was the creation of a central agency to unify, guide, and service the many hundreds of Hebrew schools and Talmud Torahs. The goal was given added urgency by attempts of

---

(of 57 Varieties fame) to place on the labels of their products 26 in number [as then under UOJCA supervision] the letter U in the letter O, indicating Orthodox Union."

non-Orthodox education bureaus in many communities to absorb the Orthodox schools, together with those of heterodox and secularist groups, into all-inclusive "non-sectarian" schools. Action to repel the takeover moves was mobilized at the Union's 1927 National Convention. At the urging of UOJCA President Herbert S. Goldstein, a resolution was adopted calling for the creation of an Orthodox Jewish National Education Board. It stressed that "the aim of Jewish education is a religious one, namely to impart to the child Jewish knowledge that will imbue it with love for and the practice of traditional Judaism in all its aspects."[5]

The projected National Educational Education Board was thereupon launched with fanfare, together with a "Million Dollar Campaign" to provide the necessary funds. The funding aim called for a $1-per-synagogue-congregant contribution. Reports of the results of the campaign have not been recorded, but apparently the drive, amateurishly conducted, was a failure. The National Education Board survived but a few short years.

One outcome of this project was the preparation and, after several years, publication of the volume *A Model Program for the Talmud Torah*, composed by Dr. Joseph Kaminetsky and Rabbi Dr. Leo Jung. This work was drawn upon to good purpose by numerous schools in the years before the day schools supplanted the role of the afternoon schools.

Of more substantial and lasting effect was the sponsorship by the Women's Branch, with the aid of the parent Union, of the establishment of the Hebrew Teachers Training School for Girls. This was to serve from 1928 to 1954, when it was absorbed by Teachers Institute for Women of Yeshiva University. In its quarter-century of service, the Hebrew Teachers Training School for Girls trained several thousand young women for their teaching role. Its graduates were noted for their dedication to their calling and their professional competence. Serving so vital a need in a field of multiplying difficulties, the school made a distinctive contribution to educational goals.

This period also saw the commencement of publication of a series of popular educational booklets that has continued, in one form or another, to the present day.[6] As early as 1925, it was reported that 250,000 copies had

---

5. Reported in the *Jewish Courier* of Chicago, November 3, 1927.

6. A number of the booklets initially published by the Union were then republished in book format, under the editorship of Rabbi Dr. Leo Jung, with the title *The Jewish Library*. This book, in turn, was subsequently republished several times under the same title, and later with additional essays under other titles. Surprisingly, the original source was credited only in the first volume. The omission was called to Rabbi Jung's attention by me, and was to have been corrected in the final volumes under Rabbi Jung's editorship published by the Soncino Press.

been circulated to that date. Over the years, millions of copies of this popular informative literature on Jewish beliefs, practices, concepts, and views on public questions have been distributed throughout congregations across the United States and Canada. The cumulative effect of these booklets, though not demonstrable in tangible terms, has undoubtedly been very large.

15

Challenge of a New Generation

By the mid-1920s, the trend of social mobility among the Jewish populace was becoming clearly marked in the American-born offspring of the eastern European migration. Aspiring to occupations and social standards beyond those of the older generation, and most with secular high-school education and but a fragment of Jewish education, their interests and outlook were not attuned to a life of Judaic integrity. Concern over this upcoming generation was much expressed in the Orthodox Union's councils. Various undertakings were intermittently essayed. One, the most meaningful up to that point, was the youth organization Habonim (The Builders). This group, together with its Women's Branch-sponsored girls' counterpart, Habanoth, reached out with a measure of effect to high-school-age boys and girls for some ten years.

Just as serious a need was felt to exist in the college-student field. Now, more and more career-minded high-school graduates, including numbers from traditional wage-worker and small-business families, were going on to the universities. In these seats of higher academic learning, the intellectual fare dispensed and the irreligious, despiritualizing attitude conveyed were at odds with the world of Jewish belief. For Jewish youth, in many cases ill-trained in the tenets of their ancestral faith, the college domain was a spiritual and moral danger zone. This problem—which was to persist and increase throughout the twentieth-century years—now insistently demanded Torah-community action. As with so many other areas of need, the deficiencies of means and the crudities of operative facility compelled a resorting to improvisations of limited scope.

Of important but eventually curtailed promise in this area was an undertaking in the student field that originated in the late 1920s. At first designated the Collegiate Branch of the Union of Orthodox Jewish Congregations of America, it was later renamed the Jewish University

Club. It seems to have functioned meaningfully for several years, with units at several university and college campuses. Some of its participants subsequently, after graduation, became active in the parent Union. Several, among them Nathan K. Gross, Bernard Levmore, and Samuel L. Brennglass, eventually served as officers of the national Union. Surprisingly, this project was permitted to lapse, for now-unidentifiable reasons. It was, perhaps, a casualty of the Depression-era strains.

Further moves in the college-student field were made over the years by the Orthodox Union, directly or in association with voluntary campus groups such as the one-time Yavneh organization. Each effort was to prove impermanent. The campus scene has not yet been an area of lasting Orthodox Union success; the challenge remains, in full dimension.

In contrast, the Orthodox Union was eventually to achieve brilliant success in its work with teenagers. This, however, came after mid-century. The earlier youth undertakings, such as the above-mentioned Habonim and Habanoth, paved the way for the birth in 1954 of the Union's National Conference of Synagogue Youth, the famed NCSY that was to become so potent a force in the Jewish rebirth.

A DISPUTED STEP

Of the various initiatives taken by Rabbi Herbert S. Goldstein during his presidential tenure, one was to occasion much perplexity and contention. This was his participation in the establishment, leadership, and functioning of the Synagogue Council of America and his bringing about the Orthodox Union's participation in it, together with that of the Rabbinical Council.[1] The Synagogue Council of America, composed of the national clerical and congregational organs of the Reform and Conservative denominations as well as the national Orthodox rabbinic and congregational bodies, was instituted in 1926. Apparently, the rationale of this "mixed" agency was to project the voice of the religiously constituted forces in American Jewry against the claims of secular, self-constituted organizations to be spokesmen for American Jewry. It is to be supposed, too, that there was hope that

---

1. This was then the Rabbinical Council of the Union of Orthodox Jewish Congregations of America, later absorbed into the Rabbinical Council of America (established in 1935). In this connection, I was once told by Benjamin Koenigsberg, in private conversation, that the Agudath Harabbanim, the Union of Orthodox Rabbis of the United States and Canada, had also indicated readiness to join the Synagogue Council of America, subject to the stipulation that the proceeding would be in Yiddish. The stipulation was not accepted.

the association would serve to influence the deviant movements toward a better course, and would, in general, make for the betterment of American Jewish life.

Diligent search has failed to disclose any record of presentation to any convention, meeting, or other organ of the UOJCA of any proposal to join the Synagogue Council of America. Nor is there to be found any record of any discussion or action taken by any organ of the Othodox Union on the matter, at the time of, or following, the establishment of the mixed council, nor yet of any consideration of the projected formation of that agency. It can be surmised that the connection was made by Rabbi Goldstein's personal presidential decision.

Rabbi Goldstein served as an officer of the Synagogue Council for a number of years, including two terms as president. Yet not for many years did Rabbi Goldstein's SCA participation, and that of the Orthodox Union and the Rabbinical Council, come under such question as eventually arose. Whatever qualms may have been felt originally in Orthodox Union quarters at this departure went unrecorded. Nor does any comment on the matter whatsoever appear in the Orthodox Jewish world between 1926 and 1954. Rabbi Goldstein's high distinction as a foremost protagonist of Jewish Orthodoxy, prominently identified with both the Orthodox Union and the Agudath Israel movement of Independent Orthodoxy, was apparently enough to obviate any possibilities of doubt as to the propriety of the step taken.

The fact that what, only twenty-eight years after its commencement, became widely challenged as a misconceived step, appeared initially as to good purpose, is a measure of outlook change among American Torah forces, within and beyond the UOJCA frame. In 1926, when the Synagogue Council was established, the Orthodox among America's Jews, institutionally and otherwise weak, were looked upon, and tended to look upon themselves, as of altogether minor weight in the land. The Reform and Conservative groups, while representing numerically much smaller but more effectively organized constituencies, had managed through successful organization to gain strong positions on the public scene. It was apparently believed that the deviant national bodies in the controlled Synagogue Council "umbrella" frame, primarily to serve in the area of relations with the non-Jewish public and religious denominations, would advance the influence and public standing of the Orthodox community. With a certain simplistic view of policy, there seems not to have been any question in the minds of the original sponsors of SCA participation as to the halachic acceptability of their move, or as to the possibility of its being interpreted as a tacit condoning of the claims of the deviant denominations to be considered "branches" or "versions" of Judaism.

By 1954, when the Synagogue Council issue was to erupt in the UOJCA

Board of Directors, following which the dispute was to spread widely, thinking among Orthodox Jewry had become more positively self-aware, and more aware of its strengths as well as its strategic weaknesses. With clearer stock of the traditional loyalist's role as bearer of Jewish authenticity, the Torah community was beginning to more clearly define the principles of relationships to other elements of the Jewish world. Realization was emerging that distinctions could be drawn of relationship conditions as within differing "umbrella" compositions and differing objective circumstances. While some favored, for tactical reasons, retention of the established Synagogue Council tie, others were sharply opposed, and there was much feeling that the notion of bridging communal gulfs by association with denominations violative of basic Jewish belief and practice was morally untenable as well as out-of-date.

The issue, encumbered by the involvement of leaders from other quarters, remained a source of debate and contention for years after the initial affray. The Orthodox Union was to await an official halachic ruling on the question by the Rabbinical Council of America, which seemed disposed to withhold such action in the anticipation that the Synagogue Council of America would simply cease to exist, obviating the question.[2] Eventually, the furor on this head died down, with matters of greater practical concern absorbing people's attention.

It is relevant to note strange contradictions that have appeared in this controversial area. One is the apparent inconsistency between Rabbi Herbert S. Goldstein's leading, on the one hand, the Union's battle against the attempted absorption—under the guise of "communal unity"—of Orthodox schools into "mixed" school auspices, and, on the other hand, his joining with Reform and Conservative figures in constituting the "mixed" Synagogue Council of America. Even stranger inconsistency is apparent on the part of the illustrious Rabbi Aaron Kotler. When SCA participation became a subject of heated dispute first within, then subsequently beyond, UOJCA channels, one of the eminent roshey yeshivah who joined in the condemnation of such participation was Rav Kotler, founder of the Lakewood Yeshivah and its kollel, and a foremost Torah-world personage. Yet it was Rav Kotler who, in 1962, personally insisted upon Torah Umesorah, the national association for yeshivah day schools, entering upon a tie with the Jewish Education Committee of New York (later renamed the Board of Jewish Education).[3]

This agency aimed to bring under its wing Orthodox schools along with

2. This actually occurred at the end of 1994.

3. Cited in the original text of Dr. Joseph Kaminetsky's memoir work (manuscript transmitted to me by Dr. Kaminetsky), *Strange Encounters*. The relevant passage reads: "The most dramatic instance of what I call Reb Aron Zatzal's breadth

schools of the Reform, Conservative, and Reconstructionist denominations—a form of the very policy that had been so uniformly opposed by the Orthodox Union and Rabbi Goldstein.

Future generations may be no less perplexed than Jews of the past few decades in contemplating these contradictions, which seem to defy resolution. The fact that both the eminent personages cited were prominently identified with the same Torah movement hardly eases the bafflement.

---

of view took place when he urged Roshe Yeshivos to make an agreement between Torah Umesorah and the [Jewish Education Committee] of New York to set up a Yeshivah Department in the J.E.C. . . . The idea was broached to him by the late Stephen Klein, who was then very active in Torah Umesorah and at the same time vice president of the Jewish Education Committee. There were some Roshe Yeshivos who were vehemently opposed to the idea and Reb Aron fought like a lion to convince them . . . it was all for the good of Torah—and he eventually prevailed. . . . So insistent was Reb Aron's desire to see the plan work that he insisted that I work—at least part-time—in the [Jewish Education Committee] department. I was hesitant . . . (but) I could not refuse his earnest request."

Subsequently, Dr. Kaminetsky further states, "a delegation of Zeirei Agudath Israel asked to meet [Rabbi Aron Kotler] on the issue. He let them have it. He told them that he did not have to be told what Da'as Torah was!"

16

Strengthening the Ramparts

Among the symptoms of the emergence of a home-grown strain of Orthodox Judaism was the rise (not within the UOJCA frame) of the Young Israel movement.

This force, a product of the American scene, began in 1912 with a group of young men and women on New York's Lower East Side who sought a youth-oriented, American-accented setting and style for their religious life. Their notion took hold, attracting numbers of the upcoming generation of the area. After a period in which the core group held services of their own and conducted a notably popular lecture series in quarters made available to them in local synagogues, they established their own shuls. Presently, in the course of the 1920s, other branches arose spontaneously in other parts of the New York City area. All were marked by the lively spirit and distinctive type of the parent group. Subsequently, additional branch congregations were formed in other cities, sharing the same distinctive character. The pattern early established, that has continued throughout, has been for each congregation, though designated as a "branch," to be autonomous. All, however, function in concert under the collective wing of the central organization that was established in the 1920s, the National Council of Young Israel.

So, Young Israel became widely known as a distinctive category within the traditional fold, with a sense of esprit de corps, and identified with a casual manner at worship services and an unostentatious but scrupulous religious observance.

Over the years, the Young Israel movement has grown into a strong force in its own right, marked among the diversity of American Orthodox Jewry by its special élan. It was to attain a roster of (circa 1996) 146 congregations, with a congregant constituency of over 130,000 almost entirely Sabbath-observant. The movement also developed strong ties with Israeli life, with American olim of Young Israel background instituting an array of affiliated congregations in the Holy Land.

At one point in the 1930s, the Young Israel force was to enter into a working relationship with the Union of Orthodox Jewish Congregations. This seems to have quietly lapsed after a few years. Thereafter, the movement's National Council was to ever cherish its independence and the movement's individuality.

In the course of time, some Young Israel congregations, among them several of the more prominent ones, were to undertake affiliation with the Orthodox Union while adhering to their original tie. Such dual attachment seems indicative of a desire for amalgamation of the two organizations, but a practical prospect of such a fusion has not appeared. Meanwhile, the spirit of mutual interest generally characterizing the Young Israel–UOJCA relationship has continued to prevail. Each has counted among its leaders figures also prominent in the other organization.

While the emergence of this self-propelled group was of little public note at first, other developments of the early twentieth century won wider attention.

YESHIVAH GROWTH: REACH INTO ACADEMIA

The Rabbi Isaac Elchanan Theological Seminary (RIETS, Yeshivah Rabbenu Yitzchak Elchanan), heretofore the western hemisphere's only full-time yeshivah gedolah, was now, in the 1920s and after, attaining new dimensions. It had grown in capacity, faculty distinction, student body, and public stature (and, along with this, in financial strain). A crucial contribution to American Jewish development, the Yeshiva had given higher Torah learning an enduring place on the New World scene in which, previously, the Jewish spiritual domain had been choked with weeds. Within the growing frame of the Torah-generating yeshivah had emerged a new phenomenon, Yeshiva College. This boldly conceived new institution, American Jewry's first college-level center of humanities studies, commenced in 1928. Subsequently to blossom into a many-schooled university, it opened a new path in the Torah world in making available, to the Yeshiva's students and others, a range of degree-granting courses in the liberal arts and sciences within a Torah environment.

Through the pioneer Yeshiva's earliest years and the ensuing period,

UOJCA leaders had been prominent in the Rabbi Isaac Elchanan Yeshiva's supportive circle. Thereafter the tie between the two diminished, and ultimately the respective orbits of primary personal attachment were to diverge. But at this 1920s point, relationships were still close, and the college, by far the greatest educational enterprise to have been undertaken up to that time by Jews in America, found strong support in Orthodox Union channels. Deeply concerned as were UOJCA circles with the problems posed to Jewish students in the free-thinking, spiritually disorienting university and college environment, they were in strong accord with the idea of providing a center for degree-granting academic studies in a positive Torah setting.

Especially meaningful to the new venture was the Orthodox Union's sponsorship of the issuance by the State of New York of the degree-granting charter of Yeshiva College. This entailed a large financial responsibility, which appears to have been duly fulfilled.

It appears, however, that later some in the active echelon of support of the Yeshiva and its College felt that Orthodox Union efforts on behalf of the twofold institution were inadequate. An undated item in the Yeshiva University Archives records a resolution establishing, at a convention for the purpose, a "Federation of all Orthodox Congregations in the United States and Canada, *with the Yeshiva as its focal point*" (underlining in text). The resolution further states:

> The name of the Organization shall be 'The National Federation of Orthodox Congregations.' This Federation shall in due course assume the sole leadership of the Orthodox communities and be empowered to act in their name in all Jewish matters. . . . The chief objective of the Federation shall be:
>
> (a) To maintain the Isaac Elchanan Yeshiva
> (b) To support the smaller yeshivas and Talmud Torahs
> (c) To unite the synagogues in each district. . . .

There is nothing in the records of the time, so far as this researcher has been able to find, to indicate any expression by the Orthodox Union in response to this move, which apparently came about in the late 1920s. Nor, as a matter of fact, is there any indication as to what extent the new organization actually functioned. The only other reference to be found in the same source is a copy of a letter from Mr. Samuel Bayer, then President of the Rabbi Isaac Elchanan Theological Seminary, to Mr. Harris Selig, asking attendance at a "joint meeting of representatives of the Yeshiva, the National Federation, and the Union of Orthodox Jewish Congregations."

No further indication is to be found of the existence of the supposed Federation.[1]

In the same later-1920s germinating period, the Rabbi Jacob Joseph School, which had arisen in tribute to the memory of New York's only Chief Rabbi, was making good progress. The few other primary-level and secondary-level yeshivoth that by then had achieved a hard-won permanence were likewise growing fast. These and others about to sprout were the advance forces of what later was to flower as the Hebrew Day School, or Yeshivah Ketanah, movement.

Presently, too, came the establishment in Chicago of the Hebrew Theological College (Beth Midrash Latorah), in Brooklyn of Yeshivath Torah Vodaath, and on New York's Lower East Side of Mesivtath Tifereth Jerusalem, with Baltimore's Ner Israel Rabbinical Seminary soon to follow. Thus emerged the next, after the Rabbi Isaac Elchanan Yeshiva, of the series that was to form the core of the Yeshivah Gedolah array of today.

～

Historical perspective as well as historical annals point to the influence of the Union of Orthodox Jewish Congregations of America in these creative developments. The Union's impetus on the religious scene and its manifestation of the purposeful Orthodox Jewish presence as well as the active support of its leading personalities were alike conditioning elements in the rise of the complex of institutions outside the Orthodox Union's organizational frame yet akin in purpose and goal.

It is pertinent to observe that if today so fertile a new growth is to be seen amid the mixed picture of American Jewry as a whole, it is because the soil was cleared, seeded, watered, weeded, and nourished by the visionaries and strivers who came before.

In the broad vista of American Torah community development, the roles of the Torah learning institutions, in all their variety, and the Orthodox Union have been complementary. So, of their nature, it must be. It was the climate of broad purpose and practical effort generated by that which was launched by Mendes and his colleagues and their successors that made possible the rise of those great schools.

The yeshivoth gedoloth, and especially Yeshiva University, have had profound effects on the character of American Jewish life. Without the leadership—rabbinic and lay—they have trained and inspired, without the

---

1. Mr. Donald Butler has informed this writer that the same figure, Harris Selig, noteworthy as a source of ideas for support of Jewish educational institutions, at one point forwarded a plan for a national lottery for the purpose.

cadres of the Torah-directed they have educated and directed, Orthodox Jewish life on this continent would not be what it has become. By every indication, the impress of the great centers of higher Torah learning, *B'ezrath Ha-Shem*, will continue to grow.

It is well to note that, just as the Union has played a necessary part vis-á-vis the yeshivoth, products of the entire range of yeshivoth gedoloth have shared in the work of the Union. All, too, with men of Yeshiva University background prominent among them, have found place in the Union's leadership roster.

17

Shadowed Course

At this point of transition in the 1930s, the Orthodox Union was caught in the throes first of countrywide and, indeed, worldwide economic convulsion, and then of mortal threat to Jewish existence.

In the course of American history, from the birth of the great union of states on, economic crises had erupted at intervals, with a force that each time had shaken public morale. Far beyond all prior experience, however, was the onset of the Great Depression. After the postwar boom had been ruptured by the stock-market collapse of 1929, the entire industrial and fiscal economy of the United States became shrouded in darkness. There ensued grim years, years of heavy trial for all, including the Orthodox Union and its constituency.

In the debacle, the populace served by the Orthodox synagogues, mostly on the economic periphery, were among the hardest hit. Countless families lost their livelihoods—livelihoods that permitted, at best, little, if any, savings. The hardships undergone then are not easily understood by a generation nurtured in an era of plenty and cushioned by the provisions of the Welfare society. But the tribulations of the Depression era, like those of the immigrant generations, ought be kept before us for better self-understanding, and, perhaps, for better self-reliance. Those, for example, who so readily avail themselves, with the encouragement of their mentors, of governmental welfare support in pursuing a cloistered religious-studies life might thus be moved to ponder a time when men and women who had toiled all their lives in unaided, proud self-dependence, now, workless and often all but penniless, would rather starve than turn—as Jews had never done before—for relief to the public channels of a basically non-Jewish nation.

Only when the mechanism of the New Deal brought jobs, work with pay—however small, and business revival that the desperation eased to some extent. Meanwhile, and long-continuing, synagogues struggled hard to keep afloat. That many collapsed is not surprising under the circumstances; rather it is surprising that so many others, with means and facilities truncated, managed somehow to hold on.

With yeshivoth and schools, the story was the same. For each of the major yeshivoth, and for the newborn Yeshiva College not least of all, it was a struggle not just year-to-year or even week-to-week—it was a struggle for existence, from day-to-day. How the rebbeyim and other staff personnel, their salaries unpaid for months, managed to subsist is an insoluble mystery.

Despite all, the movement for establishment of elementary yeshivah day schools, yeshivoth ketanoth, initially advanced by Mizrachi, the religious Zionist organization, had thrust itself into being. Perils that would have been hard to meet under any circumstances were multiplied by Depression conditions. An item I noticed in archival explorations was an announcement of a meeting called for March 10, 1932, by an Orthodox group "to consider steps whereby 8 of the 12 smaller yeshivoth closed during the past week could be reopened."

Before, Torah forces had reached a degree of momentum; now, with shattered living standards, the hope of a resurgence of Orthodoxy seemed to be foreclosed.

In such an impasse, it was to be expected that the Union of Orthodox Jewish Congregations of America would find itself in precarious straits. Here again, the wonder is not that the organization's advance was blocked or that its work was curtailed, but rather that it managed to carry on at all. It appears that even amid the adversities of so dire a situation, a degree of volition was maintained. According to the ever-ebullient William Weiss, who succeeded Rabbi Goldstein as UOJCA president, the Union's message went forth "even more vigorously than ever before." There is reason, in searching records of the time, to surmise that there was some disparity between vigor and substantial accomplishment. Various visionary new plans were now ambitiously broached, but failed to overcome governing realities; primary functions were sustained, however, and by and large the work was carried forward. Thereby the Torah community cause was upheld, to lasting good purpose. The morale-strengthening effect helped Torah forces to finally emerge from the rigors of the Depression with renewed thrust.

Among the new undertakings of continuing significance was the introduction in 1933 of the first UOJCA periodical, *The Orthodox Union*. This meaningful organ, published bi-monthly, offered a combination of communal and organizational news, informative articles on appropriate topics of Jewish interest, and editorial comment. It appeared with fair regularity until 1946, when it was succeeded by *Jewish Life*, which then made a distinctive mark in the Jewish world as the literary voice of the resurgent Torah Jew.

Besides national conventions held with continuing regularity, regional conclaves also were conducted at various times and places in the course of the Depression-burdened 1930s. One, of the Southeastern Region of the Union, in Washington, D.C., in June 1935, brought together several hundred delegates from Maryland, Delaware, Virginia, West Virginia, North Carolina, South Carolina, and Georgia, as well as the host community. At that occasion, as reported in *The Orthodox Union* and various Jewish papers of the time, William Weiss, the national president, in an address rallied the participants to "combat the spirit of religious indifference which has accompanied the economic depression." He further pointed out that while "we have lost many to the fads and fashions of more convenient and less exacting denominations, the majority of American Jews adhere to the traditional viewpoint."

A second assemblage of the Southeastern region took place the following year in Baltimore, with fifty congregations represented. Preceding these events was a convention of the New York State region, which included communities throughout the state except for Greater New York itself. At these and other UOJCA gatherings, major stress in the discussions was placed on the urgency of bringing "the message of Judaism to the Jewish youth by way of intensive Jewish education."

Concurrent with organizational initiatives, moves went forward to recharge the religious spirits weakened by the stresses of the times. One feature was a national radio broadcast on Thursday evening, July 26, 1934, from the National Broadcasting Company studios in New York. This was the first major national broadcast under Orthodox Jewish auspices since the invention of radio. With an array of noted figures speaking in the course of the program, and a "diversified religious musical program by a distinguished group of cantors," the broadcast made a strong impression. Here, too, the vital importance of effective Jewish education was emphasized: "In the stress of the economic struggle, when the morale of the community has suffered so greatly by reason of unemployment, it is so important that decisive action be taken to stabilize and rescue the institutions devoted to religion and education," Weiss said.

A further measure was the launching of a "Religious Reconstruction Fund." This was an adaptation of the plan previously advanced under the presidency of Rabbi Herbert S. Goldstein for the establishment of a National Jewish Education Board. In this case, too, the Fund was to be raised through a $1 per congregant contribution by synagogue memberships. An impressive roster of lay and rabbinic leaders of American Orthodox Jewry were recruited in support of the project, as indicated by a photo bearing the caption: "Organization Meeting of Religious Reconstruction Committee sponsored by Union of Orthodox Jewish Congregations of

America in the study of Rabbi S. Margolies, 117 E. 85th St., N.Y.C. on Sunday, October 1, 1933." Among the thirty persons shown are Rabbi Margolies, the illustrious "Ramaz"; Dr. Henry Pereira Mendes; Rabbi Bernard Drachman; Rabbi Philip Klein; Rabbi Herbert S. Goldstein; Rabbi Leo Jung; Rabbi Joseph H. Lookstein; William Weiss; Albert Wald; Benjamin Koenigsberg; and Isaac Rosengarten, editor of *The Jewish Forum*.

Unfortunately, despite this distinguished support and the earnestness of the sponsor's purpose, this project seems to have had no more real outcome than the similar one of a few years before. The plan was revived at the Fortieth Anniversary Convention in May 1938, with strong publicity. It was now keyed to "coordinate religious education throughout the country under the auspices of the National Board of Orthodox Jewish Education." The "Million Dollar Program" was prospectively to provide support for the yeshivoth, bring direction and a unified curriculum to the Talmud Torah schools, and give financial subsidies to small, outlying communities "to defray the expenses of Hebrew school teachers in these previously untouched districts."

But success again proved elusive. The response among congregants to the $1 per capita call was apparently altogether negligible. Reference to the project presently ceased.

FOR YOUTH AND ZION

Better results had attached the relaunching in 1934, on larger scale, of the youth work, now designated the National Habonim organization. This force, as previously noted, was to function with good effect for a number of years, eventually to be succeeded, after a lapse of time, by the Union's National Conference of Synagogue Youth.

A popular feature of the Habonim program was the presentation to boys attaining bar mitzvah status, by way of their respective congregations, of bar mitzvah certificates issued by the UOJCA youth agency as a mark of their assumption of Habonim membership. Many thousands of the certificates were presented up to the late 1940s.

From this time forward, the national congregational body was to continue active in the youth in one way or another—which was to register itself in the development of American Jewish life.

~

Amid the severities of the Depression times, the Jewishly concerned among American Jewry's ranks continued mindful of the upbuilding of the

Yishuv in the Holy Land. The process of bringing to reality the Jewish National Home as provided under the League of Nations Mandate and pledged in Britain's Balfour Declaration was now going forward in the face of successive hobblings by the Arab-appeasing Mandatory Power. Mobilizing support for the Zion cause, the Zionist Organizations called all elements of American Jewry to a great National Conference for the Jewish land, which took place in Washington, D.C., on January 20, 1935.

The Orthodox Union joined in response to the Conference call, "to act to accelerate the development of Eretz Yisroel and aid in opening the doors [of the Holy Land] to a larger Jewish immigration," as expressed in a report in *The Orthodox Union*.[1] The UOJCA delegation included President William Weiss, Israel S. Gomorov of Baltimore, Rabbi T.J. Loeb of Washington, and Rabbis William Margolis and I.L. Bril of New York.

The Union's delegation presented the following statement, to be recorded in the Conference Proceedings with its affirmative vote on the formal resolution adopted by the Conference:

> In passing this resolution and expressing its full sympathy with all efforts to create conditions which shall make possible greatly increased immigration of Jews into the Promised Land, the Union of Orthodox Jewish Congregations of America desires to express to this National Conference its profound conviction that only through loyal maintenance of the sacred traditions and observances of the Jewish faith can the Jewish homeland be truly Jewish in the highest and noblest sense, and genuine unity of sentiment be attained; and it is the desire and hope of the Union of Orthodox Jewish Congregations of America that all public Jewish activity in Eretz Yisrael and all public institutions in the Holy Land shall be carried on in harmony with the traditional religious precepts of our people and faith.

DISPOSING OF THE MUSHROOM SYNAGOGUE

Mention must be made of a step that led to the eradication of that unsavory eruption of "irresponsible and purely mercenary places of so-called 'worship' which annually flourish for the High Holy Days . . . that has for many years brought ruin and destruction to synagogues and Jewish

---

1. A UOJCA Convention resolution at the time (1917) had read: "Resolved:— that we favor the holding of a Congress of the Jews of America and the President shall appoint delegates from the Executive of this Union to take whatever action may be necessary in conjunction with other organizations" (YUA:CRC 11/4).

institutions." These fraudulent "synagogues" had multiplied ominously amid the difficulties of the 1930s. A bill to uproot them was introduced in the New York State legislature in 1934, most appropriately by State Senator Lazarus Joseph—grandson of Rabbi Jacob Joseph, one-time Chief Rabbi of New York.

As an amendment to the State's penal law, the measure proscribed, under penalty:

> A person who, in the person of his own interests or to derive pecuniary benefit gain or profit, for himself or for any person, firm or corporation other than a religious association or corporation, sells or offers to sell tickets for admittance to or participation in services purporting to be in accordance with the precepts of any recognized religious creed or faith or who makes any fraudulent representation as to the nature of the services to be conducted at any place designated or intended to be a house of worship. . . .

The measure bore the hoped-for effect. The "mushroom synagogue" evil, curbed, presently vanished from the Jewish scene.

BIRTH OF THE RABBINICAL COUNCIL

The establishment in 1935 of the Rabbinical Council of America was a significant step in American Torah Jewry's development. This organization of Orthodox rabbis came into being as a reconstitution of what had been the Rabbinical Council of the Union of Orthodox Jewish Congregations of America. While the predecessor had been a part of the UOJCA structure, the Rabbinical Council of America was instituted as an independent body—allied to the Union, but a self-contained, separate organization.

Into this new Council were absorbed the members of the Union's Rabbinical Council and rabbinic graduates of the Rabbi Isaac Elchanan Theological Seminary. Others presently included were rabbis ordained at other major yeshivoth in Chicago, New York, Baltimore, Cleveland, Europe, and the Holy Land. Thus it has served as central arm and spokesman for an increasingly predominant roster of Orthodox rabbis in North America.

As rabbinic affiliate of the Orthodox Union, the Rabbinical Council of America was to serve throughout as the Union's source for authoritative determination of halachah, Jewish law. The relationship between the congregationally constituted national community and the leading body of American Orthodox rabbis was to prove a force for communal stability. Thus positioned, the Rabbinical Council grew impressively in membership, service range, and public stature, becoming one of the most potent channels of the rabbinic voice in the Jewish world at large.

The office of president of the Rabbinical Council of America, first held by Rabbi Herbert S. Goldstein, came to be held by a series of personages of note in rabbinic circles and Jewish affairs. It early became prestigious among the elective posts of the Jewish world. As distinguished from the elective officers of the R.C.A., who are elected for two-year terms and serve on honorary (nonsalaried) basis, the office of executive vice president, a salaried position, is of permanent tenure. The earliest incumbent of this post was Rabbi Morris Max, who, after a considerable number of years of service, was succeeded by Rabbi Israel Klavan. The able capacities of Rabbi Klavan guided the rabbinic force on a path of growth and activity on the national and international scenes for over twenty years. Subsequent incumbents were Rabbi Bernard Walfish, and the present Executive Officer, Rabbi Steven Dworkin.

Regarding the basic role of the Rabbinical Council of America vis-á-vis the Orthodox Union, the precise terms and functions of the relationship between the two organizations were uncodified when the rabbinic body was established. In time, as given situations required some specification, various functional provisions were set forth, without incorporation into a definitive framework. With this as the continuing pattern, the resulting accrual of terms of the UOJCA–RCA relationship may be compared to the British Constitution—unwritten as a formal document, but effective as evolved in established usage.

A tangible facet of this relationship is the initially instituted policy of financial subvention to the rabbinic arm by the Union. This voluntary undertaking was conscientiously fulfilled over the years, whatever the constraints of the Union's own financial situation, which were to vary only in degrees of difficulty.

EXECUTIVE MANAGEMENT CHANGE

A turning point in the Union's processes as it emerged from the Depression era was the appointment, at last, of a full-time permanent staff executive, namely Leo S. Hilsenrad. Up to then, from the beginning of the central Torah community organ onward, its work had been conducted, operationally as well as in policy and program direction, by the president and other elected officers, all serving on an honorary basis.[2] In the 1920s and 1930s,

2. In a 1915 letter from Albert Lucas, Secretary of the Orthodox Union to the

up to that point, individuals had been engaged intermittently in professional capacity, on more or less provisional and usually part-time basis. Under varying titles, such as executive director or field secretary, these people had come and gone—some serving for several months, others for but a few weeks, but always with long, staffless intervals between incumbents. The inevitable consequence, felt increasingly as the Orthodox Union, despite all limitations, attained increasing importance in Jewish life, was the irregularity, cursory treatment, and lack of follow-through that had characterized the effectuation of the Union's undertakings.

The appointment in 1939 of Leo S. Hilsenrad as executive director, with continuing tenure, marked the inception of a transition from unreinforced volunteer limitations to organizational maturity and program continuity. Also, it proved to be a key to a clearer outlook, one that dispelled the shadows of Depression trauma.

Contributing also to the new vigor was the election at the 1942 National Convention of a new administration headed by Dr. Samuel Nirenstein as president, and including as officers Samuel Mellitz; William B. Herlands; M. Morton Rubenstein; Siegfried Bendheim; Benjamin Koenigsberg; Leon Gellman; and Joseph Schlang. The Executive roster included, in addition to the foregoing, various individuals of prior note: future officers Max Stern; Nathan K. Gross; Max. S. Rosenfeld; Solomon Rashin; Samuel L. Brennglass; Reuben E. Gross; and Bernard Levmore.

In this freshened setting, Hilsenrad's determined work cleared away

---

then President Dr. Bernard Drachman, Lucas said: "Permit me to call your attention to the fact that the duties of the Secretary of the Union and the clerical work attached to this office have been done by me for the last 17 or 18 years without any expense to the Union. I am however, today so fully occupied as the Secretary of the Central Relief Committee, and the various other engagements which that position brings to me, that it is impossible either for me to give the time, or is my sister-in-law able to give me the help, that during all these years we have given to the Union."

Further in the same letter, expressing objection to the planning at that time of a UOJCA convention, Lucas said: "I do not find that the response of the public, either financially or morally, warrants us in employing the help that would be necessary for us to have . . . even if someone other than myself takes charge and gives the necessary directions" (YUA: CRC 11/4).

An updated copy of what appears to be a UOJCA Convention resolution of the World War I period states: "Resolved: We deem it advisable that the Executive shall make the necessary arrangements towards the establishment of a permanent office and the employment of such paid assistance as may be required" (YUA: CRC 11/4).

While the office quarters were subsequently acquired after a fashion—moving from location to location—the staff personnel provision was implemented only later, on a makeshift basis, until the appointment of Leo S. Hilsenrad in 1939.

much of the accumulated functional debris, introduced new servicing features, and strengthened what at that stage had become the rather frail structure of the organization.

Through the early 1940s, services to the congregations—such as aiding in local membership campaigns, sending speakers, and providing ideological and educational direction—were improved, additions were made to the booklet literature and program materials for congregational activities, and youth groups were introduced. The spokesmanship role of the Orthodox Union was not neglected; participation was actively pursued in actions through various channels on matters of increasingly grave concern to Torah Jewry and the entire Jewish world.

With the UOJCA reaching mature years, the succession of organizational anniversaries doubtless occasioned assessments of the Union's course to the given point. These seem to have gone unrecorded with one exception: the perspective article, "Forty-two Years of Loyal Service to the Heritage of Israel" by the Union's former president, Rabbi Dr. Bernard Drachman, which appeared in the Iyar–Sivan 5700/May–June 1940 issue of *The Orthodox Union*. Dr. Drachman wrote:

> The Union cannot—and would not attempt to claim—that it has accomplished all its objectives. American Jewry is still divided into different camps. . . . [But] Orthodox Jewry has a far better and more respected position than when the Union was organized and is recognized as a great . . . force in contemporary American Jewish life. The old chaos and confusion and the overpowering sense of weakness characteristic of that period have disappeared and in their place have come dignity and self-reliance. Orthodox Judaism has learned that it can maintain itself in America. The Union has become the symbol and the center of Orthodox Jewish coherence on this side of the Atlantic.

18

Ahead: The Holocaust

As the years of the 1930s and 1940s revolved through the annals of the Orthodox Union, domestic developments increasingly reflected the chill shadow of calamity closing in abroad. The vista facing the Jewish world at that time was one of mortal challenge.

Jewish life in the Soviet Union was remorselessly crushed, severing millions from their faith and heritage, and leaving them in total isolation from the Jewish world. In Poland, amid rampant anti-Semitism, the great majority of the country's three million Jews, cut off from economic life, were reduced to destitution. Much the same occurred in Hungary and Rumania.

Blackest of all was Nazism's Germany. A nation of incomparable industrial and, at first, clandestine military might, its forces aimed at the extermination of the Jewish people, to clear the way for world conquest.

The trap was closing relentlessly on European Jewry. Every door of possible refuge was slammed shut, with very few able to escape, despite insistent external pressure. The gates of the Jewish homeland, in the grip of the Mandate-defying Mandatory Power, were barred as well.

In a hindsight consideration of the ultimate horror, the efforts of American Jewry to save their brethren abroad seem grossly inadequate. Yet it must be realized that American Jewish efforts toward that end were on a scale unprecedented in Diaspora history. This occurred in the face of a mass-mobilized surge of organized anti-Semitism beyond all precedent in American experience, and at a time when the streets of the country's major cities, its radio airways, and even the halls of the national legislature resounded with tacitly or openly expressed pro-Nazi anti-Semitic sentiment.

Sharing the work born by desperate need, the usual functions of the Orthodox Union were subordinated to the call to mobilize Jewish ranks.

Just as the Union had joined, in 1918, with the original American Jewish Congress (not the present like-named organization, but an intercommunity and interorganizational assemblage for representation of Jewish interests at the Versailles Peace Conference), so now, in 1943, did the Union join with the nationwide array of organizations and local communities in convening the American Jewish Conference for combined action. Dr. Samuel Nirenstein, who succeeded William Weiss as UOJCA president, served on the National Executive Committee of the conference.

Thus, together with the other responsible forces in American Jewry, the Orthodox Union's Torah synagogue constituency was harnessed to bringing all means to bear, through political, economic, and other channels, to stay the satanic hands; to arouse the American public to the world menace of a Nazi-ruled Germany; to open the doors of the land of Israel, America, and anywhere else possible for those who could be freed from the Nazi grasp; and to aid the settlement of the all-too-few refugees who had managed to escape. The effort was unceasing, and continued to further tasks after the Allied victory.

When the United States entered World War II, with the Japanese Empire added to the forces of Germany and Italy, the Orthodox Union again addressed itself to the religious needs of the thousands of young Jews serving in the Armed Forces. While continuing to participate in the National Jewish Welfare Board, the Union proceeded to develop its own measures for reaching out to the servicemen as they moved from installation to installation, sending them directly and by way of the chaplains kosher foods and literature, and making contact with governmental and military channels to facilitate observance to the extent military conditions might permit. During the war itself and in the first postwar years the Union was not yet equipped to conduct this work in systematic, ongoing fashion, but presently there emerged the Armed Forces Division of the Union, which, by the time of the Korean War, rendered sustained, invaluable services.

During this difficult period, the continuity of the national assemblages was somehow maintained. The call to the convening of the 1942 forty-fourth Anniversary Convention of American Jewish Orthodoxy's central arm pointed to overriding concerns. Under the heading "The Role of the Synagogue in the Battle for a Free World," the agenda set forth included deliberations on "The Observant Jew in Our Military Forces"; "The Jewish Chaplain and the Maintenance of Morale"; "Organization of Kosher Food Services"; "Co-operation with J.W.B., U.S.O., Red Cross, etc."; "Effect of the War on Religious and Communal Activities"; "The Synagogue in Civil Defense"; and "Post-war Problems."

The Convention agenda strongly focused on "The Responsibility of American Jewry for Eretz Yisrael" and on action on "The Tragic Plight of European Jewry and its Communal Institutions." Amid these pressing concerns, everyday communal and synagogal concerns were not over-looked. Sessions and workshops dealt with "Problems of Jewish Education"; "Curricula and Textbooks for Orthodox Talmud Torahs"; "Synagogue Organization and Maintenance"; "Women's Auxiliaries"; "Men's Clubs"; and "Youth Group Work." This heavy agenda occupied sessions on Sunday and Monday, June 28 and 29, at the Riverside Plaza Hotel in New York, with special programs for the preceding Shabbath at several synagogues.

In concert with the other forces in American Jewry, the Union, following the defeat of Germany, continued its efforts to save and find safe haven for the survivors. The country's Orthodox congregations were no small factor in this critical task, battling the continuing barriers to the right of Jews to enter the Jewish homeland, and supporting the heroic Yishuv and the upbuilding of the land of Israel.

While the Central Relief Committee continued to function up to the mid-1940s, its operations had, by this time, been largely absorbed in those of the "Joint," the American Jewish Joint Distribution Committee. The Orthodox Union, therefore, did not exercise so direct and distinctive a role in the wartime and post-World War II relief work as it had in World War I. Nevertheless, its share of the relief endeavors was much felt in the existing channels. This, it must be noted, was not only through the Joint and whatever remained of the separate work of the Central Relief Committee, but also through that quiet-working but potent instrument of Orthodox Jewry, the Vaad Ha-Hatzalah.

~

By now, memories of the UOJCA-sponsored Central Relief Committee (CRC) have been obscured by the vast events of the past decades. Considered, however, in the perspective offered by the century-long Orthodox Union experience, pertinent lessons for Torah community policy may be gleaned from the creation, career, and ultimate disappearance of this enterprise.

As seen earlier in this book, the CRC sprang into being as an Orthodox Jewish response to desperate Jewish need, initiating American Jewish overseas relief work. Reform-minded and Jewish labor groups followed this example, whereupon the CRC readily joined with these groups—the American Jewish Relief Committee (product of the then assimilationist American Jewish Committee) and the People's Relief Committee—in linked operations, as the Joint Distribution Committee (JDC, or Joint). Fervency, joined to the innovative means and unsparing effort of the CRC force, brought phenomenal accomplishments in both fundraising and aid dispensation. This seems to have been viewed askance by the magnates of the American Jewish Committee circle, who had gained control of the Joint.

Holding forth the call for unity and efficiency, the controlling group prevailed upon their CRC counterparts to permit a major part of its role, the fundraising and general relief disbursement, to be taken over by the Joint.

Thus, by the 1930s, the Central Relief Committee, its independence truncated, was reduced to a merely subordinate role in the JDC. It had terminated its independent fundraising activities, but participated actively in the annual campaigns of the JDC, and, later—when the United Jewish Appeal was formed by partnership of the JDC and the United Israel Appeal—in the UJA drives.

The Central Relief Committee continued its direct subventions to the yeshivoth and other Torah institutions in eastern Europe and the land of Israel, but depended on the JDC for such funds as the JDC was disposed to allocate. These fund allocations were channeled by the JDC through its Committee on Cultural Affairs (CCA), in which the CRC was pigeonholed. Serving on this unit through the 1930s were Rabbi Dr. Leo Jung, Rabbi Dr. Herbert S. Goldstein, and Morris Engelman.

In a drafted "Inventory to the Central Relief Committee Collection, 1920–1955 Organizational History," prepared for Yeshiva University's Archives department by Dr. Stephen Weinstein, it is stated:

> Despite the CRC's limited funding and its subordinate status in the JDC hierarchy, the CRC was a vital force in the world of Orthodox Jewish education in Europe, particularly in Poland and Lithuania. The CRC corresponded with the various institutions in order to collect background and statistical data on the schools, their student bodies, and their sources of income. CRC distributed funds to yeshivoth and rabbinical seminaries in impartial manner. . . . After 1933, the JDC turned its attention to German Jewry and reduced the CCA's budget. As a result, the CRC was forced to give up supporting Talmud Torahs and concentrate on institutions on the high school level and above. Nevertheless, the yeshivoth in Europe and Palestine still turned to the CRC to meet their needs. . . .
>
> Once war erupted in Europe in 1939, the CCA desperately attempted to aid refugee rabbis and yeshivoth who initially fled to Lithuania and later to Japan and [Eretz Yisrael]. . . . By 1945 the committee had shifted over 90% of its funds to aid institutions in [the Holy Land].
>
> . . . The CRC underwent a major transformation in 1948, when [it was compelled to] abandon its [fiscal] function in favor of an advisory role on cultural and religious affairs. Stripped of its official role in the CAC and replaced in Europe by the newly formed Central Orthodox Committee, the CRC closed its operations in 1950.

There emerges a picture of Orthodox Jewish initiative, responsible action, and effectiveness in a role that was not only pivotal at its inception and for crucial years, but also, if sustained in its original basis, would have been just as pivotal in Jewish welfare and collective affairs to the present time and beyond, with profound effect on the course of the Jewish world. All this might have been, had it not yielded to the blandishments of the tycoons of the American Jewish Committee. We may well ask whether any true Jewish interest was served in abandoning independence and self-reliance to a spurious call of "unity" that was, in fact, subservience to those of contrary outlook.

The call of collective endeavor in matters vital to Jews at large is one that the Torah-loyal ever honor. The Central Relief Committee experience seems to bespeak a pressing message in this connection: "Jointness" and "unity" in shared aim, as between representative agencies of the Orthodox and the non-Orthodox, can properly apply only within given limits, on thoroughly considered lines in each case, applying controlled, disciplined representation, and without compromising the self-sovereignty of the Torah community participation in any degree.

19

The Postwar Challenges

In the bleak aftermath of the global conflict, the effects of the wartime strains were registered in the limited functions of the Orthodox Union. Throughout the war, the national convocations had been perfunctory, and means of forwarding the Union's presence by its programmatic work, other than the special urgencies of the time, were limited. Now, the necessity of its function as national Torah-community force demanded heightened effort on community service and organizational reinforcements. The Union, nevertheless, was a factor in events. What had been a cosmic battle against intended extermination had become a struggle to save the survivors of the death camps and to establish the Jewish land. Withal, it was an epochal striving for Jewish rebirth—as national self, as spiritual self. In this twin endeavor, indivisible to the integrally Jewish Jew, the Union of Orthodox Jewish Congregations of America served in its own way.

The ability of the depleted central Union to rise to the postwar challenges hinged on surpassing the practical limitations of its functional equipment. Now that the organization had a permanent professional director, there emerged a tendency for the organization to turn to the "office" for the exercise of activities previously fulfilled by the elected officers of honorary capacity. To a marked extent, the *honorary* status—properly signifying voluntary, unpaid—was coming to be interpreted as *honorific*, functionally nominal. The voluntary spirit of work in the Union's service diminished. Whereas before the Union had been curbed by the lack of professional management and follow-through, its professional direction, largely deprived of lay participation, now bore a disabling multiple burden.

Concurrently, the demands upon the Orthodox Union were mounting more than ever. The ranks of the American Torah fold were shaken to the depths by a new realization of what had transpired—horrors beyond the scope of imagination. They were stirred by a sense of historic responsibility, by an urge for the upbuilding and rebuilding of Jewish life. Congregations and congregants now rediscovered the existence of the Union of Orthodox Jewish Congregations of America. More than ever before, they called upon the Union for practical aids in community activity and religious development; for their varied needs and aspirations; for guidance in addressing the perplexities of the time; for whatever services it had heretofore provided, and for all the services that they, insistently if incoherently, wanted this Union to provide for them. So now this ongoing, regularly functioning UOJCA "office" bore a burden of ever-mounting, all but crushing weight.

As previously indicated, the incumbency of Leo S. Hilsenrad as executive director had marked the Union's decisive change from hit-or-miss functioning to one of sustained character. Amid the multiplying demands and expanding work, however, Hilsenrad stood alone, except for minor clerical help and brief temporary aids for one or another occasional project, until 1946. At that time, the writer (to his own surprise) was recruited to assume the post of co-executive director, together with the editorship of the newly launched magazine, *Jewish Life*.

The clerical staff at that time consisted of a secretary, a combination bookkeeper–secretary, and a stock-boy. The Union's headquarters, then at 305 Broadway in Manhattan, consisted of a suite with a small outer area and four rooms, one of which was the executive director's office, a similar adjoining room, a room for the clerical staff, and a tightly packed stockroom. Imposing it was not, but what was accomplished there was far out of proportion to the physical dimensions and primitive office equipment.

With officialdom reinforced, a feeling of momentum emerged. Communications to the key figures of communities large and small across the land were better targeted and took on a vibrant tone. The unceasing calls from communal and congregational leaders for aids of one kind or another received more meaningful response. Also advancing constituency relations was a new house newsletter, *The Synagogue Guide*, which Leo Hilsenrad had brought into being. Issued monthly, this publication provided an interchange of community and synagogal activity, as well as information on UOJCA developments.[1] Various activities that had flagged were recharged. Recharged, too, was the opinion in the Torah community of the role of the Orthodox Union.

---

1. After several years of regular publication, *The Synagogue Guide* was replaced in 1951 by *Jewish Action*. This, in turn, appeared as a house news medium until 1984, when it assumed a new character and editorship as both a literary and an information medium, in an impressive new format. *Jewish Action* has continued as such, with high distinction, to the present.

Pending another convention, congregational leaders in a number of communities responded to a call to participate in the Union's councils. There resulted an access to figures of committed character and leadership caliber. Among them were a number of future officeholders, including Joel Schneierson, Edward A. Teplow, Harold M. Jacobs, Dr. Eric Offenbacher, and David Politi, and such influential personalities as Dr. William Weil, Earl Spero, and Julius Loeb.

THE HALF-CENTURY MARK

Stirred by a sense of mortal challenge to the Jewish being, Jews of varying background were awakening to the meaning of Jewish existence. Some saw the Orthodox Union in a new light, as an instrument of historic destiny. A current of re-envisioned purpose was beginning to stir the channels of the Mendes-charged mission.

This spirit was detected as the central Union's first post-World War II national convocation in 1948, designated the Golden Jubilee Convention. Taking place at a turn of history so epochal—a moment of rebirth, after over nineteen centuries of exile, of Israel, the Jewish commonwealth—and at the same time marking a half-century of endeavor toward the upbuilding of the Torah community in the New World, the convention rang with the note of a new era.

An article in a subsequent issue of *Jewish Life*, appraising that event, cited as "the most remarkable aspect of the occasion . . . the atmosphere of broad-visioned yet practical purpose which pervaded the Golden Jubilee convention," continuing:

> . . . for while the hundreds of delegates present . . . and the number of areas represented exceeded those of any previous gathering, it was the character rather than the quantity of the representation which made history. The delegates, the majority of whom seemed to personify the fusion of Torah Judaism with the American environment . . . had come armed with a clear perspective of religious Jewry, with a grasp of its capabilities, with an enlightened understanding of its historic needs. There was ample sober realism and there was indestructible self-confidence, faith, and determination.

From this time on, it became manifest that strong urges were rising from the grassroots of the Torah fold, and that these and the UOJCA organism were responding to each other.

Opportunity for the Union's lay leadership to absorb the new spirit was furthered by the election to presidency of the organization of William B. Herlands, whose single two-year term of office was to conclude with his pending appointment as Federal judge. While the concerned attention of the officers and Executive Committee provided requisite guidance, the practical leadership tasks, in the planning and direction as well as in operation of the Union's work, were perforce exercised on the Executive staff level. A new turn came in this regard when, in mid-1949, an attack of critical illness brought an immediate end to Leo S. Hilsenrad's services. Thereupon Saul Bernstein, now designated administrator, assumed full charge of the Orthodox Union's work, continuing under that designation throughout the ensuing decades of hard-won organizational growth.

THE BATTLE OF LONG ISLAND

One significant mark of traditional American Jewry's growing self-awareness in this period was the development dubbed "The Battle of Long Island." It was a key chapter in a struggle waged, from the inception of the Orthodox Union by Dr. Henry Pereira Mendes and his associates, to redeem from violation the Jewishness of Jewish institutions.[2]

With few exceptions, the hospitals and other welfare institutions under the auspices of the Federation of Jewish Philanthropies of Greater New York, though held forth and financed as institutions of the collective Jewish community, were violative of Jewish sanctities. Although most originally had been committed, as a matter of course, to the observance of such traditional Jewish religious requirements as Shabbath and kashruth, they had come under the control of circles opposed to normative Jewish belief and practice, who had imposed their own preferences on these communal institutions. Consistently ignored were calls, year in and year out, to cease the imposition, under Jewish communal auspices, of *terefah* food and a setting of desecration of Jewish sanctities, in disregard of communal integrity, human consideration, and Jewish self-respect alike.

It was assumed by those ruling the Federation and its dependent institutions that the protesters were powerless and could be ignored. But

---

2. The views of Torah Jewry on this matter were voiced on many occasions. A comprehensive definition and compelling presentation by Dr. David de Sola Pool, titled "The Jewishness of Communal Institutions," was given at the UOJCA Sixth Convention, 24 Sivan 5673/June 29, 1913, and was published in the Proceedings of that assemblage. It was republished in the December 1953 issue of *Jewish Life*. Expressions on the Long Island Jewish Hospital kashruth issue also appeared in various other sources of the time.

with announcement of the projected erection of a major new hospital in Long Island, a situation little anticipated by Federation circles, and startling to them, erupted. They were astonished by the reaction to their announced intent to place a non-kosher hospital to serve areas of the Borough of Queens and Nassau County to which more and more thousands of New York families were moving. There arose an outburst of demands that the hospital be kosher. With the sentiments of so very many being voiced, and with such unprecedented determination, it was clear that this time the demand for an authentically Jewish policy could not be ignored. While the Orthodox Union pressed the issue vigorously (as did the Young Israel force), the variety of individuals and circles joining the effort included some beyond, as well as the cross-section within, the Orthodox fold (although, curiously, the voices of the then-burgeoning yeshivah realm remained silent).

The Federation planners had to give way. Clinging to their determination to make this Long Island Jewish hospital non-kosher, they undertook to disarm the Jewish integrity proponents by announcing that the hospital would have a kosher kitchen also. This decree was duly fulfilled.

Although the outcome fell short of what principle warranted, what had transpired demonstrated the ripening potential of the forces for Jewish integrity. Aware of this, the New York Federation was more circumspect from that time on in its relations with the Torah-honoring. Succeeding developments over the years were to show that while "the leopard does not change its spots," the Federation, and some of its like in other communities, followed a more Jewishly conscious course.

$\sim$

The Battle of Long Island, with its broad implications, was among the numerous indicators of the spiritual awakening stirring the Jewish world and finding outlet in various channels of Jewish endeavor, not least of all in those of the Union of Orthodox Jewish Congregations of America.

The impetus of the re-envisioned mission propelled the work forward. A retrospective echo of the mood of the post-Holocaust Am Yisrael Chay was to find expression by this writer at an occasion years later (in remarks at a 1971 event marking the twenty-fifth anniversary of his incumbency with the Orthodox Union), saying, in part:

> There was an awakening to the sense that the Jew is not merely valuable or important to the world—he is essential to the purpose of the world's Maker. . . . The greater challenge to us, we begin to realize, is the inner fragmentation of the Jewish people—fragmentation not just of mind and

outlook and life pattern, but of inner spirit. The overriding task of our time is to make Jew and Jewry whole within themselves.

The extent to which such promptings spurred the central Union's reinvigoration cannot be measured, but it had become evident from mid-century on that the Union of Orthodox Jewish Congregations of America had begun to take on a new life.

20

Policy Challenge: Renewal and Organization

Along with its recharged spirit came growth in the extent and diversity of the Orthodox Union's activities. Growth brought new situations and new policy questions, placing an added burden on procedural channels. Operations hitherto had functioned through the unitary two-level composition—the officers and the Executive Board on the administration level, and the staff on the operative level. Now, however, conditions pointed to the urgent need for a more efficient setup. A particular development, which placed excessive stress on both levels, prompted structural change.

The development in question, which evoked much agitated discussion at the time, was an unmistakable, though inadvertent, mark of the rising consequence of the Union and its Ⓤ kashruth service. The Union found itself in the crossfire of rivalry between two firms engaged in the large-scale manufacture of edibles of a similar type. In each case, the products were distributed through both regular trade channels and chains of specialty shops under the same names as the manufacturers, and under their related corporative ownerships.

POWER OF THE Ⓤ

Originally, neither firm had been under Ⓤ supervision. One of the firms, seeking increased patronage among the Jewish public, found that the answer to their problem was UOJCA kashruth supervision of their products, and the firm duly submitted application. An extraordinarily massive investigational process was required, owing to the multiplicity and diversity of the ingredients, suppliers, sources, and production operations. The supervisory requirements formulated after this exacting study would

necessitate much adaptation of the applicant company's production operations and processes of supply of the materials used at the company's own
plant and those in the finished and semi-finished products made at
suppliers' plants, these in turn being subject to UOJCA supervision. The
applicant firm, however, accepted these requirements in full, and contractual agreement was effectuated.

During these negotiations and investigations, it was hoped that the other
company would see fit, in its own competitive interest, to apply likewise
for Ⓤ supervision. At one point, the Orthodox Union's administrator
personally called upon the head of that firm to point out to him the
implications of the matter. That company's chief, however, though well
aware that the negotiations between the other firm and the Orthodox
Union were far advanced—a fact known throughout the industry—
indicated no concern whatsoever, and had no interest at all in considering
Ⓤ certification of his own products. At that time, this second company's
stores were distinguished by Sabbath observance, a source of high prestige
to this firm. (At a later time it changed to a franchise policy, with each shop
in almost all cases open on Shabbath.)

In the case of the first company, the Sabbath observance matter was a
critical problem. Plant operations, with a unionized work force, were on a
six-day-week basis. The company, though corporate, was, in fact, Jewish-
owned. In this case, the opportunity to change a range of popular products
from non-kosher to kosher had to be consistent with Sabbath requirements.
The difficulty confronting both parties was met by a change, after an initial
period, to a five-day production schedule, with provision for weekday
Yomim Tovim also, plus separation of the corporate ownership of the
stores from that of the plant. The arrangement worked out satisfactorily,
with the supervised company scrupulously fulfilling its contractual obligations and winning great favor among Jewish consumers.

Then, belatedly, the other company realized that its prior unconcerned
dismissal of its competitor's move was a major mistake. In contrast to the
other firm, it had failed to reckon with the power of the Ⓤ among the
multiplying observant Jewish public. Although still refusing to apply for
UOJCA supervision, this firm aimed openly to engineer the severance of its
competitor from the Ⓤ. An unprecedented hue-and-cry was raised; a
frenzied, around-the-clock agitation pressed not only in all circles of the
traditional sphere, but beyond that in non-Orthodox channels, too, all
designed to force the Orthodox Union to withdraw its hechsher from its
rival. The pressure on the Union was intense and unremitting, but
Orthodoxy's national force stood firm on the principle of an open door to
all firms seeking its supervision that would meet its religious requirements.
This was reaffirmed at a memorable special meeting of the UOJCA

executive body, with President William B. Herlands in the chair. At this occasion, nearly all of the forty-odd members present spoke on the question, each expressing his views on a notable level of reasoned judgment. The head of the firm challenging the Union's position, who had been invited, was now admitted; President Herlands summarized concisely yet accurately all the expressions presented, and the guest was given the floor. The company head expressed his stand at length. Following his departure, a vote was taken—overwhelmingly in favor of reaffirming the established policy and its application to the case at issue.

The two companies were now locked in battle, slugging it out with every resource. They were raiding each other's personnel, store leases, and suppliers. It was a heated battle.

The time came for the negotiation of a renewal of the initial contract term with the supervised company. Now set forth to the company were additional requirements, the tightening of various procedures and the making of additional stipulations to reinforce the separation of the plant and retail stores' ownership corporations. Upon due consideration, the company informed the Union, initially by phone call from the company's attorney to the UOJCA administrator, of its decision to accept the renewal contract submitted, with the added requirements. The signed agreement was to follow.

By this point, the other company had finally abandoned its opposition to applying for Ⓤ supervision. Its application was duly submitted, and the company was investigated on the same elaborate scale that the first company had been. Thus, at that stage, arrangements were nearing completion for both companies to manufacture their products under the supervision and attestation of the Union of Orthodox Jewish Congregations of America.

But secret treaties were in process between the combatants. There resulted, thereby, a surprise phone call to Administrator Bernstein from the attorney of the first company, followed by a formal letter from the company, informing the Union that they had reconsidered matters and had decided to forego Ⓤ supervision with the UOJCA.

This writer, having been in the thick of the remarkable proceedings, has reason to believe that the decision of the original company to withdraw was a result of an "armistice" between the battling firms. Their contest had been mutually injurious, to the point of imminent mutual danger. So, by tacit or other understanding, the first company relinquished Ⓤ supervision, no doubt in exchange for given considerations by the other, which itself came, and remained, under the supervision of the national congregational body of American Orthodox Jewry.

DEPARTMENTALIZATION

The strain that this drawn-out episode placed upon the Orthodox Union's entire governing and operational centers precipitated the better ordering of the deliberative and functional structure on departmental lines. A table of operative organization, formulated by the administrator, was duly approved by the officers and adopted by authorization of the Executive Board. Under it, each of the main spheres of the Union's work was constituted as a departmental unit. Each was to be supervised by a standing commission, appointed by the president, and each was—prospectively—to be headed on the staff level by a departmental director.

Under the reorganized setup, the commissions and departments were each to operate within their assigned frames of policy and program, subject to the authority of the administration and the overall governing bodies.[1] As was inherent in the constitutional nature of the Orthodox Union, general policy and program determination remain, in principle, the province of the organization's premier governing body, the biennial convention, composed of the delegates of the member congregations. The departmental directors and other staff served under the jurisdiction of the staff head.[2]

An early application of the departmentalization concept was the establishment of the Armed Forces Division of the Union. It emerged out of the less structured activities in behalf of Jewish Armed Forces personnel in the World War II and early postwar years. Upon reconstruction as a department with a defined and extended program, this work continued as such during the further post-World War II period and the Korean and Vietnam Wars. The supervisory commission was under the chairmanship of Dr. Eric Offenbacher, for the first years, and later of Reuben E. Gross. The department's staff director for the first years was Abraham H. Eisenman.

ROLE OF THE ARMED FORCED DIVISION

While concerned with Jewish soldiers, sailors, and airmen in general, the Armed Forces Division focused on the needs of those with a traditionally

---

1. At a later time, the between-convention governing arm, previously named the Executive Committee, was redesignated the Board of Directors, with the Executive Committee designation applied to the officers and the commission chairmen.

2. In actual practice, for a long time the appointment of staff directors was only partially effectuated. In the absence of any such appointments, the pertaining functions were exercised by the administrator.

observant home and synagogue background. Through personal communications and special literature, including the division's monthly newsletter *Hachayal*, the division kept in touch with thousands of servicemen as they moved from one army installation, naval site, or air-force base to another. Contacts were maintained with the Defense Department and senior military quarters to further the adoption or implementation of provisions to facilitate Jewish religious observance to the extent feasible under military conditions. Relations with the Jewish Welfare Board were maintained, and close ties were developed with military chaplains, especially those of traditional identity. With the devoted aid of the Women's Branch of the Union, food packages were shipped to the men on frequent occasions. Communications that soldiers, sailors, airmen, marines, and chaplains sent to *Hachayal* and other publications of the Armed Forces Division, in themselves a treasure trove of historical and literary interest, show how highly these services were valued by the recipients.

KASHRUTH DEPARTMENT COMPOSITION

Pivotal to the departmentalization process was the reconstitution of the Union's Kashruth supervision and certification operations as its Kashruth Division. The supervisory commission in this facet was designated the Joint Kashruth Commission. Actually, at this time, all UOJCA commissions were given the "Joint" labeling, as an indication of the participation of the rabbinic arm. In the case of the Kashruth service, in which the RCA had a specific function, the Joint designation had particular applicability, with the provision that this commission was to include some members appointed by the Union's president on the recommendation of the president of the Rabbinical Council.

The provision referred to was the outcome of deliberations as to the definition, within the uncodified frame of UOJCA–RCA relationships, of the form of cooperation by the rabbinic body with the Union's commissions, and the cooperation between the two organizations in their respective programs as a whole. Special consideration applied in the case of the kashruth work, since the Rabbinical Council of America, in its own Kashruth and halachic committees, had specified responsibilities in passing upon any halachic questions entailed and on the acceptability, under Jewish law, of requirements of applications for the Union's supervision.

Nathan K. Gross was appointed chairman of the UOJCA Joint Kashruth Commission. He held with exceptional sagacity always, until his death in 1985. His successor was Julius J. Berman, who had previously served as UOJCA president.

For reasons dictated by experience, the restructuring required that the Kashruth Department be headed on the staff level by the director, who, it was specified, was to be a layman. The director was to have general management responsibility, including charge of the business arrangements. The rabbinic aspects were to be under the charge of the rabbinic kashruth administrator.

A long delay in effecting the departmental directorship necessitated continued handling of this work, among his other duties, by the organization's overall administrator. Excellent progress, however, was being made in the management setup. Procedures throughout were reordered on a systematic basis, relationships with the supervised firms were put on higher footing, the entrée of new firms and products was actively spurred, and public information and public relations processes were introduced.

The Ⓤ Kashruth Directory listing of products and establishments under UOJCA supervision, which previously had appeared as a feature of *Jewish Life* magazine, began to be published separately in booklet form. Some time thereafter, the large increase in the number of Ⓤ Kosher for Passover products, in addition to the multiplying number and range of year-round products, prompted the introduction of a separate Ⓤ Passover Products Directory. Distribution would eventually reach hundreds of thousands of copies annually.

The Kashruth Department's rabbinic kashruth administrator post was filled early, and by fortunate choice. The incumbent was Rabbi Alexander S. Rosenberg, a figure of distinction in rabbinic circles. With keen perception of the conditions of American Jewish life, and with a grasp of what pertained to kashruth matters, Rabbi Rosenberg was exceptionally qualified for this responsible post. Under his direction, notable progress was made in the acutely sensitive rabbinical supervisory facets of the Ⓤ program.

By this stage, at the insistence of the organization's administrator, a major change in the financial basis of the Ⓤ service had already taken place. Originally, great concern to avoid any semblance of the material interest that had so poisoned the kashruth domain had let to the virtual subsidization of the Union's supervisory operations. Increasingly burdensome deficits were incurred because the fees charged to the supervised companies barely covered, at best, the amounts paid to the supervisory personnel at the supervised premises, without regard to administrative expenses and general costs. With the constant increase of supervised firms and corresponding accrual of unpaid administrative costs, the mounting deficits became crippling. Therefore, preceding the management revision process, this untenable policy was replaced by a rationally computed fee system on an overall cost basis. Percipiently applied, the new method proved effective. From that time on, the Ⓤ service has remained financially self-sustaining.

Highly effective, too, was the smooth alignment between the respective management and rabbinic areas of Kashruth Department operation. In general, the pattern that was set made for the continuous sound growth of the UOJCA kashruth service and the enhancement of its standing among the Jewish public, religious and communal leadership, and the food industry alike.

Succeeding accomplishments over the years in this area of the central Union's work have had an important and lasting effect on the Jewish world.

In the course of time, Abraham H. Eisenman was transferred from the Armed Forces Division, where he was succeeded by Aaron Sittner, to the directorship of the Kashruth Department. This appointment contributed much to the functioning and progress of the Ⓤ program. So, too, did the appointment of Hal Stein, who succeeded to the post when Eisenman left several years later. The directorship office, however, tended to become of more subordinate level than had been envisaged. Eventually, the post of Kashruth Department director remained unfilled. Its functions, contrary to the original carefully considered intent, were effectually absorbed by the Kashruth Department's other administrative personnel.

21

A Venture in Wider Potential

The reverberations of UOJCA awakening in the mid-century period gained marked attention among the discerning, notably among the leadership circles of the increasing number of senior yeshivoth and what was, by now, Yeshiva University. By this stage, the realms of the primary vehicles of American Jewish Orthodoxy had diverged with differentiation of involved circles. Each institution had its coterie of the closely concerned, and although there was considerable overlapping, with numerous individuals active in varying degree in multiple institutions, each center became a sphere of its own. At this point, however, relations between the two primary centers of the traditional domain were strengthened by the election of Max J. Etra as president of the Union of Orthodox Jewish Congregations of America. The new president was then the chairman of Yeshiva University's governing board, as well as president of a leading New York synagogue, Congregation Kehilath Jeshurun. This situation lent itself to a connection between the central Union and a community-service undertaking that the University had previously established to aid its rabbinic graduates in the guidance of their congregations. At that time, these Y.U. community aids consisted of rabbinic placement service and the production of audiovisual materials and the monthly publication *P'rakim*, which contained a range of program materials for synagogue and men's club activities.

In March 1951 followed an agreement whereby Rabbi Irwin Gordon of Yeshiva University's community service staff and Victor B. Geller and (later) Rabbi Sol Spiro, who had been newly recruited by Yeshiva University for that work, together with clerical personnel, were transferred to the employ of the Orthodox Union, with an annual allocation by Yeshiva University toward the salary cost.[1]

The new undertaking, under the umbrella designation UOJCA Community Activities Division (CAD), included in its program the diverse but hitherto undepartmentalized community and synagogue servicing work conducted by the Union, now more focused and with more organized field service, new synagogue development, the publication of *P'rakim*, and preparation of other programmatic materials for synagogue leaders, men's clubs, and youth groups. Professor A. Leo Levin was the chairman of the supervising commission. After serving for the first two years as department director, Rabbi Gordon was called to service as a U.S. Army chaplain. He was succeeded by Victor Geller, who had been assistant director. Rabbi Spiro handled the preparation of *P'rakim* and the programmatic items. In addition, after the first year, two other individuals were engaged for field service in the New England and Atlantic seaboard regions, respectively.

Understandably, it took some time before the new Community Activities Division got into production, but once that point was reached, substantial results followed. The sense of personalized contact between congregational leaders and the central body was sparked, the materials provided were welcomed (even if not always fully utilized), regional relations took on new life, and the Union's presence registered more sharply.

One facet of the work responded to the shift of Jewish population from older-established neighborhoods to newer neighborhoods and suburban areas of the nation's cities. After World War II, the movement of the post-Depression generation to new educational and vocational levels, the aspirations of the thousands discharged from war-time military service, and the transition en masse to the automobile age all had been radically changing the entire Jewish residential locale. Although it was those more distant from Torah life who were in the vanguard of this change and put their stamp on the new communities, it was not long before observant families began to make the transition, too.

The non-Orthodox movements had early equipped themselves to adapt to this development, whereas the Orthodox Union and other traditional forces lacked the means of such equipment and were less alert to the need. Thus, the reach of the community activities work to groups in the new areas of urban settlement was especially timely.

Although the Jewishly observant usually are unwilling to move to areas lacking a shul within walking distance and other basic religious requisites,

---

1. The promised subsidy turned out to be less than half of the costs incurred, and proved to be reluctantly disbursed in small amounts.

there are generally those with the pioneer temperament. Such pioneers form the advance guard of every new traditional congregation or community: Once settled in his new home, the pioneering Jew sets out to locate fellow pioneers and organize a minyan for tephillah b'tzibbur, congregational worship services. This is how hundreds of Orthodox congregations have been established, many of them eventually becoming major institutions. In some cases, congregations have arisen without outside assistance, while others have looked for—or have gained unsought—aid in congregation formation and guidance from other sources. The Orthodox Union has, of course, been an expected resource for the purpose, as has the National Council of Young Israel for its special constituency; Yeshiva University also has been much looked to. For these institutions of rabbinic learning, joined to the desire to help new groups form Orthodox synagogues is the interest in finding rabbinic posts for those of their graduates undertaking the spiritual calling. The work of the Union's Community Activities Division was, accordingly, of special interest in various quarters.

In the course of a few years, the number of newly formed groups given practical aid in organization, membership recruitment, activities programming, and—ever of primary importance—Hebrew school establishment marked a *tachlesdik* entrée to the new-communities situation, even if not of a scale to make a major impression on that development.

The new unit's supervising commission[2] and directorship could cite, in the course of periodic reports, several of the upcoming young congregations as demonstrating the results to be achieved through the aid rendered in the new-synagogues field. The making of the Great Neck Synagogue, in the suburban Long Island community of that name, was held forth as exemplar. Here, the personal efforts of Victor Geller for the CAD were joined to those volunteered by the novelist Herman Wouk and his wife, then newly resident in that area heretofore devoid of traditional Jewish life. Careful planning and months of concentrated effort resulted in the rise of a vigorous congregation in this community, one with early promise of blooming into the Torah-loyal center of scope and renown it later became. Similar developments came about under the Community Activities Division's guidance in numerous other communities.

---

2. The lay body supervising the Community Activities Division was named the CAD *Committee*. Since, however, the supervisory bodies of permanent units subsequently were designated *Commission*, with the "committee" term applied to those instituted for special purpose, we apply here for best reference the "commission" term to the CAD body.

MULTIPLE YESHIVOTH INTEREST

The enhanced vitality of the Orthodox Union in community service and in its general work increasingly engaged the interest of the other institutions of rabbinic learning. At one point, negotiations were initiated on behalf of a group of the yeshivoth gedoloth with view to an association with the community-service undertaking of the Orthodox Union supplemental to, but not infringing upon, that with Yeshiva University. In the UOJCA files is a copy of memorandum of the matter addressed to Rabbi Gedaliah Schor and Rabbi Chaim Uri Lifschitz (of Yeshivah Torah Vodaath) and Rabbi Herman Neuberger (of Ner Israel Rabbinical College, Baltimore), from Saul Bernstein, UOJCA administrator. It refers to a meeting held on Monday, May 17, 1951, between representatives of the Union and the yeshivoth to explore relevant suggestions. There had followed, according to the communication cited, another meeting "held at the Hotel Clinton [New York] on Wednesday, Iyyar 16/May 19, at which points considered at the prior meeting were further studied." The memorandum states that "Rabbi [Herman] Neuberger, with the concurrence of Rabbis [Gedaliah] Schor and [Chaim Uri] Lifschitz then proposed the following:

1. The Union shall invite all recognized major Yeshivoth to participate in a UOJCA Advisory Council of Yeshivoth, which shall function, within the constitutional structure of the Union, as an auxiliary of the CAD Committee.

2. The Advisory Council of Yeshivoth shall be concerned solely with acting as a liaison between the Community Activities Department of the Union and the several Yeshivoth, and as a channel through which assistance can be given to the CAD by the Yeshivoth.

3. It is understood that the Advisory Council of Yeshivoth shall not exercise voice in the broad policy and functional program of the CAD. Its views, however, are to be invited and given full consideration in specific Halachic questions which may occasionally arise with respect to the content of materials published by the CAD. This shall operate in the following manner: The ACY shall delegate not more than two persons to be available for consultation with the Director of the CAD. Prior to the issuance of a new CAD publication or of a new edition of an existing publication, a copy of the text shall be submitted to the above-mentioned ACY representative or representatives for his or their suggestions. In the event that a difference of Halachic view shall be manifest on a given question as between the ACY representative and other authoritative sources, final discretion shall lie with the CAD director.

4. The Yeshivoth participating in the UOJCA Council of Yeshivoth shall furnish to the Union a contribution for the initial year of the arrangement in the amount of $10,000. The participating Yeshivoth shall be individually and collectively responsible for the prompt and full payment of this contribution. The ACY may be given responsibility for collection and transmittal.

5. The above-mentioned contribution is to be given to the Union for the unconditional use of the CAD. It is not to be earmarked in any way. Acceptance of this contribution does not entitle any commitment by the Union as to any change in or extension of the present program and functions of the CAD.

6. Payment of the contribution shall be made in accordance with a fixed schedule to be agreed upon."

The memorandum concludes:

> I [Administrator Bernstein] undertook to present your proposal, as outlined above, to the Officers and CAD Committee of the Union, following which, if such were decided, it would be submitted to a forthcoming meeting of our Executive Board.

Regrettably, this writer was unable to find any further record of this matter, and personal recollection of this negotiation, after a long lapse of time, is unclear. The probable outcome was that the proposal met with a negative response by the Community Activities Division Commission, unwilling at that juncture to go beyond the arrangement with Yeshiva University. Thus blocked, the negotiations lapsed and were never thereafter renewed.

A like blockage had resulted from a comparable occasion in 1947, early in this writer's association with the Orthodox Union. On that occasion, UOJCA Executive Director Leo S. Hilsenrad had arranged for a meeting between representatives of the Union and representatives of Yeshiva University, Yeshivath Torah Vodaath and other yeshivoth. This was to explore a coordinated process in areas of mutual interest. It was agreed that each representative would submit the ideas discussed to his authorities and report their respective decisions to Hilsenrad and Bernstein. The response from Torah Vodaath and its group was prompt and affirmative; the response from Yeshiva University was less prompt—and negative.

The failure to press for and secure acceptance and implementation of either of the aforementioned proposals was, in each case, a major blunder of the central Torah force. Much in the development of the American Torah community—its practical advancement, its better coordination, teamwork, and communal integrity—might well have been the fruit of such an initiation of interinstitutional alignment.

It must be recorded, however, that while the specific external tie of the UOJCA Community Activities Division as then constituted remained only with the one institution, its services, consonant with the character of the Union and as specified in the agreement between the Union and Yeshiva University, were addressed to the rabbinic leaders as well as to the lay leaders of all Orthodox congregations. Those congregations whose rabbis were products of yeshivoth other than Yeshiva University's Rabbi Isaac Elchanan Theological Seminary (RIETS), no less than those of the latter, were included in the servicing. All institutions benefited by the opportunity for placement of graduates in the Orthodox synagogue sphere and in all endeavors for the sustaining of Torah loyalties.

The work went ahead, with steady though undramatic progress. The personnel and resources now applied, though so much greater in number than before, were small in proportion to the size of the task before them. The very process of advancing the work brought into clearer view the enormity of the need. The conditions to be dealt with were the product of overpowering historical forces, the product of generations of cumulative deficiency in Orthodox Jewry's response to the challenges of a new age and the conditions of American life. Whatever was done, however, counted for much and bore the promise of greater fruit.

~

In reviewing the status of American Orthodox Jewry's central force at this point, it must be kept in mind that the multifaceted functions conducted by the Community Activities Department were just one part of the overall UOJCA scope.

As outlined in the Union's general report for 1950, and similarly for the years that followed, the kashruth work, reorganized as previously described, was rising to extraordinary new dimensions. *Jewish Life* was making continued gains in literary quality and influence, and, though budgetarily precluded from engaging in a capital circulation promotion, was gaining several thousand individually paid subscriptions each year. *Jewish Action* was successfully introduced as a house news organ; its initial five-thousand-copy distribution was soon to multiply manifold. The Armed Forces work was making a notable impact, as evidenced by expressions from many servicemen and chaplains. Nineteen congregations had been newly addéd to the Union's membership rolls. Pivotal to all were the progressing steps in representation in public and communal life and in public information.

These functional improvements corresponded to developments on the organizational level. The national Executive Board's regularly scheduled meetings invariably were well attended. Departmental reports were rendered by the respective commissions, and special matters arising in policy areas were acted on; discussions otherwise dealt with basic issues of religious life and of the American Jewish community, resulting in policy decisions and practical measures.

The Orthodox Union general report for 1950 stated that the organization:

> . . . [s]eeks to meet the need of American Jewry for positive coordinated activity that can combat influences which make for communal disintegration. Communities large and small throughout North America look to the Union for the practical aid and guidance that gives meaning and strength to their lives as Jews and purpose to their communal institutions, to the activities that are the basis of Jewish living. Present undertakings indicate that the Union is addressing these needs to an increasingly significant extent.

The 1950 report of the Union as a whole also stated that, consequent upon the more than doubling of professional and clerical staff, considerably increased space had been taken for the national headquarters (still at 305 Broadway in New York), and new office equipment had been added.

Within the frame of this general UOJCA report, that of the Community Activities Division, newly staffed and departmentalized, could cite the various facets of its work as pursuant to an initial development of "an organizational structure and a sound working philosophy."

Seeking to "activate the few existing 'paper' regions of the UOJCA," regional compositions had been re-established, newly established, or actively aided in the New England, Long Island, Southeast, Tristate (Atlantic seaboard), Midwest, and Northwest regions. Local city-wide Orthodox councils were activated, reconstituted, or otherwise aided in Bridgeport, New Haven, Lower Manhattan, Baltimore, Pittsburgh, and Cleveland. The report also stated: "The CAD has served and contacted for the first time, or for the first after many years, 88 congregations, of which 47 had been personally visited—throughout the U.S. and Canada." But, the report said, "It is unfortunate that limitations of staff have made it impossible to do the intensive work required."

As might be expected, this departmental report targeted the long-standing discrepancy between the Orthodox Union's capacity as central spokesman for the congregationally constituted American Torah community and the number of dues-paying member congregations. In the five boroughs of New York City alone, Gordon and Geller pointed out, there were 1,872 Orthodox congregations, and that, "allowing for 'mushroom synagogues' and 'shtiebels', there are probably 1,300 to 1,400 potential members of the Union" within New York City itself. Barely a tenth of these were, at that time, dues-paying affiliates of the Orthodox Union, although all looked to UOJCA to serve their interests.

In enumerating the department's publications activity, the same source reported that 850 copies of the program compilation *P'rakim* had been prepared and distributed for each issue; now, as transferred to the Orthodox Union, on a quarterly schedule, many thousands of copies of article reprints from *Jewish Life* and new printings of existing Union booklets had been distributed in response to orders received, and manuals on synagogue architecture, membership, and fundraising were in preparation, as well as kits of educational materials. Activities also had been initiated in men's club and youth work programming. Speakers had been provided for the many congregational and communal occasions for which this service had been requested.

~

THE PENALTY FOR SUCCESS

Yet, despite the significant promise of this venture into American Orthodox Jewry's wider reach—or perhaps, indeed, because of the implications of this very success and greater promise—the CAD arrangement was brought to an abrupt end after a few short years. This resulted from the rejection by the Union's Executive Board of an astonishing further proposal by Yeshiva University. The new plan was presented in behalf of Yeshiva University by Professor A. Leo Levin, chairman of the CAD committee, at a fully attended meeting of the UOJCA Executive body specially convened for the purpose. The plan proposed that Yeshiva University would itself absorb the Union of Orthodox Jewish Congregations of America except for the Kashruth Division[3] and *Jewish Life* magazine; the University would have the prerogative to use or not use the name of the Union, as it might see fit; and it would have the right, if it should so determine, to terminate the existence of the Union.

The motion embodying this drastic proposal was defeated by an overwhelming majority of the large attendance. Upon this rejection, Yeshiva University, by evident prior arrangement, took over the entire personnel of the UOJCA Community Activities Division. These persons withdrew from the employ of the Union immediately following the

---

3. Concurrently, a move was afoot, engineered by some members of the Rabbinical Council of America, for that organization to take over the Union's Ⓤ kashruth service.

meeting, not, however, without demanding—and receiving—payment in full of their salaries up to the end of that week, several days later.

A painful gap was left, and a desolating sense of abandonment. With what had become an accustomed major part of its broadened apparatus severed, the Union seemed, and felt itself to be, truncated. An added wound was monetary: The Yeshiva University allocation, so sparingly disbursed, had fallen far short of the added salary expense and attendant costs, and the deficit accrued was critical. Attempts by UOJCA leaders to negotiate a repairing of the breach were blandly rebuffed.[4] Predictions of the imminent demise of the Orthodox Union were now openly voiced in some quarters.

The planted, confidently spread predictions proved to be not self-fulfilling. The enlarged program was maintained—somehow!—in large part. Determination spread from the operational center to concerned circles far and near. Morale rebounded. The Orthodox Union lived—if not by the vitality of its formal composition, then by the determination of such as held fast to the Mendes idea. What had been seen as a fatal blow turned out to be a spur to major development.

CARRYING ON

After a few months, the professional staff was replenished by two appointments, one as community activities director, the other as youth department director. Under the former, Henry Siegman, a *musmach* of Yeshivoth Torah Vodaath, the work in field servicing, regional development, and new synagogues sponsorship resumed vigor.

The second area mentioned received an additional fillip with a plan, developed in conjunction with an important industrial firm, for the production of prefabricated synagogue structures. This was designed especially for groups in the early stage of congregational development who lacked the means for erecting conventional structures. The plan aroused extraordinary interest throughout the land. Innumerable enquiries flooded UOJCA headquarters, and groups from many communities conferred with the Union's Community Activities director. For all the commotion, however, only two of the congregations actually undertook the prefabricated

---

4. As, for example, when a group of Orthodox Union officers, plus the administrator, met by arrangement with Rabbi Joseph H. Lookstein, known to be a key figure in Yeshiva University counsels. It is this writer's recollection that Rabbi Lookstein manifested satisfaction rather than regret at what had transpired.

On the other hand, some in Rabbinical Council of America circles were disturbed by the situation, and sought to mediate.

structure; the rest concluded that the shortcomings of the project out-weighed the immediate advantages. Thus faded away an intriguing but transient dream.

It was at this time of shaken transition in the central union's course that the UOJCA Youth Commission was formed, with Harold H. Boxer as chairman, and with the popular Harold "Happy" Cohen as director of the emerging Youth Department. Thus was born, in an initial and as yet undefined form, a force whose designation, the National Conference of Synagogue Youth, would later prove to be much more successful and influential than may have been envisioned at the time. NCSY would bloom at a later stage and under other professional direction in the character that would bring it fame, but meanwhile the introduction and the making of the early presence of this force was in itself a signal achievement.

IV
ON A
NEW PLATEAU

22

The Turning Point

A momentous turn in the Orthodox Union story now ensued with the convening, in the Breakers Hotel of Atlantic City,[1] New Jersey, of the 56th Anniversary Convention, held on 15–18 Cheshvan 5715/November 11–14, 1954.

As the first national–binational assemblage of the Union of Orthodox Jewish Congregations of America to convene outside the New York metropolitan area, the venue added to the apprehensions about winning an attendance after what had lately transpired. In the event, all doubts were resolved. Delegates turned out in unprecedented numbers, with representation from a wider range of communities than ever before, and with a spirit of unwonted vibrancy to boot.

The Anniversary Convention program was of three uninterrupted days' duration—also a new phenomenon, since the convention Shabbath, fully programmed and with all participants sharing in its meet-and-mingle warmth, was integrated seamlessly with the rest of the convention proceedings. The event held a measure of content, arrangement, and deliberative quality, and also of color, new to the world of Orthodox Jewry. Quite beyond expectations was the *ruach* of the event, marked again and again, especially during the festive meals, by spontaneous outbursts of singing and dancing. A surprise touch was the lively participation throughout of delegates from several Toronto congregations, with Meyer Gasner, a key figure of that community, as spearhead.

The program, including the sessions agendas and all other arrangements, had been drafted (by the many-dutied staff head) for the Convention

---

1. The Atlantic City of those pre-gambling days was the country's leading convention site and a highly regarded resort.

Committee chaired by Reuben E. Gross. It proceeded efficiently. The key-note address, by famed author Herman Wouk, set a stirring mood and a strong perspective. Plenary sessions were keyed to administration and commission reports and the Resolutions Committee's carefully drafted proposed resolutions, which had been submitted in advance of the convention to congregations and their leaders and delegates. These sessions dealt with major questions of Jewish and public concern, matters of policy on various issues, and measures for new undertakings. As these were sessions with plenary decision power, there was much active delegate debate and well-considered—and deeply felt—exchange of views. Seven workshops on practical synagogue and community concerns and "know-how" exchange were well-attended and well-received by the participants.

Much treasured by all was the convention Sabbath. With hundreds of delegates and visitors joined as one family in a shared experience of spiritual elevation, elucidation of goal, and inspired purpose, the mood of joyous fellowship, lit by the aura of Sabbath sanctity, was incandescent. Among the highlights were a symposium on "Lights and Shadows of the Jewish Scene," with a panel of distinguished thinkers; expositions of Torah thought by eminent Torah personages and rabbinic figures; and vibrant open-floor discussions.

Throughout the three-day convocation, each occasion opened with a succinct D'var Torah exposition, and each day opened with a Daf Yomi study period preceding the morning service. Other *Limmud Torah* occasions were interspersed throughout the sessions.

A memorable touch of historicity came with a session marking the Tercentenary of American Jewry and its parent congregation—the Union's own founding congregation—Congregation Shearith Israel, the Spanish and Portuguese Synagogue of New York. It meant so much to those present to realize afresh that through this tie they were part of a three-hundred-year saga of the will to implant and nourish authentic Jewishness on the New World scene.

Other special features included a moving flag ceremony by a delegation of the Jewish War Veterans of America and addresses by Israel's Ambassador to the United Nations, Abba Eban, and the Governor of New Jersey, Robert E. Meyner. A musical program of rare beauty, a choral presentation with dramatic narration called "Sabbath in the Synagogue," was performed by Cantor Sholom Katz and the Jewish Music Documentation Society Choir conducted by Seymour Silbermintz.

This path-breaking convocation was to prove of more than passing significance; the policy stands and activities developments decided upon at the deliberations were to be influential in shaping the course of the American Torah community and in synagogue advancement. But beyond its impact on affairs, this convention set a pattern of substantive character that, further forwarded in succeeding conventions, continued to be felt in broadening the vista of organized Jewish Orthodoxy and enriching its sense of definition and its self-awareness.

The program format and the type of content introduced at the 1954 convention and further developed in the conventions that followed have remained the standard, not only for the Orthodox Union's convocations to the present day, but also for other Orthodox Jewish organizations. This has been much to the benefit of Torah Jewry's deliberative processes and its self-direction and public presence.

In the 1954 convocation, with its fifty-sixth-Anniversary setting of dramatic momentum, the election of Moses I. Feuerstein of Brookline, Massachusetts, as UOJCA president underscored the marks of change. The ideologically primed young leader, a third-generation American of a Torah-true family prominent in industry, communal and public endeavor, and the Orthodox Union's cause, manifested the caliber of the purposeful new breed of American Orthodox Jew. At this advent, a current of dynamism and fresh outlook infused the Orthodox Union's channels. Beyond as well as within the central Torah community force, the vibrations stirred the diverse stands of the Torah community.

With "Moe" Feuerstein as President, the Union's sphere following the 1954 assemblage bore the impress of a key personality perhaps more distinctly than at any point since the era of Henry Pereira Mendes himself. The organizational purview was readdressed to the potential of Torah Jewry as a mobilized force. The sense of volition was palpable; the organization's channels vibrated with fresh vigor.

In the wake of the new administration came further additions to the active volunteer array of organized Jewish Orthodoxy. Among those who were subsequently to make their mark in office as chairmen of commissions and committees, or in general service were Joseph Karasick and Julius Berman (both to be future presidents); Herbert Berman; Lawrence H. Kobrin; Michael Wimpfheimer; Fred Ehrman; Marvin Herskovits; David Politi; Gustave Jacobs; Marcel Weber; Harvey Blitz; Emil Ramat; Donald Butler (Pittsburgh); Gilbert Cummins (Baltimore); Herzl Rosenson (Chicago); Irving I. Stone (Cleveland); Marcos Katz (Mexico City); Marc Ratzesdorfer; George Falk; Joel Schreiber; Philip Fuchs; Gerald E. Feldhamer; Elliot Stavsky; and Saul Quinn.

The new-charged pace propelling the Union meant basic progress, but the functional apparatus was as yet outmatched by what was called for. The leadership focus on objective, as yet without equal focus on practical resources and equipment, brought added strain to already burdened operations.

With the pace quickening, the Orthodox Union's voice resounded more strongly on the Jewish and public scenes. Spokesmanship at public, governmental, and legislative channels on issues of Jewish concern bore a note of self-assurance, which was soon evident in word and action for Israel's security. In like vein were expression and action for the needs of the communities and survivor groups struggling to rebuild Holocaust-shattered lives. These efforts were under the aegis of the Overseas Commission, the initial chairman of which was Dr. Jacob Griffel, himself a survivor, who had rendered signal service to the newly liberated survivors of the extermination camps.

Such varied interests as governmental aid to education, defense of shechitah, and race-relations problems, among many others in the broad panoply of a changing society, were examined and acted on in terms defined by Torah principles. These concerns came within the scope of the Communal Relations Commission, of which Samuel Lawrence Brennglass was the long-time chairman (to be succeeded by Bernard Levmore). Within such channels as the National Jewish Community Relations Advisory Council and the newly formed Conference of Presidents of Major National Jewish Organizations, the position of the Torah community was expressed on given questions clearly and with dignity.

The news media, press and broadcast alike, now became more conscious of Orthodox Jewry as a factor in American society and of the Union of Orthodox Jewish Congregations as an articulate force. The views or positions of the central Union on topical issues were sought and reported with increasing frequency.

The established departments of the Union, including the synagogue servicing output, educational publications, Armed Forces work, and the kashruth service, kept abreast of developments. The Union's place in the daily life of its congregational and communal constituency, now more pertinently scrutinized, took on more substance. A steady flow of person-alized communications—letters, memos, issues analyses—to rabbis and presidents and other officers of congregations brought a sense of personal rapport, at the same time conveying cogent information on developments. An eloquent barometer of the impact of this process, then and in succeeding years, was the response to communications calling for action—such as presentations to the White House, key policymakers, legislators, and other sources of influence on situations menacing Israel's security, and on various other urgent issues. On each such occasion, hundreds upon hundreds of completed response cards poured into UOJCA headquarters.

The community activities and synagogue relations work also was taken to the congregations in their own local areas around the country. This work, supervised by the Commission on Regions and Councils, would assume pronounced scope in ensuing years with the further development of regional and citywide compositions. Chairman of the Commission on Regions and Councils for some years was Gilbert Commins, long-time leader of the Council of Orthodox Jewish Congregations of Baltimore. Commins was succeeded in the Commission chairmanship by Reubert E. Gross.

From this outreach, the congregations in each area gained a sense of common tie and means of continued endeavor. Particularly inspiring were the conclaves, held periodically from the late 1950s on, at a series of host cities across the United States and Canada. Participants from congregations in the communities of each such region shared in a weekend experience. These gatherings, each including a moving Shabbath in the conclave site, with all attendees participating in morning and evening worship and Torah study, were marked by idea and experience exchange, instructional workshops, and religious ideological exposition in an atmosphere of warm comradeship. Each such event, organized and programmed by the national headquarters staff in cooperation with regional leadership and host-community leadership, included a complement of national officers and eminent guest speakers. These endeavors bore continuing fruit over the years in the strengthening of Torah-loyal religious life in many communities.

The Orthodox Union's array of informative, educational, and inspirational material, a basic resource since early days, also reflected the impact of the changed climate. Then and since, this area of the organization's activity has been under the care of the Publications Commission, among whose successive chairmen have been M. Morton Rubenstein, Lawrence A. Kobrin, Sheldon Rudoff, and the present incumbent Joel M. Schreiber.

At the post-fifty-sixth Anniversary stage, *Jewish Life* had developed a widening influence. Maturing in its literary pattern, the magazine was distinctive in, among other attributes, its policy of providing a medium for writers of varying viewpoint within the spectrum of Orthodox Jewish attitudes. Tribute was won by the publication, beyond as well as within the traditional fold, for its range of timely and timeless content: topical comment, evocative experiences, exploration of ideas and issues, portrayal of personalities and of communities far and near around the world, and fiction and verse of Torah essence. Not least of all, *Jewish Life* won favor by its creative note and attitude of self-confidence.

Originally published five times a year, *Jewish Life* frequency soon was changed to six bimonthly issues per year. It remained on that schedule until 1972, when, owing to the organization's budgetary pressures, quarterly publication was imposed. The regular appearance of *Jewish Life* continued uninterrupted and—according to an appreciative readership—with consistent quality, with Saul Bernstein, the Orthodox Union's administrator, as editor, until 1976.

The editorial process was forwarded by one of a series of assistant editors or editorial assistants, each of whom also served in other capacities at the

Orthodox Union. Serving at different times, with particular value, as Assistant Editor were Thea Odem, Ricki Gordon, Judah Metchik, and Rabbi Elkanah Schwartz.

For a few years after this writer's retirement from his multiple posts in 1975, the publication of *Jewish Life* continued first, and briefly, under the editorship of Rabbi Aryeh Kaplan, and then under the editorship of Rabbi Yaakov Jacobs. In 1983, the Orthodox Union's officers decided to bring to a virtual end the career of a periodical that many people considered to be of unique value and a source of prestige and influence to American Orthodox Jewry's central force. The magazine's suspension was—and still is—widely regretted.

THE PACE OF PRODUCTION

The impetus of the 1954 biennial convocation and the advent of the new leadership, with the consequent added workload, made the need for additional staff inescapable. Thus the new administration made a number of professional staff appointments, with added clerical help, for synagogue relations work, program materials preparation, fund-raising, and a newly launched individual membership adjunct of great potential: The Orthodox Union Association.

The published *Report of Activities* for 1955 gives a comprehensive summary of the extent of the organization's work at that time. Such reports were issued annually from 1948 on (with less regularity before then), and were thereafter also included, in somewhat different form, in the handbooks issued to delegates at biennial conventions.

The 1955 report, a thirty-page multiprocessed brochure, must have been eye-opening to many of its recipients. In the years and decades to follow, the work was to continue greatly enlarged in volume and scope, but what was set forth in the 1955 report is, to an extent, illustrative of both what was being done then and what—with major growth, additions of new services (discontinuance of some others), and extraordinary multiplication of staff—was to be portrayed in future times.

Each of these nine departments, and the pertaining directive commissions, submitted data on their work. This was indicative of the needs addressed and the practical results gained. The citing of several individual items will illuminate the extraordinary scope of the Union's work.

The Community and Synagogue Activities Division reported that, having pursued the program noted earlier, it had focused on:

Establishment of citywide councils of Orthodox synagogues . . . established three such councils in 1955 and laid the foundation for an additional dozen councils. [In carrying out the previously noted in seven UOJCA Regions] these were addressed to all Orthodox congregations—whether or not affiliated with the Union—in each area. So too with many visits by officers, Commission members, and staff to individual synagogues on special occasions. In conjunction with the Publications Commission, the Community and Synagogue Activities Division distributed in 1955 large quantities of the Union's booklets, program materials, and periodicals. Also hundreds of requests were filled for guest speakers for congregational and community events; in most cases the speakers appeared gratis.

One part of the Community and Synagogue Activities report reflected the onset, in this period, of an upsurge of planning of new structures by many congregations. In some cases this was due to the need for larger or improved facilities at existing sites, while in numerous cases it was prompted by the move of congregations to new locations. In the second instance, the congregations followed the movement of many of their members to new locations, due to neighborhood change, population shifts, "upward mobility," and related social developments of the time. The same causes, which were to be felt strongly over the succeeding years, spurred another aspect of the synagogue-building need: the birth of entirely new congregations, in newly developed in-city neighborhoods or outlying suburbs.

The commission report cites the provision of architectural consultation in that year (1955) for fourteen congregations planning new buildings. The consultation was provided without charge by either the Union or the consultant, David Moed, A.I.A. Mr. Moed contributed his professional services gratis for many years, as the Orthodox Union's volunteer architectural consultant.

The New Synagogues unit reported:

". . . Organizing or aiding the birth of 12 new congregations in new neighborhoods and suburbs during the year, and providing new groups with Sepher Torah scrolls, Siddurim, Tallitoth, etc."

The Youth Division report offers a foretaste of the greater achievement to come, having inaugurated the National Conference of Synagogue Youth in 1954. The Youth report stated that, in 1955, it had already

established regional units of NCSY with ongoing programs and duly elected officers in five regions, each with its study activities and sports program. During the past year, 15 different conclaves and week-ends had been held in many communities, to which approximately 1,500 boys and girls had come, spending one to five days at the respective events. And, some 60 different communities in 20 states were serviced by the Youth Division. . . .

The Communal Relations Commission reported effective participation in the National Jewish Community Relations Advisory Council,[2] in 1955. The report stated:

> including sessions of fourteen of NCRAC's conferences and commissions; also guidance to numerous local communities on community relations problems; and the rallying of Orthodox synagogues behind efforts to amend the McCarran-Walter Immigration Acts and in opposition to attempts to have the United Nations sponsor a "Blank Day" Calendar Reform plan which would have undermined the fixity of the Sabbath.

(As noted earlier in this book, the Orthodox Union had campaigned for many years against such Shabbath-endangering calendar reform plans.)

IN DEFENSE OF SHECHITAH

In this period, much of this commission's efforts (as likewise before and thereafter) were directed at combating legislative threats to Shechitah, on both the Federal and state levels in the United States, and at Federal and provincial levels in Canada. Shechitah, although acclaimed as most humane by leading animal physiologists, has been a perennial target of self-styled humane societies of a certain transient type. These societies have shown a telling lack of concern for the conditions to be witnessed at piggeries, as well as for the countless yearly victims of animal hunters and for the agonies suffered by animals under some forms of slaughter countenanced by these same groups.

In opposing proposed legislation in this danger-strewn area, the Orthodox Union, through its Communal Relations Commission, exercised its position as the Torah community's representative in the NJCRAC to prevail upon the whole roster of major national Jewish organizations and local community relations councils to adhere to the Orthodox Union's stand. This success was scored in the face of the lesser concern—if any, in some

---

2. Originally, this association of national Jewish organizations and local Jewish community relations councils did not have the word "Jewish" in its name (abbreviated NCRAC). The word "Jewish" was added later, and the abbreviation became NJCRAC.

cases—for Shechitah itself and of their sensitivity to the disingenuous propaganda of the sources conducting the anti-Shechitah agitation.

A bill pushed in its original form by the "mushroom" humane-slaughter groups was passed by the United States Congress in 1958, but the anti-Shechitah aim was nullified by changes incorporated in the bill as passed, at the insistence of the Orthodox Union and the Rabbinical Council of America in conjunction with the Agudath Harabbanim. Shechitah was specifically designated as among the approved methods of humane slaughter, and the bill included the Case Amendment (introduced by New Jersey Senator Clifford P. Case at the urging of Rabbi Teitz of Elizabeth, New Jersey), which stipulated that Shechitah, as a religious requirement, is not subject to the law's provisions.[3]

The "humane-slaughter" forces later moved to another angle of attack: the positioning of animals for slaughter, specifically, the hoisting-and-shackling process, which had not been questioned before. This attack was dealt with under the leadership of the Union's Communal Relations Commission together with a counterpart committee of the Rabbinical Council of America, and a cross-community alignment through a Joint Advisory Committee of the NJCRAC and the Synagogue Council of America. (A key role in the process was played by Dr. Samson R. Weiss, who at that time was the UOJCA Executive Vice President.)

Eventually, different methods of pre-Shechitah positioning were developed in the United States, with the Orthodox Union's financial support, and in Canada and Great Britain as well. These methods, which were applicable to large cattle, obviated any humane-slaughter challenges in that category, and, in fact, won the approval of the legitimate, long-established animal-protection societies. Methods applicable to small cattle such as sheep continue to be researched, although the prevailing positioning methods are, in any event, not subject to valid challenge.

Meanwhile, those elements attracted to the groups that mushroomed under the "humane slaughter" banner were drawn to causes of newer vogue. Precedents indicate that the current quiescence regarding Shechitah is likely to prove temporary. Shechitah remains to be rediscovered as a target for camouflaged attack on Jews and Judaism.

ON BEHALF OF ISRAEL

To continue with citations from the *1955 Report of Activities*, the Israel and Overseas Commission pointed to:

---

3. The 1958 bill, "The Humane Methods of Animal Slaughter," was re-enacted in revised form in 1978, with the words "and handling" added to the reference to shechitah.

wholehearted cooperation both prior to and since the establishment of the State of Israel in behalf of the moral and economic welfare of and security of the Jewish State; intensified activities during the Near East Crisis of 1955, including a series of special communications to rabbis, presidents, and other congregational leaders, bringing the weight of the members of these congregations to bear on U.S. policy in this crisis. In an emergency conference in Washington, D.C. on the threat to Israel jointly convened by the Orthodox Union and nineteen other national Jewish organizations, the Union took a leading part, with the largest representation.

Also instituted by this commission was:

An effective educational campaign to assure that immigrants to Israel be provided with basic religious facilities and have proper opportunity for pursuance of their religious tenets. Responding to many calls, a study *free of bias and conjecture* made by the Union on the situation facing many thousands of deeply religious families migrating to Israel from North African lands had shown that 80% were arbitrarily sent to the settlements conducted by the non-religious parties, under a pre-established quota system.

Responding to communications from the Union, conveying its findings, very many congregational leaders joined with the Union in calling upon the responsible agencies in Israel and America to take corrective action. In the fall of 1955, the Israel government, in response, undertook to assure the Union and its constituency that "immigrants henceforth would be given freedom of choice as to type of settlement."

ADVANCES IN KEY AREAS

The report on *Jewish Life* magazine gave instances of the impact of its various articles, features, and editorials. It noted that:

scores of newspapers throughout the country picked up the story revealed by a JL article exposing attempts by Seventh Day Adventists to gain Jewish adherents to their faith by deceptive means, reproducing portions of a confidential Adventist pamphlet. *Jewish Life* thereafter received a letter from the national office of the Seventh Day Adventists in which their director expressed regrets and offered assurances, that "these activities in no way represent our true purposes and methods as a denomination."

The report noted that *Jewish Life* had continued to win plaudits not only from all elements of the Torah community but also from other "leading American Jewish personages." Cited as an example was a letter received from Dr. Joshua Bloch, Chief Librarian of the Jewish Division of the New York Public Library, reading:

> For quite some time I have had in mind to write to you about *Jewish Life*. . . . I am very much impressed with the content of each issue. It seems to me that you have succeeded in furnishing American Jewry with a magazine which is truly expressive of the sentiments and point of view of that element which calls itself Orthodox in Jewry. Each piece of literary writing which enters in its makeup seems to be permeated by sound knowledge, good writing, and a spirit of tolerance towards those whose views it does not share. Altogether, you are rendering a service which I am sure is appreciated by those who profit by it.

The Armed Forces Division, in 1955, reported on the constant updating of its central registry, whereby personalized service was rendered to Jews in the U.S. Armed Forces. A letter from a mitzvah-observant serviceman on active duty cited as typical of response to the program reads, in part:

> I am stationed 110 miles inside the Soviet Zone—if it were not for your parcels I probably would not have been able to obtain any type of Kosher food at all.

Many of the letters received expressed esteem for the "UOJCA Armed Forces Division services held in the hearts of so many Jewish soldiers, sailors, airmen and marines." Each person in the central registry was sent—with the unstinting aid of Women's Branch volunteers—appropriate booklets for each Yom Tov or other feature of the Jewish year, food packages at Pesach and other times, and other articles.

The Armed Forces Division, in 1955, also

> continued its efforts to gain from the Department of Defense official recognition that:
>
> a) Orthodox Jews in the armed forces are entitled to Kosher rations; and
> b) are entitled to observe Saturday as their Sabbath:

> The Armed Forces Division continued the Union's support of the Kosher kitchen, serving scores of Jewish soldiers, established in 1953 at Fort Devens, Massachusetts, having sponsored its creation and provided general guidance, and direct grants, contributions, and supplies to a value of approximately $6,000.

> Together with the National Council of Young Israel and the Agudath Israel Youth Council, the Union through the Armed Forces Division is sponsoring the Kosher kitchen established by a dedicated Jewish chaplain at Fort Dix, New Jersey, one of the largest military installations in the Continental U.S.

And, during the year, the Division advised many draftees on military life, and interceded in their behalf in cases where induction fell on Jewish holiday periods.

The report states further:

> among the most heartening messages received (usually from chaplains) are of those servicemen who in civilian life had had no contact with the synagogue and (in military service) have developed a love for Judaism and Mitzvoth. The Division immediately contacts the man and furnishes him with all the religious articles he requires—Siddurim, Tallith, Tephillin, etc. The response is heart-warming.

~

In the 1955 Kashruth Department report, it is stated that "the knowledge [among the Jewish public] that the Ⓤ is free of private interest and maintains the highest Halachic standards has made it axiomatic that the Ⓤ insignia of the Union of Orthodox Jewish Congregations of America assures acceptance by Jewish consumers. As a result, there is constant increase in the number of firms applying for Ⓤ supervision and certification, reaching a new peak in 1955."

The Kashruth Department report also points out that:

> The ever-increasing range of products under the Orthodox Union's supervision reflects the trend toward the increasing use of mass-produced prepared, packaged, and processed foods . . . a major factor in the social and economic life of present-day America. Thus the last year's progress has further attested the universal recognition that the Ⓤ, as the identification of authoritative, communally responsible, not-for-profit Kashruth supervision, performs an indispensable function—one which is not and cannot be performed by any other form of activity in this field.

It was also reported that "[i]n excess of 100,000 copies of the Ⓤ Kashruth Directory were given free distribution through congregations and other Jewish organizations, reaching families throughout the country," in 1955.

In the following years, this distribution was to be multiplied manifold, as were the number and variety of products, and the number of food-serving establishments added to the Ⓤ supervised list. The tempo of this upsurging trend was manifest in 1955, when it was reported that 113 products in 22 categories manufactured by 34 companies at 58 plants had been added that year.

~

This, then, was a time of great progress in both the presence and the ideological force of American Orthodox Jewry's central arm, and in its functional services. In one key area, however, progress lagged. Income development failed to keep pace with the expenses incurred by the program growth; deficits mounted, and sharp economies were in order.

Under continuing stringency, some of the newer additions to the staff were presently released pending improved circumstances; their functions were distributed among other staff members. But with the demands for the Union's services mounting from a Torah community rising to a sense of its greater self and its compelling tasks, the pressure of the organizations' daily workload was heavily burdened.

Various projects launched to increase income met with mixed success. One venture with an unhappy outcome was the chartering of a large ship for a kosher ten-day cruise to Caribbean points. Bookings being disappointingly few, the project had to be abandoned, with a commercial source taking over the charter.

The foregoing debacle and the inadequate results of other funding efforts placed the Union in a critical financial plight. This, fortunately, was partially lightened by the generosity of four figures whose appreciation for the Union's role meant a great deal: Ivan Salomon, Gustave Stern, Samuel C. Feuerstein, and Samuel Schneierson.

With retrospective thought of the trials incurred at this juncture (and at numerous other times) in meeting payroll requirements, appeasing suppliers pressing for payment of accumulated bills, juggling deficits, and otherwise struggling through fiscal quandaries, a word of appreciation is in order for those sharing this burden at UOJCA headquarters. From the late 1940s to the period under discussion and beyond, a position combining bookkeeping functions with clerical personnel management was held, in turn, by Ruth Miller (after marriage, Ruth Dubrow) and Judah Kirschblum. Both of these individuals were marked by exceptional professional ability and devotion to the work and cause of the Orthodox Union. Like qualities of competence and dedication characterized their successors in turn, Sheldon Roth and Gad Goldman. Much is owed to these unsung heroes for their signal share in enabling the Union to carry on through all its difficulties.

Later, the combination of responsibilities borne by each of those mentioned was divided into several positions, as requisite for the greatly expanded staff and the enlarged operations of later decades.

~

Fortunately, in 1956, Dr. Samson R. Weiss was appointed to the new office of executive vice president. A scholar and leader, Dr. Weiss had ripened his Torah learning at the great Mir Yeshivah of pre-World War II Poland, as well as delving into humanities studies and earning a doctoral degree at leading European universities. Noted as a thinker, ideological expositor, and bearer of a perceptive grasp of world Jewish affairs, Dr. Weiss had previously served as National Director of the National Council of Young Israel. Now, his capacities for communal direction and expression of the role of Torah Jewry would enrich the life of the Orthodox Union and its constituency through years which one member of the Union's Board, mindful of the combination of distinctive personalities then leading the Union's endeavors on both the lay and "civil" levels, has dubbed "the Golden Age of the Orthodox Union."

23

Clearing the Ideological Path

One should keep in mind the climate of the Jewish world in the post-mid-century period. Over a century of modern-age challenge to the Jew had culminated in *Shoah*—the Holocaust. An era marked by the retreat of many from essential Jewishness, yet also by the stalwart loyalty of others, had concluded with the truncated remains of a covenant-born people reeling from the atrocities of Nazism's would-be Final Solution. Jews, survivors all, were slowly trying to confront the stupefying dimension of Shoah. All was confusion of spirit; "Who, what, why am I?" was the quandry in countless minds. In the groping for meaning, for self, for direction, motivation clashed with motivation within the bosom of each afflicted Jew. To fulfill Jewishness . . . or to flee Jewishness? to accept Jewishness . . . or to *be* truly Jewish? How many wrestled thus within their inner selves? How many pondered whether to shrink from that Jewish self or to affirm and fulfill that self's verity—or even, perhaps, to somehow do both?

The groping, stumbling, and seeking, conscious and unconscious, pervaded the Jewish world. On the American Jewish scene, impulse fought impulse. To this realm of bafflement and doubt, the organism that Henry Pereira Mendes had long before brought to birth spread the Torah message. The work of the renewed, redirected Orthodox Union, with its scant, improvised apparatus, took on prosaic forms. This complex of activities was of everyday, mundane nature, without external glamour. But to those who understood, each move, each step, each function, each seeming trifle, was a victory in the battle for the spirit of the Jewish people.

This spiritual turmoil was the source of various issues that agitated Jewish religious life in the post-mid-century years. Epitomizing the erupting drives was the controversy of the mode of seating at congregational services.

THE MIXED-SEATING ISSUE

Separation of the sexes at public worship, the practice among Jews throughout the ages, was unquestioned and unquestionable until modern times. In contrast, mixing of the sexes at worship services has been the norm in the Christian world, undisputed among most of the Christian denominations. When modernity dawned on the world, there arose movements to subordinate Judaism—the beliefs, laws, and practices of Israel's historic faith—to worldly considerations. An archetypal physical token of de-Judaization was the abandonment of Jewry's synagogue separation in favor of the mixed-seating mode of the Christian churches.

From the inception of the deviant and heterodox groups, "mixed pews" had been a visible emblem of their defection from the historical Jewish faith and way of life. For the Jewish faithful, the mechitzah or the gallery marking the separation of the men's and the women's sections of the synagogue was the rampart, as it were, between the Torah way and subjection to the gentile world.

Amid the ideological turbulence of the time, the assimilative pressures that earlier had given rise to the Reform and Conservative schisms now not only brought replacements to the assimilation-prone ranks of those movements, but bore with heightened force on many congregations hitherto steadfast in the Torah faith. Most congregations so afflicted withstood the agitation in varying degrees of difficulty; others, hard-set by disruptive elements wielding blandishments, sophistries, and trickeries, were induced to yield. Some were pressured into outright heterodoxy; others sought to compromise, replacing traditional seating with mechitzah-less or even mixed seating while continuing to conduct traditional services. The latter situation, ostensibly stopping short of and deterring further deviation, was soon recognized as the more insidious—because less open—threat to religious integrity.

Through the years preceding World War II, the Torah community had not come to grips with the seating challenge. Focused with its minimal resources on the propagation and public defense of Torah observance, the Orthodox Union had combated squarely the Reform and Conservative movements, as such; but it apparently had reckoned insufficiently with the trend then beginning to appear toward a mechitzah-abandoning version of traditionalism. Following the war, however, with a new generation poorly schooled in Judaism coming to the fore, the move to suburbia sprouting, and the air astir with spiritual turbulence and ideological vagaries, the seating issue took on a weightier dimension.

It appears that the situation initially caught the central Union blind-sided.

In an era when non-Orthodox denominations stood out clearly against the Torah-true faith, it was taken for granted that no institution that had arisen and conducted itself as an Orthodox synagogue could ever veer from what Jewish Orthodoxy was universally known to be. It was inconceivable that any congregation, affiliated or otherwise, that identified itself with the Union of Orthodox Jewish Congregations of America could be—or, for that matter, would want to be—anything other than what that Union of its nature was made of and stood for. Now, however, when what had been an obscure, subterranean manifestation was revealed as a strong current battering many congregations, a far different situation was being faced. But facing the situation was one thing; countering it was quite another. That there could be no equivocation, that mechitzah observance—an immutable halachic requirement—was mandatory, was beyond question—but how to achieve the purpose?

Adequate numbers of well-schooled fieldworkers equipped to reach directly the affected portion of the thousands of Orthodox synagogues[1] and deal on the spot with the human and ideological problems was beyond possibility. What could be done had to be only within the limits of existing means.

Within these limits, the problem did not lend itself to facile methods. In the American clime, each congregation, being self-organized, considered itself self-sovereign. While many congregations were led by men of well-tried loyalty, also pushing themselves forward at this stage of American Jewish development were leaders Jewishly ignorant, with little sense of Torah law as being Divinely ordained and of binding force. The very term "halachah" had but little meaning to such men. All that was needed, they would suppose, was to engineer a majority vote of the congregation's board, or, if pushed, of its membership. Thereupon were changed the theological basis and the religious identity of the synagogue, regardless of its history, or, if necessary, of its charter or constitution.

Although very few of the congregations that had introduced mixed seating were affiliated with the Orthodox Union, the national body, in this connection as in all others, looked upon all within the Torah fold as within its constituency. Increasingly, the Union's responsible quarters were con-

---

1. A 1957 study had shown that Orthodox Jewish synagogues and places of regular worship of all kinds and sizes in the United States and Canada totalled over 3,000. Two-thirds of these were on the Orthodox Union's mailing lists, but while all looked to the UOJCA as their national arm, those maintaining an official tie were barely 1,000.

A (1960) study showed that 93 percent of all enrolled member congregations had, and scrupulously used, a mechitzah. Of the remaining 7 percent, most, although without a physical mechitzah, observed separate seating.

fronted with the policy question: Shall congregations that abandon mechitzah or institute mixed seating be dropped from servicing and, if affiliated, from the membership roster? And, if severed, might the action ultimately have disciplinary effect—or might it result in prompting the affected congregations to move to outright defection from Orthodox allegiance? And if, on the other hand, with view to holding such congregations within the Torah frame, educational persuasion without severance be the course, what would be the moral effect generally? What of nonmember, nonmechitzah synagogues seeking to mark their adherence to the Torah fold by applying for UOJCA membership?

Experience showed that the circumstances differed widely from case to case. A uniformly applicable hard–and–fast policy was beyond facile codification. Therefore, a provisional working policy adopted at a board meeting provided that such congregations as lowered their halachic standards in any regard would, if affiliated, be subject to severance, with each such case to be passed on, after due hearings, by the Union's Executive Committee. In the course of time, several congregations in breach of this requirement were dropped from the Union's membership rolls after the requisite procedures, while several others that held promise of correction by educational means were retained on probation, with ultimately successful results.

As distinguished from firefighting measures taken at points of conflagration, education propaganda was the recourse. The literature prepared and published by the Union,[2] the notes struck and reiterated at national convocations, regional conclaves, and local events, now not only addressed the mechitzah question squarely, but stressed the basic issues in such terms as:

> Behind the seating dispute was the fundamental question: The Torah way or the non-Jewish way? Shall the Jew live by the laws set forth on High or shall he yield his beliefs and practices to the pattern of surrounding society? Is a Torah synagogue subject to Torah law, determinable only by authorities in Halachah, Jewish law, or may its established religious practices be determined by vote of members?

And the further point:

> Is defection from Halachah in one regard apt to conserve observance in other respects—or must it in fact open the way to breach of observance in general, alike in synagogue practice and in the personal lives of the congregants?

---

2. Among this body of literature were such booklets as *Mixed Pews*, by Rabbi Morris Max, distributed by the thousands.

Imperceptibly at first, then more clearly, this sustained program made itself felt. The impetus to mixed seating slowed, and a reverse trend emerged.

A distinct stir was made by a *Jewish Action* article (March–April 1957) that listed by name and community, including the names of the rabbi and president of each, fourteen congregations that within a recent period had reinstated, or newly instituted, a mechitzah.[3] Over the years, to the present day, many more congregations have followed suit.

Now ensued two kindred developments with great consequences. These have become renowned in the annals of traditional American Jewry as, respectively, "The New Orleans Case" and "The Mount Clemens Case." The first-named case involved a synagogue in the Louisiana metropolis; the other one a synagogue in a Michigan resort community.

Both places were like numerous others in that, by engineered vote, the separate seating always observed by each shul had been ousted and the church-style mixed seating had been imposed. In both instances, the defenders of synagogue integrity did not, as in so many other cases, yield to the constant browbeating and pressures. In the one case one member family, in the other a single individual, had stood their ground. Both had called for submission of the issue to a Beth Din, and had met with a blanket refusal. And both the battlers—Harry Katz and his family of New Orleans, and Baruch Litvin of Mount Clemens—broke new ground by two steps: resorting to legal proceedings, and, turning to the central Torah community agency, the Orthodox Union, for both legal and procedural guidance and practical help.

The results made history. The architect of the legal strategy that was pursued was Samuel Lawrence Brennglass, a well-known New York lawyer

---

3. An intriguing instance of the impact of this article was an agitated call to the UOJCA administrator from the rabbi of a congregation in a major city. Having nursed this congregation step by planned step from its original non-Orthodox character toward a proper Torah identity, he had aimed at calling, at a strategically suitable time, for the institution of a mechitzah. But his congregation's key ba'aley battim, upon reading the *Jewish Action* piece, thereupon jumped the gun, calling for a mechitzah forthwith. The rabbi, who had planned to ease the suggestion onto his congregation to avoid controversy and possible defections, was embarrassed by the precipitate action of his lay leaders, and deemed the move to be untimely. He demanded that, henceforth, no copies of *Jewish Action* be sent to his officers or the Board (as was the regular distribution process of the publication) until after first being passed on by himself!

Notwithstanding, the mechitzah was very soon afterward installed in that shul, and the feared mass withdrawal of disaffected members turned out to be no more than five. On the other hand, there began on influx of what soon came to be hundreds of new member families. Today this congregation, with unceasing dynamism, is one of the country's powerhouses of Torah Judaism.

who was also a long-time UOJCA board member and officer and Chairman of the Communal Relations Commission, to which the matter had been assigned.

In consultation with Rabbi Samson R. Weiss and Rabbi Israel Klavan, Executive Vice Presidents, respectively, of the Orthodox Union and the Rabbinical Council of America, plus Administrator Bernstein, he formulated guidelines whose key aspects were:

1. That the laws of the Jewish religion as handed down through history have binding force in Orthodox Judaism.

2. That questions in Jewish law (Halachah) may be passed on for definitive determination only by duly qualified, recognized Orthodox rabbinic authorities, and are not subject to determination or change by vote of congregational laity.

3. That the congregation in question had been established for the practice of, and worship according to, the Orthodox Jewish religion, and had been so maintained throughout its existence heretofore.

4. That the theological commitment undertaken thereby was the condition of the contributions and participation of the members from the establishment of the synagogue onward, and hence constitutes a binding and irrevocable trust.

5. That the mixing of the sexes, or the absence of a separation between the men's and women's seating sections at synagogue public worship services, is a violation of the laws of the Jewish religion proper, Orthodox Judaism.

6. That such violation deprives the institution of its sanctity as a synagogue. Under Jewish law, Jews may not rightfully worship therein.

7. Accordingly, such change from separate seating is not only a religious violation but a breach of trust in civil law.

The briefs submitted to the respective court trials in New Orleans and Mount Clemens included, together with citations of pertinent precedents and rulings in civil law, citations from authoritative sources in Jewish law through the centuries to that date, plus expert in-person testimony by an array of eminent religious leaders. Among these were Rabbi Eliezer Silver, of the Presidium of the Union of Orthodox Rabbis of the United States and Canada (Agudath Harabbanim), Rabbi David S. Hollander, president, and Rabbi Israel Klavan, executive vice-president, of the Rabbinical Council of America, and Rabbi Samson R. Weiss, UOJCA executive vice president.

The effect was compelling. The ruling handed down in each case fully upheld the position as set forth by the plaintiffs on behalf of Orthodox Jewish rights. It was a landmark victory.

The impact of the New Orleans ruling was far-reaching, but that of the

Mount Clemens case was still greater. Baruch Litvin had been moved from the first by a sense of the countrywide dimension and historic import of the issue. He not only was in constant consultation with Orthodox Union officials, but did extensive personal research on the question in rabbinic and historical sources, and also traversed the country visiting community after community to alert key figures and the broadest possible circles as to the ultimate questions at stake.[4]

In narrowly legal terms, the force of the New Orleans and Mount Clemens cases was subsequently blunted when appeals on technical grounds—different in each case—left the principal question in uncertain legal status. This hardly lessened the force of the moral effect that had been achieved, however. Its impress had a reality that became unmistakable in the perspective of time.

Penetrating as it did the murk of confused viewpoints, this development can be seen as a moral turning point in the seating controversy and, beyond this, as a distinct influence ŏn the complex of spiritual bafflements out of which the immediate problem was spawned.

Never before had the positive Jewish stand on the matter been projected with such thoroughness; never before had the basic questions been set forth in such irrefutable clarity; never before had so many been moved to ponder the matter so deeply and, as presently became marked, with such signal effect on outlook.

The New Orleans and Mount Clemens cases were thus pivotal battles in the fight for synagogue sanctity and for all that is signified thereby. With the mentality that had promoted the breach of sanctity effectively challenged, no longer could the de-Judaization move be forwarded with the same impunity as before. Recurrences of attempts to introduce church-style seating became increasingly more rare, practically to the vanishing point. In contrast, instances of replacement of the seating separation in synagogues that had previously incurred the lapse became so common as to occasion little remark.

~

The foregoing, among assorted other occurrences of the time, gave an indication of growing realization that titanic events had demanded of the American Jew a dimension beyond all prior notions of his potential. There was a penetrating sense that pivotal responsibilities had been entrusted to

---

4. Subsequently, Mr. Litvin compiled, under his editorship, the volume *The Sanctity of the Synagogue* (New York 5719/1959; revised edition, editor Jeanne Litvin 5747/1987), a comprehensive compendium of historical and literary material on the subject.

that heterogeneous compound, American Jewry. This, not only for the support of Israel in the reborn, beleaguered homeland; for the care of brethren wherever they may be found—now including, with mounting compulsion, the rescue from extinction as Jews of the Soviet lands; but beyond all, as the last great bastion of the dispersion, co-responsibility with Israel for the living perpetuation of the heritage of Sinai.

Awareness grew that even as assimilative influences eroded Jewish loyalties, the capacity of the Torah-rooted Jew to function as an American had gained new scope; the Torah Jew, the Torah community, had taken root as a living reality within the enigmatic onrush of American civilization.

In forwarding, within this reality, the Orthodox Union's tasks as the force for cohesion, psychological tendencies as well as practical situations had to be met. Barometers of advance pointed to Torah Jewry's bolder stature on the Jewish world scene, but the Orthodox Jew, with a consciousness of past losses and intractable fragmentation, remained hesitant to take full measure of his changing capacity.

As the central Union's work proceeded on its uphill course through the second half of the twentieth century, not the least of its challenges was the nurturing of a positive yet realistic attitude to supplant inured negativism.

24

In Convention Assembled

In light of the outlook challenge, the role of the national biennial conventions stands out. Each such assemblage made its mark as a fount of mutual inspiration, broadened vistas, ideological ripening, shared endeavor, and the strength of solidarity.

After a succession of these assemblages in Atlantic City, a further change of venue, in its turn seen as daring, brought another series at famed hotels in Washington, D.C. Increasingly popular as magnets for attendance, the Orthodox Union's biennial convocations had become "the place to be" in the traditional Jewish sphere. With programs maintaining high levels of meaning and appeal, convention planning was given due scope for the course assessment and policy shaping that were the essential functions of these events.

The deliberations process on each occasion addressed domestic and world Jewish concerns of both current and long-term relevance. These included advancement of personal, family, and community life; shaping the rising generation; the role of traditionally religious Jewry in world Jewish polity; the stance of the Orthodox Union on concerns of American and Canadian society; and re-elucidation of goals. Interspersed with these sessions were daily Torah study periods and capsule expositions of Torah concepts. Practical "know-how" workshops and idea-exchange seminars on synagogue techniques and local community concerns were regularly featured. Among the highlights were symposia and panel discussions at which the delegates and other participants responded—often in lively fashion—to the Torah-directed insights on public issues or given facets of contemporary life presented by eminent thinkers and revered personages of the Torah world. The meal sessions at each biennial, occasions of festive warmth, found camaraderie at its heights. The program format also regularly included musical presentations of distinction, and sightseeing expeditions and other features for accompanying family members.

As developed through the 1950s, 1960s, and 1970s, the convention planning, agenda, and arrangements process was channeled through the successive convention committees on the basis of drafts prepared by the administrator in consultation with staff colleagues. The programs were aimed at integrating the proceedings with congregational life through the participation of the duly designated delegates. These were required to be officially delegated by their congregations on forms sent by the Union following formal announcement of each coming convention. The need was addressed to linking the deliberations to the concerns of the congregational–communal constituency, while in turn transmitting to the constituency the comprehensive view, the shared insights, and the collective policy.

In accordance with these purposes, provision was made for the congregations to submit to UOJCA headquarters their resolutions, proposals, and ideas on subjects to be addressed and problem areas to be explored. Advance drafts of proposed resolutions on policy and organizational undertakings, as prepared by the Resolutions Committee appointed in advance of each convention, were circulated to congregational leaders and the designated convention delegates, along with program drafts, for their advance consideration.

Thus the function of the Union of Orthodox Jewish Congregations of America as the representative plenary arm of the congregationally constituted Torah community was implemented and reinforced. The potential for practical fulfillment of the long-sought-for goal, a cohesive, coherent Torah community, was steadily advanced.

Thoughts on the better integration of North American Orthodox Jewry as a whole found expression at the conventions through this period. Because of its role, the Orthodox Union's channels necessarily bear a sense of Orthodox Jewry's institutional and organizational diversity as a composite of autonomous but basically interdependent units. Under the circumstances that have usually prevailed, however, this collective purview has tended to be obscured by the ongoing demands of established functions.

In the post–midcentury times now under discussion, as before and since, UOJCA circles were not exempt from the tendency prevalent among Orthodox Jewish forces generally to see the trees rather than the forest, and to focus concern on those "trees" within a given frame of responsibility. But in the case of the Orthodox Union, while its many-faceted functional range has ever commanded attention and resources, the very nature of the organization as Torah community centerpoint necessitated consideration of the all-encompassing aspects of Orthodox Jewry's collective equipment.

Hence came the realization in some quarters that stock must be taken of the deep changes in the social and institutional pattern of traditional Jewish life in North America. Convention discussions mirrored such historical realities as continuing acculturation to America's environment, and a more defined and better situated place in American society for Jews generally and for the religiously loyal among them. Reflections of this in the synagogue sphere, and in the religious domain as a whole, came into focus. Into focus, too, came the striking fact that it was now becoming prestigious, rather than unfashionable, to be marked among Jews-at-large as Torah-observant.

In informal delegate-to-delegate exchanges as well as in programmed sessions, it further came into wider perspective that the Orthodox-identified and their many now well-regulated synagogues and other institutions were learning to exercise their proper role on the local scene. Illustrative of this development was the role of the St. Louis Orthodox Jewish Community Council, the Vaad Hoeir, in embracing the several Orthodox congregations of the area, with notable success in city and state legislative matters affecting Jewish interests as well as in internal Jewish community-wide concerns.

NEW CURRENTS, NEW INFLUX

The effects of influences from a different direction playing upon Jewish life were also to be pondered. The volcanic upheavals that had revolutionized world Jewry's situation had generated powerful new waves of spiritual urge. These bore with particular force on Torah world horizons. Awareness of the new depths of Jewishness demanded of the Torah-conscious found expression, evidencing a current of rising force in the Orthodox Union's responsive processes.

A further element in the warming clime of the observant fold, reflected in the Orthodox Union's assemblages and other channels, were the powerful influences of those who had escaped Nazi clutches and of the *shearith ha-peleytah*, those rescued from Shoah. The Torah-loyal among the pre-World War II arrivals and the Holocaust survivors who came after the war were an invaluable increment to American Orthodox Jewry. Steeled by their bitter experiences, by the post-mid-century period they were already a much-felt element on the Jewish scene, and their presence in established congregations bore marked effect.

Wherever the new arrivals organized their own congregations, these communities took on a new character. A notable example was the Kahal Adath Yeshurun congregation in the Washington Heights section of New York. Bearing the *Torah im derech eretz* (Torah and modern culture) philoso-phy propounded by the great nineteenth-century thinker and leader Samson Raphael Hirsch, this congregation forwarding the Frankfurt tradition grew to number close to a thousand Shomer-Shabbath families. It created a rounded kehillah structure covering the full range of religious and social needs. Developed was an educational program, ranging from kindergarten to high schools—and to senior yeshivah for men and seminary for women—that continues to this day.

The addition of the prewar and postwar arrivals to the traditional ranks was marked in various facets of the communal makeup generally, including educational as well as congregational spheres, and in the climate of religious life, too. Besides various areas of New York City, and its vicinity, communities in Chicago, Los Angeles, Miami Beach, Boston, Baltimore, and other Jewish population hubs all benefited from the new numbers so profoundly charged with the will to live Jewishly.

The UOJCA convention settings reflected the fact that groups and individuals of these brands plucked from the burning were in varying degrees of identification with, or distance from, the central Union's involved orbit. Since whatever touches the Orthodox Jew registers in the Union's sensors and whatever the Union does touches all of Orthodox Jewry in—and perhaps beyond—North America at some point, reciprocal influences come into play, not only with the immediate fold, but also with such as might be distinct from the regular UOJCA sphere. Thus was it with many of those who settled in the most notable among the recharged communities—namely, Brooklyn's Williamsburgh, Crown Heights, and Borough Park.

All these areas had been distinguished as favored centers of Orthodox residence long before the influx of post-Shoah arrivals. It was in these especially congenial localities that the massive augmentation of the traditional reached its height. In these cases especially, the areas of new settlement took on a different character from that of the original community, for many of the newcomers, unlike most of the original Orthodox residents, were *Chassidim*. At the prompting of their revered Rebbes, thousands of surviving *Chassidim* of various sects found first Williamsburgh and Crown Heights, and then Borough Park (and, in later years, were to find other metropolitan areas, including the outer suburbs) in which to restore their devout, colorful group life in its long-accustomed pattern.

The impact of the newcomers was radical. This was an altogether distinctive element among America's Jews, one that would multiply in number and weight in Jewish affairs in succeeding years.

25

Changes in Perspective

The sense of pervading change registered in congregational life and in the Orthodox Union's processes brought into perspective not only the changes of past decades, but also those then emerging.

For that proportion of the young within the reach of meaningful Jewish education—now growing steadily, but as yet but too limited—the educational apparatus was seen as being on a much better level than before. An assessment of trends perceived that advances to that point were precursors to much greater advances as afternoon schools began to make way for all-day schools, the yeshivoth ketanoth, and yeshivoth at the high-school and college level began to bloom and multiply. Youth work outside the formal education areas by congregational forces, also by such party forces as Mizrachi and Agudath Israel, was taking on significant substance.

So, too, could it be perceived that problem-strewn though the post-mid-century synagogal and communal scene was, prevailing conditions were not to be likened to the unbounded communal chaos of the half-century and more before preceding it. Although Shechitah and the Kashruth situation as a whole still presented large problems, the evils that had flourished at the height of the mass-immigration era had been eradicated. In most communities, the kosher meat provision, though still leaving much to be desired, was much improved over earlier times. (Major further improvement in this connection was then at hand with development of modern organized processes in production, freezing, packaging, and marketing in the kosher poultry industry, with the leading companies entering this field qualifying for, and receiving, the Ⓤ supervision. Lesser, but promising, progress was also in the making in the kosher meat industry.)

Largely eradicated, too, as UOJCA channels noted with satisfaction, was the "mushroom synagogue," that perennial here-today, gone-tomorrow Rosh Hashanah–Yom Kippur phenomenon in the largest cities. Long a target of UOJCA attack, these shady entities exploited the seasonal awakenings of Judaic conscience. Developments opposite in nature to each other served to eliminate the "mushroom synagogue" aberration: On the one hand, advances by real synagogues had won some of the once-a-year ilk to better observance and regular congregant status; on the other hand, time had marked the descent of others from once-a-year attendance to none at all.

Also coming to the surface now, and noted with pleased surprise, was the early manifestation of the phenomenon presently to be labeled the *ba'al teshuvah* movement. Children of the once- or nonce-a-year services partici- pant—of the neglected, the strayed, and the alienated—were beginning to find their way past all these obstacles of assimilated background and life circumstances to the Torah faith in their people. These men and women, and the thousands to follow, were to be a force for the redemption of the Jew of the modern age.

PERCEIVING SOCIAL CHANGE

The assemblages where the local and national purviews converged proved occasions to gauge to what extent the synagogues were keeping apace of their congregants' social and economic development while pursuing wider aims in the mitzvah-constituted life. Convention participants from less flourishing congregations earnestly sought to gain helpful ideas from those congregations that had developed large, devoted memberships and well- programmed activities for community enhancement. These congregations had become prestigious centers of communal life.

Various conditions had come into play in making for progressing or lagging development in different local communities. The surrounding circumstances of each local situation, the initial direction, the evolved membership makeup, the caliber of rabbinic and lay leadership—all these played a part in the communal or congregational course. But consistent throughout was the degree to which the character of new-age American life had been grasped; how well the need was understood to apply to it authentic Jewish fundamentals; and how clearly was perceived the impact on each other of America and the Jew.

It was clear that in the stage-by-stage evolution from the world of the 1870–1924 immigration era, the specifics of the Jewish makeup had changed. Gradations of cleavage to, or discarding of, Jewish belief and practice marked, like geological deposits, the varying responses to the pressures of social adaptation, economic betterment, and absorptive influ- ences. Everyday life was of a far different pattern from that of before. The home situation—its setting, its material equipment, its occupational base, its social pattern—was irreversibly changed. The mode of personal communication and expression had changed, for by the late 1950s English was unchallenged as the mother tongue of America's Jews. Yiddish had all but lost place as a familiar tongue among the Jews of eastern and central European origin or parentage, as it had similarly with Ladino for the Sephardi Jews of Balkan or near-East origin. And by the post-mid-century point, the great majority of America's Jews were American-born.

Why was it, the assembled community representatives pondered, that in the process of Americanization[1] the Jewishness of so many had thinned, while among others it had been reinforced? Much in the shaping of communities was conditioned by the capacity to address these realities creatively, in qualitatively Judaic categories.

As earlier parts of this survey have shown, in assessment of the broad picture, the capacity to reach beyond the bleaker aspects was not lacking as the loyalist fold passed through the trials of earlier years to the 1950s and after. Those who held fast to integral Jewishness had succeeded in rearing a new generation marked by informed love of the heritage of Sinai, and, thus, brought into being the authentically Jewish, authentically American, "American Jew." The American Jew's institutional apparatus, as we have noted, was maturing.

But it was becoming noticeable that the gap of life-style between the Torah-observant and the rest of Jewry had widened and crystallized. Where before many a family may have included members with widely varying attitudes toward their heritage, more characteristic now was family-to-family differentiation, each one being either all Sabbath-observant or otherwise. The social separation was now distinct between the spheres of the Shomrey-Shabbath on the one side, and of the lesser observant, or nonobservant, on the other. The Orthodox synagogue, the spiritual home of the Jewish people, could still bridge most gaps, however.

---

1. Actually, for many of the immigrant thousands, a comparable process had been experienced prior to the New-World settlement, in the very different environments of central and eastern Europe. There, powerful modern-age currents had made a deep impact on Jewish life. In no Jewry of the Old World was universal adherence to the Torah-rooted life to be found, from the later nineteenth-century decades on, and many had deviated from the substance of Jewish belief. Among many who came to the United States, Canada, and other New-World lands in that period and up to (and beyond) the post-World War II time, the religious character of the arrivals changed, from the original vast majority of the traditionally observant, to an eventual three categories: the committed and unshakably observant; those of partial observance or with a sense of traditional ties; and those who were indifferent or in ideological breach with the Judaic heritage. Each element was felt in the shaping of American Jewish life.

A good many of those who had fallen away from the mode of life thus centered on Sabbath observance nevertheless inwardly felt themselves to be part of the traditional fold. Adhering to a measure of mitzvah observance, such as Kashruth in the home and celebration in some measure of the Yomim Tovim, they retained an attachment to the Orthodox schools of their family origins. Others, with a residual tie to Jewish life, perhaps prompted by the move to suburbia with its need for Jewish associations in a markedly and uncomfortably non-Jewish setting, joined the B'nai B'rith fraternal organization or Reform or Conservative temples. The rest remained Jewishly inert, though for the most part retaining some token symbol of Jewish adherence and not forswearing inner allegiance to their people and its faith.

Torah-community circles, through the Orthodox Union, were beginning to face in a practical if as yet vaguely conceived way that the redemption of those who had strayed from the Jewish path, and their uninstructed children, was a primary task of Orthodox Jewry.

THE TORAH LEARNING GAP

Together with this, the perspective frame brought into sharp focus the significant gains and losses between community synagogue development in areas of second-stage and third-stage settlement, and synagogues in older neighborhoods from which so many had moved. The former, in varying degree, were in a growth stage; the latter, left behind in the population movement, now remained with vestiges of their former followings, or were altogether deserted. But as the atmosphere of warm, deep-rooted Jewishness that had pervaded these older areas evaporated, what emerged in the successor neighborhoods was of a much lesser Jewish texture.

If now the worshippers in the original places were so few where of old had been such throngs of daily and Shabbath *mithpallelim*, successors in good number were yet to be found in the shuls of the newer neighborhoods. But this was much less the case with another, surely not less vital, facet of synagogue and community life: Torah learning.

How little comparable, in the synagogues that succeeded the East Side and other communities, were the numbers at their *limmud Torah shiurim* to the many who aforetime had occupied the well-worn beth *medrash* study-hall benches and *shtenders* of the synagogues of before. How shrunk from the Torah-learning numbers of before were the numbers of their counterparts in the communities of a half-century and more later.

The cross-section of congregational representatives from communities large and small across North America, pooling experience and purpose at their central organization's convocations, could assess the differences in the qualities of their own synagogues and communities and those of the earlier generation. In the one case, there was rising strength and stability, better attunement to the American world, better intelligibility, largely better physical equipment, a broader role. But, mindful though the newer-day congregations were of the centrality of Torah, it was not with such a sense of Torah learning as the pivot of a Jew's life as had suffused—in whatever varying degrees of actuality—the outlook of the core shul populace of before. The synagogue of before, as well as the innumerable free-standing Chevroth Mishnayoth and Chevroth Shas, had been *the place* of *limmud* Torah, the service of sacred study, equally with the service of *tephillah b'tzibbur*, congregational prayer. Within this duality lay the fount of the mitzvah life, of Jewish strength and Jewish eternity. In the congregational realm of the later time, Torah learning had but a lesser role, and often only a peripheral role.

Eventually it was borne in on the delegates in their collective councils that the dynamic of Torah could not find sufficient vent in an accessory role in personal or corporate Jewish life. The focal place of Torah study in daily life was constantly propagated by the organs of the national body and given strong stress at its regional events and national assemblies; formal convention resolutions drove the purpose home. Thus a resolution that was adopted at the sixty-sixth Anniversary Biennial Convention (Shoreham Hotel, Washington, D.C., Kislev 5725/November 1964) under the heading "Limmud Torah," stated:

> We reaffirm the call issued at our last Convention to all our brethren everywhere to pursue the daily study of Torah as a sacred duty, extolled by our Sages as the greatest of all Mitzvoth. The constant and intensive study of Torah at every level of achievement and at every stage of life is the principle vehicle for integrating Torah adherence into every facet of life of the individual and the community. The setting aside of fixed daily study periods is today, as it has been throughout the Jewish ages, an essential of Jewish living.
>
> With view to aiding and encouraging the observance of Limmud Torah under loyal synagogue auspices, we call upon the incoming Administration of the Orthodox Union to establish a national program under which the Torah study groups of each congregation would be linked with each other, studying simultaneously the same texts, with textual materials and study guides to be provided. It is recommended that the cooperation of the Rabbinical Council of America, and other appropriate agencies, be invited in this project.

Various measures succeeded each other in implementation of this resolution. The most consistently maintained (introduced several years after the 1964 resolution) was to be the popular *Luach and Limmud* daily diary and study publication. Made pocket-size for accessibility, its combination of daily portion of Mishnah text, with translation and capsule exposition, together with diary pages and reference items, won a following of thousands. *Luach and Limmud* retained that devotion, for individual daily study and as a text reference for group *shiurim*, through the years—with one brief interruption—to the present day.

The Orthodox Union's Torah-learning propagation was to register as an effective spur to increase of activity in this vital field among the congregations, with wider participation by their members. This was further marked in the course of time by a marked increase in the level and extent of personal, regular Torah learning among the observant fold. Thus a decisive improvement was achieved in the role of regular Torah learning in personal life. But the gains made in this regard, through Orthodox Union means and through other channels, fell far short of truly transforming the situation.

26

The Rise
of the "Yeshivah World"

Meanwhile, the pull of the Jew toward Torah and Jew had a compelling effect on the domain of Limmud-Torah centrality. Its momentum was, by mid-century, bringing such a sphere into being through the upsurge of new yeshivoth. Drawing upon Torah-community elements but with a certain distinctness from that community's evolved makeup, the yeshivoth of newer currency were opening an uncharted new phase in the American Jewish story: Torah learning as a committed way of life in the New World.

Truly a phenomenon of the American scene and of the new Jewish era, yeshivoth, academies of intensive talmudic study on every level— elementary, "Beth medrash," senior, and postgraduate "Kollel"—were springing up in the major centers of Jewish population, collectively offering a new dimension to North American Jewish life.

This development was parallel, though not identical, to another, more broadly based educational phenomenon of profound consequence to American Jewry: the day school, or yeshivah ketanah. The rise of this institution had been pioneered and given initial substance by the Mizrachi movement of religious Zionism. From the early 1950s on, the establishment of Torah Umesorah, the National Society for Hebrew Day Schools, had brought this voluntary agency to the forefront of yeshivah-ketanah endeavor. Thereafter, hundreds of day schools in communities of every size across the United States and Canada were created, some under Mizrachi's Education Bureau initiative, and more under the leadership of Torah Umesorah. This force, funded by the burning initiative and magnetic leadership of Rabbi Shragai Mendelowitz of Yeshivath Torah Vodaath, had attracted a circle of fervent devotees. Foremost among these were Torah Umesorah's inimitable national director, Dr. Joseph Kaminetzky, spearhead

of the movement's development through many challenging years. Among
the lay support group, a large role was played by its long-time president,
Samuel C. Feuerstein, a Vice President of the Orthodox Union, and several
members of his family.

Vital local support in each community was mobilized by lay leaders and
other active figures of the Orthodox synagogues of the various communities, often prompted and motivated by the rabbis of these congregations.
Rabbinic graduates of the Rabbi Isaac Elchanan Theological Seminary and
other leading yeshivoth made decisive contributions to the launching of
many of the schools.

Often, rancorous opposition by non-Orthodox elements had to be
contended with. In concert with the secular-minded and assimilation-
attuned organizational array, the Reform and Conservative forces set their
faces against the day school movement.[1] These inveterate opponents and
their followings, damning the very concept of such schools as "separatist,"
long barred aid to them by the local Jewish-community-fund channels. Not
until after many years of this stance, when the swelling prestige of the day
schools impelled the heterodox denominations to themselves institute
some day schools, did some Jewish community fund federations began to
include day schools in their allocations.

In the first years of development, all but a few of the Hebrew day schools
were on the elementary level. They were characterized by integrated
curricula of Judaic and general studies, with more or less equal emphasis on
both. This, too, was basically the pattern of the yeshivah high schools as
they presently came into being. In the equivalent grades of the yeshivoth of
earlier type, the main emphasis was on the religious—and specifically
talmudic—studies, with general studies pursued to meet state legal requirements. The senior-level yeshivoth, as colleges of rabbinics, always concentrated exclusively on talmudic and related studies.

On the elementary and high-school levels, the difference between the
newer and earlier types was accordingly one of emphasis rather than of
syllabic substance. The yeshivoth ketanoth and yeshivah high schools of
"day school" identity, as well as the elementary and beth medrash level
schools of earlier type, both served as feeders of student enrollment for the
Yeshivoth Gedoloth—the senior, college-level yeshivoth. But there was,
from early times and thereafter, a difference of orientation and atmosphere.

Another distinction was that the day schools were more closely identified with the congregational memberships at large than were other types of

---

1. Some in the pulpits of the heterodox denominations privately acted contrary
to the stand of their central institutional organs.

yeshivoth. Not only had the day schools been formed from among the local synagogue congregants, but as local schools, their pupils were entirely part of the lives of those communities, while the yeshivoth gedoloth and their preparatory schools were, with a few notable exceptions, *in*, but not *of*, the communities in which they were established. So, the Synagogue–Day school tie was more immediate, mutually rooted, and broader-based than the synagogue–Yeshivah Gedolah relationship could be.

This circumstance would have a bearing on the course of Torah Umesorah and the Hebrew day school movement. On the elementary and high-school levels, this agency served both types of schools. But the difference of ideological climate and educational goal between the two brought some pulling and pushing to direct Torah Umesorah policy in the one direction or the other. Ultimately, this tension found echoes in the relationships between the yeshivah world and the community–congregation sphere.

In the channels of the Orthodox Union, full support was in order for all instruments of education in Torah learning, and it found expression on many occasions and in numerous ways. Thus, at the 66th Anniversary National Biennial Convention, the following resolution on "The Support of Torah Institutions" stated:

> We urge all Jews to support those institutions devoted to the study of Torah in the spirit of Torah: the congregational and communal Talmud Torah, the Day School, the Yeshivah, the Mesifta and the Kolel. We urge the leaders of these institutions to foster to the fullest extent the spirit of "Torah Lishma," Torah for its own sake, so that the beauty and the majesty of the spirit of Torah may be fully manifest.
>
> Our Halachah prescribes, and Jewish needs dictate, priority in communal planning for the institutions devoted to Torah education. Unfortunately, in the development of some of the federated Jewish communal philanthropic agencies, not only has this priority been ignored but the needs of the institutions of Torah education have been served only in minimal measure, where at all. There has been perpetuated an erroneous and improper tradition of allocation which did not give due weight to the teaching of Torah and Jewish values.
>
> We therefore call upon those who are active in Jewish communal leadership and federated philanthropic endeavor to correct the mis-distribution of communal funds, giving such proper allocation as is consonant with recognition of Torah education and learning as the spiritual foundation and crowning jewel of a community. It is the particular responsibility of Orthodox leadership in every level of the community to bring to local federations awareness of the crucial role of Torah education in Jewish life and the resulting need for broad and substantial financial organizational assistance to

the institutions of Torah learning and education. It is equally their responsibility to require that the requisite allocations must in no degree infringe upon the spiritual, curricular and functional independence of these institutions.

EVOLVING RELATIONSHIPS

In their need to comprehend so fruitful a development as the new-day yeshivah upsurge, Torah community forces were hampered by the uncertainties of a new, self-propelled situation. Certain factors, however, stood out.

In the earlier stage of yeshivah development in America, "shul" and "yeshivah" were—and took it for granted that they were—of one world. As these first schools of Torah learning grew, those closely involved in each—their Roshey Yeshivah (deans), rebbeyim (instructors), and other faculty; their officers, administrators, active supporters, students, and students' families—tended to each constitute a yeshivah-focused circle. Yet, with all the attunement to the yeshivah of their particular attachment, these yeshivahs were not seen as other than an extension of the congregationally constituted community. This was so in both feeling and function: The institution had emerged from the congregational matrix, the natural nucleus of corporate Jewish life in America. From its environment had come the birth-motive of the yeshivah, its student body, its backers and supporters. To it they provided rabbis, teachers, lay leaders; above all, the nurturing and dissemination of Torah, essence of all that being Jewish means. The shul and the yeshivah complemented each other within the Torah-community frame.

So it had been in the previous stage of yeshivah development. This, it soon became apparent, was not the case with the rise of the later institutions of Torah learning. As these grew and multiplied, and as they commanded wider numbers of devotees as well as students, there seemed to have spread among them a feeling of moral—though not fiscal!—self-sufficiency. There was the *yeshivah velt*, a world of its own, apart from and not to be identified with the congregationally constituted Orthodox community. The latter, in the *yeshivish* outlook, came to be looked upon as of inferior status; it was believed to be too focused on services ceremonial and on general Jewish interests and needs, rather than on Torah learning, and, with its miscellany of participants, it was held to be lacking the degree of *frumkeit* espoused by *yeshivahleit*.

This was somewhat of a paradox, a paradox that was to await resolution through the following years. Then, as since, yeshivoth of later emergence drew their being from much the same shul–community sources as had the earlier-established Torah learning institutions. The new crop of yeshivoth, arising under the inspiration of their illustrious founders, likewise drew their initial backers and builders, their students and their lay officers, their followings of proponents and financial supporters, from among the active elements of congregational life.

That, of course, could not have been otherwise. There was not, and could not be, any other source so committed by its own inherent nature. The yeshivoth could and did glean many donations from philanthropic individuals identified with heterodox institutions, but responsive to calls from the struggling schools of talmudic learning. Yet, in the outlook that grew to mark the newer yeshivoth, the community-synagogue derivation and interrelation was blocked from attribution of shared identity. In this pervasive attitude, never formally enunciated but implicit in policy and expressions at that stage, the yeshivah and the community of which the synagogue was pivotal were seen as foreign, rather than as integral, to each other.

VARIATIONS OF SENSE OF APARTNESS

Relationships between the synagogue-constituted Torah community and the Day School (Yeshivah Ketanah), with their more familiar, everyday connection, were complicated by a different version of the separatist psychology. While further urging "increased support of Day School education by . . . local community welfare funds and federations," a 1966 convention resolution stated that:

> At the same time, it is the Orthodox Synagogue which must furnish the leadership for the needed community support of the Day School as the educational lifeline of the Jewish community. Only such leadership can protect the Day School from manifest dangers . . . particularly exposure to improper outside control of educational policy and increasing efforts to capture [the schools] by non-Orthodox elements whose beliefs and purposes are foreign to those which the Day Schools were founded to nurture and perpetuate.
>
> In the absence of organic relationships and other components of the Torah community, there has evolved an undue apartness between those who focus on Day School endeavor and those concerned with Synagogue and Community affairs . . . thus the Day School is [unduly] apt to key its budgetary policy to support by the community at large, [resulting in] dependency on non-Orthodox elements. . . .

The resolution therefore called for measures toward "the organic integration of Orthodox day schools with the Orthodox synagogues of the respective communities . . . in terms of total approach to the respective roles and reciprocal functions. . . ."

In that period, the close relations between Torah Umesorah and the Orthodox Union served to mitigate the tendency to separateness. Moses I. Feuerstein, UOJCA president, was also then Board chairman of Torah Umesorah (of which, as mentioned, his father Samuel C. Feuerstein was president, and the entire family was a central pillar of leadership activity and support of the national day schools' organization from the beginning). The moral effect of the UOJCA expression was felt through both channels, to good purpose. However, with each local institution autonomous, practical implementation of the "organic relationship" concept materialized in only a few cases.

Most of the local schools, while usually persisting in seeking financial support from the local Jewish communities at large, were sufficiently keyed to the dependency danger to preserve their independence and Torah-loyal character. Eventually however, several others did, in fact, succumb to the danger, falling into non-Orthodox hands.

REVERBERATIONS

In the other area of the "separateness" problem, the sense of otherness seems not to have been as conscious among active community-synagogue circles as among those focused on the senior seminaries. But as effects of the paradoxical outlook emanating from elements of the yeshivah velt became more tangibly felt in the community situation, concerns arose. These found reverberations in numerous congregations and in UOJCA channels and the biennial convocations.

What at first had been indulgently disregarded as understandable self-centeredness could no longer be taken impersonally with some yeshivah heads and rebbeyim persistently discouraging their students from identifying themselves with the congregations, Orthodox though they were, of their own parents. Nor could the policy of disparaging the congregational rabbinate and discouraging students from aiming at careers as rabbis or in community service fields be lastingly ignored. While all applauded and endorsed the standard of *Torah lishmah*—Torah learning for its own sake rather than for vocational aim—to carry this to the point of curtailing the availability of active rabbis and demeaning the role of the communal rabbinate itself, and of drawing away from the family congregation its own young generation, was to undercut the viability of the congregational synagogue and the very life of the congregationally constituted community.

Having themselves viewed the burgeoning schools of talmudic learning as valued assets but not as integral and pivotal to their own congregations, communal leaders and devotees found themselves at a loss when realizing that the synagogue, in the yeshivah's viewpoint, was of worth only as a reservoir of student recruitment and monetary support. For their part, while the yeshivah-focused circles deemed the sustaining of the yeshivoth a necessary obligation of the congregational constituency, they could not but be irked by the feeling that their institutions were looked upon by some synagogue-goers as poor relations. Dependence on that source thus became more resented than appreciated. Were not the yeshivoth, as generators of Torah, fully reciprocal, by this function itself, to community support without question of obligation otherwise for the welfare of the school-based community?

Indeed, at one point there was in some quarters an anticipation of the ultimate withering away of the synagogue world, with its gradual supplantation by the yeshivah itself, around which another community, yeshivah-rooted and yeshivah-fashioned, would emerge. Thus the one common trait in the attitudes towards each other of the two elements of the American Torah world was that of reciprocal separateness.

The effect of the polarization became increasingly more marked in the post-mid-century years. The community-minded and those devoted to collective Jewish interests had looked to Torah-learning colleges to produce men equipped for and zealous in leadership service to the Jewish people and its community life. It was disconcerting to find that the *b'ney yeshivah*, of the newer yeshivah efflorescence especially, had been instilled with the conviction that, together with devout personal observance and conscientious Torah learning, the only cause that mattered was the yeshivah cause; beyond that, one was not "mechuyav." It was dismaying for *ba'aley batim* to discover that their yeshivah-nurtured sons (and daughters, too, as another great phenomenon, girls' intermediate and senior-level seminaries, arose) were schooled to avoid established congregational shuls for their post-yeshivah associations. Instead, it appeared, they were encouraged to join in the fellowship of the yeshivah minyanim of their own, secluded from the contaminating rank-and-file of Jews and free of the obligations attendant upon participation in community-geared institutions concerned with their fellow Jews and their collective needs and welfare. And, failing such places of their own, they were tacitly or otherwise pointed to the shtibels conducted by *rebbeyim* as personal enterprises.

THE SHTIBEL TOLL

At the central Union's conventions and other occasions, this situation came into discussion, mostly in unfocused ways. But as the diversion from the community congregations accrued, its toll was increasingly felt. The self-sufficient minyanim and, even more, private-enterprise shtibalech multiplying in the core communities, however individually appealing, were in the aggregate an element of disintegration, sapping the institutional vitality of Torah forces. Had these enterprises undertaken to pioneer in locations where places of Orthodox Jewish worship were not yet to be found, the service rendered could have offset other considerations. But, to the contrary, they invariably placed themselves in close vicinity to established synagogues, siphoning away many families. As the years advanced, case after case occurred in which metropolitan congregations that had long been powerhouses of vibrant Torah life were surrounded on all sides by shtibalech and all but drained dry.

Though a beneficiary of the separateness syndrome, the shtibel upsurge was not actually of yeshivish origin. Had not the mood of separatism between yeshivah and congregational community been permitted to arise, had there instead emerged a feeling of mutuality, the shtibel, as a means of privatizing religion, would quite likely have made a place for itself just the same. The self-segregational motif, however, fed the shtibel and brought it collective dimension. Eventually, the yeshivoth themselves awakened to the fact that, in its effective draining of the nutrients of community vitality, the shtibel was a tax on the yeshivah, too.

Although in the blossoming of yeshivah growth from the 1950s to the 1970s the sense of apartness persisted, a more thoughtful view was beginning to emerge, too, on both sides.

There came from UOJCA headquarters periodic moves to advance relationships between yeshivah and synagogue-community forces. If without manifest practical consequences, these moves made for a better climate. Especially promising was the effect of a resolution adopted at the 68th Anniversary Biennial Convention in November 1966 (Kislev 5727). Under the heading "The Coordinated Development of the Torah Community," it formulated a visionary concept of an integrated relationship between congregations and yeshivoth. A preceding introduction, "The Torah Community," stated, in part:

> No longer do outer pressures and the reciprocal resistance to them produce the fuel of Jewish loyalty. Instead, political equality, affluence, and an open society relatively free from religious prejudices, furnish the tests and chal-

lenges to which the American Jewish community is called upon to respond. Thus, a conscious Jewish life is now the consequence of a purely ideological and faith decision.

The paramount duty of the Jewish community must be to foster the awareness and the affirmation of the ideological foundations and essential concepts of Judaism; to create the educational, communal, and social facilities for adults and youths in which the Jewish cognition can flourish and find full expression; and thereby to secure the rise of future generations of Jews who are both joyously attuned to their Jewish responsibility and equipped with the requisite knowledge to discharge it successfully. We must respond to the need to give full articulation to the specific Jewish view on the many grave issues which move the conscience of contemporary man so that the pertinence of this view to today's perplexities be established in the minds and hearts of our people and result in appropriate action.

We desire the Union of Orthodox Jewish Congregations of America to reflect in all phases of its program and activities the acknowledgement of these historic responsibilities. The Orthodox Union must strengthen Torah and its sacred institutions everywhere and create an organically interrelated Torah community in which all Torah institutions play their historic and distinctive roles. The Orthodox Union must make the Orthodox synagogues aware of their sacred obligation to represent the Torah view and the Torah pattern not only in their own programs and policies but within their respective communities. . . . Our solemn intent is reflected in the resolutions adopted at this Biennial Convention.

Then follows the furthering resolution, reading:

THE COORDINATED DEVELOPMENT
OF THE TORAH COMMUNITY

We rejoice in the manifold evidences of the growing strength of North American Orthodox Jewry, marked by the waxing of the institutions of Torah learning, the multiplication of the Day Schools, the advancement of the synagogues, the rising numbers of Mitzvah-observant families, the improvement of the facilities for religious observance generally, the enhancement of the stature of Orthodox Jewry on the public scene, and the increasing effectiveness of the voice of Torah forces within the Jewish community and in public life. However, we view with grave concern the persistence of a situation which has severely handicapped North American Orthodoxy throughout its history and which, if not radically corrected, seems bound to bring increasing penalty. This is the lack of integral relationship between the component organs of the Orthodox Community and the lack of cohesion in addressing common needs, purposes, and goals.

This basic deficiency . . . impairs the health and effectiveness of each institution and organization, it serves to dissipate strength and multiply weakness, it diminishes the impact of the Torah voice. Not least of all, this fragmentation runs counter to the all-important need for planned, coordinated development of the Torah Community as a cohesive entity, whereby the interests of Torah Jewry may be best served and whereby it can creatively shape the conditions of American Jewish life.

I. We endorse those steps taken towards intra-Orthodox unity in pursuance of the Resolution towards that purpose adopted at the preceeding National Biennial Convention of the Orthodox Union. . . . We confidently hope that, in due course, there will result joint planning and coordinated action by the major organizations of North American Orthodox Jewry for the creative development of the Torah community. We see in this process . . . an effective approach to the changing factors in surrounding society which impinge on Jewish life, and in the basis on which the Halachah can become the motivating force in the total American Jewish community.

II. The creative, dynamic development of the Torah community requires that the process of coordination and correlated effort embrace not only communal organizations but extend as well to the institutions of Torah learning. Particularly, there must be understanding of the need for mutually interdependent relationship between the two classical institutions of the Jewish community—the Synagogue and the Yeshivah. Only by the recognition and implementation of such a relationship can the needs of each and of Torah Jewry as a whole be effectively sustained.

We urge therefore that our incoming Administration undertake appropriate steps to foster and nurture this positive relationship, enlisting the guidance of the great figures of the Yeshivah world and the cooperation of the rabbinic and lay leaders of the synagogues. As a guide to such exploration, we would recommend consideration of the following:

III. The development of organic ties between the Synagogues and the major Yeshivah and other institutions of higher Torah learning, with view to:

a. The achievement of a functioning pattern of responsibility of each for the moral and material welfare of the other, of adequate communication between them, of understanding of their respective problems and needs, and of a sense of shared identity as component units of a common entity.

b. The inclusion in the programs of the Yeshivoth of courses of study and field services whereby their students may acquire practical as well as theoretical understanding of the specific situations and problems of the local congregations and communities, and of the Orthodox Jewish community at large, and whereby they can be oriented to the role of community leadership for which their Torah learning gives them both moral qualification and moral obligation.

c. The inclusion in the programs of the congregations of means whereby their memberships shall be effectively familiarized with the role and character of the Yeshivoth as the spiritual fount of Jewish religious life.

d. The inclusion in the budgets of each congregation of allocations of given amounts for the Yeshivoth. This should be based on a centrally organized funding program instituted jointly by the Yeshivoth and the Synagogues and keyed and scaled to the collective budgetary needs of the Yeshivoth.

e. The intensification of teacher training programs by the Yeshivoth, on an overall planned basis correlated to study of the needs of congregational schools.

f. The establishment of a joint committee, consisting of representatives of Yeshivoth and Synagogues, to further the above purposes.

It is our hope that such a program will bring the North American Orthodox Jewish Community closer to the classic and authentic Kehillah pattern which has been the format of Jewish community life through the most productive eras of Diaspora history.

Be it noted that the resolution's phraseology signified that "the Synagogue and the Yeshivah" were both *of* the Jewish community, and not just in *vis-à-vis* relationship. This was realistic in practice as well as in principle. By this stage, some of the newer crop of talmudical seminaries had settled down in the American Jewish situation; they were beginning to feel themselves part of the American Jewish picture rather than an entity on its periphery.

As well, visions of a self-contained yeshivah world rearing a self-sufficient community of its own were fading. Prospects of the mounting numbers of yeshivah graduates as an adequate source of financial support and second-generation student replenishment did not meet realities. Those whose Jewish-concern horizons were narrowed and whose giving standards were cramped by the shtibel-seclusion impress proved to be but sparing supporters of the institutions that had nurtured them, even after they achieved business or professional prosperity.

A weighty factor in the student-recruitment situation was the continuous multiplication of yeshivoth. With the newest ones tendering the newest brand of frumkeit and constituting the newest enrollment attraction, competition mounted for shares of the prospective student pool. As the major student-recruitment source still, the synagogue community was seen in a changed light.

THE AMERICAN IMPRINT

Withal, the yeshivah world was learning that the congregational synagogues were as indispensable as ever—to talmudical seminaries themselves, as well as to the rest of Jewry. Acclimatization particularly, now made for a tempering of the separatist mentality. In making a place for itself in America, the yeshivah had inevitably made a place, in itself, for America. With the passage of time, the tendency to associate the Torah-learning process with the environment of Poland, Hungary, and so on, receded among the scholars from eastern Europe who composed the yeshivah faculties; they were now absorbing the American clime. Without, conscious realization of the transition, for the most part, an unspoken assumption of "America-ness" of Torah was as natural and compatible as what, in the perspective of time and distance, could be recognized as having been "Lithuania-ness," "Galicia-ness," "Salonika-ness," "Syria-ness," and so on.

The America-ness impression was further forwarded as the years passed by the advancement in higher Torah scholarship of American-born products of the American yeshivoth. The selection of such American men for appointment to the faculties of senior rabbinic learning centers, even sometimes to the status of Rosh Yeshivah, became a source of recurrent *naches* to all in the circles of Orthodoxy. Although these America-nurtured Talmudey Chachamim tended to absorb the style and outlook of their European-reared seniors, the "American presence" within the yeshivah environment became an increasingly felt reality.

One more aspect of the yeshivah-community relationship must be touched on here. For all the separateness and self-confinement psychology engendered by certain of the seminaries, students of these schools shared in the irrepressible urge springing up among students of the yeshivoth in general to a life of Jewish service. These students flocked to Jewish causes—some to various channels of endeavor for Israel, some to the saving of Soviet Jewry, some to NCSY and other outreach endeavors; many among them devoted themselves to the upbuilding of the American Jewish community in Torah dimension and its synagogue base.

For these people and for their fellows of less effusive disposition, a profound experience with a permanent effect on their lives was a year or more of Torah learning in Israel. Lives so touched by the homeland of the Jewish people and the Jewish soul could never be the same again, could never be shrunk to their former dimensions. Some of these people chose aliyyah, permanent settlement in the Holy Land. More, turning from the allure of business fields, entered upon service as teachers or administrators in Jewish day schools or yeshivoth, or as professional figures in communal institutions. And there were, and still are, those undertaking the arduous regimen of study for Semichah ordination, to serve Jewish communities in rabbinic leadership.

So it was that through the forces of the Jewish nature, there eventually evolved a knitting together of yeshivah and community, of Torah shul and

Torah school. It is a process forwarded by the Orthodox Union's activities and advanced in its assemblage proceedings. Attainment of further stages in this process of continuing challenge must be deemed a measure of Orthodox Jewry's self-command.

27

Then Came "The Sixties"

It was in "The Sixties," that sorely troubled period in American and world social history, that there came to fruition a unit of the UOJCA destined to achieve a singular share in Jewish resurgence. This was the central Union's National Conference of Synagogue Youth, the now-famed NCSY.

Actually, as previously noted, NCSY was launched in 1954, but not until several years later did this project emerge in the character that became its identity: a vessel of self-discovery for the Jewish teenager.

The task to be addressed by this youth force went beyond the reinforcement of Torah loyalties among the youth of traditional-home background. It was aimed particularly at reaching out to Jewishly deprived boys and girls, at winning them to the Torah way. This twin purpose had been pursued by the Orthodox Union from its very birth in 1898. What now gave the work a special quality was the spur of the Orthodox Union's recharged volition at a point when the young generation was being exposed to new menaces superimposed on the dangers of before.

Disorders affecting society at large are apt to touch Jews in a special way; so it was when, in the so-called Sixties—actually a period from the late 1950s to the mid-1970s—peculiar forms of personality fracture appeared among adolescents and student-age youths of many lands. World War II had left humankind spiritually wounded and socially disrupted; the ills that festered during the postwar years made inroads on some of the young generation in countries east and west. The generation of postwar rearing found themselves beset by doubts—doubts about the world about them, doubts about the world within them. Reaching the threshold of adulthood, they clung to childish irresponsibilities while asserting the freedom to live as they would and to do as they pleased. The youthful glorification of self-indulgence was an unspoken commentary on the absorption of their elders in sensual satisfaction and the avid pursuit of material goods.

Permissiveness as the keynote of society joined to the technology-equipped culture of abundance had left accepted morality in limbo; the guidelines of conduct had lost force.

The complex of impulses tugging at confused members of the young generation found fevered outlet as America was caught in a fury of conflict over the Vietnam War. Outlandish spectacles were enacted on university campuses as their administrators buckled before the attacks of student mobs; civic authorities gave hardly better accounts of themselves as incited demonstrators stormed through city centers, a favorite exercise being the burning of the flag of the United States of America.

Holocaust survivors shuddered in horror at witnessing these outbursts. To them—and not only to them—it was all too reminiscent of what had transpired on the way to unutterable evil.

There was unloosed, too, a flood of what was then still commonly called "dope." There ensued the spread of addiction to narcotic drugs, those seductive poisons nowadays dubbed politely as "controlled substances." The victims, then and since, have been unnumbered thousands of young men and women, along with as many of their seniors.

Unloosed, too, was a flood of social narcotics, captors of mind and spirit. Among a wide variety of group allures were those espousing doctrines of social anarchy and sexual license. Others, which became known as "cults," bore religious trappings: some exotic idolatries, others tricked-up offspring of Eastern mysticism, and still others simply manufactured to order. Their promoters were skilled in techniques of seduction, mind manipulation, and will control. They capitalized on the inner hunger of the spiritually rootless, readily responsive to intriguing formulas of fraternal scorning of the ways of "the society."

The many thousands of recruits enticed to such groups were of all origins and social levels. The climate amid which the hippiedoms, the cult culture, and the drug culture were spawned pervaded general society.

Young Jews were not the least to be affected by the blight. Especially affected were the many youths whose preparation for life as Jews, whether in home life, community environment, or schooling, was painfully deficient at best or altogether lacking. Typically products of a life setting barren of integral Jewishness, devoid of the rudiments of Judaic knowledge, or having been given but a shallow pretense of Jewish teaching, these youths were ignorant of the Jewish self and of its place in human destiny. In lieu of a meaningful Jewish experience, they perhaps encountered the vapid theatricality of an assimilated service or the materialistic splurge of a bar mitzvah celebration that mocked the meaning of the term. Such encounters could only alienate them from any positive feeling for the meaning of Jewishness, or any idea of the heritage of a hundred generations.

For those so starved of Jewish nurture, the spiritual emptiness and tormented urgings rampant among their peers of other origins were compounded by confusion as to *self*. Theirs was but a negative self-awareness; being a Jew meant only that one didn't really *belong*. Where Jewishness was but a troubling puzzlement, the unease of its encumbrance evoked a vague sense of want. Stored somewhere in the recesses of consciousness was a dark shadow: the Holocaust. There, too, in the background of awareness, was something that pricked the spirit, a straight-backed sturdiness that challenged that spirit's infirmity: Israel.

SH'MAD AND CULT ENTICEMENTS

Beset by insecurity, these youngsters, starved of the nutrients of inner Jewish strength, were exposed to the bizarre cults, social anomalies, and mountebank-concocted oddities that sprang up in the morass of the "Sixties." Favored targets of these varied eruptions, these Jews were pursued avidly by instruments of some Christian sects devised to entrap unknowing young Jews into *sh'mad*, apostasy.

Employing modes of deceit, these missionary devices continue now, as before, to conceal their sponsorship and purpose, adopting disguises of one kind or another. A characteristic technique is a fake-Jewish "Messianic" façade. Professional apostates from Judaism—yes, there is such a species, resorted to by mission-to-the-Jews circles—are hired for the purpose, a "congregation" is mustered—fleshed out with gentiles masquerading as Jewish converts to the "Messianic" faith. Lured into this baited trap, one by one, with methods carefully devised for the purpose, are young Jews wandering in search of self, place, and meaning.

The actual members of victims cannot be determined with accuracy, but are considered by investigators to be but a fraction of the numbers claimed by the perpetrators to bolster their calls to their funding sources. It seems that, sooner or later, most of the victims realize what has been done to them and escape. The investigators who have penetrated the fake-Jewish operations have found that their prayer services and assemblies are stuffed with supposed "converts" who never were Jews. But whatever the number of actual Jews involved in this transient process, the victims of the missionary machinations—with the rest of those who, before, during, and since the Sixties to the present, have fallen prey to the varieties of apostasy seduction—are a source of heartache and self-reproach not only to their anguished parents, but to all Jews of loyalty and conscience.

With the toll of the cults and other trickeries widening as the 1960s advanced, Jewish organizations of all categories were moved to address the problem. The Orthodox Union was just one of many seeking to aid troubled youth. But what caused the Union's endeavors in this field to stand out was a perception of the root of the ailment and a realization, untrammeled by prevalent canons of youth work, of the ways to deal with it.

SELF-DISCOVERY THROUGH NCSY

This more basic grasp of the youth-alienation condition was a product of the penetrating vision animating American Orthodox Jewry's central force, under the impetus of the vibrant Moses I. Feuerstein.

The Union's Youth Commission, headed by Harold H. Boxer, was now moved to view its objectives anew. The resulting appointment, in 1959, of Rabbi Pinchas Stolper as director of the Youth Division proved to be the key to a revolution in the making.

Rabbi Stolper, who had received rabbinic ordination at Yeshivath Chaim Berlin, had made his mark as director of the Long Island Zionist Youth Commission, a joint undertaking of the Long Island regions of the Zionist Organization of America and Hadassah. Now, in assuming direction of the Orthodox Union's youth endeavors, he found its Torah-charged climate and upsurging spirit a fruitful setting for his own aims. Adapting himself to the changed circumstances, he found that what was called for was more than the revision of familiar techniques. There ensued a process of transition from the accustomed Jewish youth work mode to one keyed challengingly to the inner searchings of the Jewishly deprived young generation.

Identifying the essentials of approach to the root problem, Rabbi Stolper, in consultation with Youth Commission Chairman Boxer and senior staff colleagues, formulated, after some trial and error, the program of need and developed and led its implementation. Presently the work reached the point where "NCSY'er" became a recognized type of Jewish youth, the product of a movement that gained singular standing in the Jewish world.

In bold rejection of the prevailing climate of permissiveness, the National Conference of Synagogue Youth proffered the teenage world not the sugar-candy fare elsewhere considered mandatory in youth work, but a program of joyous challenge to spirit and mind. It was geared to the perception that youth, in an age of spiritual confusion, hunger inarticulately for a life invested with ultimate meaning. NCSY opened the way for them to a life-revolutionizing discovery: *Torah*. It brought them to the power of mitzvah, the life built on fulfillment of Divine purpose.

A central factor was the degree of self-direction by maturing boys and girls themselves, carefully fostered by the director and his staff. After the first couple of years, the staff included an associate director. Rabbi Chaim Wasserman served in that capacity with full dedication for several crucial years, to be followed by Rabbi David Cohen. In the course of the years of growth, an increasing number of professional associates were added, despite budgetary constraints. Volunteers, designated "advisers," complemented the professional staff.

The teenagers' shared experience of personal self-fulfillment was reinforced through collective self-direction in common purpose. All sprang from the central reservoir of guidance, imaginative programming, and the fount of *ruach*, the joyous exaltation of liberated spirit that was a hallmark of the NCSY atmosphere.

Of decisive importance in the NCSY story was from early times, and has been ever since, the remarkable multiplying cadre of volunteer advisers. Throughout, this corps has been composed of senior student and adult graduates of the major yeshivoth and Yeshiva University and yeshivah-trained college students and graduates. They have devoted themselves with wholehearted, contagious enthusiasm to the guidance of chapters and regions, and to their members individually. These men and women have found vast reward in the enrichment of the lives they touched and influenced—and no less reward, without doubt, in the enrichment of their own lives through this service.

Remarkable, too, from an early point, has been the fact that the Roshey Yeshivoth, the respective heads of the array of major yeshivoth along with Yeshiva University, endorsed and actively encouraged the Orthodox Union's NCSY endeavor. Several of the leading institutions, furthering the NCSY way, instituted special programs for those with minimal or no Jewish educational background seeking yeshivah learning and life, besides welcoming NCSY'ers with observant-home background and schooling. Soon, a recognized feature of the yeshivah scene—in Israel as well as in America—was the presence of an NCSY complement in each leading yeshivah, in Yeshiva University's James Striar School, and in the new crop of yeshivoth especially instituted to serve the mounting number of Ba'aley Teshuvah, those finding their way to the Torah life of their people.

Development of the organized structure also played a necessary part in the NCSY achievement. It was recognized that the "teenage" stage of life is but a passing few years, and that unbroken succession in the organizational process is needed for natural continuity. The technique introduced made for integration of each NCSY'er in the organizational channel as well as in the program process. Each took his or her course through the stages of activity and operational responsibility; each moved within a cellular formation of self-governing local chapters, collectively composing area-wide regions, these in turn interwoven in the national NCSY organism. Within this structural framework flowed the current of principles set forth and aims sought by the parent Union, as transmitted through the Youth Commission and staff.

Thus percipiently conditioned, each NCSY'er had his or her own meaningful place within his or her chapter, each chapter and region functioning within its given capacity in its own sphere of jurisdiction. The sense of self-responsibility under unobtrusive guidance in a spirit of Torah ideal was, from early days onward, to prove a potent force for character development.

The results were quickly apparent. Thus Commission Chairman Boxer reported to the UOJCA 64th Anniversary Convention (Sheraton Park Hotel, Washington, D.C., Cheshvan 24–28, 5723/November 21–25, 1962):

> The National Conference of Synagogue Youth, the Orthodox Union's youth movement, has grown . . . with unusual speed into a movement truly national in scope. Its Chapters and Regions function throughout the length and breadth of the country. New projects and objectives which in the [1960] Report of this Commission existed only on paper have been attained and exceeded. The response of our congregations has been so enthusiastic that their demands for assistance and service have long outstripped the capacities of the Youth Division, limited as it is in financial resources and personnel.

THE NEW-LIFE IDEA AT WORK

Data cited in the 1962 report included:

Approximately 10,000 young people participated in NCSY activities in the past two years (1960–62).

Each of 233 Chapters in the United States and Canadian cities in 1960 conducted its own regular meetings, Torah study groups, Onegey Shabbath, youth congregation, national projects, and a variety of social, educational, recreational, religious, and service programs.

The youth of over 200 communities participated in NCSY Regional Conventions, camp sessions, leaders' training courses, and other regional programs.

The number of Regions grew from 7 in 1960 to 15 in 1962. 130 new

Chapters were added in the same period. As compared with 180 participants in the NCSY National Convention in 1960, there were 235 in 1961 and 420 in 1962—and at least 600 expected in 1963.

The 1962 Youth Commission Report further stated:

> Major emphasis is being placed on enabling thousands of teenagers each year to experience the inspired atmosphere of Jewish living, observance, study, and leadership training at over 30 all-day, week-end, or week-long conclaves, leaders' training seminars, and summer camp institutes.

Consistently, remarkably, the UOJCA/NCSY idea worked. It has continued working and developing steadily through the decades to the present. "Working," in this case, means remaking lives. Thousands of teenage and post-teenage youths, boys and girls of high-school age and beyond, have rediscovered themselves through this movement. Those of the rising generation—often from backgrounds estranged from Jewish belief, and themselves, prior to NCSY contact, swept along with the tide of demoralization—have found their way to the Jewish life of Torah and mitzvoth.

Upon the 1976 appointment of Rabbi Stolper as executive vice president of the parent Orthodox Union, he was succeeded as national director of the Youth Division and NCSY by Rabbi Raphael Butler,[1] a graduate of Yeshivath Chofetz Chaim. Under the direction of this gifted and deeply motivated figure, NCSY continued to flourish. There then proceeded a further extension of NCSY—to reach the preteenage generation, Junior NCSY, and also to serve previously unmet, important needs with special units—one for hearing-impaired youth, Our Way, and another for the developmentally disabled, Yachad.

As a trailblazer in outreach to the searchers for meaning and identity among the young Jewish generation, this youth movement of the Union of Orthodox Jewish Congregations of America sparked the Ba'al Teshuvah phenomenon, the "on to Torah" upsurge of self-rediscovery that is a swelling current of boundless potential in Jewish life today.

It is a signal tribute to UOJCA/NCSY that it has won acclaim among all segments of loyalist Jewry as a potent force in the Jewish renaissance of our time.

∼

---

1. Later, in 1994, Rabbi Butler was, in turn, appointed UOJCA executive vice president.

CLEARER VISTA,
STRENGTHENED CAPACITIES

From the foregoing report citations and background observations, it can be seen that the post-mid-century period in the Orthodox Union story was marked by more than organizational retooling and program expansion; it was an era of sharper thinking and bolder ideas. Realization was awakening of the profundity of change in the circumstances of the Jewish people, and in the very character of the surrounding world. If the full import of the transformation was, as yet, beyond comprehension, there was a growing sense of its impact.

The outlook pervading the central Torah-community force was manifest in the communications flowing in various forms to its constituency and in the steps taken in the many matters requiring action. Recharged volition was evidenced in the quality and effectiveness of UOJCA literature; in the level of deliberations in its responsible organs; in the caliber of its spokesmanship in the councils of Jewish affairs; and in the personal presence and voice of its leadership figures at occasions in many quarters of the land. The vista animating the Union also animated the functional process of each frame of the Orthodox Union's work.

With an array of figures of distinctive talent—both lay and staff—finding in the Orthodox Union the instrument of accomplishment for historic ends, there was emerging a meaningful response to an unfolding epoch. What was to be dealt with, in Torah terms, was the remaking of the Jew and the Jewish world.

28

Meeting National and Worldwide Problems

Along with the activities discussed in the preceding chapter and the ongoing measures to illumine the path of the loyal Jew and to advance the congregational nuclei of the Jewish community, the Orthodox Union faced an unending series of problems besetting American and world Jewry. Copies of correspondence long ago filed away, meeting minutes, published and multicopied items and other surviving materials, and notably the 1960, 1962, 1964, 1966, and 1968 reports, convention agendas, and resolutions provide a heavy dossier of the flow of concern and the positions taken.

In this archival mass we see the issue of governmental aid to religiously sponsored schools evoking strong opinions over the years.

THE "FEDERAL AID" ISSUE

The phenomenal growth of the Hebrew day school movement brought, with its immeasurable benefits, massive fiscal needs. The financial strains placed on pupils' families and on the schools themselves touched swelling circles. The problem was shared with the all-day schools of some Christian denominations, notably the vast parochial-school array of the Roman Catholic Church. Strong calls were rising from these sources for some form of aid from Federal, state, or local auspices. A particular focus of the aid calls was the United States government, now geared to "Welfare State" capacity.

Proponents of what was now dubbed "Federal Aid" stressed that equity warranted governmental sharing in the schools' costs, in view of the sharing by their pupils' families, as taxpayers, in the costs of the entirely tax-supported public schools. It was also pointed out that the elementary and high schools conducted by religious denominations were providing, besides religious instruction, the legally required general subject curricula. These schools thereby were relieving the public treasury of the cost of such tuition, which it would have to bear if these children were enrolled in the public schools.

Jewish day school sponsorship circles, revered Roshey Ha-Yeshivoth Yeshivoth, and the families served by the schools increasingly joined in this publicly voiced and actively pressed stand. Among the Jewish public at large, the view found a mixture of support, doubt, and sharp opposition. The division on the question among Jews had aspects peculiar to the Jewish situation as well as those parallel to conflicting positions among the general American public.

From the first, public debate had made it obvious that the concept of Federal or other governmental aid to religiously sponsored schools was unacceptable to Americans generally. "Separation of Church and State," as a constitutional tenet in its commonly understood and juridically interpreted definition, was at the heart of the prevailing American view of things. The application of this tenet to the education sphere was taken generally as beyond question.

It was contended in some quarters, however, that the "separation" premise in application to public education was not fully consistent. The public school institutionally was not born with American independence; it was introduced in the course of the nineteenth century. Initially, it was pointed out, the schools that were made public had been under Protestant denominational sponsorship, and continued to be imbued with teachings born of Christian outlook, which then persisted on the public-school scene, in numerous communities, to the point of "nondenominational" religious exercises of one kind or another. On the other hand, critics of public-school "neutrality" held, there also evolved in the public-education arena a parallel stream of dogmatic secular "religion" transmitting an outlook and values of ungodliness—not just areligious, but unreligious. Both trends, somehow persisting concurrently and sometimes as syncrete, had become so entrenched as to be taken as the accepted norm of public education.

The general opposition to governmental assistance to religiously identified schools largely took little cognizance of the ideological and sectarian actualities in the public schools. It was the principle of Church–State separation that counted in the public mind. The issue touched Jews with special force.

The Jewishly concerned were bound to realize the imperative need, in the American situation, for effective transmission to the young generation of equipment for positive Jewish conviction—for a sense of identity rooted in basic Jewish knowledge, informed Jewish belief, and Jewish outlook. Hard-won experience had shown that the educational process for the purpose must be capable of matching the overwhelming pull of the surrounding social environment. Experience had shown, too, that by and large nothing less than the all-day Jewish school, with integrated Judaic and civil studies in a setting of affirmative Jewishness, could have the requisite capacity.

On the other hand, also stored in Jewish experience was an awareness of Jewish disability and exposure to oppression rooted in religious antagonism prevalent in Old-World lands of established religion. This has ever given Jews a special appreciation for all that is manifest in the principles that have flourished in the American clime. Jews accordingly have been keenly aware that, in the multibelief, multiorigin American society, the freedom and equal-rights foundations of the United States have ever been integral with the Church–State separation doctrine, applicable in matters of education as in other respects.

Thus, in its Jewish dimension, the question of moral equity on the one hand and American-way tradition on the other entailed in the Federal Aid to Education issue was further enmeshed with the issue of Jewish continuity imperative vis-à-vis the Jewish stake in the American pattern.

For American Jews of differing beliefs, there was a further dimension.

MAKING PLACE FOR THE DAY SCHOOL

Among the organized forces in American Jewry and among the American Jewish ranks generally, there was a sharp cleavage as to the Hebrew day school concept itself. This was a large factor in the Federal Aid issue.

The non-Orthodox organizations and religious bodies were, at that point, unanimous in inveterate opposition to Federal or any other governmental aid to religiously sponsored schools. Individual voices may have demurred, but these were too few to affect the organizational stands. This entrenched position, it was apparent, was prompted by more than objective Church–State separation principle, deep-felt though this undoubtedly was. The Jewish day school, in the eyes of those who wanted Jews to be indistinguishable from all others, was of its nature "segregational."

This view was to be combated accordingly. Insofar as governmental support would contribute to the public status as well as the fiscal underpinning of the Hebrew day school, it was all the more to be fought.

On the part of the Torah-committed forces, the stand for the day school was as positive as the opposite was the case among the assimilationist circles. Likewise, the attitude regarding the inclusion of religion-sponsored schools in Federal Aid to Education measures was equally conditioned among the Orthodox—in this case, of course, affirmatively.

However, while Orthodoxy's ranks were as one on the yeshivah ketanah idea, on the Federal Aid question there was not equal unanimity. Predominant as the pro-Federal Aid stance was among the Torah-loyal, some among them, including some day school movement activists, pondered with troubled minds the wider potential consequences of governmental role to Jewish schools.

These individuals viewed with apprehension the prospect of loss of independence, leading to the ultimate infringement on self-determination of schools' curricula and teaching. "The one who pays the piper calls the tune" sooner or later, it was argued. In the Jewish case, according to this appraisal, the potential benefit to Jewish schools must be weighed against the danger of opening their doors to government educational—and ideological—policy authority. Such a danger is implicit in a land in which Jews are but a tiny minority among a vast gentile populace of largely Christian origin or identification.

Those of the questioning attitude among the Torah-loyal perceived the issue as bearing different implications between the Jewish and the Christian schools' interests. The "Big Church" denominations, with their numbers, weight in public life, historic place in American society, and well-organized maneuverability, might well view the prospect of "Big Government" entrée in their school domain with tranquility. For them, this could be offset by their being reciprocally in position to influence government; Jewry, however, and certainly traditionally religious Jewry, surely is not so situated.

Deliberations on the Federal Aid to Education question in Orthodox Union channels thus reflected differing appraisals. Resolution formation at successive biennial convocations mark the difficulty encountered in seeking a consensus.

THE ISSUE UNDER CLOSE STUDY

At the 62nd Anniversary National Convention (Chelsea Hotel, Atlantic City, New Jersey, 19–23 Cheshvan 5721/November 9–13, 1960), policy on the disputed Federal Aid to Education measure was sharply debated. Being inconclusive, the matter was agreed to be passed on to the Executive Committee for further study.

The Executive Committee convened an all-day hearing for the purpose on Sunday, April 23, 1961, at UOJCA headquarters, then at 84 Fifth Avenue, New York. A wide array of Jewish organizations, Orthodox and non-Orthodox, were invited to present views. Presentations of position on the subject were made by official representatives of the following:

Agudath Israel of America; American Jewish Committee; American Jewish Congress; Anti-Defamation League of B'nai B'rith; Committee for Further-ance of Jewish Education (Chabad); Jewish Community Council of Greater Philadelphia; Jewish Community Council of Washington, D.C.; Joint Advi-sory Committee of the Synagogue Council of America and the National Community Relations Advisory Council; National Council of Jewish Women; Poale Agudath Israel; and Torah Umesorah.

The unprecedented hearing provided occasion for definitive exposition of the several positions and rationales, but offered no prospect of finding ground for composition of opposing views.

At the next biennial convocation (Sheraton Park Hotel, Washington, D.C., 24–28 Cheshvan 5723/November 21–25, 1962), consensus still proving elusive, the outcome was the guardedly phrased resolution:

17. FEDERAL AID TO
RELIGIOUS-SPONSORED SCHOOLS

The discussions held during this convention on the subjects of Federal aid to religion-sponsored schools and other areas of Church–State relations have indicated a variety of opinion among the delegates on these subjects. This multiplicity of views already expressed on these subjects has made it difficult because of limitation of time to reach a consensus and expression of opinion. The importance of the subjects involved clearly requires extensive delibera-tions without such limitation.

Accordingly, we defer further expression of views at this convention regarding these questions and call for the formation and election of a Special Committee which shall bring its recommendation to the Executive Commit-tee regarding these matters.

Exposition of the differing viewpoints on the governmental aid question appearing in various issues of *Jewish Life* from 1960 to 1965 were widely read and discussed in the American Jewish world and beyond. Among the contributors on the subject were Herbert Berman, Professor William W. Brickman, Reuben E. Gross, W.H. Green, Marvin Schick, and various correspondents.

On one segment of the governmental-aid issue there was complete unanimity, affirmatively, in UOJCA and all other Orthodox Jewish circles— and nearly as complete unanimity in opposition among non-Orthodox organizations, namely, the inclusion of pupils of religious-associated schools in state-financed provision of bus transportation to and from school.

Notwithstanding that secularist and civil libertarian forces were arrayed against this departure as an entering wedge for breach of Church–State separation, the policy met with wide favor generally across the United States and was adopted by numerous states. The inclusion of children of all schools in the bus transportation measures gave the cue to the administration of President Lyndon B. Johnson for an ingenious policy device that in effect put the nationwide Federal Aid debate to rest. This was the "child benefit" principle.

The aid to religion-sponsored schools issue was simply bypassed. As now reformulated, governmental aid was not to be given to the schools themselves, but to the children—of all schools. Aids supplementary to the regular schools' curricula were to be provided for all children in given categories of need, at school locations, public or nonpublic.

Surely no one could object, as a matter of principle, to aiding child needs. Legislation embodying the Johnson administration's proposal was passed by a large majority by both Houses of the United States Congress, mirroring the sentiment of the nation-at-large.

On the part of the Union of Orthodox Jewish Congregations of America, the response to the Child Benefit legislative development was expressed in the following resolution, unanimously adopted at the Sixty-eighth Anniversary Biennial Convention (Shoreham Hotel, Washington, D.C., Kislev 10–14, 5727, November 23–27, 1966), reading:

5. AID TO EDUCATION

The American democratic tradition recognizes the critical importance of the proper and complete education of the young. In this emphasis on the educational process, the secular tradition of this country is congruous with our own religious heritage with emphasis on secure and well-founded schooling for all. Recent developments in the United States have demonstrated the awareness of these needs. By passage of legislation designed to afford to all children—without regard to their economic ability or geographic location—the best in pedagogic method and curriculum, our federal government and many state governments have refused to allow any child to be limited to second-class educational preparation. In making provision for remedial assistance, for proper textbooks, for transportation facilities, and similar needs for all children who require them, most such legislation has properly adopted the test of the needs of the individual child, and has ended a policy of discrimination against children in non-public or religion-sponsored schools.

We applaud this approach based upon direct "child benefits" which we believe to be consistent with the American tradition of Church–State separation. We urge our day schools and national Jewish educational organizations to explore fully the development and utilization of all available government programs so that the students of our day schools may have full advantage of the best educational techniques and facilities and may thus be educated to their full potential and participation in the American Jewish community. We call for repeal or amendment of those state constitutional or legislative restrictions which would unfairly and improperly discriminate against some children by reason of their attendance at religious schools.

PRAYER IN THE PUBLIC SCHOOLS

Another issue in the Church–State separation frame that also came to the forefront of public concern in the 1960s was that of prayer exercises in the public schools. Unlike the governmental aid to education matters, this has remained a perennial subject of controversy to the present day.

As earlier parts of this book have shown, the Orthodox Union in its infancy had battled against what was then a flagrant problem, the imposition of Christian indoctrination on Jewish children in the public schools. This was fought unsparingly by the Union's pioneer leadership headed by Dr. Henry Pereira Mendes. Throughout the years since, successive UOJCA administrations have spoken out in opposition to religious exercises and teachings in the country's public schools.

At the same time, the Orthodox Union has recognized the menace of secularist-engineered disseminating of irreligious views in public schools under shelter of the Church–State separation tenet. Thus, the policy of American Orthodox Jewry's central arm has been directed against both religious sectarian and irreligious secularist inroads on the public schools.

In many communities of the United States, through the years, the practice of ostensibly voluntary prayer recitals at commencement of the school day had become a tacitly accepted established custom. Although the prayer recited was usually in what was deemed nondenominational form, often it was such only as within the range of Christian denominations. The practice, in any event, could obviously lend itself to the intrusion of sectarian character.

Therein, obviously, lay a serious challenge to Church–State separation as generally understood. On the other hand lay the danger to American spiritual life and human standards of dogmatic secularist pressures on the public schools. The need for some infusion of spiritual vista without doctrinal conditioning was apparent. For the Orthodox Union, the matter posed a dilemma.

The outcome of much deliberation on policy on this difficult issue was a resolution adopted at the 64th Anniversary Biennial Convention, which stated:

18. PRAYER IN PUBLIC SCHOOLS

The controversy that followed the recent United States Supreme Court decision which declared that group recitation in public schools of the so-called Regent's Prayer as contrary to the First Amendment manifests the deep commitment of American society to religious values. In the heat of this controversy, those expressing their agreement with this decision have sometimes been labeled enemies of religious faith and charged with the attempt to drive religion out of American life. We deplore the attacks on the integrity of the Supreme Court, the highest judicial body in our land.

At the same time, our concern with the importance of the appreciation and understanding of the role of G-d in the world on the part of all children, particularly the hundreds of thousands of Jewish children and millions of non-Jewish children who have no such opportunity either in the religious school, the house of worship, or the home, leads us to state that we would deem it appropriate and consistent with the First Amendment to afford the pupils of public schools the opportunity to set out on their day's task with a moment of devotion. We therefore see no objection if the school day were to start with a period of meditation. In this period of meditation, let every pupil think of the Almighty in terms of his faith and his parental religious heritage and thusly invoke His protection for himself, his family, his country, and all mankind.

In subsequent years, there has been recurrent occasion for further consideration of this question. While expression has varied from time to time, the policy trend has remained generally consistent with the 1962 resolution.

RECLAIMING RELIGIOUS PRACTICE STANDARDS FROM ABUSE

During this active period in the Orthodox Union story, the Internal Jewish Affairs Commission was activated to deal with abuses in conditions of religious practice. Under the initial and long-time chairmanship of Harold M. Jacobs, this commission focused on such concerns as kashruth observance in Jewish communal institutions, the observance of halachic requirements in the performance of b'rith milah, and propagation of general observance of taharath ha-mishpachah and mikvah, the pivotal mitzvoth of family purity. Measures to engender more general observance of these basic sanctities of Jewish life and to combat rampant abuses, as called for repeatedly in convention prescriptions, were cited in the published reports rendered to member congregations and their rabbis and lay leaders, and convention delegates.

A special focus of the Internal Jewish Affairs Commission's efforts was the problem of securing proper observance of the requirements of Jewish law and traditional practice at Jewish funerals.

THE FUNERAL STANDARDS PROBLEM

To quote from the Commission's 1962 report, submitted by Chairman Jacobs:

> The Internal Jewish Affairs Commission of the Union decided to concentrate its major efforts in a field which has been so neglected for the past decades . . . : the observance, or rather the lack of observance, of Halachic standards in Jewish funerals. . . . The clamor from the total Jewish community for "something must be done" was so great that the Commission instituted a sub-committee for the purpose, designated the Funeral Standards Committee, and directed this unit to proceed with a study of ways to combat the flagrant violations of Torah law in funeral practices and to counter the gross exploitation of bereaved families.
>
> Rabbis as well as laymen throughout the country cooperated by sending in reports about conditions in their respective communities and, in many instances, suggestions as to how the ills can be cured. The Funerals Standards Committee's findings are:
>
> 1. The American Jewish community at large has gone so far astray that most of its members actually do not know what is right and what is wrong. Countless people do not know what constitutes a "kosher" funeral. "K'riah," "Taharah," "Tachrichim", "Sh'mirah," "K'vurah" are strange and unknown terms and concepts to them.
> 2. There was in some segments of the wider community, resentment towards the Union for trying to tamper with existing conditions, as present conditions seem to fit in very well with the methods and patterns that pertain to the non-Jewish world ("fixing-up" and "dressing-up" the body; pre-funeral visitations at the chapel; metal caskets; public viewing of the remains; etc.).
> 3. The funeral has become a "social occasion." As a result of the promotion by those who derive monetary gain from ostentatious funerals as well as of the desire by many families to "live up to the Jones's", many people unwittingly expend large sums for services which are not only unnecessary, but contrary to the Halachah and traditional customs which govern the burial of the dead.

4. The arrangements and direction of the funeral has passed from the religious community, where it traditionally belongs, to the hands of professionals, some of which have taken the liberty of dealing lightly not only with the laws of burial but also with the various laws surrounding it such as K'riah, Shiva, etc.

5. The heretofore volunteer Chevrah Kadisha has slowly deteriorated and its functions have fallen into the hands of persons who fulfill these Mitzvoth for monetary gain, and ofttimes not in keeping with the Jewish Din.

6. Although numerous pamphlets and books have been published on the halachic requirements at a funeral, a large majority of American Jewry is not aware of their existence.

7. It is difficult to make generalizations because conditions vary tremendously, depending at times upon local customs and habits, and the personality of religious and lay leaders and of the local Funeral Directors.

When the Funeral Standards Committee had made but one announcement regarding its projected study and work, namely in a column of the October 1961 issue of *Jewish Action*, correspondence, phone calls, brochures, and other communications began to literally flood our office. Local rabbinic bodies as well as lay groups throughout the country began to issue statements and set standards for the members of their respective communities. Countless synagogue bulletins devoted many columns to the problem. In general, the Jewish community as a whole began to take cognizance of the chaotic and deteriorated conditions which exist in the field of Jewish funeral practices.

We are pursuing the cooperation of the Jewish Funeral Directors throughout the country in a program that:

a. will guarantee any person who so requests a "kosher" funeral for his loved one;

b. which will eventually result in such funerals becoming again the norm.

There is a Herculean task of education that lies ahead of us. Through sermons, lectures, synagogue bulletin articles, public press and radio, the Jewish public must be educated to ask for and demand that the beloved departed one be interred in accordance with halachic procedures.

The work of the commission has benefitted by the dedicated efforts of Rabbi Sidney Applbaum, spiritual leader of Congregation Beth Judah, Brooklyn, who was appointed in May 1961 to direct the activities of the Funeral Standards Committee. He initiated the nation-wide study of Jewish funeral practices and was also in charge of all other phases of our program. Rabbi Applbaum has been especially effective in dealing with the Jewish Funeral Directors Association and making its members aware of the demands of the organized Orthodox Jewish community.

From that time on, persistent pursuit of its mission by the commission's Funeral Standards Committee made a continuing impact on the Jewish public and community and synagogue interests—and notably, on the Jewish funeral directors.

The national association of the last-named, the Jewish Funeral Directors of America, found it beneficial to enter into what was designated as an "accord" with the Union of Orthodox Jewish Congregations of America and the Rabbinical Council of America to advance the observance of the requirements of halachah and Jewish tradition in funeral practice. Among a series of steps to publicize, propagate, and facilitate the observance aims, pursuant to the accord, the Union and the Rabbinical Council jointly arranged for the preparation of a basic, simply stated Jewish Funeral Guide, a one-page printed leaflet. Copies of the Guide were, from then on, continuing to the present, furnished to every member of the Funeral Directors Association for presentation to bereaved families when making funeral arrangements, as called for by the accord.

The promise of the continuing practical work of the Internal Jewish Affairs Commission's Funeral Standards Committee won tribute at the Kislev 5727/November 1964 biennial convocation of the national union, with the following Resolution:

10. FUNERAL STANDARDS

We record our gratification upon the consummation last year of the accord between the Orthodox Union, in conjunction with the Rabbinical Council of America, and the Jewish Funeral Directors of America, providing for the observance of the requirements of Jewish religious law and tradition in funeral practices and upon the development by the Joint Funeral Standards Committee of the Union of Orthodox Jewish Congregations of America and the Rabbinical Council of America of the Jewish Funeral Guide. This establishes the necessary basis for the protection of Jewish sanctities in this area. All must realize, however, that this historic accord is merely the first step towards assuring that all Jewish funerals shall be conducted in strict accord with Torah law and values. There is much more to do if we are to accomplish our objectives, and our congregations and their rabbis and lay leaders must join to help implement this program on the local level.

We therefore call upon all congregations to:

a. Disseminate periodically among their congregants an awareness and understanding of Jewish requirements and standards as to funeral, burial and mourning practices, recognizing that the most effective means of encouraging correct practice is to educate people about them before there is a loss.

b. Apprise their congregants that in case of death, G-d forbid, the rabbi of the congregation should be notified promptly so that he can offer timely counsel, guidance and advice.

c. Periodically distribute copies of the Jewish Funeral Guide to the Jewish residents of their respective communities, besides giving a copy to every bereaved family at the time of a loss.

d. Maintain continuous liaison with local funeral directors and assist the Joint Funeral Standards Committee in their respective communities, to accomplish our purposes.

The aims of the Funeral Standards Committee have been pursued in all the years since, with Harold M. Jacobs and others continuing to lend their efforts and attention. Rabbi Applbaum has directed the program through the years.

The tripartite accord met the test of time. In contrast to the initial reluctance prevalent among the funeral directors individually, an attitude of respect for and response to the standards called for by the Orthodox Union and its rabbinic arm, the Rabbinical Council, became marked among them.

It became widely recognized that although much remained unsatisfactory in funeral and related practice among the wider Jewish public, conditions as to halachic observance resulting from the work of the Union's Funeral Standards Committee showed notable improvement generally. Certainly among all elements of the Jewishly conscious, the advance over what once was a field of uncurbed abuse was impressively substantial.

Thus the program begun in 1962 took its place in the roster of UOJCA accomplishment.

29

On the World Scene

With American Jewry standing out in the post-Holocaust world as the Diaspora bulwark of Jewish life, calls for assistance or cooperation from overseas communities had taken a new tone. American Orthodox Jewry thus was looked to for leadership in the concerns of the Torah-loyal everywhere.

From its beginnings, the Orthodox Union had responded to calls from struggling communities and troubled groups and individuals around the world. Now, with world Jewry's situation so dramatically transformed, the central Union responded to calls coming from every continent with a growing perception of the new time.

The Union's records reveal a constant flow of measures broached in response to urgent developments affecting communities abroad. Often the course taken was to share in or support endeavors in the appropriate fields by agencies set up for the purpose, or to apply the Union's influence to correct disputed policies or prejudicial treatment. But in some situations the Union itself undertook a course of action, as circumstances required.

The UOJCA role in this regard in the mid-century decades and after was not such as, years before, had brought the initiation and conduct of American Torah overseas relief work, through the creation of the Central Relief Committee. But as an instrument of support and, on occasion, mediation or correction, the Union of Orthodox Jewish Congregations rendered important services. Undertakings to heal wounds, to enable the survivors of Shoah to find new life, and to guide those uprooted from ancient communities to regain their spiritual selves in a strange world, all drew upon the committed participation of America's Orthodox Jewish ranks, rallied for these tasks by the Orthodox Union.

Always uppermost in the Union's interests, amid the pressures of domestic needs, was the welfare of Israel, land and state. Just as the cause of the return to Zion, the upbuilding of the Yishuv, and the epochal struggle leading to the birth of the embattled Jewish state had ever been applauded by the American Torah community's central arm, so the development of the reborn commonwealth and its defense and security were its unfailing concern. This joined an undeviating insistence upon the awareness of the holiness of the land of Israel and of the inseparable nature of all that pertains therein to the faith and sacred heritage of the house of Israel.

Accordingly, from the birth of the Jewish state onward through and beyond the post-mid-century decades, did the Union of Orthodox Jewish Congregations of America have occasion to take public action as well as to employ its influence on behalf of Israel, subject as the reborn commonwealth was—and is—to extremes of danger. Again and again forces were rallied by the Orthodox Union at the forefront of public demonstrations, political actions, and other measures to sustain Israel's cause in defense against dire threats to its existence.

The Union also had occasion to move for the correction of wrongs in circumstances of secularistic infringement of Judaic requirements in Israel's public life and violation of the rights of the Jewishly observant. Steps of this kind were repeatedly found to be necessary throughout this period, as they unfortunately have been in the years since.

OUT OF NORTH AFRICA

From Egypt in the east to Morocco in the west, across the North African shelf of the African continent, Jewish communities of varied historical background had persisted throughout the Diaspora centuries—up to the time when, with the repeated failure of all the massed forces of the Arab nations to destroy the reborn Jewish commonwealth, there had come such an explosion of anti-Jewish hatred as compelled mass flight.

Many thousands of North African refugees found haven in France; as many others flocked to Israel. The settlement and economic integration of these refugees in Israel presented massive problems, not yet entirely eliminated in the present day. Particularly painful was the effect of the transition on their spiritual lives.

Most of those coming from North African lands had led lives steeped in traditional Jewish observance, holding fast, with but minor change under modern influence, to the ways their forefathers had pursued throughout the generations. With these refugees now uprooted and exposed, unprepared for the modern Israeli scene, disorientation took a sharp toll. The danger to their spiritual adjustment was sharpened by the placement of most, upon their arrival in Israel, in settlements and institutions of secularist or altogether irreligious forces. The effects were drastic. Efforts to deal with these problems were summarized in the 1962 report of the Israel and Overseas Commission, by its chairman, Max Stern. In it, he said:

> Rabbi Zev Segal was appointed to direct our efforts for the Holy Land and its inhabitants. He flew to Israel in August, 1961, stopping off in Geneva where he met with our President, Moses I. Feurestein, and jointly with him held several conferences with Dr. Nahum Goldmann (then Chairman of the Jewish Agency and the World Zionist Organization) concerning the North African immigrants and their children who were channeled by the Jewish Agency and [Israel] Government officials to non-religious settlements and institutions, regardless of their background and their parental upbringing.
>
> In Israel Rabbi Segal had a series of meetings with Mr. Moshe Sharett, the head [in Israel] of the Jewish Agency, and high government officials. The discussions covered not only the Israel "K'litah," the settlement on arrival, but also the atmosphere and the conduct of the transit camps in Europe, some of which were visited by Mr. Feuerstein. The forceful presentations of our emissaries brought about some important changes in the policy of the Jewish Agency and . . . assurances that there would be no repetition of the practices against which we protested so vigorously.

But, it developed, the commitments were not kept. The report continues:

> Subsequently, when we found ourselves not satisfied that these undertakings were carried out, representatives of the Orthodox Union, together with leaders of other national Orthodox Jewish organizations, met with Jewish Agency leaders. UOJCA was represented by Mr. Feuerstein, Dr. Samson R. Weiss, and Rabbi Segal. While I can report that some progress was made, the situation is still far from satisfactory and we must continue our diligence in this area.

Discussion of the problem at the 64th Anniversary convocation (Washington, D.C., 5723/1962), resulted in the passage of a resolution (no. 10) that, among other points, stated:

> We call upon the Government of Israel and upon the Jewish Agency to carry out in practice their often repeated solemn pledge to see to it that no adult immigrant and no child shall be settled in surroundings or housed and schooled in institutions which do not reflect their religious convictions and their parental preferences, respectively. We consider the enforced alienation from their previous Jewish way of life of such immigrant adults and children an unforgivable crime against the Jewish soul and a practice abhorrent to all decent persons.

Succeeding events would make all too clear the need for unceasing effort in this regard.

While the intercession of religious loyalist forces has made itself felt over the years, the problem has had lasting effect. The inculcated severance from the Torah way has exacted—as it has among their European and other counterparts—a lasting spiritual and social toll among the young generation of the families originating in Egypt, Libya, Tunisia, Algiers, and Morocco. The spiritual redemption of such segments of the Israel populace is a continuing challenge to Torah forces.

Matters affecting the Jewish state were invariably the subject of concerned discussion at all UOJCA deliberative occasions during the period under consideration here, as was the case in the years thereafter. The views expressed on this subject were consistently within a frame of ready consensus.

The resolution on Israel adopted at the 66th Anniversary Biennial Convention (Washington, D.C., 5725/1964) set forth a position that, with variations according to the circumstances, was sustained through the decades since. It reads:

16. ISRAEL

The attachment of the Torah community to Eretz Israel is unshakably anchored in the fundamentals of our faith and observances. The Torah Jew sees in Eretz Israel the land of Divine promise. Only in juncture with the Holy Land will the Jewish people reach its fullest moral and spiritual potential. Only on its sacred soil will the eternal aspirations of our Prophets and Sages come to fullest fruition. And only in juncture with Torah can the State of Israel fulfill its purpose.

a. We therefore reaffirm with renewed emphasis the calls issued at our previous conventions to our fellow Jews everywhere to continue to increase their identification with and financial and moral support of Israel; to demonstrate their devotion by renewed and frequent visits to the Land; to send their sons and daughters to make use of the Torah educational institutions which Eretz Israel offers; to invest in the economy of Israel, whether indirectly by the purchase of Israeli Bonds, or even more importantly, by direct and personal investments in its growing economic enterprises and endeavors; to support the economy of Israel by the purchase of the produce of the land, including its religious literature and other religious articles; to strengthen the language bridge between us by the learning and use of spoken Hebrew; and to pay special attention to the continually expanding needs of the religious Yishuv and its sacred institutions.

b. We voice our deep concern over repeated intrusions into the autonomous sphere of the duly authorized Israel Rabbinate. To make the Torah submissive to the State is a violation of moral right and is a perversion of spiritual and historic reality. We therefore call upon the Government of Israel to guard against any such intrusions and not to permit the bringing of pressure upon those invested with religious authority. We call upon the Government of Israel to be ever mindful of the awesome responsibility to maintain the unity of our people which was preserved on the sole basis of Torah Law during the millennia of our Dispersion. To tamper, for instance, with the laws of marriage and family status which wisely were entrusted to the jurisdiction of the rabbinate at the establishment of the State of Israel will do irreparable harm, shattering this unity, leading to the disappearance of masses of our people from the Jewish fold and undermining the relationships between the Diaspora communities and the State and populace of Israel.

c. We denounce the unconscionable proselytization practices of non-Jewish missionary groups which have capitalized on Israel's difficulties to their purpose. As the truth of this situation is becoming known, men of conscience everywhere are appalled at the exploitation by the missionaries of the plight of impoverished, confused immigrants to entice their helpless children on the path of apostasy. We look to the Government of Israel to proceed with dispatch to the implementation of measures to prevent this outrage.

d. To Jews who are concerned with the development of the truly Jewish life of which our Torah is the source and Halachah is the format, the State of Israel represents a historic opportunity for the continued and untrammelled development of the fount of Jewish law which has succored our people for so many centuries. This fount which could furnish the spiritual direction and inner communal strength, which enabled a scattered people to sustain itself in self-reliant communities surrounded by other societies, can achieve an even more glorious future in the free society which we see in the new State.

In Israel as in our own country, the education of the entire Jewish people to the benefits and supreme wisdom of the Torah society and Torah Law must be the necessary basis for the implementation of the ideals and practice of Torah in the life of the nation. The first step taken in placing the sacred area of family law in the hands of the qualified religious authorities should be followed by continued development and use of the Halachah in the modern jurisprudential setting and within the framework of the State. We urge philanthropic, educational and legal institutions to support in full measure the efforts to elucidate and present our Halachah in the language and format required for the increased juridical use in Israel.

The failure to understand and appreciate this challenge and opportunity has contributed largely to the confusion over the issue of Jewishness in the Jewish State which has misled so many of our brethren in the State of Israel, not excluding members of the Government itself. We call upon the Government and all people of good will in the State to understand that opportunity and to reject all efforts, from both within and without their borders, to exploit and distort for partisan, self-serving, un-Jewish ends the growing pains of a young nation with a glorious religious and spiritual tradition. Only within the terms of this tradition can the State of Israel fulfill the purpose for which it was brought into being, and only within these terms can Medinath Israel sustain its being and continue to develop. In such a spirit we would look to the developing State as some previsioning of the ultimate salvation for which all Jewish generations have yearned.

CALL FROM INDIA

Distinctive among the varied occurrences in the Orthodox Union's international ramifications during this period was a development resulting in a tie between American Torah Jewry's central arm and an ancient Jewish fold in far-off India. This had originated with receipt, in December 1959, of a letter from one then unknown to the Union—a leader of the community of Jews in India known as the Bene Yisrael.

The writer of the letter, Saul B. Penkar, identified himself as president of the Magen Hassidim Synagogue of Bombay, one of the largest of the congregations of India's Bene Yisrael group. He requested the aid of the Union of Orthodox Jewish Congregations of America in securing the future of the Bene Yisrael community, stating that this had become imperiled by the attempt of a deviant American Jewish denomination to ensnare his community and turn it, by deceptive means, from its age-old religious adherence to Orthodoxy.

From Mr. Penkar's letter and available sources, it was known that the Bene Yisrael had maintained their distinctive identity in India since remote times. They had remained separate from India's other recognized and long-established Jewish groups, such as the Cochin Jewish community and the "Baghadi" Jews of Iraqi derivation. The latter two groups, whose Jewish status was beyond question, did not intermarry with members of the Bene Yisrael, whose halachic status, despite their fidelity to Torah and their particular traditions, was in doubt. Then numbering about 25,000, the Bene Yisrael were mainly centered in and about Bombay, with smaller groups in Calcutta and New Delhi.

It was known that, throughout the many centuries of their history, the Bene Yisrael had been steadfast in their sense of identification with the Jewish people and faith. Their deep religious devotion, although uninstructed in halachic requirements and expressed in their own customs, was unmistakable.

Mr. Penkar, citing the efforts underway to draw his community to affiliation with a heterodox association, appealed to the UOJCA for help in maintaining "the strongholds of Orthodox Judaism in India" and to preserve "the ancient Jewish traditions which have been cherished and maintained by our forefathers in the past." He said further that his congregation and four others of the Bene Yisrael, constituting a majority of the group, had spurned the attempts to draw them away.

Upon consideration of the communication by the Union's Executive Committee, it was decided that the Union must respond to this call; accordingly, the Overseas Commission was authorized to proceed in the matter. A reply in warmly affirmative vein was sent to Mr. Penkar, leading to a continuing exchange of communications. There followed the dispatch of UOJCA literature and guidance materials to India. Rabbi Israel Brodie, Chief Rabbi of Britain and the Commonwealth, and Hacham Solomon Gaon, spiritual head of the British Sephardi community, were also appraised of the matter and were put in touch with the Bene Yisrael leadership, to good purpose.

Writing on April 1, 1960 to Dr. Samson R. Weiss, UOJCA Executive Vice President, Mr. Penkar reported that, as two additional Bene Yisrael congregations had joined the original five, they had decided to establish the Union of Orthodox Jewish Congregations of India, for which the two leaders of the Bombay Baghdadi community also had indicated their support.

At this point, the Indian Union leadership turned to the Orthodox Union with a plea for an in-person visit to India by an emissary of the American Union. There then ensued, in July 1960, a mission to India, on behalf of the Union of Orthodox Jewish Congregations of America and the Rabbinical Council of America, by Rabbi Charles Weinberger, then president of the rabbinic body.

In the course of the two weeks of his intensively crowded stay, Rabbi Weinberger conferred at length with the Bene Yisrael leaders and addressed assemblages of their members in Bombay, New Delhi, and Calcutta. He also conferred with leaders of the Indian Baghdadi community and addressed gatherings of their community, too.

Under the impetus of the presence of this emissary of the UOJCA and RCA, there took place the formal establishment of the Union of Orthodox Jewish Congregations of India. Regular contact between this body and the Orthodox Union was thereafter maintained with a continuing supply of materials, literature, and religious requisites such as tephillin, plus funds for operation expenses and publication of their bulletin. Attempts were made to provide them with a rabbi—their crucial need—but a suitable candidate could not be found.

In January 1961, a second mission to India took place on behalf of the Orthodox Union and the Rabbinical Council. The emissary this time was Rabbi Norman Lamm, then Associate Rabbi of the Jewish Center of New York.

As stated in the 1962 report of the Overseas Commission Chairman Max Stern:

> The [three-week-long] visit of Rabbi Lamm proved extremely fruitful. His addresses and lectures were received with great enthusiasm. He instituted a program for youth activities and established a productive relationship between the Indian Orthodox Union and the Torah Department of the Jewish Agency in Bombay.
> . . . The program initiated has been maintained and further developed during the intervening period. We supply our Indian brethren with most of the funds for their youth activities and a much appreciated camping program.

Mr. Stern added:

> It was also my personal pleasure to meet (during a visit to India) with the officers and other leading members of the Indian Orthodox Union. I can testify to their Jewish loyalty and pride. They feel greatly strengthened by our interest and support.

Subsequently, most members of the Bene Yisrael community, as well as those of the other Indian Jewish groups, made aliyyah to Israel. There, after the usual problems of transition and economic absorption, they presently found their way in Israeli society. For the Bene Yisrael, however, special difficulties were presented by the question of their halachic status as Jews incurred during their long centuries of isolation. The matter became a heated public controversy, eventually allayed by measures to enable the Bene Yisrael to qualify for full Jewish status.

With the migration of most of India's Jews in the course of the 1960s and 1970s, the Indian Union of Orthodox Jewish Congregations ceased to exist. Although some personal contact was maintained with their former leadership figures who had come to Israel, the UOJCA tie with Indian Jewry could not be effectively sustained with the fragments remaining in India. Thus ended—happily, with a community's ascent to the Holy Land—a distinctive chapter in the Orthodox Union story.

IN DISTANT AND NEIGHBORING LANDS

Other of the Orthodox Union's international concerns in that period did not involve such substantive organizational activity as did the Bene Yisrael, with certain exceptions to be noted later. This was not because of lesser need or concern, but because of lack of means. Thus, little beyond manifestations of fraternal encouragement and token aids could be rendered in response to calls from the remnants of communities in Europe and from small communities being born in far-Eastern points and in the isles of the Pacific.

Especially troubling to American Orthodoxy's central agency were the pressing needs of fellow Jews in other parts of the Americas. From Caribbean points, from Mexico, and from each of the lands of Central and South America came messages of critical need for aid in the sustaining of Torah-loyal life in the face of assimilative and other adverse conditions. Appeals came repeatedly, citing painful insufficiencies of rabbis, teachers, religious functionaries of all kinds, and also of instructional and inspirational materials.

In the 1962 Overseas Commission report, Chairman Max Stern was candid in stating:

> Suffice it to say that our correspondence with some of the leading personalities of Central and South American Jewry will never substitute for direct personal contacts. We can build on the Orthodox strength still in existence in these countries, but time is running out rather rapidly.

A plan to send an Orthodox Union emissary to South America in preparation for a Latin American Conference of Orthodox Jewish Congregations failed to materialize. In March 1962, however, there was convened in Panama a conference of Orthodox community leaders of the host country, Mexico, Colombia, and Venezuela. From it, it was reported, "emerged the rudiments of a congregational and rabbinic organization," for which was promised "all possible cooperation" by the Orthodox Union. Following this, in July 1962, Rabbi Pinchas Brener of Caracas, Venezuela visited Bogotá, Colombia, and Lima, Peru, on behalf of the Rabbinical Council of America, of which he was a member. He reported "a tremendous need for providing [these and other communities] with, among other things, translations of UOJCA materials, including *Jewish Life*, into Spanish and Portuguese." Subsequently, Hacham Gaon of London arranged for translation of some of the Union's booklets and programming manuals for this purpose.

In the years thereafter, efforts to aid the Latin American communities remained sporadic. In January 1970, at the occasion of a meeting of the Executive body of the World Jewish Congress, Joseph Karasick—who was to succeed Moses I. Feuerstein as UOJCA president—and Dr. Samson R. Weiss met and talked at length with Chief Rabbi David Kahane of Argentina. In response to Chief Rabbi Kahane's urgings, a tentative plan emerged for a visit of Orthodox Union leaders to Argentina, Brazil, Uruguay, Chile, and Peru, again with the view of convening a South American Conference. This, too, unfortunately did not materialize. "Neither the time nor the funds were available," was the eventual annotation. Such was the continuing pattern of gestures in this area. The fact that, despite all discouragements, notable advances were marked in a Torah development in all major Latin American centers during the later decades of the twentieth century cannot be credited to the practical contributions of the Orthodox Union or any other North American source. The example of the rise and development of the Orthodox Union itself, plus its supportive attempts, may well have been a contributing factor, however. One symptom of the Union's intent to reach out to and mark its recognition of the significance of Jewry "south of the border and beyond" was the election of Dr. Marcos Katz, of Mexico City, as chairman of the UOJCA Board of Governors upon the 1983 establishment of that new body in the Union's governing apparatus.

TOWARD FREEING SOVIET JEWRY

Seen in hindsight, the onset in the 1960s of the great campaign for Soviet Jewry by the Jews of what was then dubbed the "Free World" seems to have been curiously belated. This was perhaps because, in the aftermath of World War II, with Jewish efforts riveted on salvaging Holocaust survivors aiding in the epic struggle for the establishment, defense, and upbuilding of the Jewish state of Israel, attention was diverted from the plight of Soviet Jews. Although the "Free World's" Jews were not unaware of the ruthless suppression of Jewish life at the hands of the Communist regime, it was vaguely hoped that things would somehow right themselves.

Such was the attitude, tacit rather than expressed, of practically all organized Jewish forces—until there escaped from the Iron Curtain the cry: "Fargest uns nicht! (Do not forget us)!"

The Orthodox Union, through its literary voice, *Jewish Life*, was in advance of other Jewish forces in facing up to the situation of their hard-tried brethren in the Soviet domain. In singular contrast to Jewish periodicals generally, *Jewish Life* was unhesitant in bringing to light the conditions that, in the mid-twentieth century, updated the horrors of the Spain of Inquisition days.

At a time when the Kremlin's rulers could keep their terror-ruled domain sealed shut, impervious to intrusion from without; when few other than hand-picked visitors from the West were admitted, and these kept under vigilant surveillance during their stay; when such Western journalists as were admitted could send only carefully guarded reports or were themselves instruments of the Communist despots; when much of American news, opinion, and cultural media danced to the Agitprop tune; when the published voices of American Jewry's diverse segments were muted, if not altogether silent, about the special persecution and hardships capping the terror-imposed strangulation of all vestiges of Jewish life under the hammer-and-sickle—at just such a time did *Jewish Life* in, issue after issue, present graphic but responsibly and knowledgeably written accounts of what was happening to the Jews at the hands of the successors to the Czars.

Coverage began with an early-1950 article by Aaron Pechenik applying personal experience to "The Past and Future of Soviet Jewry." There followed reports by such other well-qualified observers as Geoffrey Neuberger, Professor William Brickman, and Dr. Erich Goldhagen, whose respective business and academic capacities had put them in position to make repeated visits to the Soviet domain during and after Stalin's time; Rabbi Bernard Poupko and Herschel H. Weinrauch, who had lived in and escaped from the Iron-Curtain stronghold; Myron Kolatch, with expertise in Kremlinology; Rabbi Murray Grauer, transmitter of the rise-and-fall experiences of the one-time Communist Party figure Izzi Barzilai, who rediscovered himself as a believing Jew in the course of twenty years in Soviet prisons and Siberian slave labor camps; and such keen-eyed visitors to a rotting empire as Michael Kaufman and Rabbi Elkanah Schwartz. Each of the foregoing was among those who, spurring the onset of the organized effort to save Soviet Jewry, brought home, in the pages of *Jewish Life*, the truth of the dark situation of the three million Soviet Jewish survivors of both prewar and postwar Communist persecutions and the intervening Nazi mass-murder onslaught. They brought word, too, of Soviet Jewish ranks astir with a sense of Jewishness, despite the decades of atheist inculcation and interdiction of knowledge of their people and heritage. Among them, "Free-World" Jews were now thrilled to learn, were those who, year in and year out, had risked all in steadfast adherence to the Torah way, and those who, led by the Eternal Hand to spiritual rebirth, were daily putting their lives on the line by proclaiming their identity with the people and faith of the House of Israel.

When, with Stalin's "Doctor's Plot" charge coming to light in December 1952, the world learned of a further darkness looming for Soviet Jewry. Jews in America and in other democracies had been shaken, but were still slow to come to grips with reality. Such moves as were instituted in various quarters in the next few years were far from the force needed to bring meaningful pressure to bear. The Kremlin could regard lightly actions such as a 1961 delegation of the Synagogue Council of America, headed by Rabbi Theodore L. Adams, then president of the Rabbinical Council of

America, to the Soviet Embassy in Washington. But mounting boldness among Jews within the Soviet realm, on the one hand, and heightened determination among "Free-World" Jews, on the other, signaled a fateful change.

Responsible quarters now grasped the realization that broadly coordinated, full-powered, and full-focused means were essential. Ensuing interorganizational negotiations presently resulted in such umbrella agencies as the American Conference for Soviet Jewry, with constituent units in all cities, and the World Conference for Soviet Jewry.

The Orthodox Union played an active part in these developments. Under UOJCA leadership, the country's Orthodox congregations played a key part in the years-long series of public demonstrations, political arousal, and propagandistic activities that were maintained at high tempo. A UOJCA delegation, headed by Emil Ramat, maintained a close liaison with the American Conference for Soviet Jewry and with another effective force, the Student Struggle for Soviet Jewry.

Various activities of its own were conducted by the Orthodox Union. Special initiative was exercised by the organization in getting food parcels to individual Soviet families whose addresses had been obtained. Once the means had been identified through which the packages containing kosher food and other useful items could be channeled for *dependable* delivery to the addresses (not easily established), the Union launched a campaign for this purpose among the country's Orthodox congregations. The results of the campaign were strong. This project, bringing together with material benefits a token of brotherly concern to those dwelling in fear, brought hope and encouragement to the grateful recipients for several years.

The Union likewise used its influence on behalf of Jewish religious sources in Russia for permission to bake a supply of matzoth for Pesach, which was previously forbidden. When permission was reluctantly granted as a sop to world opinion, it was for but a very limited amount of matzoh. Permission was also secured, through the efforts of the Orthodox Union, for the shipment of a supply of matzoth from the United States and Israel. The supply was contributed to the leading matzah baking firms. These were among indications that, despite Kremlin affectations of disregard for the protest campaigns mounting around the world, the pressure was being felt.

A particularly striking mark of the campaign's impact was the response in 1965 by the Soviet government to a request, repeatedly urged by the Union and the Rabbinical Council of America, for a visit to the Soviet Union by a delegation of the rabbinic body. Unprecedented through all the years of Communist rule, this was the first substantive contact between Soviet Jewry and the religiously constituted Jewish world. The nine-man delegation of the Rabbinical Council of America to the Jews of the Union of Soviet

Socialist Republics took place in July 1965, headed by Rabbi Israel Miller, president of the RCA.

An account of the delegation's experience by Rabbi Bernard A. Poupko, one of its members, appeared in the Tishri 5726/September 1965 issue of *Jewish Life*. One passage tells of their appearance at the Leningrad Synagogue, one of the few dozen shuls out of the thousands that had existed prior to the Russian Revolution that was permitted to survive in all of the Soviet Union. Those who attended synagogue services risked severe governmental penalty, as well as marking themselves out for hostile manifestations by the anti-Semitism rampant among much of the populace. This passage recounts:

> It is not simple to convey the spontaneous joy upon the faces of the elderly Jews who greeted us as we entered the Leningrad Synagogue for the morning service. "Just look, young rabbis from America . . . they came to visit with us and see us . . . our brothers from America, God bless them for not having forgotten us . . . are there many other young rabbis like you in America?" These wonderful elders with serene faces and tearful eyes were puzzled by the strange phenomenon of men young yet religious, by the presence in their midst of young rabbis, the age of the surviving rabbis in their country being all above seventy.
>
> It is virtually impossible to describe the fear and apprehension of these people when asked about their life and conditions. Invariably, their answer is: "We must have faith . . . we must be patient . . . we hope that God will not forsake us and that ultimately salvation will be ours." These and similar remarks were uttered quietly, with resolution and steadfastness—faith and hope from an oppressed heart and a tormented spirit.

By this 1965 stage, after the passage of forty-eight years of Communist rule, those still steadfast in the faith of their fathers were few among Soviet Jewry's remaining three million. Relentless persecution, with the provisions of a "progressive" constitution ignored, with the extirpation of leaders, the banning of religious teaching or of any Jewish schooling, the cutting off of religious requisites, the interdiction even of circumcision—all these, together with incessant drilling in atheism from earliest childhood on, had taken their sad toll. Yet it is one among the great wonders of post-Holocaust history that there sprang, out of the hearts of these—the most systematically assimilated Jews in the world—an outpouring of Jewishness. Among some, the unconquerable will to live Jewishly was integral with affirmation of their people's faith, the unity of the Torah-engendered Jewish soul. These people faced years of voluntary martyrdom, years of glowing spiritual heroism.

Eventually, the regime of despotism crumbled before the combination of social and economic ruin and moral challenge. As the regime was to strive in its last years to avert its fate, the doorways to freedom for Soviet Jewry were to open little by little, until, with the final downfall of the last of Lenin's successors, they were finally flung wide. Until that day, Jews in the Soviet domain and Jews in free lands around the world alike were to persist in the struggle. So it was with the Orthodox Union, ever foremost in concern and action.

While participating fully in all Conference for Soviet Jewry activities and in general agreement with its policies, differences of opinion arose between the Union and the Conference on two points. One was with reference to a Kremlin-sanctioned visit to the United States in 1968 by the titular Chief Rabbi of the USSR, the venerable Rabbi Yitzchak Leib Levin of Moscow. Although a well-respected figure, Rabbi Levin was seen as a captive, however unwilling, of the Kremlin regime, bound by fear of consequences to his community to speak and act with an eye to the Communist rulers' purposes.

The Conference, seeing the rabbinic visitor as suspect, and under the ostensible sponsorship of a particularly unsavory Soviet tool, generally refused to countenance his mission. The Orthodox Union, however, viewed the matter in a different light. In the words of Executive Vice President Samson R. Weiss (in the report, 1968 Convention Handbook):

> We felt that the visit, regardless of its unwelcome and hostile sponsor, was good for Soviet Jewry and tended to bring about ameliorization of their severe circumstances. We related, therefore, to Rabbi Levin with due courtesy and invited him to address a special Board meeting. Our National officers also met with him privately and offered him the hospitality of the Orthodox Union for the part of his stay no longer paid for by his original sponsor [!]. The address of Rabbi Levin at our Board meeting was a deeply moving, unforgettable experience.

Rabbi Levin was also given the opportunity to attend a conclave of NCSY, the Union's youth movement. The venerable visitor made it clear that this vibrant assemblage of fervent, Torah-inspired teenagers was a revelation to him.

Dr. Weiss further reported, in the same source:

> We also take a view quite different from the American Conference on Soviet Jewry concerning the utilization of Simchath Torah demonstrations as means of protest against the Soviet treatment of Jews. We hold that all Mitzvoth are to be performed for the sake of fulfilling the Divine precepts, and that to make them instruments of whatever lofty goal is both wrong and dangerous. We shall therefore oppose any repetitions of such Yom Tov demonstrations, should they ever be scheduled again.

The Orthodox Union's stand on the Simchath Torah demonstration issue thereafter prevailed. The cause of Soviet Jewry was on the agenda of major UOJCA assemblages from 1958 to the final collapse of the Communist regime and disintegration of the Soviet Union in 1990, bringing to an end the restrictions on Jewish life and emigration.

Formal expressions adopted concerning Soviet Jewry at these assemblages, while in consistent vein, bore varying nuances and emphases, as situations at given times warranted. This is reflected in the following excerpted passages from some convention resolutions.

FROM THE 5719/1958 BIENNIAL CONVENTION

With heavy hearts, we note that . . . the curtailment of Jewish religious life in the Soviet Union progresses with severity in contradistinction to the possibilities of organization and expression permitted to other faiths. Antisemitic publications are still being distributed, apparently with the sanction of the authorities. Unusual harshness seems to be applied to Jews charged with alleged economic crimes before Soviet courts. . . . We therefore call upon the government of the Soviet Union to put an end to the harassment of this minority and to take all necessary steps to assure this minority of all privileges and rights which the Constitution of the Soviet Union guarantees to all its citizens.

FROM THE 5727/1966 BIENNIAL CONVENTION

Our anguish over the plight of Jews in Soviet Russia is not assuaged. Religious Jews are particularly sensitive to the special discriminations imposed upon our brethren in Russia which prevents them from even the most elementary religious participation and activity. . . . We urge the incoming Orthodox Union Administration to encourage by all possible means visits to the Soviet Union and other Eastern European countries by Orthodox Jews, including youth groups, so that the frequent presence of observant Jews in these countries may bring encouragement to our brethren and dispel the loneliness of their isolation.

We commend our organization's participation in the American Jewish Conference on Soviet Jewry and take pride in the leadership that our officers and those of the Rabbinical Council of America have afforded this group. We join in the declaration proclaimed by the conference and urge our member congregations to participate and develop suitable local programs which will call attention to the crying problems set forth in the aforementioned Declaration.

FROM 5731/1970 BIENNIAL CONVENTION

The increasing number of Russian Jews who, in gallant demonstration of *mesirath nephesh*, dare to cry out against the oppressive policies of their government and to assert their Jewish identity, find themselves subject to persecution and imprisonment. . . . Alarming reports from the Soviet Union indicate that the authorities have embarked on a massive campaign against those who dare to ask to emigrate. Thousands of Jews have already lost their jobs for applying for exit visas to Israel and other countries. Similar campaigns in the past have featured "show trials" with a distinct taint of Anti-semitism. . . .

The Jews of the Soviet Union call out to us—in their letters and statements, prepared and published at great personal risk—to fulfil our sacred obligations of *pidyon shevuim*, of obtaining the release of those in captivity, by raising our voices against their oppression. We call upon our incoming Orthodox Union Administration and upon our constituent congregations and their members . . . to . . . insist that the Soviet Government permit its Jewish citizens the right of self-expression and of freedom of religion as supposedly guaranteed by the Soviet constitution . . . demand that the Soviet Government stop the arrest of, and other discriminatory practices against, Jews who request permission to leave the Soviet Union, and to cease the slanderous campaign against the Jewish people. . . .

FROM THE 5735/1974 BIENNIAL CONVENTION

In recent years the emigration question has dominated all considerations of the Soviet Jewry issue. . . . Additional tens of thousands have requested permission to join the historic exodus of the thousands that the Soviet Government, only reluctantly in the face of overwhelming world opinion, has permitted to leave, in most cases for Israel.

The present situation remains critical. . . . Soviet authorities have escalated their campaign of harassment of would-be emigrants using all the instruments available to their government to discourage those seeking to reestablish their Jewish identity. Arrests and trials on trumped-up charges, denial of work . . . are among the tactics used in recent weeks. . . .

Last month the United States Government announced the completion of a historic agreement with the Soviet Union which should result in an end to most restrictions on emigration and an end to harassment. We . . . salute the efforts of Senators Jackson, Javits, and Ribicoff and Congressmen Vanick and Mills as well as the hundreds of other Senators and Congressmen whose perseverance . . . made this accord a reality. We also deeply appreciate the unprecedented personal involvement of President Ford who played a major role. . . . We await, however, with deep anxiety, the implementation of this agreement. As long as one Jew remains in the Soviet Union, the Union of Orthodox Jewish Congregations of America is committed to fighting for his or her right to meaningful religious freedom as defined in the International Declaration of Human Rights. . . . The Soviet campaign against the Jewish religion must be halted before we are satisfied that the time has come for detente. . . .

The Union's unceasing efforts through the following years to the present in behalf of the Jews of the Soviet Union and of the successor states after the dissolution of the Soviet Union are mirrored in the resolutions adopted at the conventions and other appropriate occasions, and in other records. Activities of recent decades, including projects of large significance, will be discussed later in this book. It is pertinent to note, however, that by the early 1970s, the Union's active efforts were extended to the needs of the increasing thousands who had succeeded in leaving the Soviet domain, many settling in the United States, as well as Israel.

Thus, at the 5735/1974 National Biennial Convention (Boca Raton, Florida, Kislev/December), a resolution on "Soviet Jewish Immigrants in America" set forth a call to communicate to pursue a six-point program for facilitating the settlement and economic and social well-being of the newcomers, adding:

> Moreover, we must use the opportunity to bring to our Soviet fellow-Jews the message of Torah, which has long been denied to them. To this end, educational facilities must be available for the children. Day Schools must be prepared to admit children gratis. Teenagers must receive instruction in Jewish history, tradition, and heritage. Adults must be taught the rudiments of Yiddishkeit. . . .

30

Orthodox Jewry
as a World Force

A significant aspect of traditional Jewish development in the second half of the twentieth century was the rise of a sense of the Torah fold as a worldwide community, and as a component of, and factor in, world society.

This encompassing self-perception went beyond the accustomed tenor of leader-to-leader, community-to-community contact at occasions of special need or informational exchange. It was marked by a reaching for a functional tie between the Torah Jewries of the different lands. Manifestations of this aim can be seen in, among other sources, the records of the Orthodox Union from the early days of the Feuerstein administration onward. Correspondence and reports of the time mirror a mounting awareness of the implications of the tightly knit contemporary world, with its instant global communications and time-and-space-defying travel, its close intermeshing of national societies. The multinational domain of Orthodox Jewry, it was realized, must equip itself as circumstances now required.

Personal meetings between UOJCA leadership figures and their counterparts in other lands, as well as more frequent written exchanges, were now taking place far more often than had ever been the case. Occasions in Israel gave timely opportunity for informal discussion on mutual concerns between leading figures. Relationships between leaders of both the Orthodox Union and the Rabbinical Council of America with the Chief Rabbinates of Israel took on a more established character.

More substantive relationships also developed with the rabbinates and congregational channels of Great Britain, France, and other European countries. There resulted an association between the two American organizations and the Conference of European Rabbis, with the words "and Associated Organizations" added to the name of the latter. For a number of years, personal liaison on behalf of the Union and the Rabbinical Council with the European Conference was maintained by Rabbi Simon Langer, Rav of Congregation Orach Chayim of New York.

Contacts with the various Latin American communities continued to be maintained with some consistency, as noted earlier. Relations also developed with more distant communities such as Australia and South Africa. At the invitation of the Federation of Synagogues of South Africa, UOJCA Executive Vice President Dr. Samson R. Weiss conducted a speaking tour of the various South African communities in 1964. Received with much warmth at all points, Dr. Weiss's addresses, widely quoted in the country's press, won deep appreciation. Later, a similar lecture tour was undertaken by Rabbi Norman Lamm.

The Orthodox Union, in its turn, sponsored visits to the United States and Canada by illustrious dignitaries from abroad. In many cases, the annual national dinners of the Union were to form the venue for the visits.

THE "NATIONAL DINNER" IN INTERNATIONAL ROLE

It is opportune to note here that the Annual National Dinner, under the personal direction of Dr. Weiss, was, from its inception in 1959, a premier gala event in the social calendar of American Orthodox Jewry. Maintaining its special aura over the years, this event has invariably attracted a large attendance—usually over a thousand guests. In this setting of dignity and glamour, with an audience made up of the notables, outstanding rabbinic figures, and key congregational leaders of American Jewish Orthodoxy, Torah forces have yearly paid public tribute to chosen personages of exceptional accomplishment.

The first of the eminent rabbinic leaders from abroad to come, at the invitation of the Orthodox Union, to pay an official visit to the United States was the Chief Rabbi of Britain and the Commonwealth, Rabbi Israel H. Brodie. His address at the 1962 dinner, and his messages on several subsequent occasions during his visit, brought both inspiration and insight, evoking a warm response. In subsequent years, in a series continuing to the present, came a succession of the Chief Rabbis of Israel, as well as other eminent personages of the Torah world from several lands.

On each such occasion, the ranks of American Torah Jewry have honored their revered guest visitor at every point of his stay. Typical of the reception was that accorded the visiting Chief Rabbis of Israel, as summarized by Dr. Samson R. Weiss in his report of the 1966 Annual National dinner:

The guest speaker was His Eminence, Harav Isser Yehudah Unterman, Chief Rabbi of Israel, who came to this country upon the invitation of the Orthodox Union. Received upon his arrival at the airport with full diplomatic protocol by the dignitaries of the Jewish community, the representatives of the Israeli diplomatic corps, the representatives of the State and City of New York, welcomed at City Hall by the Mayor, and escorted to his hotel by a highly efficient and impressive police escort, this illustrious visitor remained in the United States for several weeks and was received by President Johnson at the White House. His address at the National Dinner left a deep impact upon the audience and was reported and commented upon in leading newspapers throughout the country.

The 1968 dinner similarly occasioned the visit to this country of the rishon l'tziyyon, Chief Rabbi Yitzchak Nissim. The report by Dr. Weiss records that at the airport arrival reception, with "full diplomatic honors" as before, "hundreds of students of Ashkenazi and Sephardi yeshivoth came to the airport, together with their teachers. In his stirring address at the National Dinner, the Rishon L'Tziyyon called upon American Jewry 'to join their brethren in the Holy Land in building a secure Jewish future by Aliyyah.'"

In the course of his two weeks' stay, Chief Rabbi Nissim met with the officers of the Union; was tendered a reception by the Rabbinical Council of America, at which Rabbi Joseph B. Soloveitchik delivered an address; met, under the auspices of the Union's NCSY, with delegates of American national Jewish youth organizations, "establishing a wonderful rapport with the young people"; was the honored guest on Shabbath of the Spanish and Portuguese Synagogue, Congregation Shearith Israel; received in his hotel suite a group of American Jewish leaders and "the Chachamim of the Sephardi Congregations who came to pay homage to the recognized religious authority of the world Sephardic Community"; addressed a meeting of the Conference of Presidents of Major Jewish Organizations; was tendered a reception by the Syrian Jewish Community at Congregation Shaarei Zion in Brooklyn, where the attending masses "pressed forward to kiss his hand or at least touch the hem of his garment"; and then, following a second Shabbath, this time as guest of the Fifth Avenue Synagogue, proceeded to Montreal, attended by UOJCA leaders, to attend and address the Fourth Convention of the Union's Eastern Canada Region and be tendered memorable honors by the Canadian communities.[1]

---

1. There comes to this writer's mind the recollection of a curious departure from the accustomed process of civic reception to the Union's illustrious guests. Previously, a call to the office of New York City's Mayor from the UOJCA administrator to arrange an official mayoral reception for the expected dignitary had

The personalization of relationships through visits by eminent dignitaries from abroad prompted by the Union's annual dinners and biennial conventions, and reciprocally by UOJCA leaders at major occasions of overseas commonties, furthered multinational associations.

The discussions and correspondence exchange between American, European, and Israeli Torah-community leaders were tending increasingly toward consideration of both a formal meeting of the top leaders of the several national communities and of a broader world conference. Possibilities took an interesting turn with the erection in Jerusalem of the imposing modern edifice called Hechal Shelomo. As the official seat of the Chief Rabbinate of Israel, superbly equipped and with extensive facilities, this institution gave traditional Jewry in the Jewish state a manifest public presence as well as a functional center. As such it was distinguishable from the politically constituted parties, ideological movements, and sectarian groups.

Key mover in the creation of Hechal Shelomo (and, subsequently, of the adjoining monumental Great Synagogue) was Dr. Maurice Jaffe. A figure of creative ideas and energetic drive, Dr. Jaffe was a proponent of dynamism in the advancement of the Torah cause in Israeli society. After an initial meeting with UOJCA Administrator Saul Bernstein during Bernstein's 1961 visit to Israel, contact had been maintained between them thereafter, extending presently to President Feuerstein and Executive Vice President Weiss. Project proposals resulted, including "adoption" ties between designated synagogues in America and Israel, and the provision of Siphrey Torah and other religious requisites for the hundreds of needy synagogues springing up with the incoming thousands of new olim pouring into Israel.

Perhaps prompted in part by his contacts with the American Orthodox Union, Dr. Jaffe effected the organization, for the first time in holy-land history, of a union of Israeli congregations. Presently designated the Iggud Battei Ha-k'nesseth B'Yisrael, the organization, with headquarters in Hechal Shelomo, soon numbered over 1,500 affiliates.

A 1962 visit to the United States by Dr. Jaffe advanced matters. In his dual capacity as executive director of Hechal Shelomo and chairman of the Israeli congregational union, Dr. Jaffe was presented at the Annual National Dinner that year, and addressed the Midwest regional convention of the Union in St. Louis.

---

brought, on each such occasion, a ready response. On such an occasion arising at an early point in the mayoralty of John V. Lindsay, however, the response had been: "Only if he [the incumbent Chief Rabbi of the Holy Land] comes accompanied by a Reform rabbi and a Conservative rabbi may he be received." This response was made by an official speaking on behalf of the Mayor.

Now the notion of some kind of international convocation of Orthodox communal forces that had been germinating on both sides of the Atlantic was taking hold in Israel, too. Moves by a heterodox force with aspirations to supplant the historical Jewish religion in Israel and the Diaspora further prompted for the rallying of Torah forces. In the course of a letter (Adar 2, 5722/February 6, 1962) to Dr. Weiss, Jaffe wrote:

> From my letter of Shevat 26, you will have seen that we are thinking in terms of a more positive and vigorous approach to the whole problem. Incidentally, I also discussed this matter during a very pleasant meeting with Rav Aron Kotler; he advised us to take every possible step to counteract the threat of Conservatism in Israel. . . .

Further to the purpose, a letter (3 Adar II, 5722/March 9, 1962) to Saul Bernstein states:

> . . . [A] confidential report of a very important development which has taken place. Chief Rabbi Nissim has received a letter from the Beth Din of England warning him of plans [of the heterodox movement] and a copy of the letter was sent to me. A special meeting of the Chief Rabbinate Council was convened and decisions were taken whereby the Chief Rabbinate gives its full support (1) to the Union of Israel Synagogues, (2) to the ideas of a World Conference of Orthodox Synagogues, and (3) to the proposal that a top leadership conference take place in Israel during Chol Ha'Moed Pesach. . . .

Since there was no historical precedent for such a world convocation of the communally constituted forces of Torah Judaism, translation of so unfamiliar an idea into practical reality was a slow, uncertain process. The sentiment building up, however, found expression in formal policy statements as well as in exchanges of tentative notions as to effectuation procedure. At the Orthodox Union's 66th Anniversary National Biennial Convention (Shoreham Hotel, Washington, D.C., Kislev 20–24, 5725/ November 25–29, 1964), the following resolution was adopted:

NO. 2. COOPERATION
WITH WORLD ORTHODOX JEWRY

> We consider the strengthening of the ties between the North American Orthodox Jewish community and the Orthodox Jewish communities of other countries a task of greatest importance. . . . We call upon the incoming UOJCA Administration to devote close attention to efforts to bring about the kind of unified spokesmanship of the world Orthodox Jewish community which still is missing on the world Jewish scene and whose lack has proved

to be a severe detriment to the cause of Torah. . . . We therefore recommend that the Joint Overseas Commission be invested with the responsibility to bring about an intercontinental meeting of Orthodox rabbinic and lay leaders, such meeting to take place during the calendar year 1965. This meeting shall assign on its agenda, high priority to the convening of a World Conference of Orthodox Synagogues.

The developments that followed, advancing toward the objective, are indicated in the corresponding resolution on the subject, adopted at the following 68th Anniversary Biennial Convention (Shoreham Hotel, Washington, D.C., Kislev 10–14, 5727/November 23–27, 1966):

16. WORLD ORTHODOX JEWRY

We affirm our prior Resolution on cooperation with world Orthodox Jewry and acknowledge with approval the salutary steps taken by our outgoing Administration towards the establishment of closer ties between the North American Orthodox Jewish community and the Orthodox Jewish communities of other countries, [including] the participation of the Orthodox Union in the London Conference in March, 1965 which resulted in the creation of an association of Orthodox territorial organizations representing various countries. We urge our incoming Administration to continue to foster these developments and to promote . . . sustained procedures enabling the world Orthodox Jewish community to be appropriately represented in international bodies, whenever appropriate; to achieve unified spokesmanship of world Orthodox Jewry; and to enable this community to pool its spiritual resources for the strengthening of Torah observance and the perpetuation of Jewish sanctities everywhere.

We reaffirm our resolve to bring about a World Conference of Orthodox Synagogues. We approve the decision of the outgoing Administration that the Orthodox Union shall participate in a conference to be held in Italy during Iyyar 5727 (May–June, 1967) of representatives of Orthodox Jewish communities from all parts of the world and from which shall emerge the call for such a World Conference of Orthodox Synagogues to be held soon thereafter in the Holy City, Jerusalem.

LEADERSHIP SUCCESSION

The 1966 National Biennial Convention was the occasion for the conclusion, after twelve path-clearing years, of the presidency of Moses I. Feuerstein and the inauguration of his successor, Joseph Karasick. The change, bringing a different personality to the organizational helm, was registered in certain changes of emphasis, along with freshened vigor; it did not, however, mark a change in organizational vista. The Feuerstein outlook that had brought to American Jewish Orthodoxy both a new sense of itself and new momentum was shared by Joseph Karasick. The incoming president contributed to it his own reading of Torah-community directional guideposts, as ripened in the course of his sequence of high offices in the Orthodox Union, including the vice presidency and the chairmanship of the Commission on Regions and Councils.

The new president, a figure of the business world, also had a background, from his San Francisco origins on, in Torah learning that culminated in rabbinic semichah. Karasick, like his predecessor in office, was moved by a consciousness of what the times signified. He was in strong accord with the moves toward the mobilization of world Orthodox Jewry. And now there came, in the spring of 1967, a happening that shook the world.[2]

THE SIX-DAY WAR

At this fateful point, the armed forces of the nations of the Arab world joined together in armed might to attack Israel. Once and for all, they proposed, the Jewish state was to be smashed, its people slaughtered and

---

2. Under the terms of the new UOJCA Constitution adopted at the Sixty-second Anniversary National Biennial Convention (Atlantic City, NJ, Cheshvan 5721/ November 1960), presidential incumbency in office was limited to a maximum of three successive two-year terms of office.

The Constitution, adopted in 1962, had been prepared over a period of several preceding years by a Constitution Committee headed by Chairman Herbert Berman. An initial draft had been submitted by that committee to affiliated congregations well in advance of the 1958 Biennial Convention and to delegates at that convention. Various changes having been proposed, it was then referred back to Berman's committee; thereafter, various revisions were made in the course of committee deliberations. The text, as revised, was then resubmitted to member congregations prior to the 1960 Biennial Convention and to the delegates at a special session of that convention. The Constitution was then adopted as submitted. Similar procedures were followed in amending some of the provisions effected in 1969.

This responsible, painstaking process of constituency consideration and action, together with committee deliberation, was retrospectively seen in striking contrast to that leading to the announced adoption of another change of Constitution at the 92nd Anniversary Biennial Convention (Wyndham Franklin Plaza Hotel, Philadelphia, Kislev 5751/November 1990).

driven into the sea. The time of doom had come for all that had come into being with the rebirth of Zion, it was proclaimed.

The world and its nations heard this in stunned silence. The world's Jews heard, and what they heard touched the innermost hearts of all. In the land of Israel, all stood steadfast; in the Diaspora, all were moved to stand with their Israeli brethren in their mortal danger.

The Orthodox Union led the way in mobilizing a great national demonstration in Washington. There, the massive throng joined in calls for immediate steps to counter the impending calamity. Whether or not a response would come from government sources will never be known, for one came from the Highest of all sources.

Anyone present at that time will never forget that moment in Lafayette Square when the Union's President reached a height of fervor in his impassioned address—at that very moment there came the message of a miracle:

> Within six days, Israel's defense forces had driven the entire oncoming array of armies, with air forces, tank forces, infantry forces, armaments and all, into total defeat.
>
> The enemy hosts were fleeing wildly. For them, not for their intended victims, all was lost.
>
> Within the six brief days, instead of the predicted doom, all of the Land of Israel west of the Jordan was freed, all in Jewish command.
>
> All of Jerusalem, holiest of cities, was united in Jewish hands. Jewish soldiers, shaken with outpouring tears, were kissing the stones of the Kothel Ha-Ma'aravi, the Western Wall, fragment of that pivot of earthly sanctity, the Beth Ha-Mikdash of old.
>
> Who could fail to see the guiding Hand behind the incredible victory? Who could fail to ponder the ultimate meaning of the lightning-swift reversal of so mighty a military undertaking? Who could fail to sense the deeper reality of what had transpired?

As that moment reverberated across the world, the peoples of the world were bewildered. As that moment penetrated Jewish hearts, every believer and nonbeliever resounded with its touch. To Jews of Torah, it came as a message from on High.

Now, the call from Jerusalem to the Torah-loyal came with new force, and leaders of Diaspora Torah communities were quick to respond. Among the first to arrive was UOJCA President Karasick. Gathering there, in the aura of Divine purpose, they decided that the long-considered World Conference should now be made a reality.

REALIZATION OF
THE WORLD CONFERENCE DREAM

It was agreed that the official call to this first convocation in history of the synagogal-constituted communities of world Torah Jewry should emanate from the Conference of European Rabbis and Associated Religious Organizations by the president of that body, Rabbi Israel H. Brodie, Chief Rabbi of Britain and the Commonwealth.

The call was duly issued. The assemblage, designated the First World Conference of Ashkenazi and Sephardi Synagogues, was to take place, with Heavenly blessing, in Jerusalem, *Yerushalayim Ir-Hakodesh*, on the 7–10th Teveth, 5728 (January 8–13, 1968).

The following objectives were held forth:

To bring together, for the first time in history, representatives of the congregations of Torah Jewry throughout the world, both Ashkenazi and Sephardi, to discuss their common problems and aspirations.

To add a new tie between Israel and the Golah.

To foster sustained communication and cooperation between the congregations and Kehilloth of the world, so that they may share experiences, aid each other and join in the sacred endeavor of maintaining authentic, Halachic Judaism and the traditional Jewish way of life.

To strengthen the bonds between the Ashkenazi and Sephardi communities.

To strengthen the position of Orthodox Jewry on the world scene.

It was announced that Chief Rabbi Brodie had accepted the invitation to serve as Convener of the World Conference and that Israel's Chief Rabbis, Rav Isser Yehudah Unterman and Chacham Yitzchak Nissim, and Israel's Minister of Religious Affairs, Dr. Zevach Warhaftig, had accepted invitations to serve as Patrons of the World Conference.

There proceeded meetings in Jerusalem and London of the interorganizational Planning Committee, composed of the heads of the major participating organizations. Dr. Samson R. Weiss, Rabbi A. Moshe Rose, then Executive Secretary of the British Chief Rabbinate, and Dr. Maurice Jaffe played key roles in the basic planning process. Rabbi Rose was designated Secretary of the Planning Committee, and Dr. Jaffe, designated Coordinator, was assigned direction of the technical arrangements.

Since the World Conference was projected de novo, there was no pre-existing structure or formula on which to base its procedures. It was therefore necessary, besides formulating the program of sessions and events, to initiate a format of procedural arrangements. This was worked out in advance and proved effective.

The functioning of the assemblage was placed under the direction of the Steering Committee. This committee, numbering thirty-four, was composed of leaders of all the participating organizations and national delegations. Joseph Karasick served as Chairman of the Steering Committee. Lawrence A. Kobrin, Chairman of the Orthodox Union's Israel Commission, was designated Chairman of the Resolutions Committee.

Throughout, as noted by the *Report to UOJCA Congregations on the World Conference* that was issued by the Orthodox Union following the unprecedented assemblage, "All benefited by the aid of Saul Bernstein, Administrator of the Orthodox Union."

MULTIPLE TASKS

Beyond the initial work of the Planning Committee lay the larger tasks of developing participation, setting up the facilities and technical arrangements, formulating the conference program in all its facets and details, and selection and enlistment of the sessions chairmen, speakers and specialists, and other program participants. This, under the circumstances, with the multinational and multiorganizational setup requiring clearance at all points, was unavoidably cumbrous.

Much of the burden of these tasks was borne by the Orthodox Union's staff, reporting to the Israel Commission, which "devoted requisite attention to the responsibilities entrusted to them," as the *Report* stated, continuing: "[Chairman] Lawrence H. Kobrin's unsparing dedication to this endeavor through many months, and the percipient thinking he brought to bear throughout on all facets of the undertaking, were key factors in the entire achievement."

The ongoing work of conference implementation was directed by the ad hoc operations trio of Maurice Jaffe, Saul Bernstein, and Moshe Rose. The three, in continuous communication with each other and meeting together in London and Jerusalem, put together the program with its array of ceremonial occasions, plenary and workshop sessions, series of special events, selection of and communications with the program participants, and site provision for each function. They also handled the arrangements for accreditation and registration of delegates and their hotel accommodations.

Besides handling the promotion of the Conference in the Union's North American constituency and recruiting the UOJCA delegation, the Union's administrator journeyed to Britain, France, and Holland to meet with various groups there to advance Conference participation. Additionally, a series of special pilgrimage tours to precede and follow the World Conference was devised and publicized. These tours, in light of the unfamiliarity of the World Conference concept, served to bring home the uniqueness of that event, together with the opportunity of a post-Six-Day War Holy Land pilgrimage.

The carefully planned Pilgrimage Tour itineraries encompassed a range much surpassing the offerings of other sources. The previously quoted report says, in this connection:

> We get deep satisfaction from expressions voiced again and again by participants in the UOJCA Delegation and Pilgrimage Tours. Rarely, if ever, has an undertaking involving so large a number and so broad a program been accorded such unanimous, enthusiastic plaudits.
>
> The Pilgrimage tours gave our delegates opportunity not only to travel throughout the Holy Land, including the areas formerly under Arab rule, but also to meet with and be seen by a large portion of the Israeli public. Furthermore, these specially designed tours took our participants to an especially wide range of points of religious interest, including various types of religious settlements and Torah centers as well as sacred sites numerous of which were, prior to the Six-Day War, for decades or centuries barred to Jewish visitors.

The same source noted that "the large task of processing the delegate enrollment arrangements was conducted by Judah Kirshblum, UOJCA Office Manager and Controller, whose work contributed to the successful functioning of the Pilgrimage undertaking. A contribution to be recorded too was that of Victor B. Geller, who, as our Special Consultant for the Pilgrimage Tours, gave expert guidance in the itineraries planning and travel arrangements." Victor Geller's capacities proved further invaluable when one of the pilgrimage groups completing its post-conference tour back in Jerusalem was stranded by an unprecedented snowstorm. Led by Geller, the group members made it to their flight connection.

The promotional work for the World Conference resulted in the enrollment of 530 participants in the delegation of the Union of Orthodox Jewish Congregations of America. This was second only to the Israeli delegation of over 600. The Orthodox Union delegates were from fifty-six communities in twenty-one states of the United States and three communities in two Canadian provinces. Other delegations were of varying sizes. The total number of registered delegates was nearly two thousand.

While it was to be expected that this great convocation of Torah forces would be unwelcome to antireligious or heterodox circles, more disturbing was a show of opposition from an element within Orthodoxy. The pretext of a few, that the conference would deal with halachic matters, was patently specious. It had been made clear from the first that such matters were excluded from the conference purview, and, in fact, there had been no thought at any time, by any source, of inclusion of any discussion of halachic matters. There was reason to perceive the mark of opposition as emanating from a political source concerned with narrow partisan and personal aspirations of its own. In this connection, the report of the Executive Vice President in 1968 was to say:

> Unfortunately, some quite irresponsible elements utilized these tensions to their own, less than noble ends. It is to the honor of the Orthodox Union leadership that we did not respond, in spite of the grave provocation, and rested our case simply on the text of a cable which Chief Rabbi Unterman, one of the Conference honorary Sponsors, sent to an outstanding Torah authority[3] in this country.

Petty jealousies being disregarded, all arrangements for the first-time-ever World Conference of Orthodox Jewish communal and synagogal bodies advanced and successfully fell into place.

There flocked to Jerusalem a swarm of delegates from twenty-six countries around the globe. Included were delegations from England, France, Argentina, Australia, Belgium, Canada, Colombia, Denmark, Eire, Greece, Holland, Israel, Italy, Luxembourg, Mexico, Portugal, Rhodesia, Scotland, South Africa, Spain, Switzerland, the United States, and West Germany. Also represented were, by public acknowledgment, Romania and—unannounced—the sub rosa representative of a community in another eastern European country then under Communist sway, Czechoslovakia.

The participants came not in individual capacity, but as members of the delegations of the participating organizations, the kehilloth and central synagogal bodies of the several countries. Each organization was committed to bringing responsible and representative communal leadership.

The registration procedure, at Hechal Shelomo, moved swiftly and smoothly. The Orthodox Union's postconference report says:

> It was an exciting sight in itself to see the colorful throngs of delegates, coming from so many lands, speaking a diversity of tongues, and from so many walks of life, . . . each in turn being checked rapidly against the previously-submitted Delegation list, being given his badge, tickets of admission to the various events and "tik" of delegates' materials, each then blending into the variegated Conference scene of which he was now an integral part.

---

3. This writer believes that this was Rav Moshe Feinstein.

The emotion of the occasion is conveyed in an introductory expression in the report, under the signature of Joseph Karasick, that reads:

The thrilling success of the World Conference of Ashkenazi and Sephardi Synagogues exceeded our fondest expectations. Right up to the opening on Monday, Teveth 7/January 8, none of us could clearly envisage what it might all add up to. This, after all, was something without precedent in Synagogue history. We had been working in uncharted territory, dealing with undefined factors. But who could tell what the outcome might be?

Then came the historic moment—the opening, with all its inherent drama. In that moment, every one of us gathered there in Jerusalem knew, by a single instinct, that something decisive was happening. There, in the vast expanse of the Binyonei Ha-Ummah, the audience overflowing into the aisles and lobbies, we knew, every one of us, that world Orthodox Jewry had crossed the threshold to a new era.

The very air was electric with charged purpose. And so it was to remain, through all the events and sessions that followed. Right up to the last event, the post-conference symposium on Motzai Shabbath, there was not the slightest lag in or lapse of mood participation.

This feeling of the World Conference experience is, I know, shared by every one of the nearly 2,000 delegates. Coming together from 26 countries in six continents, they shared thoughts and joined mind to mind; coming together from the four corners of the earth, they became knitted together, joined in a week-long program that was executed, to the last detail, with a finesse that in itself placed Orthodoxy in a new light.

A variety of service facilities was provided for the delegates, and bus shuttle service brought the delegates to and from the conference events with prompt convenience. Notably, although the timetable for each session or other event was calculated to the minute, the schedule was followed precisely. The report pays tribute to the commitment of the delegates who "attended on all occasions with exemplary promptness," continuing:

Thus, for example, the morning sessions were scheduled to start at 9:14 a.m., for program needs left no alternative; what actually happened was that far from coming late (as had been feared), many delegates came ahead of time. By 9:00 a.m. on Tuesday morning, the Hechal Shelomo auditorium was already filled for the first plenary session!—and so it went throughout the Conference.

Among the World Conference innovations was the multiple translation system used for the sessions, believed to be its first such use at any Orthodox Jewish assemblage. At each session, all delegates were provided with earphone equipment from which, by moving a switch, each could select his choice from the three languages—Hebrew, English, and French—

into which all proceedings were being simultaneously translated by teams of Israel's most expert translators. At the opening assembly, Yiddish was also provided. Potential of special significance was seen in the role of the Steering Committee. As the postconference report issued by the Orthodox Union said:

> The knitting together of this top leadership group, coming from many lands, was one of the most valuable results of the World Conference enterprise. Meeting daily face to face around a table, learning to think in common terms and developing a mutual understanding—this opened new vistas for all and laid a foundation for a continuing channel of liaison, mutual aid, and joint endeavor among the organized forces of the world Orthodox Synagogue and Kehillah community.

THE PROGRAM

The official printed program of the World Conference was an impressive 88-page book, in three sections—Hebrew, English, and French. All events set forth there took place precisely as listed. At the opening session, in Binyonei Ha-Ummah, keynote addresses were given by Hacham Dr. Solomon Gaon, Chief Rabbi Isser Yehudah Unterman, and Chief Rabbi Immanuel Jakobovits, as well as messages by several other notables.

All plenary sessions except for the fifth took place at Hechal Shelomo. The first plenary session had as its topic: "Israel and Golah: Shaping the Horizons of the Synagogue World." The second plenary was on "Aliyyah"; the third had as its subject "Responsibility for the Rising Generation"; the fourth plenary dealt with "The Day School, the Synagogue, and the Community." The location for the fifth plenary session was Yeshivath Porath Yoseph, with "Chizzuk Ha-Torah: the Strengthening of Torah Life in Israel and Golah" as its theme. The sixth plenary session dealt with "The Relationship Between Ashkenazi and Sephardi Jewry in Israel and the Golah."

The deliberative sessions of the World Conference closed with the concluding assembly. This was the occasion for expressions on "The World Conference in Historical Perspective," and for discussion and action on a series of resolutions previously formulated and submitted in multicopied form to the delegates by the Resolutions Committee.

The structure of the session was designed to further the basic objectives of bridging Israel and the Diaspora communities, and linking the Sephardi, Ashkenazi, and Oriental communities. Thus each session featured one presentation by an Israeli figure, another by one from a Diaspora community—one in each case being of the Ashkenazi, the other of the Sephardi, or Oriental, fold.[4] Similarly, the discussion and the concluding summation panels that followed the opening presentations included distinguished figures from the various countries represented at the conference.

Except for those plenary sessions that were followed by Workshops, a given period was allotted for general discussion on the topic of the session. With many delegates availing themselves of the opportunity to voice their views, the intensity of their involvement in the issues under discussion was marked. This, the Orthodox Union's report noted, "was characteristic of delegates from all countries . . . notably those from Oriental communities, whose articulateness and fervor were alike striking."

A feature of the World Conference novel to some delegates was the fourteen workshop units. Their respective topics stemmed from, and were designed to particularize the application of, the subjects deliberated more broadly at the preceding sessions. Succinct presentations by distinguished workshop leaders, and the contributions at each workshop of an international faculty of lay and professional experts in the relevant fields, served as guidelines for the ensuing free-flowing exchange of ideas among the participants. This proved highly rewarding.

Commenting on the notable success of the conference workshops, the postconference UOJCA report said:

> To the delegates other than those from North America, the workshop concept was unfamiliar. . . . Some delegates initially approached them hesitantly. Within minutes, the hesitancy wore off and the participants soon joined with gusto in the intimate and informal pattern of discussion. The new-found popularity of the workshop technique was much apparent at the second series, each one of them having a capacity complement.

WOMEN'S SESSIONS: SPECIAL EVENTS

The women delegates joined in all World Conference sessions and events, and in addition participated in two sessions especially for women. These, on Wednesday and Thursday mornings, January 9 and 10, had as their theme "The Woman's Role in the Synagogue World." Panels of outstanding

---

4. The delegates originating from the ancient communities of Eastern lands repeatedly expressed their objection to being included among the "Sephardi" segments, since their ancestors did not come from Spain or Portugal. They wished to be in a category of their own, distinguished from and equal to both Sephardim and Ashkenazim.

women leaders from nine countries followed presentations by Tova Sanhedria, Deputy Speaker of Israel's Knesseth, and Pearl Wadler, president of the Women's Branch of the Orthodox Union, with Rabbanith Sara Herzog of Israel and Rabbanith Brodie of Britain chairing the very-well-attended sessions.

This facet of the World Conference also was a first. This was the first time in history that Orthodox Jewish women's synagogue and kehillah forces convened on a worldwide scale.

An open-house reception for the women delegates by Rabbanith Herzog, at her Jerusalem residence, provided a warmly festive occasion for social mingling. A special tour of religious institutions and schools under women's sponsorship offered further reward.

~

For the delegates in general, various special events, in addition to the deliberative agenda, had memorable qualities of their own. A lavish reception for the delegates tendered by Jerusalem's Mayor Teddy Kollek at the Israel National Museum was a popular social occasion. In a different mood, one of profound, soul-stirring feeling, was the Yom Ha-Kaddish ceremony at the Yeshurun Synagogue.

Not to be forgotten by any of the participants was the spiritual impact of the Asarah B'Teveth Minchah assemblage at the Western Wall:

> When, marching together 2,000-strong in solemn procession to the Western Wall, all of us from our many lands and diverse backgrounds, shoulder to shoulder, and we then stood, amidst the vast multitude of our fellow Jews on that soul-shaking Asara B'Teveth before the Kothel itself—we knew that this was a moment distilled from the very essence of Jewish history, being, and purpose.

Sharing Shabbath festivities in the aura of Jerusalem's sanctity, the World Conference participants reached a new peak of their never-to-be-forgotten experience. While many delegates davvened together at the Hechal Shelomo Synagogue, others attended services at other of the Holy City's many battey k'nesseth, each of which offered a warm welcome to the World Conference participants. Oneg-Shabbath gatherings were conducted for the participants at the King David, Kings, and President Hotels. Each one featured guest speakers of distinction, and were marked by lively discussion and by fraternal warmth. Following Shabbath morning services, each conference participant was a guest, by special invitation, at one of the ten kiddush receptions tendered by ten distinguished Jerusalem personages at their respective homes.

All of those who had flocked to this unique assemblage from around the world flocked again, in the course of the Sabbath, to the Kothel "to offer their prayers and to be suffused with the profundity of emotion which this most sacred of all sites evokes in the Jew."

The series of World Conference events came to a close on Motzai Shabbath, 12 Teveth/January 13, with a symposium on "How Diaspora Communities View Their Future." Discussions were led by a panel including Rabbi Ralph Pelcovitz, past president of the Rabbinical Alliance of America and member of the UOJCA Board, Rabbi Trzaskala of the Consistoire Central of France, Rabbi A.N. Lapin of the Federation of Synagogues of South Africa, and S.S. Levin, Vice President of the United Synagogue of England. Here, the insights gained during the days of deliberation and thought exchange were applied to what lay ahead.

The ten resolutions adopted by this first World Conference of the synagogal-constituted Torah community were framed with much care to encompass the full consensus of its diversity of constituent organizations. They were prepared, for submission to and final adoption by the delegations, by the Resolutions Committee composed of representatives of the participating bodies, under the chairmanship of Lawrence A. Kobrin. The titles of the resolutions, indicative of the nature of each, are as follows:

1. The People of the Torah	2. The Sanctification of Existence
3. The State and the Land of Israel	4. The Synagogue and Israel
5. Our Rising Generation	6. The Synagogue and Torah Learning
7. Our Oppressed Brethren	8. Aid to Isolated Communities
9. Our Sacred Observances	10. Future Cooperation Among Our Communities

Within the frame of these unanimously adopted formulations are expressed, severally, the affirmation of unity in "our Faith and our Torah whose commandments are obligatory and binding for all Jewish generations"; the obligation of the synagogal community to "provide the inspiration and means both for individual observance and for community fulfillment of the Mitzvoth Ma'asiyoth which are at the core of Jewish life"; to bring Torah conviction to bear "on the endeavor to create a better future for all mankind"; and for Synagogue and Kehillah forces to devote fullest energies to satisfying "the spiritual thirst of those who now yearn for the knowledge of Torah and who seek the nearness of God."

Further within the resolutions frame is the call to each community and congregation to "have its share among the Olim to Eretz Yisrael," while sustaining "the struggle to ensure the preservation of Jewish Life in the Diaspora." The "sacred obligation" was stressed "for our community synagogues to activate young people in the functions and affairs of the congregation, to devise special cultural and social programs, guided by the letter and spirit of the Halachah, to satisfy their cultural and social needs," and to "befriend our children and to act as their guides in free-time activities suffused with Torah content and Jewish value," and to develop programs for Jewish students and support the establishment and functioning of Torah-committed student organizations on the campuses of universities and colleges.

The resolutions further called for the extension of programs of Torah learning to "every congregant—man, woman, or child—so that each may personally participate in the fulfillment of the command of Torah study"; for synagogues and kehilloth "to see to it that every Jewish child receives a Yeshivah education; that the synagogue program assumes responsibility for the maintenance of Torah day schools in every community, of a Mesifta or High School in every region or group of communities, and of at least one Yeshivah Gedolah or Kollel in every country or area." In turn, the yeshivah domain must be looked to "to view it as part of its responsibility to furnish from among its best students the personnel for training and service as rabbis, teachers, and lay leaders." Called for, too, was "the reaffirmation of the Rabbinate as the recognized custodian of Jewish destiny, as essential for our common task."

Extending on behalf of the organized Torah Synagogue world "the call of brotherhood to our brethren in the Soviet Union to whom religious and cultural freedom is being so shamefully denied," a resolution also called upon "the entire civilized world to apply all means possible to put an end to the physical persecution of the Jewish citizens in certain Arab countries."

The conference, in these expressions, also called upon "the vibrant centers of Jewish life" to "accept the historic responsibility for the small and isolated Jewish communities," by helping them to obtain rabbis, teachers, shochatim, and mohalim, and conducting programs of periodic visitations and ongoing contact. Among various expressions regarding Israel was one pointing to "special problems which have arisen in the State of Israel where Jewish verities have been cast aside for the sake of transitory considerations." No secular authority, the World Conference protested in this resolution, "has the right to abrogate, under whatever pretext, the Shabbath Kodesh."

The final resolution called upon the leaders of the participating national communal and synagogal bodies "to continue to maintain communications . . . and to take any steps they may deem desirable towards the all-pervading goal . . . in our mutual sacred endeavor to maintain Torah life ever based on the sanctity and immutability of Torah, the Written and Oral Law."

~

In summary, it may be said that:

The World Conference of Ashkenazi and Sephardi Synagogues was a potent demonstration of the strength and solidarity of the Synagogue-constituted Torah Community. It forged ties of mutual understanding and common purpose between the Jewries of east and west, and of Israel and Diaspora.

This first-time-ever assemblage of Orthodox synagogues and communities the world over enabled them to apply teamwork in the pursuit of shared goals.

The World Conference brought Orthodox Synagogue and Kehillah forces a new awareness of their role in the contemporary world; of their integral ties with each other and their combined power; and of their capacity to shape the direction of Jewish life.

~

As a newly born undertaking of multiple organizations, the World Conference of Ashkenazi and Sephardi Synagogues was not empowered to institute a mechanism for continuing activities. A remarkable practical achievement in itself, its effects were moral rather than material. Yet were there some specific practical consequences, as shall be cited below. Withal, the effect of the path-breaking conference was such that demands for a repetition were widespread and compelling enough not to be denied.

As directed, the key figures of the several organizations, with UOJCA president Karasick at their center, remained in communication and met together at opportune occasions during the months after the conference. The outcome was an agreement to convene a second World Conference in Jerusalem in Teveth 5732/January 1972.

It was further decided that, as reported by Dr. Weiss in his report for 1970, "The presidents of the participating organizations would not convene such a Conference unless called upon [to do so] by the Chief Rabbis of Israel and to maintain the principle of the original Conference not to place any Halachic matters on the agenda nor to permit their discussion from the floor, such matters being the preserve of the Orthodox rabbinate exclusively."

The calls from Israel's two Chief Rabbis jointly were duly forthcoming; arrangements then proceeded along the lines previously originated. The event, this time designated The Second World Conference of Synagogues and Kehilloth, took place in the same Jerusalem settings as before, running from Teveth 22–25, 5732/January 9–12, 1972. The pivotal figure in the guidance of the event, as before, was UOJCA president Joseph Karasick,

Steering Committee Chairman. The Bernstein, Rose, and Jaffe trio again arranged and directed the proceedings.

The attendance of the Second World Conference, this time, was from twenty-seven lands. If not reaching the emotional post-Six-Day War and first-time-ever pitch of before, this successor event was marked by sustained enthusiasm throughout.

The program of this second world assemblage of Torah forces followed the lines of its predecessor. An array of Torah-world personages and figures of high distinction from many parts addressed the various sessions and special events. Discussion at each session was on an impressive level throughout, and again the workshop sessions proved their value and appeal. Receptions and other social occasions contributed their informal warmth, and the aura of Jerusalem exercised, as ever, its incomparable spiritual magic.

In short, this second event of its kind—the World Conference of Synagogues and Kehilloth—was, as before, an experience ever to be treasured by every participant, and an accomplishment of surpassing value to the Torah cause.

31

From Departmentalization to Compartmentalization

Moving into its seventh decade, the Union of Orthodox Jewish Congregations of America had taken on a multitrack capacity with its diversity of activities. The Union had made itself felt across the Jewish world, as well as establishing a meaningful presence in regions across the United States and Canada. Its role in the renaissance of Torah spirit was manifest in the Karasick presidency, as it had been in the Feuerstein era. So, too, was its effectiveness as a leadership channel for the synagogue-constituted Torah community. Withal, the central congregational Union had gained recognition as a weighty force in Jewish world affairs and a factor in American public life.

The continuing course of the congregational Union paralleled the evolving state of its constituency. From the mid-1960s through the 1970s, Orthodox Jewry was visibly taking on further shape within the frame of American society. Economically, Orthodox Jewry was on a substantially higher level, as a whole, than the generations of before. Standards of education, both Jewish and secular, were notably beyond what had prevailed when the multitudes born of the immigrant flood were scrambling to find themselves spiritually while straining for livelihood. The Orthodox Jew was now *of*, as well as *in*, America, taking his due place in American life. This was occurring in larger measure, both numerically and sociologically, than at any previous time.

As yet, a large proportion of the gainfully employed among the Torah-observant ranks were, like many of their fellows of lesser observance, skilled or semiskilled wage earners in commercial or, in fewer cases, industrial fields. Among the mounting proportions of Jews in the various levels of ownership or management in business enterprises were those of the Orthodox fold. Now the Jewishly observant were increasingly visible in the professions—as physicians, lawyers, dentists, accountants, teachers, musicians, and scientists.

Of notable significance was the rise of the Association of Orthodox Jewish Scientists, a force new to Jewish history. The appearance of the Torah-loyal Jew in the fields of modern science was an aspect of response among the shomrey mitzvoth to new-age life. It was a mark of the capacity to maintain spiritual balance while finding the Torah way among the innovations of modern civilization.

The Orthodox scientists' organization, then newly coined, flourished over the years with its membership mounting to a thousand or more, and added branches in Great Britain and Israel. The presence of the association was to be felt in two spheres—that of the modern sciences and that of the Torah world. For a number of years, the Association of Orthodox Jewish Scientists, while always an autonomous body, was housed at the headquarters of the Orthodox Union, where it was provided, at its host organization's expense, with the necessary facilities. Subsequently the association moved to quarters of its own in Brooklyn.

At this time, the computer age, though already born, was yet to thrive. Not yet had arrived the fantastic technological development that was subsequently to provide a career field for thousands of Jewish men and women, a high proportion of whom were of the Orthodox fold.

In the 1960s and 1970s, numbers of the observant were also making careers in the Federal, state, and municipal civil services. Their abilities were suitably accommodated in these fields, together with provision for their Shabbath and Yom Tov requirements. In New York, the numbers of the observant in public-school teaching posts had, by this point, prompted the organization of the Association of Orthodox Jewish Public School Teachers. This organization was to function through the years since with a meaningful program. Membership, believed to be in the 1,500–2,000 range, later, according to report, experienced a decline currently owing to fewer young Jews entering the New York city schools system under circumstances of social change.

SHIFT OF RELIGIOUS CURRENT

In this period, religious currents took on a tendency curiously different from those prevalent in prior stages of American Jewish evolution. Leaving aside the earliest colonial and postcolonial era, with its unique characteristics, the consistent trend through the generations of American Jewish life had been the decline of religious-observance standards accompanying the rise of economic and social level. This trend was by no means absent in the years of the 1970s; but, remarkably, an opposite trend was also being simultaneously felt. In fact, prevailing standards in the traditionally observant domain were now more scrupulous and more consistently fulfilled than previously. Observance of Shabbath and the mitzvah life as a whole was now more conscientiously maintained than in the past, and in larger and steadily increasing numbers.

The seven decades of educational and ideological endeavor by the Orthodox Union had thus, by this stage, made their cumulative mark. Synagogues, better equipped and largely better led, were bringing a more defined Torah influence to their communities. With this, the rise of the yeshivah domain, rising in tempo from the early days of *"the* yeshivah" trailblazer in the New-World maelstrom to the latest of the continuing "new yeshivah" series had produced a generation whose influence, by the 1970s, was beginning to be strongly felt. The yeshivah ketanah day-school phenomenon was also, by this time, showing its revolutionary promise. And, under UOJCA leadership, Orthodox Jewry was beginning to address itself and the world coherently, and in its own terms of value.

In this ripening setting, the Union of Orthodox Jewish Congregations was proceeding along a rather loosely integrated network of distinct tracks.

RANGE OF "TRACKS"

One track—the main one essentially, but increasingly overshadowed in the public mind by others that touched more immediate personal interests— was that of the basic organizational capacity. This represented pursuit of the Union's primary mission: to serve as central force, plenary arm, and common voice of the synagogue-constituted Torah community. Functionally, this included conduct of the Union's everyday affairs; financial provision; general guidance and service to the congregational constituency in their collective and special needs; literary and vocal propagation of the tenets and beliefs of authentic Judaism and expression of its aims and views; representative spokesmanship in collective Jewish affairs and the channels of public life; relations with overseas Torah communities; and maintenance and functioning of the organizational structure—membership relations, the elected officers, the Board and Executive Committee, the commissions, the regions, and the Biennial Convention, parliamentary forum and highest governing body of the organization, its determinant of policy and program.

Within this "main track" was its complex of subtracks, and from it diverged others devoted to special functions that were adopted in the course of time. Each had a life of its own, intermeshed only in limited degree with that of the rest.

Outstanding, by the 1970s, was the kashruth service track. Of its nature, the Union's Ⓤ service was not so much a facet of the integral Union–congregation relationship as a relationship between the congregational Union and the individual Jew's home. It was also a relationship, by way of the Orthodox Union, between the home and the food industry.

The functions of the kashruth service were of a technical, specialized nature that could not fall into the general pattern of the Union's procedures. Hence, the Kashruth Division and its supervisory commission evolved into a self-enclosed area. As time went by and the Ⓤ operations became even more vast, the departmental staff necessarily grew, and the tasks of the departmental director at the time, Herman (Hal) Stein, the department rabbinic administrator, Rabbi Alexander S. Rosenberg, and his chief assistant, Rabbi Philip H. Reiss, grew more complex and more distant from the daily operations of the rest of the Union. Thus, the self-containment went beyond what the definitive 1956 departmentalization had envisioned. This tendency did not go unchecked, but it remained marked over the years.

The youth work constituted a self-contained track, not so much by its inherent separateness of character as by the impetus of its need and direction. Countless numbers of teenage boys and girls and student-age youths were "out there"—a boundless reservoir of young people likely to respond to what NCSY could offer, could they but be reached. Every community, every locality, had its numbers. Just as limitless was the recruitment urge of the Youth Division, headed by its director, Rabbi Pinchas Stolper, and his successive associate directors, Rabbi Chaim Wasserman and Rabbi David Cohen, plus Rabbi Louis Ginsberg as National Projects and Metropolitan Region Director, several other regional directors, and a steadily growing corps of Advisor enthusiasts. The staff was setting a pace that the lay commission was schooled to facilitate rather than to curb.

Balking at budgetary restraints, NCSY operations were forwarded, with the Karasick administration's keen support, at high pitch. Again and again, accomplished facts of unbudgeted expenditure were presented, with the UOJCA national administration under constraint to make good. Although the departmental leadership felt itself to be hobbled, the fact was, increasingly, that an ever-swelling proportion of the central Union's resources was being absorbed by the NCSY work. Since the Orthodox Union's income resources, though growing, were not keeping up with the rise in expenditure, other activities gave way before the Youth Division's surge. Thus, the needs of other departments and services were thrust aside to give right-of-way to NCSY growth.

The Union's leadership manifestly realized that the National Conference of Synagogue Youth, in serving so successfully a universally felt need, was fulfilling a basic Torah-community aim. Although for a period there was a curious tendency in NCSY operations and in its literature to underplay its Orthodox Union identity, the NCSY achievement was widely seen as adding to the prestige of the Union. These realizations caused the UOJCA administration to relax restraints on the Youth Division's budget-infringing course; only in the oft-recurring times of extreme fiscal crisis were temporary checks imposed. So, second only to the Kashruth Division, the Youth Division emerged as a self-contained compartment, a track of its own.

STAFFING

While the two foregoing departments had staff personnel engaged exclusively in their work—as did the Armed Forces Division during its years of function—others, although also of such individual nature as to constitute "tracks," had no staff assigned to them exclusively. These departments were conducted collectively by the Executice Vice President, Dr. Samson R. Weiss, and the Administrator, Saul Bernstein. Working under them at this time were two staff members of professional standing, and the clerical staff. These two were Sheldon Rothberg (in succession to Judah Kirshblum), serving as combination controller-head bookkeeper-office manager, and Rabbi Elkanah Schwartz, community relations and public affairs director and also the assistant editor of *Jewish Life* and *Jewish Action*.

Spreading forth from the "main track," whose responsibilities were as summarized earlier, were such subtracks as Budget, Finance, and Development; Membership Relations; Synagogue Servicing; Regions and Councils; Publications and *Jewish Life*; Communal Relations and Public Affairs; Israel and Overseas Jewries Relations; and Organizational Functioning—procedures of officers, Board of Directors and Executive Committee, Commissions, Special Committees, and the Biennial Convention.

The Budget, Finance, and Development track was, at this period, the concern of the Resources and Development Commission, with Morris L. Green, UOJCA treasurer, as Chairman. Together with the projecting of overall income and expenses, entailed here was the provision of funds for overall budgetary needs. This included conservation and development of the basic—in principle—income resource, namely the annual dues payable by member congregations. Originally of nominal amount, the dues rate had been set in the 1950s at $2 per year for each member of member congregations, and was now set, by 1968 convention action, at $5 per capita annually. But the new dues rate, at this early point in the 1970s, was not yet implemented, and the prior rate was, in fact, fulfilled by only a limited number of congregations; the rest remitted smaller, or even mere token, amounts.

A resource supplement of growing importance was the dues revenue of the Union's individual membership auxiliary, the Orthodox Union Association. Growing quietly from year to year, the OUA in future was to stand as a major supportive force, drawing membership not only from the Union's constituent congregations, but also from Torah-community individuals of all associations.

One UOJCA unit at the time, the Kashruth Division, fully covered its operational budget and—within the frame of the service-at-overall cost principle—shared equitably in the general administration and maintenance costs. Another function, the National Biennial Convention, covered under the administrator's direction most of its costs of preparation, promotion, programming, and in-hotel expense through registration fees and markup on the convention-site hotel-accommodations rates. Beyond this, however, with the conventions providing appropriate occasions for fund appeals, the sums contributed, beyond covering any balance of convention expense, provided large amounts toward the Union's general administration and maintenance costs.

The operations of most units were not such as could provide any fraction of their costs. Exceptions were Publications and *Jewish Life*, with the advertising and subscription income of the latter and the booklet-sales income defraying part of their operating costs. The Youth Department, too, through NCSY membership dues—though these were absorbed by their regions—and sales of regalia and such, raised some fraction of its expenditures.

The dues income, as yet very much short of the part it should properly play, and all the other sources cited combined, were far unequal to the total funding need. Filling the gap was the job of the Development arm of the track. Apart from planning ways to advance departmental income channels, the development process involved a focus on special contributions. The major project here, other than the fundraising occasions at the conventions, was the Annual National Dinner. This was a major element of the executive vice president's tasks. Innovative special projects were essayed, too, from time to time.

SPANNING THE REGIONS

Such areas as Synagogue Relations and Servicing, basic as they inherently are to the function of the Orthodox Union, warranted special professional staff of their own, but under the conditions of the Union's seventh decade, this was as yet hoped-for but not realizable in the light of other priorities. So, too, was it with the widespread undertakings on the Regions and Councils track, likewise under the administrator's charge.

Each regional convention or conclave involved planning, programming, and conducting events that were mostly on a three-day weekend pattern. Each, held at a different site, entailed publication and the recruitment of participation from widely dispersed communities. While these undertakings were conducted from the late 1950s on, continuing in varied forms to the present, of outstanding note were the number in close sequence over a fifteen-year period in the 1960s to 1970s. The nearly fifty regional conclaves in this series had an electric impact in bringing a sense of Torah-world renaissance to communities awakening to a new day. Each had registered attendances ranging from 150 to nearly 400, plus hundreds more visitors, and the audiences of up to 700 and more at the customary Saturday-night banquet sessions.

The locations of the 1960s to 1970s series were:

SOUTHEAST REGION: Atlanta; Memphis, Tennessee (2); Charleston, South Carolina (2); Nashville, Tennessee; New Orleans; Miami Beach; Birmingham, Alabama; Jacksonville, Florida

MIDWEST REGION: St. Louis (2); Skokie, Illinois; Kansas City, Missouri; Minneapolis–St. Paul; Milwaukee

CENTRAL STATES–GREAT LAKES REGION: Cleveland; Pittsburgh; Southfield, Michigan; Louisville, Kentucky; Cincinnati

ATLANTIC SEABOARD REGION: Baltimore; Richmond, Virginia; Washington, D.C.

NEW ENGLAND REGION: Brookline, Massachusetts; Hartford, Connecticut; Springfield, Massachusetts; New Haven, Connecticut

SOUTHWEST REGION: San Antonio, Texas; Galveston and Houston, Texas

NORTHWEST REGION: Seattle; Vancouver, British Columbia

Each region had its board, composed of leaders of the participating congregations. With most regions covering wide interstate areas, meetings of regional boards were infrequent, communications otherwise being irregular. The president and other regional officers were elected at regional conventions or assemblies. In varying degree, the leadership echelons of the several regions tended also to become figures in national UOJCA affairs, a valued complement to active circles.

Among those serving as presidents of regions in the 1960s to 1970s period were:

Abe Rabham of Savannah, Georgia, succeeded by Sam S. Margolin of Memphis, and he in turn by Al H. Thomas, also of Memphis, Southeast Region; Joseph R. Friedman of Chicago, succeeded by Ronald Green of St. Louis, Midwest Region; Ben Genauer of Seattle, later succeeded by Joseph Russak, Northwest Region; Donald Butler of Pittsburgh, Great Lakes–Central States Region; Edward S. Gerber, followed by Saul Isserow, both of Brookline, New England Region; Gilbert Cummins and Emanuel Reich, both successive presidents of the Baltimore Council of Orthodox Jewish Congregations and of the Atlantic Seaboard Region.

Many of the foregoing have continued in regional or national leadership roles in the years since.

Of special character was the Midcontinent Conclave and Leadership Conference, held at the Ambassador Hotel, Chicago, on Kislev 17–20, 5730/November 27–30, 1969. This event was projected and programmed as a national assemblage. With Herzl Rosenson of Chicago as chairman, it drew participation from several regions, including a complement of national officers and board members. Among the guest speakers was Chief Rabbi Immanuel Jakobovits of Great Britain.

In the Regions track, special effort was addressed to the Eastern Canada region and the Pacific Coast region.

CANADA CALLING

Several Montreal rabbis had turned to the Orthodox Union in 1963 with pressing requests for active work by the central Union in Montreal and other Quebec communities. In response there ensued successive visits by Dr. Weiss and Saul Bernstein, meeting with the leadership of the numerous Orthodox synagogues in the area and planning collective organization. These visits resulted in the recruitment of an intersynagogue representative body and the institution in 1964 of the Eastern Canada region. Officers were elected, with Dr. Melvin Schwartben (later succeeded by Moe Seidman) as regional president. Various activities were projected, and strong emphasis was placed on the development of chapters of the Union's National Conference of Synagogue Youth.

In each of the following several years, one-day and two-day regional assemblies were held that, together with actions taken in communal questions, lecture series, youth work and various other means, conveyed a sense of the Eastern Canada region of the Union as a significant and creative presence on the public scene.

It was quickly realized that without regular professional direction, an effective program and organizational continuity could not be maintained. Establishment of the regional director post being agreed upon, salary and expenses were to be met from regional dues income and fundraising projects, supplemented by an allocation from UOJCA headquarters. Appointment from among available candidacies was then made; the results not being satisfactory, the first incumbent was replaced. With income provision falling short and the regional promise being overshadowed by disappointments, the second incumbent in the regional directorship post eventually left. The search for another candidate with the necessary qualifications being unsuccessful, the Eastern Canada region endeavor thereafter languished, after several years of promise and good efforts by both the Montreal leadership group and UOJCA headquarters support. Since then, NCSY chapters have continued, but otherwise the Eastern Canada region retained but a shadow existence.

A Central Canada region, centered in Toronto, was also projected in this period. An initial regional conclave was held in 1969 in Hamilton, Ontario, with the attendance of representatives of a dozen or more congregations, and every mark of keen interest and promise. Thereafter, moves toward the formation of a regional body gained continuing interest, but without practical result. Here, too, the need for a regional director was felt. With Toronto taking on new dimension as a world metropolis and with its Orthodox Jewish community taking on dynamic development, there was every prospect of a large regional role under the Orthodox Union banner. Here, too, the NCSY has made a good foothold; otherwise, the notion of uniting the congregations of the area in a regionwide force continues to hold forth its promise, but the fulfillment is still sought.

THE WEST COAST

On the Regions track, among the toughest nuts to crack was the Pacific Coast region, centered in Los Angeles. Here was multiplying daily what soon came to be the second-largest Jewish population of any American city, and the second-largest American city. The character of Jewish life emerging in Los Angeles was likely to be important for the whole Jewish picture, but in the post-mid-century period, Jewish life in Southern California reflected the rootless swirl of its surroundings. Heterodoxy abounded, as did a good deal of the kookiness that flourished in the atmosphere of sunny California. There were by now a number of congregations of traditional tendency, but only a few of them were of definitive Orthodox commitment in practice and outlook. These, however, were sensible of the wider need and the opportunity that lay beyond the haze of transient makeshifts. So, the

Union's executive vice president, followed by the administrator, were duly dispatched on the California trail.

Through repeated visits by Dr. Weiss, some of several weeks' duration—with Administrator Bernstein coming also on occasion to build on the foundation laid by his colleague—the Pacific Coast region was duly established. In the face of the difficulties encountered among the quickly spawned conditions of the Southern California Jewish community scene, a good deal of improvisation was required. However, a representative regional board, with the backing of the more far-seeing among the rabbis, was set up, officers were elected, and an initial program of intercommunity and intersynagogue activities was launched. Earl Korchak of Los Angeles was installed as regional president, to be succeeded by Julius Samson of Beverly Hills, and he, in turn, by Sanford Deutsch.

Going beyond a number of regional meetings, the concept of a three-day weekend conclave was conveyed to the California communities by Saul Bernstein. Such a coming-together in shared multicommunity fellowship, with a thoughtful, purpose-enriching program, was a new experience for the participants recruited from across California. The event, at an attractive Palm Desert location, was highly successful and relished by all.

Among the undertakings launched were further intersynagogue occasions, youth work involving development of NCSY chapters, and means of bringing the Torah viewpoint and the combined influence of the traditional synagogues to bear in collective Jewish affairs on the West Coast.

A major project undertaken, designed, and formulated by Dr. Weiss was a full-scale institute of adult Jewish studies. This, offering a range of courses with a distinguished faculty, was launched in 1969, attracting a strong enrollment. Successful though it was, the institute was a strain on the young region's capacities. When Yeshiva University offered to absorb the institute in its new West Coast branch, the transfer was agreed upon and effected.

The need for a regional director being self-evident on the West Coast, there ensued a succession of incumbents. The right choice was finally made with the engagement, as regional director, of Lee Samson. His perceptive work was effective, and the Region now functioned meaningfully. Meanwhile, however, financial problems that had been felt from the first became increasingly burdensome; fundraising projects bore inadequate results. Differences between the regional leaders and national UOJCA headquarters as to allocations from the Union's funds were a recurrent irritation. When Lee Samson withdrew after several productive years, the region remained with but a semblance of existence, although the NCSY work was sustained. After languishing for some years, a reorganization in the 1980s brought the Pacific Coast region to new and vigorous life, functioning to the present day—and, by all indications, permanently—with sound accomplishment and every prospect of further achievement.

The years of earlier effort paved the way for the radical change in the religious complexion of the California Jewish scene. What was done in those years of path-breaking made possible the rise of Torah-committed life that was to come.

CITY AND INTER-CITY COUNCILS

Part of the regional composition were two units of lesser geographic range, the Eastern Pennsylvania and the Upstate New York districts. Each had its group of officers and undertook activities on an intercommunity basis. Periodic district conferences were held—for the Eastern Pennsylvania unit in Scranton and Harrisburg, and for the Upstate New York district in Syracuse, Rochester, and Utica.

A number of citywide councils of congregations were newly established or—in several pre-existing cases—reorganized during the 1960s and 1970s. Some of these were short-lived; others persisted, with ups and downs in their courses, for greater or lesser terms of years.

Already flourishing as an exemplar of community-wide intersynagogue cooperation was the Vaad Hoeir (Jewish Community Council) of St. Louis. Long headed by its revered chief rabbi, Rabbi Menachem Eichenstein (succeeded after his decease by Rabbi Sholom Rivkin), with Ben Hoffman as its long-time-chairman and ably directed by its executive secretary, Hyman Flaks, this kehillah-type body conducted a program of scope that is still maintained. Included were shechitah, providing the local kosher meat and poultry supply; kashruth supervision for other locally produced products; maintenance of the local day schools and the yeshivah; various educational and communal activities; and important public-affairs work, with effective results in local, state, and Federal measures affecting Jewish interests.

Hyman Flaks was presently invited to serve, in addition to his Vaad duties, as director of the Midwest region. He occupied this post, along with his original responsibilities, for several years, until settling as an oleh in Israel in the 1980s.

On the Councils subtrack, ever-notable has been the Council of Orthodox Jewish Congregations of Baltimore. Almost all of Baltimore's Orthodox synagogues are joined in this body, a fruitful channel for intercongregational community teamwork. The council acts on local and state issues of Jewish concern; conducts educational activities; supports kosher dining clubs in the area's universities and colleges; cares for Jewish patients in hospitals; and sponsors local NCSY chapters. The Council consistently forwards the application of various facets of the UOJCA national program on the local scene.

The high point of the Baltimore Council's program is its annual Torah Institute. This three-day retreat is held in early summer of each year at a picturesque mountain location. The scores of participants—originally men only—engage in informal Torah study groups and in informative, inspirational lectures on subjects of topical reference given by a chosen faculty, amid a woodland setting and an atmosphere of intimate friendship.

Numerous traditional communities across North America have drawn from the Baltimore retreat concept in adaptation to their own Torah Institute and retreat patterns. Almost all of these diverge from the Baltimore Council's original format in including women as well as men, and often children, too, making for a family atmosphere. Long an exemplar of success in this format was the Gatlinburg Torah Institute of the Union's Southeast region, popular and highly influential for many years and attracting participants from many points.

THE "HOME" TRACK

The development of a functioning region for Metropolitan New York itself, with the largest urban Jewish population in the world, has presented special difficulty, precisely because of its massiveness, through much of the Orthodox Union's history. Here, the hundreds upon hundreds of Orthodox congregations have less a sense of need for identification with and support of a strong central force than those of "out-of-town" communities, and often have less community consciousness. Each congregation is a world unto itself—until, that is, a problem situation arises, when its leaders are apt to turn to Orthodoxy's national force for aid.

A regional format for the Union's home area was essayed a few times in earlier years, and once again during the 1960s upsurge. Upon the realization that the possibility of practical results in this massive area necessitated hands-on, ongoing professional direction, a regional director of promising qualifications was engaged, and some months of effortful probing and project-launching ensued. Despite his diligence, the director had permitted himself to follow unfruitful trails, was daunted, and left for a position overseas. The hoped-for Metropolitan New York region became dormant again.

But the time was coming for the Metropolitan region of UOJCA to be reborn, this time to an active life. Its rebirth in 1980 came under the leadership of a broad-visioned vice president of the Union, Gerald E.

Feldhamer. Productive of fruitful undertakings, the Metropolitan New York region made a strong, enduring place for itself on its multisynagogue scene and bore, this time, a sound prospect for growth as the unifying arm of New York's congregations of Torah Jewry and in their voice in the affairs of the metropolis of the Western world.

32

With the
Printed and Spoken Word

Jewish Life, in a category by itself among Jewish periodicals, was continuing to win distinction at the 1971 quarter-century point of its publication history. Besides a following across the spectrum of Orthodox Jewry, the magazine was well-respected among the Jewishly concerned at large. "Be it noted that our subscription lists (consisting basically of voluntary paid subscriptions) include readers in a score of overseas countries and Israel as well as in all parts of the United States and Canada," it was pointed out in the report on *Jewish Life* in the 1970 convention delegates' handbook.

A supplementary report in the same source by Rabbi Elkanah Schwartz, in his capacity as assistant editor of *Jewish Life*, said: "The hallmark of *Jewish Life* has always been quality. The readers, in their many categories, have come to expect a quality magazine, in content, in variety, and in timeliness."

Listing, with brief annotations of each, a selection of articles from the preceding two years' issues of *Jewish Life* that had evoked wide discussion, Rabbi Schwartz stated:

> The attention won by such *Jewish Life* contributors as these were underlined by letters and calls from readers, by requests for quantities of copies of the issues in which they appeared, for bulk copies of reprints in pamphlet form, and by requests for permission to reprint by other publications. Reprints of the articles listed [above] and numerous others appeared, by permission, not only in various U.S. and Canadian publications but also by others in England, Australia, and South Africa and also, in translation, in Israel, France, and Latin American countries.

The extent to which editorial expressions in *Jewish Life* were particular subjects of attention in diverse circles—non-Orthodox as well as Orthodox—was itself a matter of remark among observers of the Jewish scene, it was also noted here. According to one commentator, "These editorial views are echoed in pulpits across the land."

While devotees of *Jewish Life* constantly urged the increase of its bimonthly publication frequency to monthly, some in the Union's administration saw the budgetary preferences in a different light. Under budget-paring pressures, with other needs having greater priority, it was officially decided that the magazine's frequency, instead of being increased, would actually be reduced—to a quarterly schedule. In light of the standing and influence of *Jewish Life*, this decision may be taken retrospectively as a measure of the pressure of the Union's financial plight rather than of objective assessment.

The Publications Division, with the perceptive Lawrence A. Kobrin as chairman of the supervising commission, otherwise continued its established program. This included *Jewish Action*'s regular appearance and range of content. Its character as house news organ, featuring principal UOJCA activities and major events, with some items of noteworthy developments among the synagogues, served the purpose to rather minimal extent in that period.

A resource as much drawn upon as previously was the array of booklets—the festivals series, popular expositions of Judaism and the mitzvoth, items on contemporary issues, biographies of great figures, and others. These resources were drawn upon by congregations for distribution in their communities in scores of thousands of copies annually. Serving more specialized needs, for categories of synagogue leaders, were practical manuals on synagogue programming, administration, membership development, and fundraising. The utility of these manuals in bringing instruction to those serving responsible synagogue posts needs no underlining. Especially so, when the turnover of office with greater or lesser frequency brings an annual crop of new incumbents with need for qualified means of guidance in their respective spheres of responsibility.

The output in these categories, large though it was in serving the central Union's normative constituency and the Jewish public generally, was now dwarfed by that of the Youth Department. Now rapidly emerging was a veritable library of contemporary youth literature, from pamphlets and booklets innumerable to full-size volumes. Written for the contemporary teenager or student, these publications addressed questions spoken and unspoken; shed light on the what, why, and how of the authentic Jewish way; and brought guidance to the seekers, information to the learners. All this, plus an array of organizational programmatic and procedural matter, was now being written, produced, and proffered to its youthful audience and their adult leaders in unprecedented abundance. Much of the material was well presented, other material less so; but, all in all, the NCSY literary arsenal was beyond comparison in kind and range among the reading fare presented for Jewish youth by Jewish sources or otherwise available to the searching Jewish teenager.

Many of the items published by the Youth Division were written by Rabbi Stolper himself. Others were products of the outpouring genius of Rabbi Aryeh Kaplan. Much of the editorial production was handled by the diligent Yaakov Kornreich.

This NCSY output had taken on such proportions, as the 1960s became the 1970s, that—in the hope of lessening printing costs—in-house type-setting and printing equipment was installed. This included computer word-processing equipment, with senior clerical staff trained to function with what was then mysteriously unfamiliar technology; photo-offset and printing machinery was also acquired, and the requisite qualified personnel engaged for these operations.

After several years, however, with the availability of these facilities as unshakable stimulus to an increase in publication, the economics of the innovation was viewed askance by responsible quarters. The photo-offset and printing equipment was then sold at a fraction of its cost. Thereafter, the NCSY literature output was modified from a flood to a controllable stream, and so continued over the years.

The Kashruth Division, too, was making its own special and substantial contribution to the Union's publications output. As with everything in this department's ever-swelling frame, its printed and published material con-tinued to multiply spontaneously from year to year. The Ⓤ directories for year-round and kosher-for-Pesach products were in mass demand around the country, distributed in the hundreds of thousands of copies. The Ⓤ *News Reporter*, listing new additions to the products and services under official UOJCA supervision, published frequently, appeared often on syna-gogue bulletin boards everywhere. Press and food-industry sources were sent materials especially prepared for them.

THE EXTERNAL AFFAIRS TRACK

Legislative matters, the communal relations field, and activities for the support of Israel and defense of domestic and worldwide Jewish interest constituted another area of vital concern and heavy demand that lacked the special full-time professional staff so manifestly warranted. In these areas, hands-on participation by senior administration and commission personnel, as well as by the Union's top officials, was requisite, but continuous attention and expert command of a boundless range of developing situa-tions and intricacies of relationships was essential to effectively facilitate and complement the actions of the aforementioned in determining and pursuing applicable UOJCA policy. Later, the incorporation of these various fields of involvement into the Institute of Public Affairs established a departmentalized format for them, with special staff provision. At the 1970s stage, prior to this innovation, Rabbi Elkanah Schwartz, as previously mentioned, counted the Communal Relations Commission's sphere among his multiple duties.

At the time, matters of law and legislation, heretofore under the Communal Relations Commission umbrella, was designated a separate commission, with Samuel L. Brennglass as its chairman. Serving successively as Communal Relations Commission chairman were Joel Balsam and Dr. Marvin Schick.

A major focus of Communal Relations Commission attention in this period was the National Jewish Community Relations Advisory Council, popularly referred to as NJCRAC. Technically, the commission's jurisdiction also included the UOJCA delegation to the Synagogue Council of America, but this group, chaired by Julius Berman, in actual practice reported directly to the administration.

UOJCA association with the National Jewish Welfare Board now consisted of appointment of a member of its national advisory board. Since the original NJWB composition as an interorganizational body had been replaced by a self-contained organizational makeup, the relationship, on the part of the Orthodox Union, was without substance.

Important among the Union's external-affairs ramifications was the recently devised Conference of Presidents of Major National Jewish Organizations. Although unduly loaded by the ingenuity of its originator, Dr. Nahum Goldmann, with inclusion of a number of organizations whose factual existence was a mystery, this book, otherwise including the heads of all leading organizations, had quickly acquired status and influence. It had proved to be an effective means for consultation and joint action on developments affecting Israel's security, winning attention in highest governmental and congressional quarters. With the personalized basis of the composition of the Presidents' Conference conditioning the relationship, the Union's concerns here were under immediate administration direction.

So it was, too, with a new addition to the Orthodox Union's "roof association" affiliations, the World Jewish Congress. The association with this valued channel of international activity on behalf of Jewish welfare had been undertaken when an invitation to the Union to affiliate with the WJC was referred to a special committee headed by Joseph Karasick; a favorable recommendation resulted; the UOJCA Board in 1970, upon recommendation of the officers, approved the affiliation. It was reported subsequently that the participation of UOJCA representatives at World Jewish Congress meetings was both warmly welcomed and highly effective. Joseph Karasick was designated chairman of the North American section of the World Jewish Congress.

The Orthodox Union was now also represented on the Board of the former Jewish Claims Conference, the Memorial Foundation for Jewish Culture and Education. This, too, was effectuated under direct Administration attention.

The Union's participation in the various roof organizations was not free of questions as to the propriety of placing Orthodox Jewry in the position of being but one among a multiplicity of Jewish associations of, in principle, equal standing. There appeared no tendency from any quarter to press this point, and the practical utility of such participation, subject to proper projection of Torah view, was well recognized. The disputed Synagogue Council of America remained under a cloud, and all moves within and by the Synagogue Council were under scrutiny, to assure that they were within the frame of external relations and free of infringement on religious outlook. In contrast to the delimited and hesitant Synagogue Council association, that with the National Jewish Community Relations Advisory Council was thought of at this time in UOJCA circles as valuable and important.

The NJCRAC in this period had gained in public standing. Its composition bore weight, including, as it did, most of the leading national Jewish organizations and the full roster of local and regional Jewish community relations councils. Adequately financed, its professional staff, headed then by Isaiah Minkoff—well seasoned in Jewish affairs—was of expert caliber in that agency's fields of concern.

The National (Jewish)[1] Community Relations Advisory Council had been born as an undertaking of several participants in the 1943 American Jewish Conference, which, as was noted in an earlier chapter, had been organized on pro tem basis to act for Jewish interests. The NCRAC was constituted as an interorganizational mechanism for coordination through consensus on issues touching Jewish–non-Jewish relations.

In the NJCRAC structure, standing committees were instituted to give close study to developments in the various ongoing areas of concern, with appointment of special committees to deal with new problems as they arose. Their findings—with majority and minority reports as occasion might require—were acted on at the agency's annual plenary assembly. Policy stand, with recommendation as to procedure on each matter dealt with, was then published for common guidance in the annual NCRAC Joint Program Plan. Where unanimity was not reached, the rules provided that

---

1. The word "Jewish," not originally included, was added later.

publication of the majority position be followed by statement (or statements) of dissent by the source or sources of minority stand.

The Orthodox Union had not been among the original participating organizations of the NCRAC. In 1959, a formal invitation to the Union to affiliate had been tendered by the National Jewish Community Relations Advisory Council. Following consideration by the Union's officers and Board, the invitation was accepted and thereupon the Union of Orthodox Jewish Congregations of America became a participating organization of the National Community Relations Advisory Counsel, on the same basis as the rest.[2]

The participation of the central Torah-community arm enhanced the status of the NJCRAC and its scrupulously observed consensus process. With the joint community-relations advisory body otherwise rising in public influence, the American Jewish Committee was also presently moved to join, too. This agency, determined to be considered in an authoritative spokesmanship class by itself, had hitherto held aloof; its affiliation now further reinforced the array of participating organizations. In time, however, the benefit of this was qualified by the tendency toward domination of the affairs of the National Jewish Community Relations Advisory Council by three groups: the American Jewish Committee, the American Jewish Congress, and B'nai B'rith. It is within the climate of weighted influence thus operative that UOJCA participation has functioned.[3]

Both Dr. Marion Schick and Joel Balsam, as with Samuel L. Brennglass previously, manifested a keen grasp of the attitudes to be dealt with and a deft mode of procedure in conducting their Torah-professed way through NJCRAC channels. Each, in turn, together with Rabbi Schwartz, personally participated in a number of the NJCRAC committees, including its Executive Committee, and guided other Communal Relations Commission members in their participation. Both men, in their successive terms of Commission chairmanship service, contributed on behalf of the Orthodox Union Torah-keyed views on the matters under consideration in the

---

2. This writer recollects that Isaiah Minkoff, executive vice-chairman of NCRAC from its inception, addressed the Union's Board by arrangement at the time to further the invitation. Falling short, on this occasion, of his usual informed sagacity, a patronizing expression used in the course of Minkoff's presentation left an unfortunate impression. This was discounted, however, in arriving at an affirmative decision.

3. It is to be noted, however, that over the years, until the "Orthodox bashing" affray of 1989 and after, scrupulous adherence was maintained to the basic provisions of nonintrusion into matters beyond the constitutional community relations purview of the NJCRAC, and its established procedures.

NJCRAC processes that bore influence on the deliberations. Each in turn formulated, in consultation with senior Union officials, Joint Program Plan statements of dissent from the majority stand on such contested issues of the period as governmental support of religious-related schools and inter-religious relationships.

The abovementioned figures benefited much by consultation with Dr. Weiss, as well as by the work in this area by Rabbi Schwartz. Dr. Weiss also personally participated, together with the administrator and each Communal Relations chairman, in the NJCRAC plenary assemblies. At these multiple-day and heavily programmed meetings, the attending top figures of the national and local organizations from across the country were impressed by the caliber of the UOJCA representatives, who, in these years, played a notable part in the deliberations.

It is useful to be cognizant of the means afforded by the Orthodox Union participation in NJCRAC to contribute to the collective Jewish community the Torah outlook on social questions facing American society. Apart from issues of special concern to Torah Jewry, the moral and social well-being of American life has been recognized since the Union's earliest days as among its vital concerns, in themselves and in their effects on Jewish life.

Since matters of community relations derive largely from the social and moral currents stirring American society, these necessarily fall within the NJCRAC purview. It is accordingly seen as important that, in the formulation of the collective American Jewish stands on such circumstances as arise, the outlook of Orthodox Jewry be voiced and heard—*in its distinctiveness.*

Reciprocally, the NJCRAC participation has stimulated the consideration of questions facing American society and humankind-at-large in the ever-crowded UOJCA agenda itself. Over the years, Biennial Convention resolutions have marked the trend of Torah-community thinking in these areas.

Examples of these expressions in the 1960s to the 1970s are appended to this chapter.

In the late 1960s–early 1970s period, the Union's participation in NJCRAC seems to have been more sustained and with stronger impress than was perhaps to be the case thereafter. As was expressed in the 1972 Communal Relations Commission report by Rabbi Elkanah Schwartz, in his capacity as director:

> The policy formulation and program planning process with which the Commission is charged is done to a significant extent within the framework of the larger community, both for the purpose of strengthening its thrust in those issues where there is consensus, and for exerting our influence in the issues where the Union's stand differs from that of other communal bodies.

In the nine national organizations which with 93 local and regional community relations councils constitute the National Jewish Community Relations Advisory Council, UOJCA is the only voice of a wholly-Orthodox constituency, representing the Torah viewpoint. Often, ours has been an influential voice. But even when we differ, it becomes known that the collective voice of the other organizations cannot speak for the totality of the Jewish community.

Thus our policy direction to the community is supported by other groups on domestic issues such as the Jewish poor, integrated public education, religious practices in public schools, Shechitah, and Sabbath observance protection, and on such international issues as support for Israel's position in the world, interpreting the Holocaust, Genocide Convention, and Jews in Arab lands.

However, . . . where the policies we seek to project are not supported by the other agencies, we abstain or record dissent from the majority position and state opposing views. . . . It is the Union's position, dissenting from the views of the non-Orthodox agencies, that government aid to the secular programs of religiously affiliated schools, through direct grants or such means as vouchers and tax credits, does not breach the separation of Church and State. In the past, we had found it necessary to similarly dissent on the subject of inter-religious dialogue. Recently, however, the non-Orthodox agencies, which had heretofore advocated such dialogues, have come to accept and support our view.

Torah thinking, combined with our greater communal strength, has moved the Commission to adopt in behalf of the Orthodox Union different positions on some social issues. Notable among them are equal rights for women (the proposed 27th Amendment), where we dissented, and the general issue of affirmative action, preferential treatment, and quotas, where our position differed somewhat from that of the non-Orthodox community.

Rabbi Schwartz also cited as products of commission effort the securing from NJCRAC of a "Statement of Responsibility of Community Relations for Jewish Education"; and, through participation in recent General Assemblies of the Council of Jewish Federations, emphasis for the first time in its formal policy statement on Jewish education. Synagogues were then mobilized to press for implementation of these calls by the local fund federations.

It is useful to note that UOJCA experience with "roof agency" participation, here and generally, shows that the mandatory condition for such participation is continuous, fully informed attention to what is before the given agency, full perception of the ramifications of any given question, the ability to properly assess the matter in terms of Orthodox Jewish values, and the capacity to convey the Torah community stand, in its distinctive terms, lucidly and effectively.

Selections from Resolutions on Social Issues Adopted at 1960s–1970s Bienniel Conventions

1962   WORLD PEACE AND NUCLEAR WARFARE

The specter of a nuclear war which can result only in the destruction of all civilization and from which there cannot possibly emerge any victor, hovers perilously close over the nations of the world. The continued tests of nuclear weapons and the resulting radioactive fallout and the failure of the big powers to agree on the cessation of such tests, weigh heavily upon the souls of men everywhere.

The Messianic vision of universal peace, as pronounced by the prophets of Israel and as daily uttered in the sacred prayers of our people, is the only realistic goal of world statesmanship. We call upon the community of nations and their leaders to utilize all avenues of international diplomacy to bring about the climate of international understanding in which alone this goal can be realistically pursued.

We call upon the President of the United States to intensify the efforts of our government to bring about the complete cessation of all nuclear arms tests and to achieve subsequent general disarmament, seeking in concert with the other nations the appropriate means to obtain the necessary international agreements on inspection and control.

We further call upon the President and the Government of the United States to accelerate the American effort to make available to the nations of the world the results of scientific advances in the peaceful use of nuclear energy, turning into blessing what is now a universal bane.

1962   SPACE EXPLORATION

Mankind is witnessing the unlocking of new horizons by the genius of man who is transforming yesterday's scientific dreams into today's bold realities, penetrating into outer space and gaining new insights into the mysteries of the universe.

Great Jewish thinkers throughout the ages have always perceived of the scientific quest as one of the great portals to the knowledge of the Almighty. Accordingly, we firmly believe that these explorations can lead mankind to a deeper recognition of the dominion of the Creator Whose wisdom established this universe and its rules and Whose glory is recounted by the expanse of the heavens. We also firmly believe that the exploration of space can bring untold benefits to humanity if pursued with peaceful aims secured within the framework of binding international covenants.

The exercise of moral control over all physical power is a basic Biblical postulate. Any increase of power unaccompanied by such control breeds evil and destruction. Thus, man standing at the threshold of a new age is called upon by Divine Providence to match his scientific genius by the proportionate development and exercise of his moral genius, a genius vouchsafed to him by being created in the image of his Maker.

We therefore see great danger in the over-emphasis and glorification of science in education, tending to make science a goal rather than a tool, a purpose in itself rather than an instrument for the good. We call upon the leaders of education everywhere to stress the moral direction of the scientific endeavor in the curricula of elementary and high schools, colleges and universities.

We call upon the United Nations to establish a covenant regulating the exploration of space, assuring humanity that such exploration will be undertaken in its service and for peaceful purposes only. We call upon the governments of the United States and Canada to lend their good offices to this end and accordingly to instruct their respective delegations to the United Nations.

1962   MORAL SAFEGUARDS

The moral fiber of American society is gravely endangered by the rising tendency to disregard any standards of decency in the field of publications, motion pictures and television.

An avalanche of filth is inundating newsstands, drugstores and bookstalls. Under the guise of artistic expressions, pornography is flooding this country. Lurid portrayals, in words and pictures, of sexual passion and perversion, fill paperbacks, hard cover books and magazines. Domestic and foreign motion pictures often vie with the printed publications in suggestiveness and actual depiction of moral depravity, concentrating on sexual excitement and scenes of brutal violence. The television industry to an extent follows suit.

Chastity and marital integrity are all too often depicted as outworn notions and sexual license and adultery as the norm. The foundations of society are likewise undermined by the glorification of cunning and brutality, with the triumph of justice and goodness more often than not presented as a most unconvincing appendage and afterthought.

We affirm our basic commitment to the concept of freedom of expression which is enshrined in the Bill of Rights and the constitution of the United States. We oppose, therefore, censorship by government action, deeming legislative restriction upon freedom of speech and freedom of the press a last resort. We are persuaded furthermore, that the present obscenity laws, upheld by the United States Supreme Court as properly proscribing utterances of so-called "hard core pornography", are extremely difficult of administration and application, for the absence of any "intended" social or literary idea or scientific interest must be proven.

Accordingly, it becomes the imperative duty of all responsible forces within American society to join in combatting this onslaught upon the moral health of this nation. We therefore urge the establishment of a voluntary Council composed of representatives of the several religious communities, the arts, the sciences, and appropriate civic bodies and of the publishing, motion picture, radio and television industries. It shall be the function of their Council to serve as a medium for the interchange of ideas and views with respect to these media of public expression and to establish self-policing procedures binding by common and voluntary consent upon all members of these industries.

We call upon the President of the United States to convene as soon as feasible a White House Conference on Public Morals for the purpose of exploring the best ways and means for the early establishment of such a voluntary nationwide Council.

1962   IMMIGRATION

The planks of both the Democratic and Republican parties contain clear statements on the need for revision of the Immigration and Nationality Act of 1952. Both parties state in their respective planks that the National-Origins quota system must be replaced and our immigration policy be based upon the individual merit of each applicant for admission and citizenship. A Bill introduced in March of this year by Senator Philip A. Hart of Michigan, co-sponsored by 26 senators of both parties, addresses itself to this racist quota system which more than any other provision of the Immigration and Nationality Act has engendered severe criticism from leading American religious and civil national organizations as contrary to our democratic principles and as damaging to our foreign relations.

While affirming our support of this bill, we call upon the Congress of the United States to enact, in addition to the Hart amendment, also such additional amendments as will bring about:

the elimination of the present harsh deportation provisions; the elimination of the present unjust distinction between native-born and naturalized citizens; the establishment of fair appellate procedures in immigration and nationality matters.

We urge President Kennedy to use the power and prestige of his office in behalf of such legislation, in keeping with the platform of his party and in keeping with his own declarations, while a member of the Senate, advocating the revision of the present Immigration and Nationality Act.

1964   CIVIL RIGHTS

The people of the United States has entered into a new era with the enactment of the Civil Rights Act of 1964, which definitively implements the basic American principle of the equality of all citizens, of whatever ethnic origin or creed.

We are deeply aware of the fact that laws do not necessarily create new human attitudes nor change overnight prejudices instilled by long habit and social tradition. Yet, the law is the fundamental expression of moral direction and intent of a nation. While mindful, therefore, of the many difficulties and frictions the American people must reasonably expect in this area of civic life, we call upon all citizens not to be deterred by these difficulties, but rather to accept them as the almost inevitable price of human progress. We call upon all American Jews to give the full cooperation to the Community Relations Service, established under the Civil Rights Act of 2964, and its National Citizens Advisory board, which will assist community leaders in resolving racial tensions and assuring harmonious observance of the law.

We note with satisfaction the contributions made by the UOJCA Communal Relations Commission, directly and through the Union's participation in the National Community Relations Advisory Council, to the advancement of Civil Rights and look to the said Commission to give continued leadership and direction to the Torah Community in this area of human need.

1966   CIVIL RIGHTS

America is today in the midst of a major revolution as Negroes and other disadvantaged minority ethnic groups demand as human beings the true measure of the equality granted by the Creator but sometimes denied by human beings. Jewish tradition and Jewish history make the Jews particularly sensitive to the needs and rights of minority groups.

We recognize the need for minority groups to conduct and man their own agencies for securing civil rights, and to pursue such policies and programs as represent their autonomous views. However, we deplore the fact that efforts towards this purpose have on occasion been accompanied by overtly Anti-semitic and other clearly racist, anti-White expressions on the part of militant extremists.

Such manifestations, contradicting the very principles on which the civil rights movement rests, are bound to undermine the attainment of its objectives.

We call upon all Jews to resist the sterile reaction of the "backlash" and to continue to erase bigotry, intolerance and prejudice from their own business, professional and personal lives, and to support all endeavors to secure equal rights or special assistance for Negroes and all minority groups in employment, housing and education so that the victims of racial or ethnic discrimination may achieve their complete rights as Americans and as human beings.

In furtherance of these purposes, we call upon our member congregations and Jews everywhere not to patronize or sponsor activities at public accommodations which discriminate against anyone because of race or religion; to further fair employment practices by including non-discriminatory provision in contractual commitments; to institute and enforce non-discriminatory employment and promotion practice in business endeavors and to patronize those businesses and enterprises which have such policies, and to give active support to the passage of strong local, state and federal civil rights legislation.

1966   MORAL STANDARDS

We reaffirm our prior resolution on Moral Standards calling upon the
American community to affirm the immutability of the moral law established
by the Creator, to base the policies of public and private education on the firm
moral values of chastity, honesty, personal goodness and integrity, and to
pronounce the primacy of the spiritual and intellectual endeavor over the
current hedonistic quest for sensual satisfaction.

In recent years, new and even more threatening danger signals have
appeared on the scene of the American society which indicate the severe
threat to which its very fiber is exposed. Pervading sexual license on
the college campus, the use of hallucinatory drugs, and similar excesses are
rampant among young people, endangering the ability of the American
community to preserve and to transmit its ideas and its values. In an orderly
society, the natural rebelliousness of youth is a great asset which calls for a
constant review of accepted values and promoting, by its challenge, human
progress. Present trends, however, appear more akin to a denial of fundamental decencies and a rejection of all established authority without which
society can neither function nor undergo meaningful changes.

When the exercise of license and excess is claimed as a right, we must fear
that the vital distinction between personal freedom and anarchy is slowly
being eroded. We consider this danger so serious that we call upon the
President of the United States to convene as soon as possible a conference of
leading educators, sociologists and thinkers, among them religious leaders, to
a White House Conference on Moral Standards for the purpose of earnestly
considering the great problems inherent in these developments and of
proposing the methods and techniques to secure and to promote the moral
foundations which will insure the integrity of the American community.

Such a Conference would give recognition to the pervasive nature of the
problem of moral standards and personal code of life which is not merely a
concern of religious teachers and institutions but must always remain a basic
component of civilized life for which all people are responsible.

1968   THE URBAN CRISIS

The struggle for equality by Negroes and other minorities of the American
nation has entered a new phase. Its emphasis has turned from efforts to
eliminate discrimination through law to the social action arena. The pursuit of
improved conditions and greater local control of community affairs have
become focal issues. A racial character has thus been added to what were
already critical urban problems. The passions of the civil rights movement
now threaten to erupt violently unless the problems of the slums are solved.

The problems of our cities—deteriorating housing, widespread unemployment, poor schools and rampant crime, among others—have been increasing
over the years. The cities lack the financial resources to cope with them.
Negroes and other minorities inhabiting the inner cities have become

increasingly frustrated in their inability to improve their lot and some have taken to the streets to protest their cause. Rioting and looting have followed in a number of areas. Jews, tending to live in urban areas and owning businesses in the inner cities, are especially affected by this turmoil.

In this matter as in all aspects of life the Orthodox Jew looks to Halachah for direction. Numerous precepts of our Torah teach the collective responsibility of society to care for its underprivileged. In the formulation of the Rambam the highest degree of charity is to assist a person in becoming self-supporting. Basic to the Torah approach to this problem is the concept that man, created in the Divine Image, must in the conduct of his life imitate the Divine attributes, such as mercy and compassion. For these reasons Orthodox Jews have always been in the forefront of the battle for social justice.

The Orthodox Union believes that the time has come for our nation to recognize its obligation to improve the quality of life for all Americans. We believe that our great nation has the resources to give every individual as much education as he can absorb without regard to ability to pay; to provide employment for all who are able to work and job-training for those who wish to work at better jobs; to assist the needy in obtaining decent housing; in short, to permit all Americans to live lives of dignity. We believe that such an effort is not only right as a matter of social conscience, but will result in a stronger and more prosperous America.

Only the Federal Government can marshal the financial resources to underwrite such a program. Yet, it is important that the private sector of our economy be utilized as much as possible and it is essential that the poor who are to be the beneficiaries be active participants in administering the program.

Any pursuit of these goals must respect the rights and legitimate interests of others. We reject blanket application of a concept of reverse discrimination as immoral and self-defeating. We deplore the anti-Semitic and racist expressions of some extremists and trust that they will not deter the majority of Jews from continuing the pursuit of social justice. We call upon the incoming Administration of the Orthodox Union to formulate guidelines for its constituent synagogues to aid them in taking more active roles in local community councils and in establishing lines of communication with the leadership of other minority groups.

1970   CAMPUS UNREST

The passivism and lack of concern that held sway on the college campus during the 1950's has turned to the activism of the Sixties and Seventies. Some students, not content to pursue this activism by peaceful methods, have resorted to the rhetoric and use of violence. In the process they have transformed many of our great universities into battlegrounds, resulting in the death and maiming of innocent people, destruction of property and disruption of education.

We view with anguish and deep concern the violence and disruptions that have taken place on college campuses. For the University to play its vital role in our society, the hallowed tradition of academic freedom must be scrupulously guarded or, perhaps we should say with a note of sadness, restored. Heckling, shouting obscenities or otherwise preventing others from voicing their opinions have no place on campus; nor do students or faculty who seize buildings or otherwise disrupt the educational process.

We call upon college administrators to act resolutely in curbing these disruptions, using as much restraint as possible, but being prepared to call in the legal authorities if necessary. Where disruptions consist of criminal acts, college administrators have the duty to make certain that the offenders are prosecuted. Students or faculty who commit crime have no right of sanctuary on campus.

At the same time, we recognize that the long-range solution to the crisis on campus lies in coming to grips with those problems disturbing our youth that play such a large part in campus ferment.

As bearers of the tradition that introduced the concept of social justice to the world, Torah Jews are the first to recognize the basic goodness of the bearers of the new youth culture. However, young people must recognize that man's duty to his fellow man, important as that may be, does not constitute the totality of his obligations. In addition he has a duty to God to live the kind of life ordained by Him, the kind that may be truly be termed the good life.

We recognize as our challenge and obligation the need to carry this message effectively to our youth.

1970   DISSENT AND ITS LIMITS

The Bill of Rights of the United States Constitution commences with the guarantee of freedom of religion, speech and the press; and with the right to assemble peacefully and to petition the government for redress of grievances. Thus, the right to dissent constitutes the very foundation of our government.

This constitutional guarantee covers diverse forms of peaceful dissent, such as worship, speech, publishing, picketing, organizing, assembling, protesting and petitioning. A healthy society will not cringe before the dissenter who criminally exceeds the legal boundaries of democratic dissent, for no society can hope to survive unless it defends itself against such abuse of this noble right of free men and women.

No group can be permitted to compel by force the acquiescence of those who disagree with it. No cause, no matter how just, can be used as a rationalization for violent means. Prompt governmental action at all levels, using only lawful force, i.e. the minimum necessary under the circumstances and with particular care to avoid harm to the innocent, will insure that our democracy is not destroyed by revolutionary activity masquerading as legitimate dissent.

We appreciate that sincere individuals, especially among our youth, have become impatient with our nation's pace in moving to eradicate war and social injustice. We ask them to understand that in a democracy it is not enough to espouse good causes. Equally important is the need to convince the electorate of the correctness of these causes. We call upon the youth of this country to increase their participation in the political process and we welcome as an important step facilitating such participation the recent passage by Congress of legislation granting the voting right to eighteen-year-olds.

We also strongly oppose the practice of dealing with non-violent dissenters in a manner tending to intimidate them or make them appear less patriotic and loyal because of their dissent. These tactics, by undermining the reasoned discourse so vital to the democratic process, only serve to polarize our nation and to poison the political atmosphere.

In all of history there has never been a nation that has afforded more opportunity to the disadvantaged and more freedom for all people than the United States. No group is more appreciative of this than we Jews, whose history is one of dissent from tyrants and majorities and from prevailing morals and methods of the many societies of which we have been part throughout the millennia of Jewish existence. We reaffirm our conviction that the rule of law is an essential condition of individual liberty and that only under the rule of law is the creative exercise of dissent possible.

1970   THE URBAN CRISIS

The critical problems of our cities—deteriorating housing, environmental contamination, widespread unemployment, poor schools, drug abuse and violent crime—have worsened during the past two years. Meanwhile, white people have continued their exodus from cities to suburbs, furthering the conversion of our largest cities into black and other minority enclaves. These minorities, either because of economic circumstance or outright discrimination, are unable to join this move, thereby also being disadvantaged with regard to new employment opportunities created in the suburbs.

Our nation's response to this crisis has been to concentrate on only one of its aspects, namely the crime and violence that have made many parts of our cities unsafe to live or work in. While no one can dispute the immediate need to take all necessary steps to deal directly with crime, it is obvious that we must at the same time act to eliminate the underlying social inequities and other urban problems that breed crime and violence. Unfortunately, as the National Commission on Causes and Prevention of violence noted, fear of crime and violence are "making fortresses of portions of our cities, dividing our people into armed camps, jeopardizing some of our institutions and corroding our political processes", in some places "law and order" has become a code word for refusal to spend the necessary funds to attack the problems of the inner city. This refusal has disastrous implications, since the blacks and other minorities of the inner city rightly demand that society help them, and help them now, to attain decent living conditions.

We repeat the call expressed at our last convention for a massive effort, underwritten by Federal Government, to improve the quality of life for all Americans by providing them with employment and without regard to ability to pay, with decent housing, job training, and education. This vital effort alone can restore the faith of our less fortunate citizens in our nation's ability to cope with their problems.

1970   ENVIRONMENTAL POLLUTION

Having "conquered" nature in the process of developing a wondrous technology and an urban society, Western man is beginning to turn in revulsion from the contamination he has wrought upon his environment. His cities have become largely unlivable, with air unfit to breathe, adjacent bodies of water polluted, land strewn with garbage and debris, and unwanted noise everywhere. The beauty of his countryside is marred by such eyesores as strip mining and billboards. His food supply is threatened by toxic pesticides; his safety by cancer-producing radiation.

The Torah-observing Jew throughout the ages has regarded the protection of his environment as a basic tenet of his faith, for "the earth and the fullness thereof belong to the Lord". Although man has been given the right to develop and consume Earth's resources, he may not engage in their wanton destruction (*bal tashchith*); nor may he disregard the effect his acts may have upon his neighbor's welfare. To achieve the life of holiness demanded of every Jew, the Halachah has numerous rules that require cleanliness and purity, not only of man's mind and body but of his environment as well.

The struggle for a pure environment will not be an easy one. The principal polluters of our environment, the automobile industry, the industrial burners of coal, gas and oil, and the industrial producers of waste, are a powerful political force in resisting the legislation needed to cope with this problem.

We call upon the incoming Administration and our member synagogues to give high priority in their social action programs to the subject of ecology and to join with other conservation-minded groups in mobilizing public and legislative opinion to take all steps necessary to restore our environment to its natural purity and pristine beauty.

1974   ABORTION

Judaism regards all life—including fetal life—as inviolate. Abortion is not a private matter between a woman and her physician. It impinges upon the most fundamental right of a third party—that of the unborn child.

The concern with which Jewish tradition views the destruction of a fetus is reflected in the provisions of the Noachidic code. Judaism teaches that abortion, for the sons of Noah, is a capital crime. The Talmud renders Genesis 9:6 as "He who sheds the blood of a man within a man, his blood shall be shed." "Who is 'a man within a man'?" queries the Talmud. "This is a fetus in its mother's womb."

For Jews, fetal life is inviolate unless continuation of pregnancy poses a serious threat to the life of the mother. The life of the mother takes precedence over that of the unborn child. Situations in which maternal health, rather than maternal life, are involved post complex problems requiring rabbinic adjudication. Similarly, situations involving psychiatric components require authoritative determination in each individual case. Performance of an abortion cannot be sanctioned unless the relevant medical facts are submitted to a competent rabbinic authority who will review the medical data and render advice in accordance with Jewish law.

1974   WORLDWIDE HUNGER

For centuries, most of mankind has known hunger as a daily condition. In recent years, however, one-third of the human race has burst out of the "poverty cycle," while the remaining two-thirds sink into ever deepening squalor and poverty. It is thus particularly ironic that in this age when hundreds of millions of North American, Europeans, and Japanese are enjoying the highest standard of living in their history, the spectra of impending mass starvation threatens hundreds of millions of their fellow human beings.

The brutal drought in the Sub-Sahara, the apparent shifting of climatic conditions in the temperate zone, and the shocking escalation of the cost of essential petrochemical fertilizers have all brought entire sections of the globe to the verge of unprecedented tragedy. The governments of the United States and Canada have responded to this situation with their characteristic humanitarian concern as have many of the other relatively wealthy nations of the world. It is shocking, however, to note that with the exception of Iran, the oil states, whose actions have helped contribute to this crisis, remain aloof from the international effort to assist their fellow Third World nations that now face disaster.

As encouraging as these international efforts have been, they fall far short of the scope and magnitude of actions that are required in this time of world-wide crisis. The Orthodox Union accordingly calls upon President Ford to convene a world-wide "summit conference" to be exclusively devoted to the problems of international famine and food supply. In the interim we call upon the governments of the United States and Canada to increase their relief aid to those areas that face the gravest immediate danger.

1974   AFFIRMATIVE ACTION

Until recently, the standard approach towards equality in such areas as employment and education was to fight against discrimination. Recently, this approach shifted to one of active measures on behalf of those who were victims of discrimination. This active approach is known as "affirmative action".

The results to date of this new approach have been mixed, because of the confused manner of its practice. While it benefited some, others found themselves losing jobs or student status, or finding promotional opportunities denied them.

This confusion in the practice of affirmative action results primarily from the confusion in its definition. At the very least, affirmative action means taking steps to assure job and student opportunities to members of minority groups. This concept is universally approved. At the other extreme, affirmative action is defined by quotas and reverse discrimination. This concept is universally condemned. Between these extremes lies a variety of other concepts. For example, in the DeFunis case before the United Status Supreme Court, the most publicized legal battle on this issue, *amicus* briefs from Jewish organizations were submitted on both sides of the issue. Yet some of the opponents of affirmative action in the DeFunis case are on record in support of affirmative action. There is no contradiction: the affirmative action procedure challenged by DeFunis involved a law school admissions policy which predetermined a fixed number of admissions for minority group members, on a racially determined basis. The other form of affirmative action makes allowances for an individual's background, which permits flexing of standards administratively.

The Orthodox Union is opposed to any form of affirmative action which in any way compromises, or opens the way to compromise of, the principle of merit as the sole standard of qualification for admissions and promotion opportunities in employment and education.

Mindful of the gross inequities suffered by members of minority groups and women in the areas of employment and education, we support those programs of government and the private sector which seek to end discrimination on the basis of race and sex.

We do not, however, support those programs that would allow for special "group" privileges, which would have the affect of remedying this situation by wrongfully discriminating against others. We do not believe it would be morally or legally proper for any group in American society to be given special advantage over others to redress past inequities.

We heartily endorse those programs which provide for remedial education and special job training, if these programs are open to members of all groups and if the criterion is one of individual need.

1974   SEXUAL PERVERSION

The Jewish religious tradition treats homosexual relations, both male and female, not merely as a deviation from normal sexual practice but as a capital offense. Such practices are included in the overall Biblical injunction against indulgence in the abhorrent sexual practices which were associated with the ancient Egyptians and Canaanites.

The traditional Jewish opposition to any form of sodomy, unnatural sexual practice, clashes head-on with tendencies of today's permissive society where the pursuit of pleasure is idolized. The dominant mood of contemporary culture places a premium on "self-expression" and "self-fulfillment." Within this basically hedonistic socio-cultural setting, maximum gratification of the individual's wants and needs becomes the overriding imperative. Unless necessary for the protection of the rights of others, any interference with self-gratification is regarded as unwarranted, or even immoral.

Under such conditions, considerable pressure has been brought to bear upon the Jewish community to align itself with "enlightened" progressive opinion and to sanction all kinds of perverse sexual practices as long as they yield gratification to the individuals involved. It is argued that a ban on homosexual relations between "consenting adults" constitutes an infringement of the rights of individuals seeking homosexual indulgence.

The Jewish community, however, cannot yield to these pressures without undermining the very foundation of its moral structure. Judaism has always insisted that moral values are not simply fabricated by individuals or society to suit their individual or collective needs, but are ultimately grounded in a Supreme source and, therefore, possess objective validity.

Since the Jewish moral code categorically forbids homosexual relations, it is inconceivable for any agency that is concerned with the preservation or promotion of Jewish values to condone, sanction, let alone advocate or foster homosexual relations. The establishment of "gay synagogues" or of any institution designed to place the mantle of acceptability upon homosexuality represents not merely sacrilege but an act of Jewish spiritual self-destruction.

Uncompromising and all-out opposition to any legitimization of homosexuality must, however, not lead to the exclusion of homosexuals from the Jewish community. They must be treated as individuals who have violated fundamental Jewish ethical religious beliefs. In keeping with classical Jewish teaching, our opposition must be directed to the sin itself but not to the sinner as a person. Homosexuals deserve our compassion for the terrible plight under which they labor and should be given every possible assistance to overcome the perversion with which they are afflicted. All the resources of the Jewish community should be placed at their disposal to encourage them to attain a meaningful Jewish life.

33

The Wider Reach

The successive world conferences greatly enhanced Torah-community relationships across the globe. Since, however, those shining events did not, for various reasons, provide for establishment of a functioning world organization of synagogues and communities, relationships on the international level remained unstructured. The complex of informal individual community-to-community associations that had emerged continued to prove beneficial, but this did not equal the stature and practical force that a duly constituted common arm could attain.

The two initial world conferences were seen by some as, of themselves, demonstrating the need, in light of modern-day realities, of a permanent world format of the multinational synagogal domain. Then and since, advocates of the creation of such an organism have seen this purpose as bearing the same timely urgency as that which, in an earlier era, had led to the birth of the Union of Orthodox Jewish Congregations of America. Whether an organization equivalent in scope to that envisioned earlier by Henry Pereira Mendes will appear remains an unanswered question.

Meanwhile, the Orthodox Union's ties with communities abroad bore fruit from time to time, as occasion arose. Of particular note was the cooperation between the Union and the Consistoire Central of France, the constituted religious corporate body of France's Jews. Prompting this development was the revolutionary impact on French Jewish life of an influx of several hundreds of thousands of Jewish newcomers from North African lands. Under the difficult circumstances that arose, the religious leadership of French Jewry turned to the American Torah community's central force for fraternal guidance. The American response was immediately forthcoming.

The influx had come when, upon the termination of French rule over Tunisia, Algeria, and Morocco in the 1960s, the Jews there, exposed to the hostility of the inflamed Arabs, had fled en masse. About a half of the more than 700,000 in flight found haven in Israel; most of the rest, as French citizens, settled in France. The mass inpouring, doubling French Jewry's numbers, posed vast problems. The tasks of resettlement and economic integration were borne mainly by government sources, but meeting religious and communal needs fell largely on the shoulders of the Consistoire Central of France, along with the self-directed efforts of dedicated figures among the new arrivals themselves.

While touched in the era of French rule by modern-day French culture, the communities in Tunisia, Algeria, and Morocco had been largely of deeply rooted, traditionally Jewish texture. The qualities, pattern, and atmosphere of Jewish life in France were much different. Products of Oriental and Occidental worlds, respectively, the newcomers and their established fellow-Jews were strangers and puzzlements to each other. Yet, for all the massive difficulties of the situation, an effect that presently became visible was the revitalization of Jewish life in France. At the same time, however, also visible was the force of conditions impelling the young among both the newcomers and the established away from Jewish loyalties.

On the one hand, the apparatus of Jewish living was undergoing radical reconstruction. Synagogues were newly born or reborn; sources of meeting kosher food needs came into being on a new scale; facilities for children's religious instruction were extended or improvised; Shabbath and Yom Tov found observance in a measure long absent from the French scene; Jewish consciousness was reawakened, the Jewish spirit was recharged; Torah study found new participants, including among university students and graduates; yeshivoth on several levels were established, some jointly by Jews of Western and of Eastern background.

But even as the will to live Jewishly was making itself so meaningfully felt, it was being sapped by the absorption of many into the life of the French environment. Especially ominous was the toll being evoked among schoolchildren; France's public schools had, and continue to have, classes on Saturday, with attendance and the fulfillment of written exercises being compulsory. Along with the drastic effect of preclusion of Sabbath observance was the prevailing atmosphere of shared Frenchness, undifferentiated between Jews and gentiles.

Wider awareness among American Jews of the paradoxical conditions in the suddenly enlarged French community resulted from an article by Rabbi Elkanah Schwartz in the January-February 1970 (Shevat–Adar 5730) issue of *Jewish Life*. Meeting, during an extended visit to French Jewry, with a series of grassroots-level activists, Schwartz had the opportunity to take the pulse of life among the former North Africans and to see what, against all obstacles, was being accomplished in the creation in various parts of France of day schools, yeshivoth,[1] camps, and other Torah life-generating undertakings.

From France, Rabbi Schwartz went on to examine Jewish conditions in the Soviet Union. He summarized with:

> When on my return people asked how things are in Russia and France, I said that while the two are not to be compared . . . in Russia, Jews know that little can be done, so they look only for that little. But in France, they know they could have more [of aid in Jewish upbuilding]. And until that more is forthcoming, the vacuum grows ever more dangerous.

For its part, the Consistoire Central was wrestling with radical change. Heretofore, while committed to traditional Judaism, its mode had reflected, since the Napoleonic era, a cultural, as well as a civic, Frenchification. In moving to meet the religious needs of the mass of new arrivals, the Consistoire itself, and the sphere of Jewish society under its spiritual care, underwent an awakening. The challenge before the Consistoire circle, of a magnitude beyond prior experience, proved to be not only a challenge to *do*, but a challenge to *be*.

Stirred by the positive new spirit, the Consistoire leadership, headed by Chief Rabbi Jacob Kaplan, manifested anew its identification with the Torah way of Orthodox Judaism. Providentially, an occasion arose at which UOJCA president Joseph Karasick met with Baron Alain de Rothschild. This scion of a famed family, moved by his own spiritual searchings as a concentration-camp survivor, had assumed a lay leadership role in the Consistoire Central. The meeting of these two bore powerful results over following years.

In 1967, Baron de Rothschild, at Joseph Karasick's invitation, visited the United States to consult, on behalf of the French community, with the Orthodox Union's leadership. He conferred with the Union's officers and officials, and had thorough briefing sessions with the department heads. Additionally, Baron de Rothschild visited Yeshiva University and other major yeshivoth, and in Boston visited Maimonides Institute and conferred with Rav Joseph B. Soloveitchik. He also addressed the Conference of Presidents of Major Jewish Organizations, reporting on French Jewry, and was tendered a formal reception by the Orthodox Union.

The French community leader thereafter bringing his colleagues in the Consistoire leadership a sense of the moral and practical guidance gleaned by his visit, the French organization became imbued with fresh outlook. Measures were taken to better equip the Consistoire with personnel and

---

1. In one of these institutions, Yeshivath Ha-Torah, every student was either a university graduate or a student on leave, according to the article.

facilities to conduct its reconceived tasks. The program was reformulated in new terms to serve the religious advance of both the original and the newer components of the community. A relatively large delegation sent to the World Conference gained much from the experience.

Over the years, the ties between the French Consistoire and the American Union remained close. Orthodox Union materials for adults and youths were furnished liberally, and the Union's experience and thinking were brought to bear in response to concerns on given points conveyed by Consistoire figures, including Consistoire director Albert Horouche.

An exchange of personal visits contributed much to the cooperative process. Among the French visitors was Chief Rabbi Jacob Kaplan, who was received with appropriate courtesies and met with leaders and officials of both the central Union and the Rabbinical Council of America. Another visitor was the personable Jean Paul Elkan, president of the Paris Consistoire.

A further facet of the UOJCA–Consistoire cooperation followed a 1968 visit by Grand Rabbi Schilli, head of the Seminaire Israëlite de France. In 1969, three rabbinic graduates of the Paris seminary, guests of the Union and the Rabbinical Council, came on a study and field-training mission. The three spent two months in advanced study as guests at the Rabbi Isaac Elchanan Theological Seminary, then proceeded to in-field training experiences in, successively, congregations in Long Branch and Perth Amboy, New Jersey; Savannah; and Montreal. A similar mission in 1971, this time with two rabbinic graduates, included guest stays with congregations in Springfield, Fall River, and Brookline, Massachusetts; Atlanta; Kew Gardens, Monsey, and Far Rockaway, New York; and Montreal. In each community, the visiting rabbis of both groups were guests of, and received orientation from, the rabbis of the respective congregations.

Then subsequently came Admiral Louis Kahn, newly elected as president of the national Consistoire. This dignitary, a hero of the Free French forces battling the Germans in World War II, was received with honors at the Union's 76th Anniversary Biennial Convention (Boca Raton, Florida, 13–17 Kislev 5735/November 27–December 1, 1974). Admiral Kahn and all present were deeply moved when the delegates of Yavne, the then flourishing Orthodox Jewish university students' organization, saluted the French leader with singing of the Marseillaise—in Hebrew.

At about this time there came an extended visit of observation and field training by the then recently appointed youth director of the Consistoire Central. Over the two months of his stay, he was given the full attention of the Union's Youth Division director and associates. From these, the visitor received grounding in Torah-keyed techniques in youth work. He was escorted to a variety of NCSY events and was enabled to gain a grasp of the NCSY concept, process, and methods.

These personalized contacts and the cooperative program otherwise were recognized by the French and the American participants alike as contributing signally to the endeavors to forward Torah-loyal religious life among France's Jews. Persisting to varying degree through the years, this work has been a strengthening force in French Jewish life.

~

The developments on the international scene viewed here and in previous chapters show that, by the Union's seventh decade, this aspect of its program also was of "track" dimension. This work, under the respective jurisdictions of the Israel Commission and the Overseas Commission, was among the multiple cares of the Union's executive vice president. Here, too, assignment of departmental professional staff was not to be hoped for at the time.

Events had given added force, in this 1970s period, to persisting urges for America's Torah community arm to make a direct contribution to Israeli life. Translating the intent into an actual project might have continued to remain an elusive goal, however, but for the initiative of George B. Falk, a member of the UOJCA Board who later became a vice president of the organization. Falk conceived the idea of establishing in Israel a permanent UOJCA institute of educational and outreach activities; in fact, he made it his mission in the 1970s to get the plan formulated, approved, and carried out, with initial budget provided for. Thus was born in Jerusalem, in 1980, the Israel Center of the Orthodox Union. Quarters were provided—presently to be much enlarged—at a central Jerusalem location, 10 Rechov Strauss.

The Israel Center program as it presently developed was addressed, free of political associations, to seekers of Jewish knowledge and searchers for meaning of all backgrounds. Those coming to Israel to find themselves, and Israeli residents pursuing broader spiritual horizons, were alike, from the beginning on, within the Center's purposes. A range of classes, lectures, discussion groups, personalized projects, and private consultation services was introduced. Once the Center became known, it drew a large, devoted following that has been constantly replenished to the present day.

From its beginnings, the Union's Israel Center has been directed by Shai Solomon. The guidance of Dr. Weiss was drawn upon in the formation of the program, along with the prescriptions of the Israel Center Committee, of which George B. Falk was chairman throughout. In the course of time, as the Israel Center proved itself and enlarged its scope, two assistant directors were ultimately added to the staff.

Many of the Israel Center's activities being in the youth and student areas, it is often referred to by its younger participants as the NCSY Center, or the UOJCA–NCSY Center. Throughout, this institute has functioned in understated style, focusing on results in shaping the minds and lives of its circle of devotees rather than on self-serving publicity. The role of the Union's Israel Center nevertheless has been applauded by the discerning as a distinctive, creative service on the Israeli scene. Seen in the frame of the Orthodox Union's century-long experience, the Israel Center in Jerusalem is to be accounted as one of the Orthodox Union's enduring accomplishments.

～

A further development in relation to Israel in this fruitful period was the institution of the Aliyyah Department. In an arrangement with the Jewish Agency negotiated by Board member Emanuel Gruss, a member of the Israel Commission, a shaliach to act as director of the new department was appointed. The budgeted cost of this undertaking was provided for.

The initial shaliach was the first of a series, each one serving for a designated term, then returning home to Israel. The Aliyyah Department, thus pursued, under the supervision of the Israel Commission through Emanuel Gruss and others, an active program. Besides generating interest through various channels in settlement in Israel, consultation and practical guidance were furnished to those undertaking or contemplating Aliyyah. Effective results were shown as the program developed.

V
IN GREATER
DIMENSION

34

1972:
A Year of Changes in Key Posts

This seventh decade in the experience of the Union of Orthodox Jewish Congregations of America was marked by changes of large import as well as by accomplishment in areas both new and old.

Early in 1972 Dr. Samson R. Weiss, fulfilling his lifelong desire to dwell permanently in the Holy Land, resigned his post as executive vice president of the Union. His sixteen years of leadership service had meant very much to the conduct of the Union's affairs. Dr. Weiss, with his insights and outlook on the organization's processes, had been a source of strong, Torah-directed influence on the Torah community. Now he would find new outlets for his special capacities on the pulsating Israel scene.

After a search period, with numerous candidacies considered, Rabbi Berel Wein was chosen and accepted invitation to serve as executive vice president in succession to Dr. Weiss.

Rabbi Wein, ordained at the Hebrew Theological College in Chicago, also had a law degree. In his years as Mara D'asra of Beth Israel Congregation in Miami Beach, he had become noted beyond, as well as within, the south Florida communities as a personality of exceptional caliber. While his assumption of the national post was warmly welcomed throughout UOJCA circles, Rabbi Wein's departure was deeply regretted by the congregation he had served, which had grown in activity, stature, and numbers under his spiritual leadership.[1]

It was to be expected that the transition in the occupancy of so central an office would slow developments while the new incumbent "learned the

---

1. The injured feelings of Rabbi Wein's former congregants were brought home to this writer when, on a subsequent visit to Beth Israel, he found himself taken to task by members and personnel present in the synagogue: "You took away our Rabbi!"

ropes." With the cooperation of his colleagues, however, Rabbi Wein quickly developed a grasp of his tasks. By the time of the 74th Anniversary Biennial Convention (Boca Raton Hotel, Florida, 16–20 Kislev, 5733/ November 2–26, 1972), Rabbi Wein had marked his capacity in his leadership post.

Meanwhile, however, the Orthodox Union was shaken by the death in that same year of Rabbi Alexander S. Rosenberg, rabbinic administrator of the Union's Kashruth Division. In the course of his twenty-two years of service in this post, Rabbi Rosenberg had become the central figure in Ⓤ operations. When, with the appointment in 1951 of a Kashruth Division director, the overall UOJCA administrator had been relieved of the daily management of the kashruth service, the relative status in departmental direction of the director and the rabbinic administrator of the department had been reversed from what, in light of early experience, had been originally envisaged. Rabbi Rosenberg's personality, together with his rare grasp of the complexities of the kashruth area, had lent themselves well to the timely need, and had become predominant accordingly.

Under Rabbi Rosenberg's skilled piloting and the judicious guidance of the Kashruth Commission headed by Nathan K. Gross, the spontaneous, ever-burgeoning growth of the Orthodox Union's kashruth service had been conducted wisely and effectively. Food-industry development, coinciding with powerful manifestations of Jewish consumer insistence on the Ⓤ, now pointed to an expansion of the Ⓤ service as much beyond the great advances already achieved as those in turn had outdone earlier gains.

The position of Rabbinic Administrator of the UOJCA Kashruth Division had thus become a pivotal office in the kashruth domain, and one of extraordinary sensitivity. Choice of a successor was problematic.

With the need to appoint a successor to the rabbinic kashruth administrator post a daily urgency, the officers turned to Rabbi Wein to serve in the required capacity. Aware of the pressure of the situation, he agreed, withdrawing from the executive vice presidency for the purpose. Once again the difficulties of transition in a key executive area. But Rabbi Wein quickly took hold of his new responsibilities.

It was decided to leave the office of executive vice president open for a time, with the long-tried Administrator counted on to maintain effective continuity. For some months Reuben Savitz served in Associate capacity, until leaving for a position elsewhere.

Now came another aspect of change: The election at the 1972 Biennial Convention of Harold M. Jacobs, as successor to Joseph Karasick, as president of the Union of Orthodox Jewish Congregations of America.

Although the new president had been part of preceding administrations, his election heralded the advent of a new era. The six years of the Karasick presidency had continued the character of the preceding years of the

Feuerstein presidency. In this eighteen-year period, the distinctive personalities of these lay leaders and their associates had been complemented on the staff level by correspondingly "quality" figures, two of whom were now to be missed. So, the composition of key leadership, both elective and staff, was in new hands.

While now a resident of Lawrence in suburban Nassau County, New York, Harold M. Jacobs was a product of New York City's Borough of Brooklyn. As such, he was the first "Brooklynite" to hold the UOJCA presidency; moreover, within the Brooklyn frame, Harold Jacobs was identified with the Crown Heights community, an area with marked nuances of its own and, prior to the population changes of the post-mid-century decades, with a compact neighborhood character of substantial private homes and apartment houses. The Jewish climate of Crown Heights had been subtly different from that of the uptown parts of Manhattan in which most UOJCA presidents had been nurtured.

The new president, a successful businessman, thus bore the stamp of the comfortable, folksy Orthodoxy of the Crown Heights community in its prime with its center in the Crown Heights Yeshivah. The yiddishkeit of Crown Heights was baale-batish, but unstarched. One lived Jewishly as a matter of course; one worked for Jewish causes as a matter of course; one gave of one's means as a matter of course. The Orthodox Jew of Crown Heights' past great days was a figure of spontaneous, thoroughly relished Jewishness.

Prominent among the Crown Heights *askanim* was Harold Jacobs. All endeavors of valid Jewish character had benefited by his participation. The Orthodox Union, from the late 1940s on, had been one of his major interests. Having gained the top rung of the organizational ladder after holding office upon office, he was now in position to make his special mark on the national and international ranges of Jewish life.

The incoming president's active interests had extended to the political and civic spheres as well as to Jewish affairs. He was of consequence in the Brooklyn political domain, with influence beyond. One of the various positions he held in public life was membership on the New York City Board of Higher Education.

Harold Jacobs did not discourage expectations that his presidential course would reflect, to some degree, his training in politics. It was therefore to be expected that President Jacobs would want to have, in important positions, persons of his choosing who were likely to have a sense of personal loyalty. What ensued now, however, was not a marked change in the Union's program and policies, which continued basically as before. The change was more apparent in personal relations.

Tacit emphasis was placed on the personalization of presidential authority. A lesser degree of collegiality than previously became felt between the president and his fellow officers, according to some observers, and little cognizance was given of the roles of the Executive Committee and the Board. As distinguished from the mode of leadership of a volunteer force, the presidential mode tended to be that of the head of a business firm. However, while the atmosphere took on a different tone, the departments and commissions continued on their respective courses. The several "tracks" manifested a measure of built-in self-sufficiency not unduly affected by top-level currents, while in the exercise of his jurisdiction President Jacobs showed perceptive judgment in various decisions reached.

Presently came staff changes. Rabbi David Cohen was promoted from his position as associate director of the Youth Division to the new post of national director of the Orthodox Union. Rabbi Wein withdrew to undertake the establishment of a yeshivah and the rabbinate of a related congregation in Monsey, New York. For some months, the rabbinic management was under the pro tem charge of Rabbi Jules Lipschitz. Succeeding as rabbinic administrator of the Kashruth Division was the present incumbent, Rabbi Menachem Genack, the choice of whom was made on the personal recommendation of the illustrious Rav Joseph B. Soloveichik.

Thereafter was to follow the departure of Rabbi Cohen, and then the appointment of Rabbi Pinchas Stolper, architect and guiding spirit of NCSY, to the high office of executive vice president of the Orthodox Union. Another change to be noted was the withdrawal from the Union's service—especially regrettable, in this writer's opinion—of Rabbi Elkanah Schwartz.

Rabbi Stolper was succeeded as youth division director first by Rabbi Baruch Taub, and then by Rabbi Raphael Butler. Rabbi Butler was to make so notable a mark in that position as to lead again to his succession to Rabbi Stolper when, after further signal service to be noted lately, Rabbi Stolper was designated senior executive.

Perhaps the ultimate mark of change of era came with the retirement, in 1975, of Saul Bernstein as UOJCA administrator and editor of *Jewish Life.* His retirement, following a near-fatal illness, culminated twenty-nine years of total absorption in the work and cause of the Union of Orthodox Jewish Congregations of America. His sense of identification with this work and cause has not diminished.

35

Jew and Jew in Changed Context

At the mid-1970s point in the Orthodox Union's course, the durability of the congregational Union was well marked; so, too, was the resilience of its constituency of the Torah-committed. Under UOJCA leadership, the fold of the Torah synagogue had weathered crucial times. The vitality of the mitzvah-observant Jew amid America's dynamics and modernity's anomalies was a manifest reality. Purpose had endured the challenges encountered along the way, a path marked by endeavors to nurture Jewish Orthodoxy's inherent vitality and to contain its ingrained tendency to fragmentation. The forces of the Torah heritage were now better aware of both strengths and weaknesses. Moved by broadening aim, they looked outward, addressing themselves more deliberately to the Jewish totality.

Facing the organized forces of Orthodox Jewry, and more especially the echelons of the Orthodox Union, was the gap between the world of the Torah-observant and the range of others. The accruing effects of unceasing modern-age years of spiritual attrition had solidified. The previously variant levels of Judaic practice within families had run their course, to the point where familial links had all but disappeared between observant and nonobservant.

While those steadfast in faith were advancing in the Torah way, a great fraction of the Jewish people was now not only lost to active Jewish life, but was without a sense of deficiency in their nonobservance. Many had been habituated from birth to gentile ways and an assimilated outlook; the experience of Jewish life was unknown to them, and Jewish life was incomprehensible to them.

In personal regard, the observant and the nonobservant, the believer and the beliefless, might each go his own separate way without contact with the other. But in collective Jewish affairs, in matters touching all Jews, there were compulsions bearing strains. In the tight-knit world of the late twentieth century, it was realized that the need for a mode of relationship and a common medium between the organized instruments of Orthodox and non-Orthodox Jews was inescapable. Here, though, were perplexities. The collective Jewish affairs situation for Torah-community forces was made problematic by matters of both principle and means. On what basis, morally and halachically, might the upholder of historic Jewish belief and practice as immutably requisite in Jewish corporate life join in collective Jewish undertakings with those rejecting such premises? This question has been wrestled with ever since the rise of defections that came with the onset of modern civilization. A definitive answer has yet to come forth, and under the force of circumstances pragmatic improvisations, varying under varying conditions, have been resorted to. The difficulties of the question in principle are compounded in practice by the fact of non-Orthodox control of most instrumentalities established in fields of collective Jewish affairs.

On the international level, such vehicles as the Jewish Agency, the World Zionist Organization, the World Jewish Congress, and the Jewish Memorial Foundation for Jewish Culture are, one and all, under the control of non-Orthodox participants. In the United States, the array of community fund federations and their National Council, the United Jewish Appeal (UJA), the Conference of Presidents of Major Jewish Organizations, and the National Jewish Community Relations Advisory Council (NJCRAC) are all under non-Orthodox control. So, too, is it with individual membership bodies claiming a communal spokesmanship and defense role, such as B'nai B'rith, the American Jewish Committee, and the American Jewish Congress.

Aspects of relationship questions with various of the foregoing have been examined in other parts of this book. Our treatment of other aspects is in order to see how the matter is affected by trends in relationship within the Torah-community fold.

TORAH COMMUNITY REALIGNMENTS

Over the years of Jewish settlement in America, traditional believers in each layer of arrivals had tended to look questioningly at the religious mode of the settled communities. Presently, though, at each acclimatization stage, a process of integration between newly settled and already-settled elements came about. Traces might survive of religious–cultural differences between those of different eras of settlement or different origins, but usually they were not of real weight. An exception in this connection, however, seemed to apply when the religious among the immediate post-World War II arrivals were, in turn, settled; they tended to remain in spheres of their own. This was not universally so; many did, in time, become absorbed into the congregations and social circles of the communities of their residence. Many others, however, remained apart from the institutions and associations of the established Orthodox domain. This was conspicuously the case among the Chassidic groups and among those who attached themselves to the proliferating privately instituted shtibels and to the newer flock of yeshivoth.

This development has affected American Jewish life substantially and in various ways. Among these has been a shift in organizational attachments.

Zionism had found favor from the first among the Jewish mass-immigrant generations in America. The Torah-loyal religious Zionism represented by the Mizrachi movement had commanded wide support among America's Orthodox Jews from the 1902 founding of that organization onward. The Mizrachi organization had come forward as a self-constituted force within the collective Zionist movement when the latter fell under the control of secular-minded groups that imposed educational policies fundamentally unacceptable to the religious loyalists.

Also arising presently (1912) was the Agudath Israel movement of independent Orthodoxy. It was formed in part by some withdrawing from the Zionist fold (as being irrecoverably in the grasp of the nontraditional), and in part by others of various trends within Orthodoxy who also viewed Zionism askance.

Up to the later decades of the twentieth century, the prevailing outlook among America's Orthodox Jews had been in accord with the philosophy of the Mizrachi movement and its companion force, the Torah-socialism, self-labor pioneering co-movement Hapoel Hamizrachi. From their own experiences, the many with memories of Old-Country pogroms and disabilities were attuned to the Zionist-borne call of a dynamic rather than a passive approach to basic Jewish policy need.

America's Torah-loyal ranks were responsive to the Mizrachi–Hapoel Hamizrachi policy of association with all elements dedicated to the Zionist goal of self-achieved restoration of Jewish nationhood in its homeland, but under the banner of "The Land of Israel and the People of Israel Under the Torah of Israel." Thus the preeminence of Mizrachi–Hapoel Hamizrachi among traditional Jewish circles in the United States and Canada was long unchallenged.

The Agudath Israel movement, holding forth the aim "To solve, in the spirit of the Torah, all problems arising in the life of the Jewish people," had also found American votaries through the years, including, for a time, as noted earlier, some leading figures of the Union of Orthodox Jewish Congregations of America. But, up to the 1960s, the Agudath Israel following in the United States and Canada remained few in number and of minor standing in domestic Jewish affairs. Then began certain changes affecting Mizrachi and Agudath both.

A potent source of change in this connection—as in so many others!—was the epochal establishment in 5708/1948 of the state of Israel.

EFFECTS OF AMERICAN ALIYAH

There soon ensued a flow of aliyah migration to the reborn land of Israel from the United States and Canada. It was not comparable to the massive inpouring of the *shearith ha-p'leytah*, these who had survived the Holocaust; nor was it in proportion to the many Jews from Europe and the East who joined in the homeland resettlement movement. But it was a sustained flow, and of the finest human quality. Predominantly, the aliyah inflow from the United States and Canada was composed of the very cream of North American Torah Jewry's ranks. Year by year, in a process continuing to the present day, dedicated idealists from America and other advanced Western lands have undertaken the transition from the familiar comforts and economic well-being of Western life to the rigors and challenges of Israeli settlement. The leadership of the North American Mizrachi and Hapoel Hamizrachi movements (which presently merged in "Mizzug") was inevitably drawn to settlement in Israel. Not only the leadership echelon itself, but also the ranks of leadership potential, the most ardent of the movement's upcoming generation, were drawn there.

As the years passed, with the American aliyah numbering from several hundred to several thousand every year, the American religious Zionist movement was drained—by the fulfillment of its own tenets—of its experienced leadership and its top cadres. The movement's capacities in the North American setting diminished; its status declined.

The case of the Agudath Israel movement in America was quite different. While the goal of return to Zion is basic to the faith of the House of Israel and is interwoven with every facet of Jewish religious life, the redemption of the land of Israel and the deliberately projected return of the Jewish people to the land as a practical undertaking, the credo of Zionism, is not shared by Agudath Israel. Therefore, there was no equivalent urge to aliyah in Agudath channels. Nevertheless, the opportunity to fulfill the great mitzvah of *yishuv la'aretz*, with the allure of the Holy Land in its effervescing rebirth, drew numbers from the Agudist fold, too. But in this case the migration was not of comparable proportion or numbers, with no question of the siphoning away of its domestic leadership and active elements.

A source of American Agudath's post-1960s upsurge was a growing sense of kinship with the Agudist way among those originating in the post-World War II influx that had remained apart from the Orthodox mainstream. Some had been adherents of Agudath Israel in Europe, which in the prewar era had commanded a mass following there. Many, perhaps, whether or not of prior Agudist background, may have had feelings of self-doubt at having foregone, after having escaped or survived the Holocaust, the opportunity to go to the long-sought homeland. Shrinking from the hardships and dangers of the embattled newborn Jewish state, they turned rather to the material well-being and security of America. Implicit sanction for their chosen course, it would seem, was seen in the path pointed out by the independent Orthodoxy of Agudath Israel.

The newer yeshivah circles, now growing, also formed a ready pool of support and recruiting ground for Agudath Israel development. The key figures of these schools, their roshey yeshivoth, were mostly advocates of the Agudath cause, and so, too, were many of the yeshivah rebbeyim. While some of the yeshivah students were from Agudath-inclined families, the parents of most of those who increasingly flocked to the multiplying yeshivoth after the mid-century years had been of Mizrachi outlook. What now transpired was the ideological "capture" of yeshivah-absorbed youths from Mizrachist homes as recruits for the Agudist force—if not, in most cases, as actual "card-carrying" Agudath members, but followers with attitudes on Jewish policies shaped by Agudist influence.

This trend had a bearing on the realm of the national congregational union. The "community synagogue" sphere was, by and large, of Mizrachist outlook, although there were some congregations under Agudist leadership. So, too, it was, if less clearly, with the older bastions of higher Torah learning, such as the Rabbi Isaac Elchanan, Torah Vodaath, Ner Israel (Baltimore), and Beth Midrash Latorah (Chicago) yeshivoth. In contradistinction, the yeshivoth of later origin, now multiplying, were of Agudist-inclined complexion. Among the secluded yeshivoth minyanim and the "rebbishe shtibalech," although they drew their share of the Mizrachi-minded, Agudist influence was common. The sense of relationship to the Union of Orthodox Jewish Congregations prevalent in the community synagogue fold was little found among "yeshivish" and shtibel circles. It was in the latter circles, together with the Chassidish domains—as was daily becoming more evident in the 1970s and after—that the burgeoning growth of American Jewish Orthodoxy was most marked. And it was in this period that the raw weight, so to speak, of these multiplying increments of the traditional fold was beginning to be counted in the American picture.

MULTIPLE VOICES

In an objective sense, with the Orthodox Union's historical primacy as Torah community voice and arm of American life, any element of growth in the traditional fold contributes to the Union's advancement. In practical terms, however, this has force only to the extent of relationship between the element of growth and the central Union. In the case of the yeshivish and shtibel spheres, ties of any substance with the Orthodox Union did not readily materialize.

In Brooklyn's Williamsburgh and Borough Park communities, the largest concentrations of deeply observant Jews in the Diaspora, where yeshivish and Chassidish vehicles abound, the Orthodox Union's presence has been only indirectly felt. Among the residents is being found, in more recent years, the occasional Orthodox Union Association individual member. Among their thousands of devout homes, Ⓤ-certified food products became staples, as elsewhere. And by the 1970s period, as much more so later, numbers of Williamsburgh and Borough Park residents were employed as *mashgichim, shochatim,* and *bodekim* by the UOJCA kashruth supervision service. As well, young women from these communities have found employment in UOJCA headquarters.

Beyond these incidental connections, the Orthodox Union seems to have been disengaged from the affairs of such pulsating locales of chareidi-keyed Jewish life as Borough Park, Williamsburgh, and their offshoots. Records of the UOJCA administration under the presidency of Harold M. Jacobs bear some indications of concern with the gap, without resulting in remedial action.

Understandably, the unit of the Orthodox Union to manifest concern about reaching out to Borough Park and its like was the Union's Metropolitan New York region. In the 1970s, however, when these major centers of Torah life were taking on the character that was to define them thereafter, the Metropolitan region had not yet been brought back to life. Later, from the early 1980s on, under the prompting and active leadership of Gerald E. Feldhamer, aided by Avery E. Neumark, both national UOJCA officers, various of the activities then newly introduced were effectively aimed to reach, among others, the yeshivish and shtibel circles.

Particularly popular became the annual spring-holiday weekend Torah retreat and the annual four-day early summer Yarchei Kallah, both held at a Catskill Mountains resort location. The first-named, featuring an array of noted rabbis whose lectures on selected themes served as the basis for group discussion, was soon to become a not-to-be missed annual event for several hundred family participants. The Yarchei Kallah enabled "ba'aley-battim" to devote themselves to study with renowned roshey yeshivah assigned parts of Gemora and halachah, with their wives separately studying appropriate Torah subjects. This, too, gained an enthusiastic following in which, as with the Torah retreat, Borough Park and like areas were always well represented.

These openings for outreach and diverse other innovations—lecture series, Shabbatonim, Speakers Bureau, and "singles" events—were facilitated by staff assignments, with Melanie Shimoff and Rabbi Yoel Schonfeld to serve, successively, through the 1980s as regional director. When Rabbi Schonfeld was assigned to another department without replacement, the pace of regional development slowed. While the maintenance of the main annual events continued to retain the Borough Park-type portions of the followings, ties with this area were not further forwarded.

Not so limited, however, was the pace of the Agudath Israel organization. With its ties, as aforementioned, to the yeshivah and shtibel followings, the Agudath force was well attuned to what Borough Park and its offshoots were becoming.

~

A change in the stance and thrust of the American Agudath movement, first becoming visible in the 1960s, became strongly marked from the 1970s on. Under the leadership of Rabbi Moshe Sherer, who, after having long served in other capacities, became designated executive president of the organization, a series of new activities began to unfold, together with a new posture in the public arena. Although not diverging from the ideology of "independent Orthodoxy" that was the hallmark of the Agudath Israel movement, and loyal as ever to the standard and discipline of the world organization of the movement, the American Agudist force launched a path of its own.

From its earliest years, the Agudist movement had been marked by a defensive psychology. It had been concerned to protect its following from contamination with those of other views; it was ever reacting against the moves and positions of other forces. Apart from organizational activities, positive initiatives and constructive projects for Jewish purposes were few. Outstanding among these projects was the adoption, by the central echelon of the world Agudah movement, of the Bais Yaakov schools. Originated in post-World War I days by a great woman of modern Jewish history, Sarah Schenirer, sponsorship of this system of schools for girls and young women was a revolutionary step for Agudath Yisrael. The system was to grow to include a range of schools on elementary, high-school, and seminary levels in several lands. In the land of Israel, the foremost practical accomplishment under the Agudist banner was also in education: the creation of the

Chinuch Atzmai religious school system, serving many thousands of children.

On the Israeli scene otherwise, Agudist endeavor remained confined mostly to the political sphere, bearing no comparison in practical developmental undertakings to the many accomplishments of the Mizrachi-Hapoel Hamizrachi religious Zionist movement. The advent of the state of Israel, however, led by Zionist forces, posed new problems for Agudist policy. These were met in the ensuing years more by pragmatic process than consistent principle, and by a recharged sense of need for creative response to a changed situation.

In America, the Agudath awakening took its own form. Those taking over the helm of the American wing of the organization were alert to the "modern-day America" setting and recognized the need to deal with the realities of the time.

While disclaiming any identification with "modernist Orthodoxy," these leaders saw the Agudath Israel movement as a modern-day product, promoted by the need to deal in contemporary terms with modern-age forces and conditions. The initiative for the movement's founding had, in fact, come from the circle bearing the *Torah im derech eretz* (Torah and modern culture) philosophy of Rabbi Samson Raphael Hirsch, and within its eclectic makeup this element was represented along with certain yeshivish and Chassidic forces. Thus keyed, the awakening American Agudath now brought modernity to bear with concentrated force on its organizational apparatus.

While maintaining its intensive traditionalism in full, the literature of the American Agudath Israel was updated in form and content. The organization's structure was enlarged and reconstituted, and addressed in totally new ways to the American political scene. New undertakings and procedures of the reborn American Agudath evidenced lavish—and unacknowledged—borrowings from the projects and methods of the Orthodox Union, as well as from those of the National Council of Young Israel and Torah Umesorah. Notably, contacts with governmental channels were assiduously pursued, and intimations of Agudist influence on segments of the electorate were disseminated.

Effort went into establishment of ties with various governmental agencies in social-welfare fields. Among the results were projects in occupational training, in which the Agudath Israel organization established well-recognized training-course institutions in numerous modern technologies and clerical skills. The extent of political involvement and governmental ties became such as to cause the American Agudath organization to be seen as a political body, if not an arm of government.

∽

Also asserting itself more on the public scene in the 1970s was the National Council of Young Israel. With continuing expansion in the number and geographic range of chapters, the Young Israel movement's national leadership sought increased recognition for their growing force as a major institution in Jewish life. Progress in this regard was marked by inclusion of the National Council of Young Israel in various interorganizational "umbrella" agencies, but not until events in the 1990s shook the Jewish world did the voice of the national Young Israel movement, strong, unequivocal, and eloquent, come to the forefront of Jewish affairs.

It was in the 1970s, too, that the Lubavitch movement, with its "Chabad" version of Chassidism, was proceeding to take on the bold, imaginative slant that was to bring it so special a place on the American scene.

A movement all to itself, free of ties to any and all other organized or informal forces and institutions of the Jewish world, the Lubavitch enterprise was distinguished by its focus on outreach to Jews of all kinds, including, especially, those beyond the observant fold. While this had been a mark of Chabad philosophy since its late-eighteenth-century origins, under the incumbent Lubavitcher Rebbe, Rabbi Menachem Mendel Schneerson, it was given unprecedented driving force.

Devotion to the Rebbe was the ruling motif in the life of each of his followers. In this spirit, his followers executed his purposes as directed, going wherever sent, across the land and around the world, to establish and conduct instruments for winning Jews to the Jewish way—within the frame of the Lubavitch fold.

The Lubavitch leadership apparatus manifested rare skill in winning financial support, as well as adeptness in organizational technique. Especially remarkable was the mastery shown in public relations and publicity. Equipped with its schools and literature, its apparatus and institutions spreading from its center in Brooklyn's Crown Heights section throughout the far corners of North America and to all points of the world, the Lubavitch Chabad movement was already, in the 1970s, well on its way to becoming a weighty force in American Jewish life.

A further complication for the Union was the developmental disparity among Orthodox congregations. It was not simply a matter of differences of membership size or physical equipment or communal situation, widely varying as those were and still are. Beyond such differences were differences of response—or response capacity—to the challenges of an epoch.

At many points in this period, for example, the shul-going populace was more Torah-conscious, better informed, and more open to positive Jewish purpose than its forerunners. The level of observance among them was rising markedly above its previous casualness. Correspondingly, an increasing number of congregations were acquiring lay leaders of finer caliber than those of prior years, in terms of both Jewish knowledge and personal characteristics.

Yet, in contrast, there were at numerous other points—in larger and smaller communities both—congregations that remained locked in slow decay. Such places had not yet been swept by the renascent spirit stirring much of the Torah community. Not yet carried forward by the widening waves of rebirth, they were without vista of the future. Their diminishing memberships were skeptical of reports of the reawakening.

Wide variances of ideological disposition at the personal level echoed on the congregational and communal scenes. There were those afire with the will to carry the Torah banner afar; for them, the synagogue task was to widen the ramparts of the Torah community and to win all Jews to their heritage birthright. There were others, though, for whom the synagogue was to enable such as themselves to focus on their own personal fidelity to the way of Torah and mitzvoth, close-guarded against infection by others.

Thus it can be seen that with the assortment of institutional and organizational forces taking on scope and weight in the 1970s and after, together with the constituency disparities, the situation of the Union of Orthodox Jewish Congregations of American bore new complexities.

～

Along with internal complexities went further dimensions of world change. Never, since the birth of the Industrial Age, had the capacity to convert the Earth's resources into a means of satisfying human desires or serving humankind's material needs reached such a point as was now changing the face of the world. Now reigning supreme were two forces: "technology" and "consumerism." With the flood of new availability came the appetite to utilize them. In America and all lands of advanced industrial development—conspicuous among them Germany and Japan, risen from wartime destruction and defeat—material living standards rose, for most, to unprecedented peaks. Elsewhere, the urge to catch up and share in the bounties of modern technology became itself a key factor in world affairs.

For Orthodox Jews, along with the rest, the world about them was widening. The automobile having become universal, personal mobility opened new dimensions of accessibility to parts heretofore distant. Jet airplane flight had brought any part of the globe within a few hours' reach. A variety of new communications devices, with the fax machine starting to become an everyday tool, were now affording instant communication with anybody anywhere. Withal, the immediacy of the effect of the rise of the Jewish state, magnified in the life of every Jew, was now emphasized by the airplane-borne visits of many thousands each year to Israel and by the soon-spreading pattern of a year of study in the Holy Land by Diaspora youth.

Horizons were widening for the observant Jew of America or other Diaspora lands who experienced visits to Israel, or who engaged in travel in his own country or to lands abroad: the Orthodox Jewish businessman who periodically flew to Singapore, Tokyo, or Bombay; the Torah-loyal scientist, scholar, or technological specialist whose vocational circumstances required a stay in places far from the centers of Jewish life—such, mitzvah-observant Jews, were no longer bound by the horizons of their customary or original residence, whether in Forest Hills, New York; Englewood, New Jersey; West Rogers Park (Chicago); or some outspreading neighborhood in Kansas City, Memphis, Seattle, St. Louis, Hartford, or wherever. And this horizon-widening was not merely geographic.

⁓

To steer a course amid such a tangle of factors was a responsibility not shared in its diverse range by any other Torah-community force. It was a responsibility that hung heavily on the Orthodox Union, pulled this way and that by cross-currents and pressed by multiple urges. American Jewish Orthodoxy's central organ might well have become marooned in confusion, as the ill-kept records of the period and the recollections of some may indicate. But the historical role and the force of established services, under earnest if untried leadership effort, checked the floundering.

Understandably, then, the course of the Union of Orthodox Jewish Congregations of America in the middle and later 1970s was marked by uncertainty, and also by some contradictions. On the other hand, there was accrued growth, fruit of the years of prior effort. It was a growth spurred more by uncharted response to pressures of need than by planned process. The Union of Orthodox Jewish Congregations was enlarged because the Union, alone in its capacity, was "there"—where, otherwise, would have been chaos. Still, at a time of great shifts in the pattern of human life, in the conditions of Jewish life and the situation of the Jewish people, in the composition of Orthodox Jewry and in the currents of Torah-committed life—at such a time there was an acute need for clear, mature, insightful direction.

The officer corps of the Union at this time included most of the previous incumbents, with some changes of capacity. Yet the collective ability to address the scope of emerging circumstances in clear purpose—a need now especially acute—was clouded. The personalities new to the Union's executive staff brought new abilities and a freshness of outlook, plus strong commitment. But still missing after the departure of key figures of before were certain resources of insight and experience needed to enable the lay leadership to function to best effect as a team.

Under the circumstances, the role of the Orthodox Union as guidance source for its constituency underwent a strained test. It was nevertheless upheld—if not on the level that might have been looked for, then better, all things considered, than some may have feared.

SHIFT OF POLICY PROCEDURE PATTERN

The notably scant records of the 1970s indicate leadership uncertainties on new policy situations, regarding procedure and substance both. Thus, a development involving a complex of new international relationship commitments of major consequence was considered—and ultimately acted on—with apparently minimal concern for the constitutional process requisite in such case, and without thought of constituency voice.

The matter arose with a proposal by Dr. Maurice Jaffe, president of the Iggud Battey K'nessiyoth, the Israeli synagogue union, and director general of Hechal Shelomo, seat of the Israel Chief Rabbinate, for the convening of another World Conference of Orthodox Synagogues and Kehilloth. This was conceived as a successor not only to the memorable first and second world synagogal convocations, in which the Orthodox Union had played a leading part, but also to a third event so designated. The Union and other major national bodies, such as those of Great Britain and France, had declined to participate in that third project, which Jaffe had then pieced together with small numbers of token participants from a few places. At that occasion, provision had been made for the designation of the World Conference of Synagogues and Kehilloth as a permanent body. This was contrary to what had been stipulated in convening the original World Conference, as being incompatible with the situations or constitutions of some of the national communities. Also arranged at the same occasion had been the designation of Maurice Jaffe himself as president of the organization. In that capacity, Jaffe had arranged affiliation of the World Conference with the World Zionist Organization, and thereby with the Jewish Agency, with himself as representative on the key boards of both.

Now, broaching a fourth World Conference, the participation of the Union of Orthodox Jewish Congregations of America was urgently sought. Such participation was the key to giving the proposed assembly, and the convening body, the needed substance and structure.

At a meeting of UOJCA officers (November 16, 1977), President Jacobs had reported conferring on the matter with the leadership of the National Council of Young Israel, whose participation in the projected World

Conference was similarly solicited by Jaffe. Apparently, with view to possibilities of attaining a position of influence on Jewish agency policies, positive interest had developed. According to the meeting minutes (recorded by Michael C. Wimpfheimer, UOJCA secretary), "The two issues before the Union at this point are a) whether to take part in the February, 1978 assembly of the World Conference [of Orthodox Synagogues and Kehilloth] and b) whether to join a permanent body and through that to obtain participation in and representation in the Jewish Agency and the World Zionist Organization. . . ."

It was noted that "there is no way of obtaining Jewish Agency representations without joining the WZO." President Jacobs, in pressing for an affirmative decision, called for seeking the approval of "the Roshei Yeshivoth" on the question—a remarkable innovation. The minutes also recorded that advocates of an affirmative decision had reasoned that "in order to avoid the prospect of Dr. Jaffe serving as permanent head of this permanent organization a rotation would be asked for the rotation succession in office of the leaderships respectively of Israeli, American, British, and French representation."

Apparently, an out-of-hand authorization for the president to proceed was sought, but the objections of a few, including Secretary Wimpfheimer, to "making a hurried decision on a policy issue without proper examination of the constitutional and halachic aspects," could not be ignored. (It is to be presumed that the "halachic aspects" point was intended to apply to the Halachah Commission of the Union's rabbinic affiliate, the Rabbinical Council of America, as distinguished from external channels.) However, a motion was made and seconded (and presumably carried, although the minutes transcription does not so state) "which recommended that subject to the approval of the Board of Directors and Roshei Yeshivoth who will be consulted that the Union work in conjunction with the National Council of Young Israel toward joining the World Conference and through it the WZO and that in this connection the President shall appoint a committee to further explore the matter."

This writer has been unable to find minutes or other record of a Board of Directors meeting with reference to this matter. Nor has there been found any record of proceedings of any "committee to further explore the matter." Action was, in fact, taken on behalf of the Union in this matter, though apparently unburdened by constitutional processes.

In the Union's files is a copy of a communication, dated February 29, 1978, from Rabbi Pinchas Stolper, UOJCA executive vice president, to "Members of the Executive Committee," headed, "Report: World Conference of Synagogues—World Zionist Organization, February 14–19, 1978," stating, in part:

The UOJC and Young Israel attended the Fourth World Conference of Synagogues and Kehilloth as a united delegation. The decision to attend was made with the approval of the Administrative Committee [and] our Joint Committee and after a meeting with Dr. Jaffe in New York to determine if he was prepared to be flexible. The delegation of the UOJC to the World Conference of Synagogues and Kehilloth, while in small numbers, achieved extraordinary success.

   a. We went beyond the minimum conditions laid down by the officers, and obtained much more stringent conditions.
   b. The UOJC–Young Israel delegation was the major factor in restoring the World Conference of Synagogues to its former ad hoc status. At the same time, the World Conference has been transformed from a paper concept into an instrument capable of practical involvement.
   c. . . . The name of the between-conference body henceforth will be called the Committee for the World Conference of Synagogues and Kehilloth.
   d. We created a closer, trusting partnership and ongoing working relationship with Young Israel. . . .
   e. We entered the World Zionist Organization on our terms which protect the interests of the American contingent in every way.

By entering the World Zionist Organization we accomplished three things:

   a. We perceived that . . . the Zionist leadership was anxious to have an across-the-board representation and needed a world Orthodox structure to complete the picture. . . . If we did not enter, we would be represented and spoken for, in any case, without safeguards, controls, or [responsibly authorized] representation.
   b. We ended a situation of "taxation without representation"—one in which American Orthodox congregations raise millions for UJA and we have no say in how these funds are spent.
   c. We opened a new era of cooperation between the UJOC/NCYI and the partners in the new Israeli coalition (Mizrachi, Agudah, Herut) by giving the UOJC and other Orthodox bodies a voice in how major funds are to be spent.

Rabbi Stolper's communication then summarized "the major points," citing an agreement to draw up a constitution for the World Conference; defining its structure and function as an ad hoc body; reporting that "Maurice Jaffe gave us his acceptance of the provisions of the agreement in writing and gave us a signed letter of resignation"; and that "all appointments, and the system of rotation (to the WZO) to be set up and set forth in writing before the opening of the World Zionist Congress."

Putting aside the question as to the merits, or otherwise, of the associations undertaken with the World Zionist Organization and (prospectively) with the Jewish Agency—although the anticipated benefits are so far not clearly identifiable—the mode of proceeding itself bore, and has continued to bear, troubling implications. As with some other matters of the time, the precedent was established of bypassing the processes requisite for a responsible, representative communal body. The pattern of policy determination that was then forwarded was thereafter taken as more or less the established norm. Subsequent UOJCA administrations, with the procedural standards of earlier eras all but forgotten, have tended to follow suit in the pattern set in the mid-1970s.

The rationale offered—"It works, doesn't it?"—is sophistic. What can only really "work," without ultimate penalty, is a process conformable with the inherent requirements for such a conception as the Union of Orthodox Jewish Congregations of America.

36

Era of Enlargement

The era of the UOJCA administration headed by Julius Berman as president was marked, among various developments, by the inception of major enlargement of the Union's scale of operations, fiscal capacity, and practical equipment.

Previously, from the 1950s to the 1970s, there had been radical advances in organizational vista, ideological thrust, and program; there had been accompanying growth of staff and facilities. Now, although without an equivalent to the advent of the Feuerstein administration in dramatic upsurge of spirit and emboldened attitude on the Jewish scene, what emerged at this juncture led, as it developed, to an altogether new dimension in material areas, as well as to continued advances in general program.

Whether or not greater, in the sense of creative leadership in Jewish life, the Orthodox Union's rise to its present "bigness" in operations extent, staff, headquarters capacity, and advanced equipment, and surely not least of all in budget, undoubtedly gained its impetus in the Berman administration period. Along with the president's team of officers and commission heads, Rabbi Pinchas Stolper and his staff colleagues proved a force for practical growth.

From the first, Berman as president had set his sights on practical upscale. With broad grounding in the Union's affairs, he had seen its work expand under the compulsion of need, but always a strained expansion, painfully hobbled. With all too inadequate means for fulfillment of its assumed tasks, its finances were a make-do patchwork, yielding ever-mounting deficit. Now, what so quietly began to come about was an operative and fiscal transformation.

It was not that the vistas of the personalities directing the Union's course at this point were fixed on mere enlargement; aims were those of spiritual

310

elevation. Such a note was echoed at the occasion at which Julius Berman was elected as president—the 80th Anniversary Biennial Convention, held at the Capitol Hilton Hotel, Washington, D.C., 22–26 Cheshvan 5739/ November 22–26, 1978. But there was a realization that the time called for ways and means of different order from those of before.

The policy of realism now stressed signified that to tackle the Union's tasks realistically, concepts of workforce, of tools and facilities, of budget and finance must be in scale with what was to be done. There was the realization, too, that operations funding for the 1980s was subject to terms different from what had been the measuring stick since the 1950s. The 1980s dollar was, after inflation years, but a fraction of that 1950s dollar, and was on its way to becoming the yet more shrunken dollar of subsequent years. And, further, it was to be seen that the economic status of the observant Jew of the 1980s differed greatly from that of his equivalent of an earlier generation.

Together with the beginning of a new day in the "how" of the functions of the Union of Orthodox Jewish Congregations of America came a change in tone of the Union's "what."

In the perspective of the interpreter of a century-long organizational course, the crux of historic change at this period may be seen as the new grasp of practical means. For those who introduced the change process, however, the crux of change was to be seen rather as enabling "the Administration to devote its time to substantive programming, both current and long-range," on which innovative achievement "ever since . . . successors in the Presidency have been able to capitalize."

EAST OF THE EAST RIVER

Each successive figure at the helm of American Orthodox Jewry's central force has brought to it the impress of his personality. Something of the outlook born of his life experience, his ideas and goals, has been registered in the organization's direction, as well as something of the mind-frame colored by the environment of his own community. In Julius Berman's case, this was a sequence from his growing years in Hartford, Connecticut; years, crowned with semichah, at Yeshiva University; then law school and a law career; and the establishment of his home in Forest Hills, Queens. His assumption of the presidential office, following years in preceding UOJCA elective posts, marked, among other things, the rising influence of that borough's communities in the affairs of the national Orthodox Jewish body and of the Jewish world at large.

Forest Hills, along with such Queens locales as Kew Gardens, Jackson Heights, Rego Park, Kew Gardens Hills, Flushing, Jamaica Estates, Briarwood, Bayside, Hillcrest and—earlier—the Rockaways, had been the site of great growth of Jewish population since mid-century. Thousands of shomer-mitzvoth families were among the swelling numbers. The rise of numerous Orthodox congregations and yeshivoth resulted.

These growing centers of the Torah-loyal, each with its own characteristics, were collectively rising to prominence on the Jewish map. Attitudes and thinking generated in these quarters were now well felt in the Union's leadership channels. The Forest Hills contingent, especially, had become prominent in the organization's active circles, with such figures as Bernard Levmore, Herbert Berman, Gustave Jacobs, Dr. Bernand Lander, and, of course, Julius Berman himself as the long-time advance guard. Now also making their mark in Orthodox Union endeavors were others of Forest Hills identity, among them Prof. Shimon Kwestel, David Fund, Elliot Stavsky, Allan Fagin, Zev Berman, and Franklin Snitow. So, with the Union then headed by one bearing that community's distinctive stamp,[1] it is perhaps appropriate to see in the enlargement phase of the Orthodox Union something of the newer, "outer-borough," stage of New York's, and America's, Jewish development.

---

1. This writer hastens to note that the community referred to, though exceptionally represented, was but one of many from across the continent with figures in the Union's leadership team. In addition to those aforementioned (and to others, of various locales, cited earlier), the array in those years of national officeholders, commission and committee chairmen, and key regional figures, plus others then newly coming to the fore in various capacities, were from diverse areas, all contributing to the progress being made. Among them were: Harry Bearman; Harvey Blitz; Daniel Chill; Philip Fuchs; Samuel E. Eisenstat; Emil Fish; Dr. Mandell I. Ganchrow; Ronald Greenwald; Benjamin Mandel; Joseph Miller; Donald Press; Howard Rhine; Solomon T. Scharf; Joel M. Schreiber; Neal Twersky; Saul Quinn; Dr. Jacob R. Ukules; and Marcel Weber.

The foregoing were all from various communities of the Metropolitan New York–New Jersey area. From other parts were: Earl Korchak and Jack M. Nagel, Los Angeles, and Sanford Deutch and Ernie Goldberger, Beverly Hills, California; Charles Batt, Hartford, Connecticut; Alan Lapping and Gerald I. Fishman, Chicago; Joseph Macy, Brookline, Massachusetts; Emanuel Reich, Nathan Futeral, and Dr. Noah Lightman, Baltimore; Dr. Heschel J. Raskas and Dr. Issac Bonick, St. Louis; E. David Subar and Dr. Ronald Berger, Rochester, New York; Irving Stone, Cleveland, and Herman Herskovic, Cincinnati; Donald B. Butler, Pittsburgh; Al Herbert Thomas and Larry Brown, Memphis, Tennessee; Marcus Rosenberg, Dallas. Canadian representation in this key group included Max M. Richler and Edward B. Wolkove, Montreal; and Hy Bergel and David Woolf, Toronto.

OPERATIVE AND
BUDGETARY PROGRAMMING

The direction to be taken by his administration was set forth by Julius Berman in an "informal" meeting of officers in early November 1978. Emphasis was placed on tightening ties with the congregations and development of the regions. "The goal is to develop UOJCA as a true grass roots movement." Each of the Union's departments, its range of services and activities, was to function on specifically programmed lines, and each was to function within a specified budget and "with lay chairmen and officers to participate actively" in the supervision of the departments or areas assigned to them for oversight.

The emphasis on "lay direction" was—and remained—a key nuance of President Berman's outlook on the character of the organization. It signified self-conduct of the Union by its congregational participants, through their representatives, the elected apparatus, as distinguished from operative command by the professional staff, as had become the established fact in some organizations. It was in this sense that, according to the minutes of the "informal" meeting, the new President took occasion to emphasize that "the Union is a lay organization."

Notwithstanding the doctrine of lay-operative "hands-on," the policy set forth called for fuller professionalization, especially of the NCSY staff. Provision was to be made for regional directors to be regularly paid, and various active workers on irregular semi-staff, semi-volunteer basis were to be put on full-time professional standing, with appropriate, regularly paid salaries. Staff appointments were to be made for departments lacking professional staff, such as synagogue servicing, education, and religious development. Important changes were in view in Kashruth Division procedures.

The funding, as envisioned in the administrative program, was to be projected on businesslike lines, in accordance with the overall budgetary needs. The funding operation was to be conducted under direction of the officers by the executive staff and the professional operation of a director of development. The program was to be geared to the elimination of accumulated deficits, as well as to cover the ongoing needs of all facets of the Union.

It was agreed at this initial meeting, as recorded in the "informal" minutes, that the fundraising program was to be initiated by the officers themselves. "Each officer will be individually contacted for his personal pledge toward the National budget." While the personal commitment formula adopted as the basis for major fundraising was a familiar one, in this case it was notable for the fact that it was actually fulfilled. Out of the fulfillment was to come a new, thoroughgoing fundraising structure.

This would not be an overnight accomplishment. Actually, it would take a stretch of years, going well beyond the six years (three successive two-year terms) to the Berman presidency to reach what would become the budgetary and fiscal makeup of the Union of Orthodox Jewish Congregations of America of the 1990s. But this structure, keeping apace of the extraordinary functional expansion, is the outcome of the fiscal transformation of the 1980s.

There was much trial-and-error along the way. After the first year of the new program, with staff increases and other added expenditures weighing against increased income, a $250,000 deficit remained. While the administration leadership played a full part, a key role was exercised by Rabbi Pinchas Stolper. Several fundraising specialists succeeded each other in turn, each to advance the progress in one way or another before leaving for easier associations. In time, what was to be seen as the right match for the Union's need—with its hard-to-package appeal—was to be found in the present director of development, Sheldon Fliegelman, in whom the title finds full meaning, and his similarly percipient and devoted associate director, Steven M. Karp. These two, under the guidance of Rabbi Stolper and with sound grasp of the inherent meaning of the Union, were to manifest an adept application of the requisite technique.

SUPPLEMENTS AND BASICS

What was thus to take form was still—as in the nature of the situation it must be—in principle supplementary to the membership dues of affiliated congregations. Chronically overshadowed as this basic source has been by other funding means, the essential importance of the dues principle is apt to be lost sight of in both UOJCA circles and the congregations at large.

It is as the corporate embodiment of its community that the community synagogue has its being. It is as the collective embodiment of the congregational totality, the Torah community as national entity, that the Union has its being. The tie between Union and congregation is one, in high principle, of mutual indispensability. Effectuation of the tie requires, on the part of the Union, the serving of the common needs of its constituents; on the part of the congregations, the sustenance of the Union's work, including participation in its budget through membership dues.

As the 1980s succeeded the 1970s, the dues rate payable to the Union by its member congregations, up to then $5 per capita annually, was raised to $10. Then and since, some congregations have remitted on the new basis, but others have fallen short. In contrast to the notable progress in income by other means, this basic source continued, through this period and thereafter, to make only limited progress.

This problem, which has fettered the Union of Orthodox Jewish Congregations of America throughout its history, was not among those overcome in the Berman years—or since, for that matter. For some time, an "Achdus Committee," set up by the Union and the Rabbinical Council of America jointly, addressed itself earnestly to the dues situation. Some improvements were gained, but some feel that fundamental change awaits far-going development of organic ties between the congregations and their members, and the Union.

Strikingly better results were gained in the individual-membership category. Here, the rise in the sense of personal identification with the national Torah community arm, which had been building up year by year, now sprouted freely. Propagated now with applied technique, personal membership in the Orthodox Union became a widespread, accepted practice among the communally concerned of all shades of Orthodoxy. Voluntary choice of annual dues amount—in several categories—being offered, a surprising proportion chose the higher rates, although there was no difference in membership benefits—all alike receiving the Union's periodicals and other publications and special communications, plus the universally popular pocket-calendar diary. Year after year, unfailingly, from the 1980s on, the pace of growth of individual membership rolls has set new records.

A new category of support now introduced was the Orthodox Union Associates. Here, too, the participants choose the contribution amount, on annual basis, of their preference. Here, however, the amounts of optional choice are in categories of multiples from $1,000 yearly upward. Remarkably successful and constantly growing, the Orthodox Union Associates has become a major pillar of the UOJCA budget.

The primary fundraising occasion for the national body continued, in that era and since, to be the Annual National Dinner. Unfailingly gala, this event has been unfailingly productive for both public aura and financial benefit. And, as before, the Biennial Conventions have continued to provide occasion, in the course of the events and deliberations, for significant financial contributions to the Union's work.

The totality of all these funding developments was to take the Orthodox Union far, indeed, from its budgetary boundaries of old. Income growth, for all its attained magnitude, has been hard put to keep abreast of growth of expenditures. The multiplication of personnel and their manifold diversification of function; the spread, relative to the headquarters space of the "old days," of the space of national headquarters; the fine conference and meeting rooms; the many office units; the array of costly computer equipment, office equipment, copying, printing, folding and mailing equipment; and many etceteras—all these things, to those who remember what existed previously, are remarkable. One welcomes the knowledge that all is being done to the right purpose, efficiently and productively.

IMPLEMENTATION

The operative aim of the Berman administration was forwarded with some irregularity. There was considerable fluctuation in both lay and staff assignments and in the objectives of the several units of the Union's activities.

Among the successive figures who served for varying periods as commission chairman were some who would later appear in changed capacity; others presently no longer appear in the active leadership roster. For a while, Rabbi Herschel Schacter[2] served as chairman of the Communal Relations Commission, to be succeeded by Dr. Joel Rosenheim. Sheldon Rudoff, chairman of the Publications Commission, served also for a time as Campus Commission chairman, with Harvey Blitz as associate chairman. The chairmanship of the Limud Torah Commission passed, under the sad circumstances of death, from Charles Batt to Sender Kolatch; later, Rabbi Sholom Rephun took over. The vaunted Achdus Commission, a joint Union–Rabbinical Council undertaking, under the chairmanship of David Fund, after its first productive months lost volition and then faded away. So too, apparently, did the Adult Education Commission, which Dr. Henry Horowitz served as chairman.

A number of staff appointments were made in the early 1980s. In several cases, however, the appointees were assigned to more than one commission of department. This limited the applicable focus and the time needed for meaningful fulfillment of the programs.

Whether due to the above mentioned circumstances or other causes, the appointments made in some areas proved to be short-lived. Synagogue Servicing (sometimes called Synagogue Activities), Regions and Councils, Adult Education, Soviet Jewry, and Campus, were areas thus affected.

There can thus be seen in this period, alongside relatively sound development, a degree of makeshift planning.

The Limud Torah Commission, however, earned its keep with the

---

2. Rav for many years of the Mosholu Jewish Center, in the Bronx. Not to be confused with his near namesake, Rabbi Hershel Schachter, rosh yeshivah of Yeshivath Rabbenu Yitzchak Elchanan.

launching, after long preparation, of the highly prized *Luach and Limud*. This pocket-sized diary struck an imaginative new path with its sections for daily Mishnah study portions, in Hebrew and English, plus succinct explanatory commentary in English. Well received from the first, the *Luach and Limud*, published monthly, retained a following of thousands of individuals and groups over the years.

A less enduring project teamed the Limud Torah Commission with the more irregularly functioning Adult Education Commission and a unit of the Rabbinical Council of America. This project entailed the institution of a national chain of synagogal Torah-learning courses, for the regularly scheduled group study of Mishnah Yomith or Halachah Yomith, the assigned portions of the Mishnah and standard expositions of Jewish law and practice. Under this program, each participating group would study the same Mishnah or halachic source. At the completion of each segment of the course, the participants would receive credits, and, at a later stage, a certificate.

The idea of generating a sense of sharing with like groups across the country in a common Torah-learning course held much appeal, and numerous congregations joined the program. But it appears that the requisite follow-through was lacking. In the absence of continuous, focused central direction, the project languished.

The activities of the Campus Commission in the period under consideration seem to have gone unrecorded. Earlier, this field had been under the care of the Youth Division. The then chairman of the Youth Commission, Ronald Greenwald, had urged, in a 1979 communication to Julius Berman, the appointment of a full-time director for the "collegiate program," despite "three aborted attempts at collegiate effort." There is no reason to assume that any measure of lasting accomplishment was gained at the time in this area, whether under the aegis of either the Campus Commission or the Youth Commission.

MISSION TO WASHINGTON

The Communal Relations Commission had for a time the benefit of a staff director, David Merzel, who was also assigned to the Publications Commission. So equipped, the Communal Relations unit went beyond its previous range with a new project, the Mission to Washington. Launched in 1981, this activity has been renewed periodically.

At its origin, the Mission to Washington followed a pattern that was to prove effective over the years. A call initially went out, through the Union's channels, for volunteers to join in a mission of fact-finding and individual meetings with government figures, senators, and congressional representatives on behalf of Israel and other Jewish interests. The response for this first mission was immediate, has been the case ever since. The assembled group of volunteer researchers and lobbyists proceeded on the specified date, as arranged, to the nation's capitol. In Washington the group was given special briefings on major matters of Jewish concern at the White House, the Israeli Embassy, and AIPAC (the American–Israeli Political Affairs Committee), after which it proceeded to similarly arranged visits with members of the United States Senate and the House of Representatives.

The initial 1981 Mission to Washington enrolled fifty participants, a convenient number for the purpose. Subsequent missions were of similar number, although at times participation went as high as a hundred. Quickly adopted as a permanent program, the Mission was the basis of what was at first designated UOJCA's Commission on Political Action, of which Samuel M. Eisenstat was the initial chairman.

At the third Mission to Washington in 1984, Dr. Mandell Ganchrow served as mission chairman. He also chaired what was now designated the Political Action Advisory Commission. Dr. Ganchrow's various communal activities, in addition to his Orthodox Union endeavors (not to mention his busy medical practice!), included chairmanship of a leading AIPAC chapter.

∽

While the Union's relationships with its constituent congregations is obviously at its very heart, this central facet of the organization's concerns did not, at this time, gain the intensive attention given some other areas.

SPOTLIGHT ON NCSY

The starring role in the Orthodox Union's overall program at this point (as previously and since), the Youth Division's ever-growing National Conference of Synagogue Youth, enabled the effectuation of the staff appointments envisioned in the initial Berman administration meeting.

A key position to be filled was that of associate director. This position had been held over the past thirteen years by Rabbi Jack Simcha Cohen and Rabbi Chaim Wasserman—each of whom, had in turn, after devoted NCSY service, accepted calls to the rabbinates of noted congregations— and Rabbi David Cohen, who was transferred to new duties in temporary service as national UOJCA director. Now appointed to the associate director post, joined to that of director of regions, was Moshe Greenwald, previous director of the NCSY Midwest region. He was shortly succeeded by Rabbi Baruch Taub, who, in due course—after serving for a period as national NCSY director—left for a Canadian rabbinic post.

Subsequently, in a successor administration but upon the recommendation of Julius Berman, there came the engagement of Rabbi Raphael Butler, who was to make a lasting mark first with NCSY as associate national director, then as national director, and, ultimately, as executive vice president of the Orthodox Union.

One early-1980s appointment that proved to be enduring was that of Rabbi Yitzchak Rosenberg as NCSY's national program director. Rabbi Rosenberg assumed, within a broadened range of activities, the program work that had been conducted for several years previously by the talented Anne Weinrauch.

The NCSY regional appointments of the early 1980s were on a relatively large scale. Eighteen regional directors were then appointed, eight of which were on full-time basis, and the other ten part-time. In addition, three assistant regional directors were engaged, one on full-time and the two others on part-time basis.

While the NCSY regions as such were to have responsibility for their respective budgets, this proved, as a practical matter, to require a greater or lesser subsidy allocation from national UOJCA headquarters.

Eventually, the staffing of both the national and the regional NCSY, along with their activities ranges, outstripped the Berman-era expansion. Some of the NCSY regional directors were also expected to serve the "adult" Union regions, a circumstance that has not proved meaningful. The world of the congregation and the world of the teenager are vastly different; rarely can be found those who can function effectively or can be motivated to serve organizationally or programmatically in both.

YACHAD AND OUR WAY

Born in the 1980s were two auxiliary NCSY forces serving heretofore unmet needs of two disadvantaged segments of Jewish youth: Our Way, for the hearing-impaired, and Yachad, for the developmentally disabled. Each of these forces grew and flourished in the succeeding years, winning appreciation far and wide for their enrichment of the lives of many hundreds of boys and girls guided to light and happiness in the Torah way.

Looking back with particular satisfaction on the UOJCA's establishment of these two additions to its community services, Julius Berman has said:

What we did here was to focus upon a totally ignored segment of our community and project the cause to the forefront of the community agenda. We were the first—and in a sense the only—organization within the Orthodox Jewish community to underscore the responsibility of the community to these individuals, and, of almost equal significance, to their parents and siblings.

I shall never forget the letter I received from a parent who informed me in all candor that, due to the fact that her child had virtually no social interaction with other children, in the event the *church* across the street had a program for such children, she would have been willing to have her children participate there—anything to get the child "out of the closet." But, Yachad came along to save the day.

Here we are dealing—almost literally—with the saving of lives. And we at the Union were specially equipped to adopt such a beautiful chesed project, since we had a broad-based youth movement to which Yachad and Our Way children could be attached. Thereby the mainstreaming of many Yachad and Our Way activities could be accomplished.

~

It fell to the Youth Division, too, to reach out on the Union's behalf to the young people of the rising tide of immigration in this period from the Soviet Union. The Orthodox Union, with other of American Jewry's organized forces, now faced a new reality—the presence of thousands of newcomers who were products of three generations of the extinguishing of Jewish life; Jews with not a shred of Jewish background, to whom Jewishness was completely alien.

Various activities were undertaken or sponsored by the Union for aid to this mounting influx, among them the distribution of Russian translations of UOJCA and NCSY literature. These publications were chosen for their basic understanding of, or introduction to, the Jewish way. Another project was undertaken in cooperation with the B'er Hagolah Yeshivah, which had been established to give the Russian immigrant children and youths a basic Torah education in preparation for their integration into established yeshivoth.

On the Union's part, "the expertise of NCSY was desperately needed to conduct Shabbatonim, discussion groups, etc., using informal education approaches," as reported to a UOJCA Board meeting by Youth Division Director Stolper. The report continued: "the professional [to be engaged by the Union for the project] would initially work with the Brooklyn community, and the formula and programming to be developed would then be transplanted to other regions and communities around the country" (Minutes, Meeting of Board of Directors and Board of Governors, December 1979). In 1980, Rabbi Dov Shurin was engaged to direct the joint project with B'er Hagolah. After months of effort, however, it appeared that the *shidduch* between the two institutions was not working out. The undertaking was terminated, the Union pursuing programs of other kinds for the Soviet emigres.

~

It was in this period, too, that the kashruth service of the Union of Orthodox Jewish Congregations of America sprouted into what became an era of spectacular expansion.

Julius Berman continued, as president of UOJCA, to keep in close touch with the Kashruth Commission, of which he had long been a key member. He appointed Joel Schreiber and Shimon Kwestel as associate chairmen of that commission to aid the veteran Chairman Nathan K. Gross, then in failing health. Kwestel, in particular, devoted himself to the needs and problems of the Ⓤ service. He viewed with a fresh eye the procedures and methods that had been developed over the years, and saw, as did President Berman, the need for major changes to facilitate what would be a veritable explosion of calls for Ⓤ validation by new companies.

The ensuing studies bore fruit, in the succeeding Kwestel administration, with the enlargement of the Kashruth Department's administrative staff and plant supervisory personnel.

~

The additions to the professional and clerical staffs of the several departments, as well as equipment and other physical needs, necessitated larger headquarters. The quarters at 84 Fifth Avenue (the Union's address following that of 305 Broadway) being too small, there followed a move to 116 East 27th Street, and another move, in late 1981, to 45 West 36th Street. Before long, this site was also outgrown, resulting in the establishment of the present quarters on two full floors at 333 Seventh Avenue. At this writing, another floor of this large building is being prepared for the Union's use.

~

It was in his third term as UOJCA president that Julius Berman was called upon to serve concurrently as chairman of the Conference of Presidents of Major American Jewish Organizations, a post that is considered as in a class by itself in the Jewish organizational realm. The post entails spokesmanship on behalf of the entire organized American Jewish community on matters of Israel–U.S. relations. As presiding officer of the instrument of collective American Jewish organizational leadership, the chairman meets and confers personally with the highest personages in American government and public life, including, as occasion might require, the President of the United States. He is responsible for leading his fellow presidents in the determination of policy in questions of large import, and in achieving consensus on sharply disputed issues.

Nominations for election as chairman of the Conference of Presidents of Major Jewish Organizations are made by a committee designated by the group for the purpose. The choice is made from among the participating organizational presidents, who are the electors. The term of chairmanship office is one year, re-electable for a second year.

This was the first time since the association was established that the incumbent was head of the Orthodox Union.[3] While looked upon as a signal recognition of Orthodoxy's rise on the American scene, there was also apparently among the leaders of the assorted constituencies a sense of exceptional regard for the character and qualities of the UOJCA president.

Needless to say, Julius Berman distinguished himself in his handling of this office. He brought pride to all and naches to Orthodox Jewry at large—by his skill in dealing with a succession of sensitive issues; by his quiet assurance; by the dignity of his bearing and the clarity of his voice before the determiners of policy and the great of the land; and by his expression, under all circumstances, of the Torah outlook.

An added benefit was the series of published reports on developments as they occurred that Julius Berman composed for distribution to UOJCA members. These publications were marked by lucid, succinct reportage that gave insights on what had transpired and elucidated the background.

Thus, the Berman presidency closed on a note of distinguished service to the American Jewish community.

---

3. Two other notable Orthodox Jewish figures, Rabbi Herschel Schacter and Rabbi Israel Miller, had earlier served—but not in UOJCA capacity—as Conference of Presidents chairman.

37

Amid Shifting Currents

At the 86th Anniversary Biennial Convention (Hyatt Regency Hotel, Baltimore, 27 Cheshvan–Rosh Chodesh Kislev, 5745/November 22–25, 1984), Shimon (Sidney) Kwestel was elected as the fourteenth president of the Union of Orthodox Jewish Congregations of America. A native of Brooklyn's Borough Park, Shimon Kwestel was, like his predecessor in office, a lawyer and a resident of Forest Hills, New York.

In the six years of his active participation in UOJCA endeavors, Kwestel had made his mark among the emerging new generation of leadership. His devotion to the national Torah community force was characterized by the premise, voiced on more than one occasion, that "the Orthodox Union's pivotal role rests on the fact of its very existence; beyond its manifold services, invaluable as these are, it is the Union as Union, as embodiment of American Torah Jewry's corporate self, that is unique, indispensable, and irreplaceable."

Within the compass of this philosophy, the incoming president's programmatic vista was set on integrating the Union with the lives of all in the Torah synagogue fold, through services to their daily needs as well as to their common interests. "The Union and the school-goer at large must share life, and they must be aware of the sharing," he stated. Kwestel's outlook was furthered by his capacity as Professor of Law at Touro College.

(At this juncture it is opportune to take note of Touro College, a curious development on the higher-education scene. This institution, named after Judah Touro, the noted early nineteenth-century philanthropist, sprang from the ingenious mind of Dr. Bernard Lander, also of the Forest Hills community. A sociologist long on the faculty of Yeshiva University, Dr. Lander had aspired to a collegiate undertaking shaped by his own ideas and addressed to Jewish students of diverse backgrounds. With a creative flair that surprised many, Dr. Lander first brought into active being a college in

Manhattan that offered academic credit courses for male and female students in both liberal arts and Judaic studies. Then, in rapid succession, he created a series of additional college-level schools, all under the Touro College umbrella, with a range of humanities, professional, and Judaica courses in various parts of the metropolitan New York area. Touro College and its various schools, while open to students at large, was instituted to bear a warmly Jewish atmosphere. It early won a response among Jewish students seeking to advance themselves in both academic or professional studies and in Jewish life. One of the accomplishments of Dr. Lander's enterprise was the establishment of a law school.)

Actually, much of the day-to-day burden of the UOJCA presidency during the final years of the prior administration had been shared by Shimon Kwestel, Julius Berman then being heavily taxed with his responsibilities as head of the Conference of Presidents. Kwestel had served then as part of a steering committee of which Sheldon Rudoff had been chairman.

POLITICAL, MILITARY, AND EMOTIONAL VARIABLES

The Kwestel administration period was set in a time when the Jewish world generally was on a sort of rollercoaster. In the years after the Six-Day War, euphoria had ebbed; the unifying effect of that soul-stirring experience had faded, too. Each one of the diverse compositions of Jews had remained fastened to its particular doctrinal or outlook pattern. Divisions, rivalries, and hostilities had resumed their full sway.

Then had come the Yom Kippur War of 1974–1975, shattering complacency. Confidence was partially restored by Egyptian President Anwar Sadat's astonishing visit to Jerusalem. Then had come, under U.S. President Jimmy Carter's pressure, the yielding of the Sinai Peninsula to Egypt, as the price of what proved to be but a cold peace.

There had by now spread in Israel a widely deplored, but widely shared, lapse of the idealism theretofore characteristic of the Jewish state's populace. The social goal gave way before the struggle for personal advancement and material benefit. Yeridah, the abandonment of life in Israel to pursue the allures of advanced Western lands—including even Germany—took on massive proportion. Those leaving were largely the irreligious. They far outnumbered the aliyah, the continuing stream of those—almost all shomrey-mitzvoth—choosing to settle in the land of Israel at the sacrifice of the familiar comforts and security of the economically advanced democracies.

The yeridah, composed as it was of elements generally indifferent to—or even derisive of—the Jewish heritage, had a negative impact on the public Jewish mind. Its effects, felt wherever the *yordim* settled, were sharpened by the traits now seen as prevalent among them: an absence of both yiddishkeit and mentshlishkeit.

Spirits among the Jewish ranks at large were recharged by the dramatic development of the mounting migration of Jews at last released from Soviet bonds. At first, most sought and found new life in Israel; later came a change. The drama was heightened by the transfer to Israel—in two migrations, 1984 and 1990—of the Beta Yisrael communities from Ethiopia. Through uncounted centuries, these Falasha in the African heartland, completely isolated from the Jewish world, had cleaved to their sense of Jewish identity and their loyalty to the faith of Israel as maintained by their own distinctive traditions and rites.

FORWARD STEPS

As with all developments touching Jewish life, the preceding events were registered in the concerns of the Union of Orthodox Jewish Congregations of America. They found response among the congregations across the continent through the various facets of the Union's program, as well as by special actions of the Union, and by the Union's voice in the collective councils of Jewish affairs.

Continuing the pace of development pursued by the previous administration, the Kwestel presidency was marked by the introduction of new services, the expansion of established departments and significant moves in communications. A policy of "openness" brought the Union's constituency and the general Jewish public better knowledge of processes of the organization's departments, including kashruth.

ENTER KETUBAH

An entirely new addition to the services roster of the national body, launched in 1985, was that soon gaining wide note as "Ketubah." This program was the arm of the Orthodox Union in the "singles" field.

This new department, with specially appointed staff, was instituted at the initiative of Moses I. Feuerstein, formerly president and now an honorary president of the national body. Over the years that had passed since the conclusion of his terms of presidential office, "Moe," as this widely admired figure was popularly known, had actively maintained his devotion to the Union. In pressing for a constructive program to facilitate marriage among the growing singles population, he was addressing what had come to be a serious problem in American Jewish life. As chairman of the UOJCA Commission on Family and Marriage, he led the way in organizing the research and planning of the undertaking, and would head the Commission's activities over the years to the present.

As was stated in a Kwestel presidential report:

> The Orthodox Union's National Marriage Program addresses one of the most critical problems facing the Orthodox Jewish community—the proliferation of non-married and very late marriages. The resultant personal frustrations, and the loss to our people's historical continuity, spurred us to undertake a multi-faceted singles program in which matchmaking is the goal. We are encouraged by our success to date and are confident that by working together with our synagogues the Union's national marriage program will continue to build on its immediate record of achievement.

The anticipation was warranted. Within less than two years from the time of its launching, Feuerstein, as commission chairman, reported to the Executive Committee that Ketubah "had accomplished fourteen marriages and six engagements." He had also reported active participation in the Ketubah/Marriage program by the Women's Branch of the UOJCA and the Family Commission of the Rabbinical Council of America.

Serving as co-chair with Moses I. Feuerstein, and continuing actively to the present, was Beverly Luchfeld. The members of the Family and Marriage Commission showed consistent devotion to its purposes throughout. Ketubah also was fortunate throughout in its staff, headed for several years by Department Director Victoria De Vidas, who, following departure upon (appropriately!) her marriage, was succeeded by the present incumbent, Chanah Cohen, with Leah Kalish as department secretary.

~

The presidential report cited in the preceding also noted progress in several other activity fields. Sustained professional direction, for example, was brought to the Synagogue Services Division with the appointment, as director, of Rabbi Bertram Leff. The resulting annual series of regional retreat-type weekend institutes, Shabbatonim, and other activities were making a decided mark.

Regional leaders had reason to believe, however, that were these inspiriting gatherings to be built upon by a force of trained staff fieldworkers, comparable on the congregational level to the NCSY regional staff on the youth level, their effect would be far more enduring. This, however, was a need that is still awaiting fulfillment—with one notable exception. This was the West Coast region, with the appointment, as regional director, of Rabbi Alex Kalinsky. This appointment, together with the induction of a new set of officers headed by Marcus Nachimson as region president, marked the vibrant rebirth of the West Coast region.

Similar professionally staffed reconstruction was blueprinted for other regions. In the West Coast region, the momentum of active progress was maintained over the succeeding years. This had a marked effect on Torah-loyal Jewish life in the Pacific Coast communities, among which that of Seattle had always been outstanding. Upsurge was felt in far Western communities, with particular effect in Denver.

After the mid-1980s, the progress of the Synagogue Services Division was marked, according to presidential report, by a busy, productive program. It ranged from "trouble-shooting, arbitration, and consultation" with problem-beset congregations to a coast-to-coast sequence of "hundreds of retreats, Shabbatonim, Yarchei Kallah, Lectures and Synagogue Leadership Conferences."

In the years 5747 and 5748 (1986–1987 and 1988–1989), the weekend retreats conducted by the Synagogue Service Division, each fully programmed or program-aided and with guest faculty provided, were held in: Dallas, Texas; New Brunswick, New Jersey; South Bend, Indiana; St. Louis, Missouri; Newport, Rhode Island; Newport, California; Atlanta, Georgia; Miami Beach, Florida; Syracuse, New York; Chicago; Newport News, Virginia; and, in Canada, Vancouver, British Columbia; Toronto, Ontario; and Montreal, Quebec. The foregoing were, in some cases, resumptions after a lapse of some years of earlier series of regional assemblies; others were new innovations. Different in both regards was a long-established perennial, the weekend Torah Institute of the Baltimore Council of Orthodox Jewish Congregations, held in these years, as before, in a rural Maryland location. So too, it was, in this case with lesser seniority than the Baltimore event, with the Metropolitan New York Region's annual Torah Retreat and annual Yarchei Kallah.

The Kwestel presidential report cited also noted that the Funeral Standards Committee which "has established national standards and grievance procedures, publishes educational materials, and conducts seminars for Chevroth Kadisha, has established recently a community Chevra Kadisha for the Los Angeles area, and in the past few years has conducted a most successful National Conference on Funeral Standards." He indicated that reports received at various points by the Funeral Standards Committee and through other channels attested to the positive cumulative effect of this program.

THE ⓤ EXPLOSION

The ⓤ kashruth service, by now a heavyweight performer in the UOJCA array, attained extraordinary new levels of development in this period. Functioning with a high degree of self-containment, this department of the Torah community's central force continued to be supervised, as long established, by the Union's Kashruth Commission. As with all UOJCA commissions, appointments to the Kashruth Commission are made by the Union's president, usually at the beginning of his term of office. They are chosen from among members of the board of directors, in the case of the Kashruth Commission with the addition of some members of the Rabbinical Council of America appointed, by the Union's president, upon the recommendation of the president of the Rabbinical Council.

Under the Kwestel administration, the membership composition of the Kashruth Commission included some who had served before, as was warranted by their well-marked attentiveness to their responsibilities, plus some new appointees. The commission, together with the department's professional staff headed by the rabbinic kashruth administrator, Rabbi Menachem Genack, was now geared to notes of wider opportunity struck at the preceding Biennial Convention. They were prompted in this motivation by the outlook of both the administration of the Orthodox Union itself and the figure at the Commission's helm, Julius Berman—former, and now honorary, president. Berman had been appointed Kashruth Commission chairman following the passing of its honored leader of many years, Nathan K. Gross.

There now ensued a veritable explosion of applications for the Union's kashruth supervision. Applications came from firms of global scope, from processors of long-established "national brand" products and from newly launched processors; from food types familiar and food types novel; from domestic places near and far and lands near and far. They brought new dimensions of familiar halachic and supervisory situations, and situations and conditions of new kind and complexity. It was a veritable tidal wave.

REORGANIZATION OF STRUCTURE

Reorganization of Kashruth Division makeup, procedures, and equipment was now mandatory. At the prompting of President Kwestel, the reorganization was duly effected. The number of senior rabbinic representatives in cities central to the food industry was largely increased, and their status was elevated. At national headquarters, numerous carefully selected additions were made to the kashruth rabbinic staff. The added rabbinic staff personnel were assigned different functions in alignment with the multiplication not only of supervised firms and products, but of the vast diversity of items; sources; ingredients; technological, chemical, and industrial processes; and global dispersion of product origins. All this entailed a corresponding multiplication of intricate halachic problems requiring fresh research.

The dramatic development was summarized in a 1996 letter to this writer by Julius Berman that stated the following:

> Looking back at that period, the major expansion of Kashruth occurred during the past ten years. . . . The expansion of the Ⓤ Kashruth certification service into over 45 countries, with close to 3,000 plants under supervision; the arrangement with the Chief Rabbinate in Israel sanctioning the establishment by our Union of an office in Israel for our Ⓤ supervision and certification, jointly with that of the Chief Rabbinate, of Israeli-manufactured products to be sold throughout the world; the expansion of our internal Rabbinic headquarters officials to 30 Rabbinic personnel; plus corresponding additions to the secretarial and clerical staff; the introduction of computerization of critical facts; the necessary income growth; and on and on—all this occurred during my tenure as Chairman of the Kashruth Commission, during which I had the full cooperation of my successors as President, i.e., Shimon Kwestel and Sheldon Rudoff.

Appropriately complementing this is another extract, this time from a 1988 report by then-President Shimon Kwestel:

> It is a major source of pride for the American Jew to find Ⓤ products in airports, hotels, hospitals, and thousands of supermarkets and retail stores. Over the last six years, our Kashruth Division had experienced meteoric growth—from a six-person headquarters professional staff a few years ago to our present department headquarters complement of over 30, with equivalent multiplication of the Kashruth field supervisory force, with the world's most sophisticated computerized Kashruth control system. The Kashruth Division published hundreds of thousands of copies of the Ⓤ Kashruth Directory listing all Ⓤ products and facilities as well as hundreds of thousands of copies of the Ⓤ Kosher for Passover Directory. The Kashruth Division of the Union of Orthodox Jewish Congregations of America is the world's hub of Kashruth information.

Professor Kwestel has also expressed particular satisfaction in the effectuation, during his presidency, of the agreement with Israel's Chief Rabbinate for the extension of the Union's Ⓤ kashruth service to Israel. Duly sanctioned by then-Chief Rabbi (Ashkenazi) Avraham Shapira and

Chief Rabbi (Sephardi) Mordechai Eliyahu, the arrangement was successfully designed to further foodstuffs exports from Israel to Diaspora lands.
The arrangement proceeded through the years under a committee of which
the eminent Rav Simcha Hakohen Kook is chairman.

~

It is, perhaps, in order to suggest that the ultimate "hero" (or heroine) in
the remarkable Ⓤ accomplishment is the observant Jewish home and
homemaker.

By this stage, the unique role of the Ⓤ program in the Jewish world had
captured the interest of the broadest segment of the food industry as never
before. Along with it came a fresh recognition of the scope of the "kosher
market." Through the UOJCA, the observant Jewish public made its fealty
to Kashruth authenticity and communally responsible hashgachah a powerful force for Jewish resurgence. At the same time, these Jews of Jewish
conviction—the ultimate heroes of the Ⓤ's remarkable accomplishment—
had made their special food needs known and their religious standards
recognized by that giant marvel among these times, the modern-day food
industry.

Jewish history has so many strange chapters. Among them, one of
unique character is the way the keepers of Jewish homes exercised, through
the Union of Orthodox Jewish Congregations of America, the means to
shape to their spiritual needs a key area of the American economy. In final
analysis, the place of the Ⓤ in hundreds of thousands of Jewish lives in
America and beyond bear testimony to the force of personal Jewish belief.

NCSY: "BEYOND NORMAL PARAMETERS"

For the Union's Youth Division, too, progress took on new dimensions in
the years (1984–1990) of the Kwestel administration.

By the mid-1980s, close to 25,000 teenagers were reached each year by
NCSY programs, as reported by Youth Commission Chairman Harvey
Blitz, who had succeeded Sheldon Rudoff to that office originally held, until
his untimely decease, by the long-devoted Harold H. Boxer. Fully 11,000 of
the participants were regularly dues-paying members. The total NCSY
annual budget at that time, national and regional combined, was reported
to be almost $3.5 million.

It was pointed out in the same report that, pursuant to a Biennial
Convention recommendation, the Youth Commission had advanced a
policy of "outreach beyond the normal parameters of NCSY . . . a very
aggressive outreach program having contact with Jewish youth in non-

Orthodox congregations as well as the still-existing Hebrew Schools." Lave and Ta'am, respectively for teenage and preteenage boys and girls of those backgrounds, were the NCSY vehicles instituted for this purpose. The well-tried NCSY Shabbaton programs were effectively adapted to the Lave and Ta'am undertakings.

Also instituted was the development of free "Hebrew high schools," for attendance, after their regular school times, by students of public high schools. After the initial establishment of three such schools in "three geographic areas," this project was expanded nationwide. A 1988 report by Rabbi Raphael Butler, then National Youth Division director, stated:

> A Teen Torah Center of Free Torah High is now operating in each of the following communities: Baltimore, Maryland; Toronto, Ontario; Mineola, New York; Queens, New York; Merrick, New York; Coram, [New York]; Cleveland, Ohio; Detroit, Michigan, and soon, Los Angeles, California.

These centers and schools were designed, with great success in most cases, to enable their participants to voluntarily pursue Torah studies on a regular weekly after school-hours basis.

Another NCSY innovation was the "Jerusalem Experience." Introduced initially in the New York and Miami-area communities and then in Toronto and New Jersey, it was thereafter conducted for teenagers in many other parts of North America. This project was hailed in a presidential summation by Professor Kwestel as:

> having almost a magical effect on apathetic and "unaffiliated" young people which transforms them in only eight days [of Holy Land encounter] into concerned and searching Jewish youth who wish to savor the taste of Torah.

With these newer projects and the established National Conference of Synagogue Youth range of programs, the Orthodox Union's NCSY won recognition by the mid-1980s as the largest informal Torah-educational institution in the country. More than 50 percent of its participants came from nonobservant homes—in many cases, from homes entirely devoid of Jewish ties. In many instances, the parents (or other family members) were moved by the example of their NCSY children to find their own way to Torah and mitzvoth.

"NCSY's Torah message and unique educational approach," President Kwestel declared in this summation, "continues to appeal so powerfully to the hearts and minds of third- and fourth-generation of assimilated Jews."

Beyond the "informal" education outreach services, there was added to the apparatus of the UOJCA Youth Division in this period the Schottenstein Youth College. This generously sponsored educational instrument was instituted to incorporate the array of NCSY study programs into an integrated academic composition. The Schottenstein Youth College took on an increasingly substantial role as it ripened and developed over the years to the present.

STAFF STABILITY

In a mid-1980s report to the UOJCA Executive Committee on behalf of the Youth Commission, Rabbi Butler said:

> The problem we have encountered is the need for serious, committed professional personnel who treat their position not as a way station for further advancement but rather as an end to itself.

Fortunately, however, the Youth Division's national director was able, in a subsequent report, to state more optimistically:

> Thanks to the encouragement of the Union, the Regional NCSY Directors now view their position as a career move . . . the average tenure of a NCSY Regional Director is now at least four years.

Since then, according to the records, the duration of tenure has further stabilized.

Also introduced in the 1980–1990 decade was NCSY's Jewish Overseas Leadership Training Course, "Jolt." This project, providing a travel–study course, bridges "the pain of Eastern Europe with the joy of Medinath Yisrael," with on-site contact. Well received from the first, this project has continued as part of NCSY operations through the years.

Yachad, the Orthodox Union's program for developmentally disabled youth, and Our Way, for hearing-impaired youth, both steadily advanced their programs as the 1980s became the 1990s. The first, with Torah study groups, Israel summer seminars, summer tours, the Achim Gad Yachad fellowship, family retreats, and their own *Yachad* magazine, greatly expanded their numbers. In this period, Yachad chapters were established in ten U.S. states and one Canadian province. Similarly, such Our Way projects as special-educational Shabbatonim, the *Let's Get Together Friendship* and *Torah Correspondence* magazines, the special telephone-teletype, and the establishment of the Association for Jewish Parents of the Deaf were seen as further manifestations of the creativity of this special UOJCA–NCSY service.

In the presidential summation previously referred to, Professor Kwestel said:

As Yachad and Our Way bring the developmentally disabled and the deaf into the Torah way and into the mainstream of Jewish Life, it also provides the Jewish community with the privilege and tremendous joy of focusing on their abilities, not their disabilities.

ISRAEL CENTER IN JERUSALEM—
NEW LAURELS

In large measure, the progressively advancing Orthodox Union Israel Center in Jerusalem functioned in this period, as it has since, under the Youth Division umbrella. Of its development at that point, a presidential expression said:

> Thousands find a home from home in which they are exposed to the Torah way of life where both "religious" and "non-religious" feel welcome and comfortable. Each week its yellow doors welcome almost a thousand people who enjoy the Center's broad range of programs. Most recently, Russian immigrants who are being newly awakened to their Jewish heritage are participating in the UOJCA Jerusalem Center's program for Jews from [then] Soviet lands, it included sponsorship of Sedarim throughout the Jerusalem area for 1,000 of these brethren freed from bondage to an atheistic autocracy.

With a view to the extension of the Union's NCSY movement to Israel, the Israel Center also provided a base for experimental pilot projects for the purpose.

PUBLICATIONS, A LA CARTE

The advances noted on the previous pages were not equaled in other areas. The communication process, though not escaping administrative attention, was forwarded during the Kwestel presidency with the same absence of overall planning or interdepartmental coordination as before.

The aggregate publications output, in its unsystemized fashion, reached new quantitative heights in the 1980s. A publications catalog of the period lists 240 items in many different subject areas. Catalog items range in size from one-page leaflets to full-size books, with a range of expository, informational, inspirational, educational, and practical reference topics. The largest number of titles listed in that catalog, as in prior and current listings, emanated from the Youth Division.

It is shown in a separate source that the largest distribution of given items was the Kashruth's Division's Ⓤ Directory and Ⓤ Kosher-for-Passover Directory, each of which was distributed in the hundreds of thousands. Altogether, it seems that the total distribution of all Orthodox Union publications was well over a million copies annually. Although the absence of coordination in the planning of the diverse multidepartmental literary, informational, and educational output impaired the potential for collective impress, there can be no doubt of the practical influence of this work in the various areas addressed.

From this abundant constellation, though, one star had fallen. It seems from the minutes of officers' meetings during the Berman presidency that the Union's administration had been in doubt as to what to do with the previously bimonthly, and now quarterly, magazine *Jewish Life*. Formerly a source of prestige for the Orthodox Union, with widely felt influence and a significant subscriber following, the magazine's distinction had declined with changes in its long-time editorship. The physical appearance of the publication had been enhanced by a new format introduced by its final editor, Yaakov Jacobs; this, and some changes in content and circulation methods reported on hopefully by the chairman of the Publications commission, Sheldon Rudoff, did not prove satisfying to the organization's officers. It seems that with the needs of other UOJCA undertakings having strong priority on the Union's strained financial resources, it was decided that the costs involved in the publication of *Jewish Life* should no longer be absorbed. So, in 1983, publication of this magazine was summarily suspended.

To many then, and to those now who recollect the place *Jewish Life* had occupied in the Jewish world, termination of this organ was, and is, seen as among the Orthodox Union's serious mistakes.

THE RISE OF *JEWISH ACTION*

With the extinction of one literary star, however, another was soon to rise. In 1985, the Publications Commission, now under the chairmanship of Joel Schreiber, came forward with a plan to repair the loss created by the suspension of *Jewish Life*. His idea was to transform the Union's house organ, *Jewish Action*, into a magazine combining literary content with other matter. The plan was approved by the Kwestel administration, and arrangements proceeded forthwith.

Over the years, *Jewish Action* had mostly carried news of UOJCA events and activities, with some items from local congregational scenes. More recently, several quarterly issues under the editorship of Yaakov Kornreich had been of superior journalistic and editorial quality, with wider news coverage. Kornreich was presently succeeded by Brachah Orlovsky, under whom further improvements were made, including some magazine-type articles. Now, under the new plan, the periodical was reborn as a quarterly magazine with an entirely new literary program and new physical format. The first issue of the new *Jewish Action* was dated Fall 1985. It appeared under the editorship of Heidi Tenzer, with Matis Greenblatt as literary editor. The masthead listed, in addition to Joel Schreiber as publications commission chairman, a distinguished roster of contributing editors. In standard magazine format, printed on coated stock and with an attractive color cover, the magazine made a pleasing appearance. The content— which was subsequently to develop further while retaining much of the same general character through succeeding issues—was of a rather curious twofold nature. The first half was composed of serious articles of literary quality that treated subjects of Jewish interest both topical and conceptual, plus book reviews and some special features. All articles were knowledgeably written, and the overall editing was manifestly creditable. While this part of the publication was clearly aimed at the reader attuned to Jewish thought and contemporary Jewish issues, the other part was as patently addressed to "the Jewish consumer." It contained items on kashruth developments and questions, plus the ⓤ News Reporter, previously issued in leaflet form.

For all the incongruity of its twofold makeup, the reborn *Jewish Action* was well received. While some personal subscriptions eventually developed, circulation was basically with members of affiliated congregations, on basis of per capita dues payment, plus individual members and supporters.

In 1992, Heidi Tenzer (after her marriage, Heidi Pekarsky) was succeeded by the magazine's present editor, Charlotte Friedland. Like her predecessor, editor Friedland, together with literary editor Greenblatt, has shown creative and accomplished editorial ability in the course of the magazine's continuing career. Throughout, the constant attention and perceptive judgment of chairman Joel Schreiber played a large part in the *Jewish Action* picture.

In the years since its rebirth, *Jewish Action* has won the interest and good opinion of the discerning. Content quality and range have been well-maintained; reader correspondence, book reviews, and other features have been on intelligent levels. Particular attention was won by the series of symposia and the numerous special articles on issues of major concern. The technical production was likewise of professional quality, the lavish use of color adding to its appeal. The "homely" matter was handled deftly to increase its utility while mitigating its coupling with the literary fare.

Two other periodicals were newly introduced under the Kwestel administration: *Mesorah* and *Jewish Thought*. *Mesorah*, a project of the Kashruth division, has served since its 1989 origins as a journal "exploring in depth

Halachic issues relating to contemporary questions in Kashruth observance and supervision" and offering "articles by talmidim of Rav Joseph B. Soloveitchik *zatzal* on his *Chidushey Torah* and *sh'urim.*" It is published semiannually, under the editorship of Rabbi Hershel Schacter, rosh kollel of Yeshivath Rabbenu Yitzchak Elchanan, and Rabbi Menachem Genack, Kashruth Division rabbinic administrator.

Jewish Thought, a journal of Torah scholarship under the editorship of Moshe Sossovesky, is sponsored jointly by the Orthodox Union and Yeshivath Ohr Yerusalayim of Israel. The literary content, in advanced areas of Jewish thought on a range of topics of timely and permanent significance, is prepared under the yeshivah's auspices, while the publication and distribution are handled by the Union. While published semiannually, specially bound copies containing two issues are sent each year to individual members of the Orthodox Union.

~

THE AGUNAH PROBLEM

Among the diversity of developments transpiring during the Kwestel presidency was the formation of a special committee on the agunah problem, sponsored jointly by the Union with the other national Orthodox organizations. As set forth at a meeting (October 31, 1987) of UOJCA officers, the committee was designed to seek an arrangement "to establish a set of procedures which would be followed by all the participating organizations regarding what is permissible Halachically in terms of exerting social and communal pressure upon the husband to present (or upon the wife to accept) a Get (a document of Jewish religious divorce)." (The aim was to help resolve situations in which one of the parties to a Jewish marriage, despite a civil divorce, obdurately refuses to give [if a former husband] or to receive [if a former wife] a get, without which, under Jewish law, remarriage may not take place. Unfortunately, in most such cases, the wife is exploited for money or for spite by the unscrupulous husband.) The committee, headed by Michael Wimpfheimer, held a number of meetings attended by representatives of each organization. A practical problem of implementation means arose, however, that could not be met at the time.

However, in a subsequent development, a law was drafted under interorganizational auspices (not initiated by the Orthodox Union) dealing with the agunah problem. It was introduced in the New York State legislature, passed by a near-unanimous vote, and signed into law by then-Governor Mario Cuomo. A debate on the merits of this bill was held at a meeting of UOJCA officers, in 1989, between Nathan Lewin, prominent attorney, author of the bill, and Dr. Marvin Schick, professor of political science. Both of these figures, equally ardent exponents of Jewish Orthodoxy and members of the Orthodox Union's Board, are distinguished in matters involving constitutional and halachic issues.

In the course of his presentation, Nathan Lewin said:

> The law involves the courts in a matter of religious divorce in only one very peripheral way: It requires the party who wants a civil divorce after a marriage [originally] solemnized in a religious ceremony to state under oath that he or she has taken all steps in his or her power to remove barriers to remarriage.

Dr. Marvin Schick, on his part, held that:

> The Get legislation turns the concept of accommodation [to prevent coercion of religious Jews . . . in discrimitory practices in American society] on its head, [requiring] civil authorities to adjust their practices to accommodate our norms.

Dr. Schick also held that the law in question is "unconstitutional on its face . . . and also runs afoul of the First Amendment." Dr. Schick was undeterred in his objections to the bill, apparently expressed mainly in this context, by the fact of the strong opposition to the measure taken by the American Jewish Congress and, very actively but to no avail, by the [Reform] Union of American Hebrew Congregations.

A second bill dealing with the agunah problem was also later submitted to and adopted by the New York State legislature. The Orthodox Union was not involved in the sponsorship of this bill, which included provisions whose halachic validity came under fire.

～

ENTER IPA

Notable among the innovative moves of the Kwestel Administration of the Orthodox Union was the 1986 establishment of the UOJCA Institute of

Public Affairs. This new department has served since then as arm of the Union in public life, combining the spheres of the various commissions and of the units in external relations.

The vigorous new IPA department had been founded "to more effectively represent the Union's bi-national constituency on domestic and foreign issues in which the Jewish community in general and the observant community in particular have a stake," as stated in a pronouncement of the time. Incorporated within the Institute for Public Affairs were the jurisdictions of the Communal Relations, Law and Legislation, Israel, Overseas, and Soviet Jewry Commissions. "The Orthodox Union's Institute for Public Affairs represents the Orthodox Jewish viewpoint in public affairs on the national and local levels and in national, international and regional umbrella agencies," it was stated.

A unique highlight of the period was the UOJCA Mission to Soviet Jewry. This truly soul-stirring event in August 1985 grew out of the launching, at the 1984 Biennial Convention for use among the Jews of the Soviet Union, of the writing of a sepher Torah. Later, at the formal completion of the writing of this sacred scroll amid the memorable celebrations in Moscow described below, this sepher Torah was dedicated to the memory of Joseph K. Miller.

Joseph Miller, dear to many as "Joe," met his tragic death as one of the 259 victims of the Arab terrorist bombing of an American jet passenger airplane in December, 1985, over Lockerbie, Scotland. UOJCA treasurer and Finance Committee chairman, and one who held the Torah cause dear, Joe Miller had been deeply devoted to the efforts for Soviet Jewry. His widow, Rhoda, carries forward her late husband's purposes, currently serving as chair of the Union's Kharkov/Soviet Jewry Commission.

The Mission to Soviet Jewry, motivated by the sepher Torah undertaking, took place in the days, as a *Jewish Action* report (Winter 5751/1990–1991) tells, "before *glasnost* and *perestroika* [as Communist rule was crumbling] had taken hold."

The *Jewish Action* article recounts:

> The Orthodox Union's historic Torah Mission was witness to one of the miraculous events of modern Jewish history—the reawakening of Russian Jews to their Judaism. For ten momentous days, 110 Orthodox Jews [leadership figures from communities across the U.S. and from Canada and Mexico] forged spiritual ties. . . . The emotional highs, the tears, the joy, the excitement, and most of all the electric atmosphere by the tens of thousands who came to the Torah celebration in Moscow, Leningrad, Kiev, and Berdichev were beyond anything we might have anticipated.
>
> Who would have believed that in the Moscow Youth Palace, in the

Ukrainian Palace of Culture in Kiev, and the Leningrad Yubilayim Stadium—built by those oppressors who had suppressed their heritage—the Torah would reign supreme!

. . . Throngs pushed to touch and kiss the Sepher Torah as it was taken around the huge halls [each in turn] to the tune of *Ki Mitziyon Tetzeh Torah*. As we completed [the writing of] the Sepher Torah in Leningrad the entire audience of over 10,000 stood and sang forth *Shema Yisrael Hashem Elokenu Hashem Ehad* . . . the ceremony was repeated for an additional 7,000 who could not be accomodated the previous time.

The Mission to Soviet Jewry was led by the Union's president, Shimon Kwestel, who addressed the successive audiences, with translators provided. Directing the arrangements and serving key roles in the programs were Rabbi Pinchas Stolper and Rabbi Raphael Butler, then respectively executive vice president and NCSY national director, and Elly Edelman, administrative director. Also participating at different occasions were Zevulun Hammer, then Israel's Minister of Education, and Rav Simcha Kook, Chief Rabbi of Rehovoth, Israel. Shlomo Carlebach, famed Torah troubadour, added his talents to the Mission. Technical aid was provided by the Shamir organization.

The *Jewish Action* report explains that technical difficulties had prevented the inclusion of Kharkov in the sequence. Instead, Professor Kwestel, accompanied by New York City Councilman Noach Dear, went to Kharkov to participate in a public ceremony marking the return of the remaining synagogue structure to the local Jewish community. It was out of this direct contact that the Orthodox Union's Kharkov project subsequently took place.

38

From Bigness to . . . ?

In the historical course of the Union of Orthodox Jewish Congregations of America, the span from the mid-1970s to the early 1990s can be seen as a continuum of pattern. The period of the administration headed by Sheldon Rudoff as president bore the stamp of this continuity. The governing trends were much the same as those of the preceding two administrations.

By and large, the policies and program lines pursued by his predecessors in office were maintained, with diligent attention, through President Rudoff's two successive terms of office (5752–5757/1990–1994). Such innovations as were introduced during these years were few, but important.

The areas of activity marked by preceding expansion continued to grow in the Rudoff era, largely by their built-in processes. And, as before—in contrast to the striking progress in such fields as youth activity and outreach; kashruth service; individual membership and associates support; budgetary scope; headquarters equipment; and, to a lesser extent, in regional and synagogue servicing and publications—other areas continued to limp along as before. The deficiencies were those that had been long-entrenched through the mid-1970s to the mid-1990s. Especially in need of thoroughgoing repair were constituency relations and communications, organizational integration, and public relations.

Gone now for several administrations past, and little remembered, was the previous two-way flow of communications and contact between UOJCA headquarters and the rabbis and presidents and other congregational officers. In the outward flow, synagogue and community leaders had been briefed on the many issues and developments of concern, enlisting their close participation in Orthodox Union moves on public measures and on activities for meeting communal and congregational needs. The incoming flow brought local and regional responses and their own ideas, information, and concerns.

Little remembered now and scarcely attempted, after a several-administrations gap, were the earlier time processes in engaging constituency involvement with preparations for the biennial conventions—preparing the agendas and drafting the policy and program resolutions, and otherwise engaging the input of the leaderships of the congregations of which, in principle, the Orthodox Union is the common instrument. How little was done in the mid-1970s to early 1990s—unlike the earlier time—toward advance preparation of congregational delegates for consideration of the issues to be acted on, the policy stands to be debated, and the organizational program steps to be considered at each biennial convocation, which, in constitutional principle, is the ruling body of the congregationally constituted Union.

The Board of Directors, constitutionally the governing body of the Union between conventions, had now come to be all but devoid of either deliberative or active role in policy and program matters. Its occasional meetings were now used mainly to provide audiences for visiting dignitaries of note. Even the Executive Committee, composed—in addition to officers and commissions chairmen—of a number appointed from the Board membership, were left with a limited factual role.

As matters developed through the post-mid-1970s, the principal commissions functioned with so high a degree of autonomy as to be internally self-ruling. The collective affairs of the Torah community's central body were governed, with little reference to organizational process, by the officers, functioning through the executive staff.

This state of affairs had become entrenched, beyond all previous inadequacies in these regards, since the close of the Feuerstein and Karasick presidential eras. In view of the dramatic growth of the Union's operations and budget, the bona fides of the directive course had been little questioned; that is, not in such form as to gain wide attention. But indications can be detected that among those with a long view of Torah community development as an organized force and the capacity of the central Union, thoughts of a more valid, and in the long run healthier, structural functioning were germinating.

Regarding public relations in the sense of a planned and operated process for projecting awareness of the organization's role, appreciation of its work, and cognizance of its policies, it is to be recognized that this is an area in which the Orthodox Union has rarely shone at any point in its history. The fact that the Union's public relations blind spot is shared with the Orthodox Jewish domain as a whole offers no consolation to such as recognize the need in today's world for an effective, clearly conceived, and systematically and professionally conducted public-information process.

As the 1990s opened, marks could be seen of dawning awareness in the

Orthodox Union's leadership circles of the distinction between public relations in the broad sense and spasmodic reaches for press publicity. This was reflected in measures toward some coordination, through a staff publicity appointee, of the publicity items and informative materials disseminated by the several departments. The previously launched UOJCA Institute for Public Affairs, in the 1990s, also has served, apart from its prescribed function, to contribute to public relations purpose.

THE IPA IN ACTION

The annual two-day mission to Washington of the central Torah-community body was now under the active leadership of Gerry Gontown-ick, one of a group of rising new young figures on the Orthodox Union scene. Functioning within the IPA program, it was supplemented by periodic Congressional Dinners at which Senatorial and House legislators came together with Orthodox Union leadership figures from around the country. Another meaningful IPA project originated during the Kwestel presidency and further forwarded in the Rudoff term was the Congressional Internship Program. Those placed as "interns" serve for a stated time with the staff of one or another cooperating Congressional figure, an experience that "affords our future leaders an opportunity to participate in public affairs."

The IPA was actively headed as chairman by its architect, Dr. Mandell I. Ganchrow, until his election as UOJCA president at the Kislev 5755/ November 1994 Biennial Convention. He was succeeded as IPA chairman by Sheldon Rudoff, then by Marcel Weber, and finally by Professor Richard Stone, the present incumbent. The initial professional director of this department was Mark Friedman, who was followed by William Rapfogel. Since 1992, the post (now bearing the title of [departmental] executive director) has been held, with recognized ability, by Betty Ehrenberg.

The multiple facets of the IPA program seem to have been forwarded at full pace, with strong administrative support, through the Rudoff presidential years. By then, it had become firmly established as a key arm of the national body and a force in Jewish and American public life.

A new Synagogue Services Commission constructive undertaking, with interdepartmental participation, was instituted for annual recurrence during the Rudoff administration: the National Leadership Conference of Community Synagogues. Its first session was held in 1992 in New Brunswick,

New Jersey.[1] In following years, the conference was held in various communities around the country. The planning and arrangements direction have been under the care of Rabbi Yitzchak Rosenberg, national director of Synagogue Programs.

The National Leadership Conference of Community Synagogues has provided the opportunity, on each occasion, for close consultation on both shared and special local needs. National Orthodox Union leadership figures and a roster of staff heads of various UOJCA departments have joined with leaders and activists of both larger and smaller communities in sharing know-how and experience in dealing with circumstances that develop and problems that arise, and in gleaning new ideas in congregational activities programming.

The practical value of this project, indicated by following the initial assemblage by postconference participant responses, has been further attested to by attendance increases each succeeding year.

AMID A SHIFTING BALANCE

Records of the period indicate a ripening awareness, among the organization's leadership, of the need to reposition the role of American Jewish Orthodoxy's central arm on the shifting Jewish scene. In the setting of new situations affecting Jewish life was the changing weight of segments of Jewry. It seems that the implications thereof were sensed, but not clearly grasped, by UOJCA. Amid all shifts had gone forward the continuing phenomenon of the resurgence of the Torah-loyal world; Israel and America were its main settings.

Unceasing growth in numbers, intensifying self-awareness, new scope of educational and institutional development, steady rise in public status: Such was the consistent trend of Torah-constituted life. With the previous shadow of decline all but forgotten, there was now the manifestation of growth; growth in every category, in fact, but rational integration.

Division, with all its self-penalizing consequences, continued to mark the overall makeup of the world's Torah community. The segments were individually larger, the aggregation was potentially far stronger than for a century past; but it was a potentiality unrealized in the shaping of collective Jewish policy.

---

1. Initially, these events were designated "Smaller Communities Conference," but later conferences were designated as noted.

Efforts of the Orthodox Union, under its successive leadership, to further the integration of Torah-world forces had been repeatedly undertaken, but they were not of the scale or force to gain a measure of real success on either the international or the domestic scene. One move in this area, favored by the Kwestel regime, for some mode of alliance between the Union and the Young Israel force had fallen short of the aim. On certain issues that arose in the public area, various of the Orthodox organizations joined the Orthodox Union in statements of common stand. Steps toward the establishment of a regularly functioning mechanism of continuing broadly inclusive coordinated action could not overcome the barrier of limited resources.

In a valedictory address at the 1994 UOJCA Biennial Convention, outgoing President Sheldon Rudoff recalled:

> Four years ago from this platform I called for a union of yeshivoth, the synagogues, and the Rabbonim in an Orthodox Jewish Council of America to serve as the authentic collective voice of the American Torah community.

The expressed aim was not realized, however. A number of the leading national Orthodox organizations banded together in 1983 as the North American Orthodox Jewish Leadership Conference. Not being fully inclusive, however, and not being equipped for ongoing function, this grouping bore more indication of potentiality than actuality.

In contrast, outside the religious loyalist fold, the organizations and institutions, though diverse in character, seem to have effected a tacit alignment with each other in areas where their interests converged. Their voices bore ebullience. Yet, there could be detected an undertone of unease.

The uncertainty underlying the assurance of the non-Orthodox instrumentalities had manifestations in Israeli political life and in American Jewish organs such as the United Jewish Appeal; in the Zionist organization; and in the "umbrella" agencies, such as the Conference of Presidents and the National Jewish Community Relations Advisory Council. There resulted relationship tensions of a new ideological sharpness between these various areas, that resembled the tensions between the non-Orthodox organizational array and the Orthodox Union. Under the best of circumstances, the Union had been at chronic disadvantage in these multiorganizational channels; participation, with its provision of means for exercising voice in major channels of Jewish policy, invoked the status of being but one among several or many organizations, rather than of being morally in vis-à-vis status to the collectivity of non-Orthodox constituencies represented. Now, matters worsened.

WITH AND WITHOUT LIFE FORCE

Structurally, these organized forces outside the observing domain in Israel and America were, typically, well constituted and well placed. The apparatus of each was the product of studied experience, careful planning, and the application of ample resources of funds and skills. Their respective placements in central Jewish channels had been adroitly maneuvered toward centerpoints of influence. Each, in its particular location in the scheme of things, seemed at a plateau of organizational success.

But now permeating these various forces was a question as to their own basic vitality. Their literature and their recorded deliberations reveal the emerging consciousness that their diversity shared a common problem: They had all the attributes of life, except for the seed of life itself.

Troubling now to devotees of established forces not rooted in Torah was the increasing evidence of their common inability for organic continuity. Lacking was the capacity to hold the young generation, to replenish their numbers from within. Further troubling, to their leaderships, were the marks of the upsurge, among the observing fold, of that life-generating capacity so painfully absent elsewhere.

The problem common to the otherwise widely differing movements, organizations, and institutions could be seen, from their internal exchanges of view, as arising from their common subjection to non-Jewish criteria of life values and outlook. The problem was of long standing, but had become more visible in the 1980s. It was difficult for their leaders to digest the reality that ideologies keyed to intrinsically non-Jewish criteria, assimilating forces of their nature, not only cannot beget intrinsic Jewishness in their exponents' and followers' offspring, but, as a mixed species, cannot beget definitively Jewish life at all. Tough to swallow, for exponents of spiritually assimilative ideologies, was the lesson of Jewish history: that only out of the life rooted in authentic Jewish belief and practice can Jewish life renew and bear the qualities of the House of Israel.

Failing the capacity for Jewish fertility, non-Torah forces must resort to the siphoning of vitality from external sources. By the 1980s, the siphoning pace had perforce quickened. There now ensued, among the Jewish deficient forces, a race against what mathematics made clear.

As the 1980s took their course, the contrast between the growth within traditional religious ranks and the reverse among circles oriented to worldly criteria sharpened on all sides, demography having outpaced ideology. The religiously observant were having large families, and, with better tools to deal with modern-day challenges, were retaining youth loyalties; they had also developed increasingly effective outreach to the Jewishly deprived. On the other side, the heterodox factions in the United States and the doctrinaire "secularist" and nonreligious segments in Israel were marked by small families and the loss of their disaffected youths. Basic arithmetic pointed to ultimate majority numbers of the traditionally observant populace. Ahead was restoration of the norm of Jewish history.

BORROWING LIFE

In Israel, the siphoning technique for replenishment pursued by the secular and antireligious forces was their hold on the governmental apparatus, on means of livelihood, and on the press and electronic media and the organs of public information generally. Thereby they continued to maintain influence over that large part of the Israeli populace in ideological limbo. Many of these, inwardly attached to the faith of their fathers, have retained in their daily lives vestiges of traditional religious observance; as yet inadequately reached out to by Torah agencies, however, they have remained exposed to opposing influences. Thus this source could be exploited to sustain secularist social dominance and to replenish anti-Torah party ranks.

The assimilative currents in Israel emanating from such sources have resulted in constant pressure against Jewish norms in the Jewish state. Violative as this pressure is of the very nature of the land of Israel, as well as of the life conditions of believers, it has brought repeated eruption of internecine conflict throughout the years. In the 1980s, the growth in the numbers and weight of the Torah forces, and the vista of their oncoming impetus, brought heightened animus to assimilationists. Hostility to integral Jewishness became a raging fury among these circles. The battle lines were drawn with the "Who is a Jew?" issue. This move sought to compel Israel to accept as Jews gentiles who underwent the conversion procedures, not in accordance with Jewish law, of heterodox bodies.

The Israeli populace being mainly Jewish, the assimilative trend among them is obscured. Intermarriage, for the most part, is out of reach. The rabid assimilationist envisions a "pseudogentile" society and nation made up of Jews. In Diaspora lands, the situation is obviously different. Under prevailing circumstances, the difference had become a source of apprehension to all concerned with Jewish being. Inroads on the Diaspora populace were now, by the later 1980s, taking on ominous proportions.

The cumulative toll of assimilation, with its inevitable consequence of intermarriage and absorption, was by this period demanding the attention of the Jewish public. Although, as studied by this writer, the incidence of mixed marriages has been far less than what has been claimed and widely propagated by certain sources[2] (with the implication of "You can't stop it"), it has been, and remains, a dire threat.

For the Union of Orthodox Jewish Congregations of America, concerned with Jewish well-being as a whole, the problem loomed large. The fact that intermarriage and its associated conditions are but little encountered among the observant has not been permitted to deflect attention from the problem. The Union's youth movement, NCSY, has been the organization's foremost instrument for the purpose. In the Rudoff administration, as in previous periods, the notably successful endeavor to win young people from Torah-less homes to the Torah way has continued to have full priority in the Union's resources and budget. For the American organizations and institutions outside the religious loyalist fold, the tide of mixed marriage and absorption was a matter of institutional life-or-death. As the 1990s came into view, their constituencies were awash.

Most imperiled among these groups was the Reform Judaism movement. Its assimilative posture being inherent, the effects were progressively drastic, and could be little checked by random gestures of moving from de-Judaization to re-Judaization. Tacitly or openly, the Reform temple had

---

2. Examination of the various widely publicized surveys of mixed marriages and other trends among the American Jewish populace reveals that none of them have valid claim to authentic scientific basis as representative of the populace. The survey the most ambitiously publicized, most widely cited, and most preposterous in its claim to constitute an actual statistical representation of "the national Jewish population"—that is, all Jews in the United States—is the one sponsored by the Council of Jewish Federations. Examination of this survey, as published under the title *Highlights of the 1990 Jewish Population Survey*, shows that their claim is altogether untenable.

That source reveals that the study was *based solely on 2,441 telephone interviews to randomly chosen people*, at diverse locations, without reference to distribution of Jewish population or any acceptably qualifying criteria of sample representation. They were selected as "Jewish" for the survey purpose, "from 125,813 American households" called simply by "random-digit" phone calls to numbers in all parts of the continental United States plus Alaska and Hawaii.

The 2,441 interviewees, claimed to constitute a cross-section of the estimated 5.5 million to 5.9 million Jews in America, were chosen for inclusion on the following basis:

Any person one of whose parents was a Jew; or anyone of any origin, religion, or belief married to a Jew; or yet anyone of any origin, religion, etc., with some family relation to a Jew; or again, even anyone of any origin, etc., in whose household is a Jew.

The unquestioning acceptance of such balderdash speaks poorly for the judgment of those contemporary figures in Jewish life who have given it currency.

become the nurturing ground of mixed marriages. In its chronic need to replenish its intermarrying and assimilating numbers, the Reform forces, with their Conservative counterpart following suit, had strained to recruit mixed-marriage couples and their offspring for inclusion in their fold. A form of conversion, one incompatible with age-old Jewish requirements, was drawn upon for the purpose; even this, however, was not insisted upon.

Reform forces had resorted extensively to the siphoning process. Like their Israeli equivalents, their recruitment aim was among those of persisting but vestigial Jewish ties—but, in this case, among the more well-to-do of this kind. That resource was now diminishing, however, for the trend now was to either of two opposing directions—a turning toward the Jewish way, or the abandonment of Jewish ties. And now, Reform's built-in problem was compounded with difficulties in filling established pulpits.

The Reform leadership, haunted by their movement's no-win situation, saw at the crux of their dilemma the nonrecognition of Reform in Israel as equivalent to the historical Jewish religion. Its status in the Jewish world was thereby shadowed, and doubts as to its legitimacy pervaded its own ranks. Thus pressed, further threat was seen in the advancing current of Torah loyalism. The Reform leadership was under compulsion to act. Pulling the leaders of Conservative Judaism in tow, they moved to an all-out attack on the constituted position of the Jewish religion of the ages in the Jewish state.

TORAH UNDER SIEGE

The attack was mounted on wide fronts in America, as well as Israel. All institutions of collective Jewish endeavor in the United States were stormed in the openly orchestrated campaign. Each, in flagrant overriding of its relevant constitutional prohibitions, was made to serve as an instrument, under the banner of "religious pluralism," toward forcing Israel to declare the Reform and Conservative denominations as legal equivalents to the Jewish people's traditional faith.

In this way, the professed converts to Reform and Conservative Judaism would then be able to legally claim their Jewishness, with status as such under Israel's Law of Return. This outrageous notion brought an outpouring of support, from religious loyalists throughout the Jewish world, for the drive in Israel to clarify, in the law, what had always been understood and unquestioned—to add the phrase "in accordance with halachah" to the reference to converts in Israel's Law of Return. The Orthodox Union, together with all other Orthodox Jewish organizations in the United States and Canada, joined in a public statement on behalf of this stand.

Telling as was this public expression, the situation pointed all the more sharply to the need for an established medium whereby the combined weight of Torah forces could be consistently wielded with the requisite force and continuity. What then followed was injurious to all that Torah-loyal forces stood for, but the needed means of combined channel to public opinion and policy makers was lacking. The heterodox campaign continued full-force: Such bodies as the Jewish Agency, the United Jewish Appeal, the Zionist Organization, and the Council of Jewish Federations; many local welfare funds; and the cross-organizations umbrella agencies—the Conference of President of Major Jewish Organizations and the National Jewish Community Relations Advisory Council—were engineered, for the purposes of the Reform force and its Conservative ally, to impose on Israel's self-sovereignty.

The voices from abroad were without counterpart in Israel itself, where neither of the two schismatic movements had any established following to speak of. Antireligious elements in Israel joined in the agitation, but the Israeli public was not disposed to be browbeaten, and even the secularist organs hesitated to further affront public sentiment.

The "Orthodox-bashing" crusade, as it became known, was not confined to Jewish channels. Connections with leading U.S. newspapers and radio and television media were utilized without scruple. The outrageous use of this tactic by Jews against their fellows was capped by the appearance, in *The New York Times* of November 17, 1988, of a damning opinion expressed by the widely syndicated columnist William Safire. Safire charged that ". . . a cabal of politico-rabbis is making a grab for ecclesiastical exclusivity. At issue is the cabal's attempt to arrogate for itself the authority to determine 'who is a Jew.'" An accompanying boldfaced sidebar read: "Orthodox Power Grab." None of the many letters of protest submitted to the Letters to the Editor department of *The New York Times* were ever published.

In response to the culminating volley of the 1988 Orthodox-bashing drive, the American national Orthodox organizations, including UOJCA, issued a widely published joint statement refuting and denouncing the canard disseminated by Reform quarters that Torah forces do not regard Jews of the Reform fold as Jews. Except for this and such statements of valid information as occasions called for, the Orthodox Union and most other responsible Torah community sources did not otherwise permit themselves to be drawn into the morass of vituperative exchange.

Floundering in its outpouring of venom, the Orthodox-bashing crusade failed in its aim. Efforts to renew the assault recurred thereafter from time to time, with little prospect of result other than refueling animosities.

~

The frenzied drive to break the bond between the faith and the people of Israel had been interrupted by the epochal foundering of the Communist-ruled Soviet domain. This world-shaking development resulted, amid its vast political upsets, in the fall of barriers to Jewish life in what had been the imperial Soviet Union and in the outpouring of mass aliyah from thence to Israel.

FROM THE DOWNFALL
OF AN ATHEIST AUTOCRACY

All Jewish efforts were needed now to be concentrated on the transfer to Israel and the resettlement there of the hundreds of thousands seeking haven in their people's land. The congregations of Orthodox Judaism across North America, under the leadership of their central force, were brought to bear as one in support of this vast task. In response to the Union's calls for the purpose, the resultant outpouring of material and active support made a significant contribution to the absorption of the incoming thousands.

The aid to the physical mass resettlement was also felt in the sensitive task of bringing the rudiments of Jewish life to the newcomers, products of three generations of subjection to a despotic atheist regime. This work has persisted and, as is widely realized, must continue to persist, not only for the spiritual welfare of these olim, but for the character of Israeli society as a whole.

Along with the efforts for Israel-bound emigrés came the need to aid the increasing numbers choosing to settle in the United States. Various measures for this purpose were launched by the Orthodox Union under Sheldon Rudoff's presidential leadership. Some were designed for implementation by the congregations in the communities of settlement, others by the national body directly.

The practical aid rendered through these programs was strongly felt in providing for the immediate needs and settlement process of the newcomers, now numbering in the scores of thousands yearly. In the accompanying endeavors to awaken and nurture their atrophied spiritual lives as Jews, the difficulties encountered were more elusive.

Some among the Jews leaving the former Soviet Union had been moved by the urge to a Jewish life; others sought to escape anti-Semitic hostility, still others ought material betterment. Most of the emigrés governed by Jewish spirit settled in Israel; many of those who settled in America were of the other categories.

Thus a most superficial response met the programs developed by the Orthodox Union—and joined in by many congregations—to evoke the Jewish spirit among the forcibly assimilated products of Communist teachings, and to draw them to the synagogue sphere. Here and there, heartwarming results were gained; more often, little impact was made. So the situation continued in the following years, but the hard-won gains among the disappointments point to better prospects ahead. Those devoting their lives to the Jewish destiny of their brethren from Russia are found in numerous congregations and in and beyond UOJCA circles. They see, beyond present appearances, a germinating Judaic potential among the ranks of the influx, with special promise for the rise of Torah-inspired leadership from among the upcoming generation. This is especially so from among the young people attending the schools especially instituted and maintained for them by far-seeing sponsors.

KHARKOV: THE TASK
WITHIN FORMER SOVIET LANDS

Meanwhile, Torah-community concern focused on the needs, additional to those of the great numbers settling in Israel and the United States, of those Jews remaining in Russia and the now-independent lands of the former Soviet Union. Once drawn to this need, which embraced many hundreds of thousands of Jews, the leading organizations of the Torah world, with the Orthodox Union prominent among them, plunged into undertakings for the spiritual renewal of what, prior to the Russian Revolution, had been a bastion of Jewish life.

By tacit understanding, each organization focused its efforts in a given area. That chosen by the Union of Orthodox Jewish Congregations of America was the community of Kharkov, in the now independent state of Ukraine.

In Czarist times a vibrant center of traditional Jewish life, what existed in Kharkov now, after Communist terror and Nazi invasion had taken their frightful toll, was but a grim reminder of what had been. In the post-World War II years, numbers of Jewish survivors found their way to this slowly recovering former economic hub of a broad area of Ukraine. With nothing but the "Yivrei" stamp on their internal passports and the lurking hostility of their gentile neighbors to give them any sense of Jewishness, they were spiritual orphans; but Jews they were, to be reclaimed for their people and their people's faith. The challenge was to reach out to this Jewry devoid of

Jewishness, devoid of community form, and to bring them, with understanding, patience, and love, the lifeline of Torah heritage.

The challenge was grasped by the Orthodox Union. "Kharkov," the project of Jewish rebirth in a far-off land undertaken by the Orthodox Union during the presidency of Sheldon Rudoff, was of a kind unlike any other in the annals of American Torah Jewry's central force. It was spearheaded and led from the first by former president Shimon Kwestel. With the support of the Union's designated Soviet Jewry Committee and the organization's administration, Professor Kwestel journeyed again and again to Kharkov to weld together the Jewish populace, bring them a sense of Jewish purpose, and inculcate a positive awareness of Jewish meanings. Schools were established; groups were formed for children, youths, and adults. A living Jewish community was brought into being. The Union's Kharkov endeavors were joined, in close cooperation, with those conducted by Sha'alvim. This kibbutz and yeshivah in Israel, an affiliate of Bnei Akivah—youth movement of the Mizraḥi Religious Zionist Organization—had also sent its emissaries to the aid of Soviet Jewry. Their pioneering work in Kharkov made possible the Orthodox Union's program there.

"Kharkov" is to be numbered among those facets of the work of the Union of Orthodox Jewish Congregations of America that bear the quality of Torah nobility.

"PEACE PROCESS"?

The Union's strengthened grasp in representative and community service fields, in that period, was not equally marked in what stood out as the great Jewish issue of the time: the eruption of the "peace process" negotiations between Israel's Mapai-led Labor government and the anti-Israel Palestine Liberation Organization.

The intent of Israel's government leaders to yield most of Judea, Samaria, and the Gaza area to PLO rule aroused opposition in Israel, echoed throughout diaspora communities. Never, in all of Jewish history, had the concept even arisen that part of the land Divinely given to the Jewish people should be voluntarily ceded by a Jewish source to gentiles. The deception practiced in cloaking the negotiations, and the police-state means applied to combat the opposition, caused further embitterment.

At the forefront of the struggle for defense of the Holy-Land heritage were those who had chosen to settle across the "Green Line" in "Yesha" (Yehudah, Shomron, and the Aza region). These 150,000 banner-bearers of the Jewish heritage were Israel's finest idealists, lovers of the Torah who lived Torah in forwarding the Zion goal. It became apparent that in Israel and the Diaspora both, the great majority of those of Jewish conviction stood together with the Yesha pioneers for holding fast to the land of Israel.

Others, wearied by endless years of embattlement capped by the grinding, murderous depredations of the PLO-led Intifada, leaned on hopes that presenting what seekers of Israeli surrender had dubbed the West Bank—Judea, Samaria, and the Gaza strip—to the PLO would slake the terrorist force's blood-lust and the urge for the destruction of the Jewish state, the land of Israel.

With Jews everywhere shaken by the development, it was an occasion for careful but clear leadership of its constituency by the central American Torah-community arm. But, instead, there were indications of equivocation, of strangely divided counsels, within the UOJCA administration. Expressions by certain administrative figures, the featuring in *Jewish Action* of articles supporting the Rabin–Peres course with priority position over articles bearing the views far more prevalent among the Torah-committed, and other troubling manifestations were seen as far from what was to be expected from such a source.

What came forth at this juncture from the Rudoff administration was seen as lacking in clear perception, out of character with the historical stance of the Union of Orthodox Jewish Congregations of America,[3] and inadequately mindful of the deeply felt views on the "peace process" by the great majority of the Orthodox Union's constituency.

Speculation as to the promptings of some in the congregational Union's leadership circle found no warrant for surmise that any among them were influenced by the policy that had been espoused by the Agudath Israel movement's Council of Sages. Well before the Israeli government-PLO negotiations came to light, this body had spoken in favor of yielding parts of the land of Israel in order to save increasingly endangered Jewish lives. But, for the nonce, this expression, though from a revered source, had found little support among Agudist circles themselves, and surely not among Orthodox Jewry's ranks otherwise.

The equivocation was evidenced in the program of the Union's ninety-sixth Anniversary Biennial Convention in November 1994. On the agenda were presentations touching on the "peace process" by speakers from both

---

3. As expressed in the words of the Union's founding president, Dr. Henry Pereira Mendes, at an occasion in 1905:

> I consider that the spiritual side of Zionism doesn't mean only the possession of a legalized home in the Land of our Fathers. It means that, and much more. *Our possession is already legalized by Him who gave it to us forever,* and who gives all lands to whom He pleases.

sides of the issue, including even a member of the Rabin–Peres cabinet notorious for his hostility to the Torah way, and who was known to be a principal factor in forwarding the plan. Many delegates among the 1,200 or more in attendance voiced sentiments on the issue obviously shared, in contradistinction to those partial to the Rabin–Peres course, by the overwhelming majority of convention participants and of the congregations they represented. The manifestation being so unmistakable, it stood as a message not to be ignored by the successor administration elected at the convocation.

~

In a letter reviewing some of the developments undertaken during his Administration, Sheldon Rudoff has stated, in part:

> Move of the national headquarters [of the Union of Orthodox Congregations of America] to spacious "state of the art" offices occupying two full floors [later a third floor added] at 333 Seventh Avenue, New York.
>
> The demise of the [mixed] Synagogue Council of America as a result of quiet diplomacy moves without the tumult that had characterized the issue in previous years.
>
> The Union's response to crises with T'phillah and Limmud Torah, as well as such as the incredibly successful Torah Vigil [participated in by congregations across the U.S. and Canada] in response to the Gulf War; the learning program in memory of Rav Soloveitchik. . . .
>
> The great growth of the Individual Membership program, which reached its apex during this period. . . .
>
> The unprecedented expansion of the Union in the years prior to the 1990s then resulted in a tremendous deficit, which was compounded by the economic recession. . . . An enduring accomplishment was facing and solving this fiscal crisis. Through the efforts of men like Fred Ehrman and Avi Blumenthal, we raised unprecedented capital funds and made necessary cuts . . . but maintained the programmatic integrity of the Union in every respect.
>
> The attempts to reach out to the Yeshivah and Agudah communities . . . which opened lines of communication if not cooperation. The attempt to unify the Orthodox community not only through the historic formation of the NAOLC. . . .
>
> The infusion of new leadership . . . Moshe Bane, Richard Stone, Frank Snitow, Alan Fagin, Morton Landowne, Steve Stavistsky, Al Blumenthal, Manny Adler, Elliot Gibber, Zvi Friedman, Steven Spira, Saul Kamelhar, Matty Maryles, Alan Miller, Henry Rothman, Carmi Schwartz, William Schwartz, and Harvey Wolinetz . . . surely represent the future leadership of the Union.
>
> At the conclusion of my Administration, the Orthodox Union was in better

fiscal position than it had been for decades . . . had a new professional head [Rabbi Raphael Butler] capable of replacing the . . . leadership of the past; and a physical plant with staff, equipment, and talent capable of implementing its programs.

The letter also cites, as among outstanding developments of the period:

> . . . The unprecedented two-day conference of Union leadership in Ossining, New York, which clearly showed a path to follow . . . concentration on . . . an effective "delivery system" to enable our traditional synagogue constituency to provide effective outreach programs which have begun to change the face of American Jewish life.

The conference referred to, held in Ossining, New York, on October 31, 1993 to November 1, 1993, united national and regional officers and a number of Executive Committee and Board of Directors members for two days of intensive analysis of the operations of the Union. The deliberations were keyed to a research study of the national congregational body done through preceding months by the Ukeles organization. The findings of the research study were presented in a report prepared for the Ossining conference.

39

As the Centenary Nears

The 96th Anniversary Biennial Convention of the Union of Orthodox Jewish Congregations of America took place at the Hilton Seasons Hotel, Great Gorge, New Jersey, on 21–24 Kislev, 5755/November 24–27, 1994. The delegates, in great number as usual, were, as also was usual, from congregations and communities throughout the United States and Canada. Pervading their deliberations was the mindfulness, with the Union's centennial anniversary nearing, of their historical role. As successors in office and in purpose to their earliest predecessors, the delegates bore the mission advanced unceasingly through a near-century of world upheaval since the representatives delegated by forty-seven congregations came together in Iyyar 5659 (June 1898) to establish, on behalf of the American Torah community, this Union.

In electing Dr. Mandell I. Ganchrow as sixteenth President of the Union of Orthodox Jewish Congregations of America, the delegates may well have seen him as bearer of the spirit of the Union's founding president, Dr. Henry Pereira Mendes.

It was clear from the first that the new president was to pursue active policies in both the makeup of the organization and its functioning. It was also clear that Dr. Ganchrow was to be a hands-on leader. To date, his undertaking to restrict his medical practice in order to devote himself totally to his presidential concerns has been punctiliously fulfilled.

In many respects, the Ganchrow administration began with advantages. All established departments were functioning, most of them with competent staff and generally well conceived programs. Expenses were high, with a seventy-five-person national and regional executive and professional staff, a larger number of clerical staff, many part-time personnel and full-time mashgichim, large costs for headquarters and utilities, and assorted operating expenses. Although there were recurrent periods of sharp cash-flow strains and budgeting demanded constant close scrutiny, income, on the whole, was in relation to costs. In short, there was a solid functioning base on which to build further, and the incoming administration had its sights set on building further in all areas.

STAFF APPOINTMENTS, NEW VENTURES

An important early change on the top executive level was the redesignation of Rabbi Pinchas Stolper as senior executive, plus his resumed charge of the Youth Division, and the designation of Rabbi Raphael Butler as executive vice president.

There followed further new appointments designed to strengthen areas of service needing attention. One was the engagement of Rabbi Moshe Krupka as director of Synagogue Services; another was the appointment of Rabbi Jacob Haber as "the Orthodox Union's National Director of Jewish Education."

The department assigned to the directorship of Rabbi Krupka functions under the supervision of the UOJCA Synagogue Servicing commission, of which Carmi Schwartz is the current chairman. Rabbi Krupka was quoted, following his appointment, as envisioning "a nationwide network of revitalized Kehilloth, the hundreds of OU congregations bonded to each other and their central headquarters by unity of purpose and shared experience."

Certain areas within the Synagogue Servicing frame were now assigned to the continuing directorship of Rabbi Bertram Leff. Foremost among these is the Union's Metropolitan New York region, which is expected to develop vigorously to its larger potential as a strong force in the religious concerns and public life of an area with the largest Jewish population of any metropolis in the world.

An early event under the redirected Synagogue Services auspices was the Northeastern Leadership Conference, held at the Newark Airport Hilton on November 19, 1995. Participating were representatives of congregations in Maryland, Pennsylvania, New Jersey, Massachusetts, and New York; joining them were national leaders and key staff figures. The all-day session focused on ways to channel the resources of the range of Orthodox Union departments to the enrichment of congregational programs, and on exchanges of ideas and information on synagogue development.

The Limud Torah Commission, of which Moshe Bane is now the chairman, supervises the Jewish Education Department, with Rabbi Haber as departmental national director. Chairman Bane and Director Haber have stated:

A presentation for a massive educational program was made to the UOJCA Board of Directors. They unanimously agreed that however we respond externally, we must also respond by *inreach*, by creating and maintaining a sustained educational program. . . . The mandate of our Department is to create a deeper spiritual awareness of what it is to be a Jew, to rid ourselves of "lifetime Judaism" and to help our synagogues across the country flourish as centers of spirituality.

Quickly, the newly mandated department swung into action with its Pardes Project. This innovation, the brainchild of Executive Vice President Butler, under the slogan "One Thousand Hours of Dialogue," called for volunteers to invite and host ten persons each for shared Friday-night Shabbath experience, discussion, and spiritual enrichment.

The inaugural occasion of the Pardes Project was on Shabbath Chanukah, 5756/1995. A remarkable number of families—720[1]—responded to the call to participate as hosts. The information thereafter received as to how the gatherings went marked the initial undertaking an "overwhelming success," as reported to the Limud Torah Commission and UOJCA administration. This encouraged the permanence of the Pardes Project and the introduction of other innovative and creative programs.

A forward step in meeting the Orthodox Union's public presentation needs was marked by the response of Herbert Berman to a call to serve as chairman of the Public Relations Commission. Prominent in civic affairs and long active in the Union's cause, Herbert Berman was well aware of the importance and sensitivies of image projection and information presentation. Professional implementation of the Public Relations Commission's program was provided for by the appointment of Mike Cohen in directive capacity. A professional specialist in public relations, Mike Cohen said, in a statement following his appointment:

Public relations is . . . an overall evaluation of an organization's relationships with its "publics." . . . We at the Union have several such "publics". Our job is to evaluate our relationships with these various publics and then establish mechanisms to serve them even better.

The foregoing and other developments in the extension of the Orthodox Union's direct service to, and relationship with, its constituency went forward while a spate of matters in external relations made heavy demands. The Ganchrow administration found itself dealing with relationships with non-Orthodox bodies that had grown more problematic over the years.

---

1. Actually, the number of responses was larger. The number given is of those who verified having conducted their gatherings.

The needs of Jews migrating from or remaining in the lands of the former Soviet Union also demanded continuing attention. Climaxing all was the eruption of the "peace process" in Israel and its decisive significance for Jews everywhere.

To understand how this array of massive developments has stood, with the Ganchrow administration at the Union's helm, some recapitulation is in order.

"UMBRELLA" EMBATTLEMENT

The demands on Jewish resources resulting from the collapse of Communist rule had deflected the Orthodox-bashing fray engineered by the Reform group, but the effects lingered. By the later 1980s and into the 1990s, "roof" organizations that previously had maintained a "non-partisan" façade were openly dancing to the tune of anti-Orthodoxy.

The change had become painfully apparent in the proceedings of the National Jewish Community Relations Advisory Council (NJCRAC). There, because of the sensitive relations between the rival "defense" organizations, the mode of consensus on policy prescriptions had heretofore been scrupulously maintained, with partisan rancor in disputed matters kept under wraps. Stipulated provision for expression of dissent from majority positions, in published documents such as the annual Joint Program Plan, had been conscientiously guarded. But, with anti-Orthodoxy openly unleashed, expressions in committees or plenums of NJCRAC of UOJCA positions that differed on given issues from those of the others met with open hostility, rather than the courteous hearing of before. Time and again, the Orthodox Union's representatives found themselves in a position of futile opposition—not merely a minority of one, but a "one" deliberately overridden.

The responsible channels of the Orthodox Union repeatedly had to consider the question of whether or not to withdraw from an association made so untenable. The situation was not so inherently problematic in principle as had been that with the mixed Synagogue Council of America. The disbanding of the Synagogue Council, in this period, rid the Torah community of a gratuitous problem. Heretofore, the disadvantages entailed in participation in a composite agency such as NJCRAC had been deemed outweighed by the advantages to Torah-community interests. Now, however, it seemed that the balance had swung sharply in the opposite direction, in this case, too.

Already, at an officer's meeting of October 30, 1985, Dr. David Luchins, then chairman of the Communal Relations Commission, had reported:

The Reform and Conservative groups are attempting to make [the NJCRAC] a more politicized forum, which can result in problems. Both the issue of "who is a Jew" and the statement with respect to Rabbi Meir Kahane created sensitive relationships with this agency.

At a later point (officers meeting, May 1988), Marcel Weber, in turn as chairman of the Communal Relations Commission, reported that, adopting a position contrary to that of the Union:

An overwhelming majority of the membership of NJCRAC urged adoption of a resolution approving "religious pluralism" in Israel and opposing the amending of Israel's Law of Return, to specify Halachic requirement for conversion. This was despite the expressed stand of the Union that it is inappropriate for NJCRAC to deal with an issue which is, by its very terms, contrary to the views of some group or groups within the NJCRAC and is contrary to the avowed purposes of NJCRAC. NJCRAC policy formulation should be limited [as required by its composition] to those issues deemed desirable for American Jewish community relations agencies to take position.

Notwithstanding the futility of the situation, the decision regarding withdrawal from NJCRAC has continued to be held in abeyance (to this writing). The time was to come, however, when the problem of participation in the National Jewish Community Relations Advisory Council would be shared, with UOJCA, by none other than the very "defense" organizations that had joined so readily in the perversion of the NJCRAC process for the "Orthodox-bashing" aim.

This occurred in 1995. The Reform leadership, frustrated in Israel, had sought to capitalize further on its penetration of American Jewish umbrella bodies. The Council of Jewish Federations, along with the local welfare funds, had been made a Reform stronghold. The American Zionist movement had become effectively subject to manipulation by the once so bitterly anti-Zionist Reform force. Such organizations, however, as the American Jewish Committee, the Anti-Defamation League of B'nai B'rith, and the American Jewish Congress, though themselves instruments of non-Orthodox elements, had their own jealously guarded spheres, and were indisposed to fall under the dictates of their ideological kin wielding the Reform course. The Reform movement, it seems, then set afoot a move to challenge the recalcitrant groups in their own defense and social-action domains, through a radical change in the character of the NJCRAC.

The strategy this time was to mobilize the local and regional Jewish community-relations councils to collectively seize control of the NJCRAC from the dominant defense organizations, and change its capacity from that of a cross-organizational advisory and consultative medium, functioning through consensus, to that of an autonomous action force, with majority rule.

In its sought new capacity, the NJCRAC would be in the position to both make and execute policy. Its infringement on the national organizations in community relations, intergroup relations, and public-spokesmanship matters would, necessarily, be drastic. Beyond that, with command of the local community-relations councils combined with control of the community welfare fund federations—directly and through their central Council, plus the United Jewish Appeal, now in merger negotiations—those directing the Reform moves would have a controlling influence over the affairs of the entire organized apparatus of American Jewry.

With this challenge facing them, the Anti-Defamation League, the American Jewish Congress, and the American Jewish Committee found themselves losing their appetite for the downing of Orthodoxy. Rather, it became their tactic to seek restoration in NJCRAC of the kind of atmosphere and consensus mode under which the central Torah-community arm can continue its participation—and under which the imperiled defense organizations can better defend themselves and safeguard their own standing.

At this writing, the ultimate outcome of this peculiar state of affairs is unresolved. The UOJCA administration and the Union's Institute for Public Affairs are keeping an attentive eye on the situation.[2]

CORRECTED STAND

In the different context of the Conference of Presidents of Major American Jewish Organizations, the situation confronting the Orthodox Union was not identical with the NJCRAC experience. The Orthodox-bashing operation had been felt in the Presidents' Conference, too, but here, where major U.S.-Israel and Israel-world relations were the sphere of concern, internal Jewish matters were of lesser weight. What now impinged more significantly on the Union's position in the Presidents' Conference setup was the "peace process" issue.

The Conference of Presidents of Major Jewish Organizations, designed as

---

2. More recent information is to the effect that while the sought change in the character of NJCRAC was eventually made, it was modified to an extent, safeguarding the interests of the national organizations, with a special "religious exemptions" provision to meet Orthodox Union stipulations. Under this provision, the Union would have veto power on official NJCRAC expressions or actions on matters deemed by the Union as having bearing on religious concerns.

a vehicle of communication for organized American Jewry with Washington, found itself at times utilized for purposes in the opposite direction. There had been occasion to learn that such moves, adroitly applied by weighty sources, could be compelling. Among indications of this was the quietly forced addition, to Presidents' Conference membership, of a group whose credentials as a "major American Jewish Organization" were nonexistent. This smallest of mini-groups, "Americans for Peace Now," espoused a policy of Israel submission to Arab demands.

When the Rabin-Peres government's negotiations with the PLO first became known to the Presidents' Conference participants, most of them, stunned, found such a turn beyond belief, and a wave of opposition ensued. But then the Presidents' Conference was subjected to influence and attitude-reshaping from a combination of the White House and government instrumentalities in Washington, and governmental and party channels of Israel. It was hardly a secret that the whole peace-process business had been instigated in Washington. With President Clinton performing the "nice cop" role to the "tough cop" role previously played by then-President Bush, Israel's Prime Minister Rabin had been prevailed upon to adopt a course he had previously totally, and vocally, opposed. Now, in turn, the Conference of Presidents of Major American Jewish Organizations was being turned around.

Resistance to the turnaround was not confined to the Orthodox participants—the presidents of not only the UOJCA, but also the Religious Zionists of America, National Council of Young Israel, and Poale Agudath Israel—but included, prominently, the president of the Zionist Organization of America. The rest of the members were made to fall into line.

Prior to Dr. Ganchrow's assumption of the UOJCA presidency, the equivocation as to the "peace process" issue within the Union's administration circle had been manifested also in its positions on the matter at the Presidents' Conference exchanges. Thereafter, however, there developed a clear-cut stand. While still bearing traces of the prior attitude, the policy now voiced on the disputed matter was more consistent with the historical Orthodox Union stand on Israel's rights and more forthrightly attuned to the Union's constituency leadership role.

The policy now manifested was arrived at in the way that had become more or less customary through the past several administrations: namely, by internal administration consideration. The necessity for deliberation and decision by the Union's Board of Directors on a major new question had not been grasped as yet by the organization's current leadership. What had transpired was set forth in a letter to members of the Board dated (per civil year calendar only) August 29, 1995. Together with it was enclosed a copy of a letter sent to Yitzchak Rabin, Prime Minister of the State of Israel, on behalf of the Orthodox Union, with the signatures of the Union's president and executive vice president.

This writer has not been informed as to written or verbal communications from Board members or synagogue leaders indicative of opinions on the administration's action. It may be assumed that sentiment was largely in accord with what was set forth in the letter to Rabin, together with concern that the unfortunate aspects of the "peace process" and the procedures engaged in to subjugate opposition had not been publicly challenged by the Union before this. One Board member took occasion to set forth in the pages of a popular Jewish weekly journal a drastic criticism of the letter to Israel's Prime Minister as inexcusably late and inadequate.

~

There now occurred a tragic happening that placed the whole situation in a violently changed context: the assassination of Prime Minister Yitzchak Rabin. The evil deed was committed by a Jew who, it became immediately known, was a religiously observant student at Bar-Ilan University. This fact was immediately seized upon to impugn the Orthodox Jewish world at large as the source of militant opposition to the government's course, implying that therein lay responsibility for the crime.

Horrified by what had happened, and burdened by the wave of obloquy poured upon religious loyalism, the institutions of the Torah world were moved to impassioned public statements in denunciation of the assassination. Each voiced high tribute to the slain figure, expressing shock and grief at a crime so outrageous and so violative of all that Torah and its laws stand for.

Among these, the Orthodox Union was prompt to publish its own expression of pain, horror, and sorrow at what had occurred. Under stormy circumstances, the Ganchrow administration strained to find a footing in treacherous ground. In a November 28, 1995 letter to Board members, President Ganchrow had written that at the initial postassassination Presidents' Conference convening, "the anti-Orthodox attitude created a distinct danger to our community . . . the anti-Orthodox attitude was almost universal . . . the atmosphere, in the words of one of our colleagues, was simply threatening."

In the face of this situation, the UOJCA leader struggled to prevail on the Presidents' group to reverse the hostile note to be struck at a planned mass rally in tribute to the slain prime minister. Under Dr. Ganchrow's persuasive moves, the original plan to make the occasion an endorsement of the peace process was shelved and reprogrammed as a "unity rally" held at New York's Madison Square Garden. Besides participating in the unity rally, the Union, together with several other Orthodox organizations and institutions, held a *hazkarah* memorial gathering in tribute to Yitzchak Rabin on December 4, 1995, at Congregation Kehilath Jeshurun.

Nothing could have served so well to sustain the "peace process" and undermine the opposition as the killing of Prime Minister Rabin. From that point on, the Israeli public generally, previously unsure and divided, seems to have viewed the policy as an irrevocably accomplished fact. Unceasing murderous forays by terrorist Arab forces, however indicative of what to expect from an enemy entrenched within Israel's narrow borders, shook, but did not reverse, wishful sentiment.

Along with a sense of basic, though threatened, security, was a feeling among Israelis of material well-being. Israeli's economy was now flourishing as never before.

$$\sim$$

What had transpired, shaking the Jewish world, had ramifications far and wide throughout the greater world. Along with the President of the United States, the leaders of many other nations—including several Arab countries—journeyed to Israel to attend Rabin's funeral. Along with its sadness at what had occurred, Israel basked in the unwonted glow of international sympathy. This, of course, was short-lived, and soon events resumed their accustomed pattern. Part of that pattern was the unremitting pressure from diverse sources to wrest Jerusalem—or at least some part of it—out of Jewish hands.

Remarkably, this aim is shared unabashedly by institutions of both Islam and Christianity, and is forwarded by the chancelleries of nations west and nations east. It parallels, so many centuries later, the aim of Rome, executed by Vespasian and Titus of evil memory. Against this modern-day version of *Hierosalem est perdita* stands the spirit of Avaraham Avinu, ascending Mount Moriah with his son Yitzhak, and the voice of David Ha'Melech who, some three thousand years ago, freed the Holy City for its central place in the heritage and life of the House of Israel. Against today's would-be dividers of holy Jerusalem stand the steadfast ones who, like their long-ago predecessors, fight to perpetuate Jewish life in Jerusalem's sanctity and those who for all the centuries were bonded in prayer and spirit with this heart of the Jewish world. Jerusalem, the eternal fount of Jewish being, reborn capital of the Land reborn, regained in its completeness by Jewish valor, resounding now with Jewish vigor, with Jewish life—this Jerusalem to be sliced away? Never!

The stand of the Orthodox Union regarding Jerusalem was, and is, necessarily beyond question. All have stood as one for the integrity and inviolability of Jerusalem—all of it. The troubles besetting the Ganchrow administration served rather to reinforce than to weaken the plan previously made to convene an assemblage in the Holy City. The assemblage was to be within the frame of the "Jerusalem 3000" celebration, marking the original establishment, by King David, of Jerusalem as Israel's capital.

~

The event took place in Jerusalem, as planned, on 29 Teveth–7 Shevat 5756/January 21–28, 1996. The attendance of several hundred was invested throughout with the spirit of profound commitment to all that the Holy City signifies.

Both the Sephardi and the Ashkenazi Chief Rabbis of Israel were among the array of notable figures who addressed the convocation. Most sessions, and many of the special events, were held at the Jerusalem Plaza Hotel. The program provided occasion for delegate dialogue with political figures, including Prime Minister Shimon Peres and Likud Chairman Benjamin Netanyahu. Key Knesseth figures of all religious parties, and of most of the other parties, were available for discussion with delegates.

Among the special events were moving assemblies at the Western Wall. Besides the tours of sites of special interest in Jerusalem, a tour of "Yesha" areas provided vistas of settlements in Yehudah (Judah), Shomron (Samaria), and the Aza (Gaza) outposts. Subject expositions by selected speakers spurred discussions on current concerns and inspirational topics interspersed through the days of the program, and shiurim were conducted several times each day. Several receptions were tendered the conclave participants by Jerusalem hosts.

Beyond the rich rewards of the convention program, it was marked by a prevailing sense of the greater significance of the assemblage. There was vivid realization that, convening at a fateful moment in history, the Jerusalem 3000 convocation evidenced the unceasing vitality of the Jewish being, flowing from the timeless strength of destined purpose. In the beloved theme, "From out of Zion shall go forth Torah and the word of the Lord from Jerusalem," was to be seen the outlook of the Union of Orthodox Jewish Congregations of America.

~

The spiritual upsurge of the Jerusalem assemblage brought lasting momentum to Orthodox Union forces. At the present writing, and with every indication of continuity, the Ganchrow administration has made itself felt in all channels of the Union and its constituency. The president's intensive (virtually full-time) concentration on UOJCA and its objectives appears to have primed his fellow officers in their own areas of responsibility. The various commissions under their respective, much loved chairmen appear to have maintained, by and large, consistent effectiveness. Correspondingly, standards of enthusiasm and application are seen as marking the staff echelon.

Administration figures have found repeated occasion to voice praise for the way Rabbi Raphael Butler had distinguished himself as UOJCA executive vice president. Increasingly, his personality is seen as making a major impression on the atmosphere, as well as the practical implementation, of the Union's work. Now seen as bearing fruit are expectations that the qualities of creativity in leadership that "Rafi" had shown during his tenure as NCSY national director would be manifest in his present, larger role. Much promise is seen in new, innovative service undertakings, along with marks of the capacity for forwarding, and integrating, the Orthodox Union's program and operations as a whole.

The abilities and experience of Rabbi Pinchas Stolper are recognized as an invaluable resource to his successor in previous office and of high guidance to his other colleagues of all departments as well as of the NCSY staff. With NCSY again under the aegis of the figure who formed and led it to greatness, this force for Jewish rebirth is marking further achievement.

Very much a key figure in the organization's operations, though insufficiently known to the Orthodox Union world in general, is Elly Edelman, UOJCA administrative director. It is under this figure of quiet competence that the thousand-and-one activities at the national headquarters of the Torah community's central force mesh together, the clerical and operations staff function as a team, and the work gets done.

The array of departmental directors and professional personnel, too, are seen as marked by commitment, competence, and diligence. America's Orthodox Jewish community has reason to consider itself fortunate in having at its service so able and so highly purposed an array of men and women as those composing the directive and professional staff of the Union of Orthodox Jewish Congregations of America.

The caliber of the foregoing is credited as reflected in the entire clerical and operative staff. It is not to be wondered at that positions at the Orthodox Union are so ardently sought.

∿

Some of the recent developments at the UOJCA are illustrative of current progress trends.

In response to a call from Dr. Ganchrow, representatives of Orthodox Jewish communities in thirty countries participated in a conference in Jerusalem following the Union's convocation on the occasion of the Jerusalem 3000 celebration. A coordinating committee, to formulate an ongoing program and structure for the group, was chosen, with Dr. Ganchrow named as the chairman.

The Union's Youth Division is to develop an NCSY program in Israel, addressed to students in government public high schools. In response to an impromptu appeal made at the Melavah Malkah feature of the Union's Jerusalem 3000 conclave, $150,000 was raised for the purpose, to which was added another $150,000 contributed in memory of parents by Mr. and Mrs. Fred Ehrman.

Provision was made, under the Ganchrow administration, for Orthodox congregations "throughout the world" to affiliate with UOJCA. The first to join under this arrangement was the Young Israel of the Old City of Jerusalem, led by Rabbi Nachman Kahana. Thereafter followed the affiliation of a group of eighteen congregations in Efrat, under the leadership of Rabbi Shlomo Riskin.

Among innovations in outreach introduced by the present administration is the "Jerusalem Experience," a traveling museum. This graphic presentation, conceived by Rabbi Butler, is reported to have visited "several hundred communities, reaching tens of thousands of Jews with the message of the sanctity of Jerusalem." Another of Rabbi Butler's innovations currently is *Torah Insights*, an appealing leaflet-format weekly Torah message sent for reproduction to member congregations. It is edited by Rabbi Bertram Leff, with Rabbi Yisrael Epstein as co-editor.

The publication frequency of *Leadership Briefing* was increased in 1996 to eight issues per year. This informative news organ, which began publication on a quarterly basis during the Rudoff administration, reports UOJCA activities and developments on the synagogue and community scenes. In the recent period also, additions were made to the Union's film library and audiotape collection. These items have been much drawn upon by constituents since their introduction several years ago.

Professor Richard Stone, Chairman of the Institute for Public Affairs, has reported that the continuing growth of IPA work has warranted the addition to the staff of Nathan Diament as managing director. Diament is to serve also as IPA director for Domestic Affairs, while Betty Ehrenburg will concentrate on International Affairs. Also reported for IPA is a major increase to the Washington Internship program. "We sent 42 collegiates to Washington for 1996 summer internships. Students come from 18 different universities and colleges." It was further recorded that in 1995 the Orthodox Union received full membership as a nongovernment organization (NGO) in the United Nations, "facilitating further involvement in world affairs of Jewish concern."

Announcement was made by Herbert Berman, chairman of the Public Relations Commission, of the appointment of Stan Steinreich as director of Public Relations. With Mike Cohen continuing to serve as associate director, plus the requisite support personnel, the need for a broadly planned public relations program is now expected to be effectively served. It is also reported in this connection that "we are now heavily involved on the Internet and Web sites whereby each synagogue will have a Web page. This is in addition to all our Torah programs."

As reported by Kashruth Commission Chairman Shimon Kwestel, the Kashruth Division inaugurated in 1996 a six-week internship program, open to rabbinical students at all major yeshivoth, for instruction in the intricacies of Kashruth supervision. In addition to the two interns initially appointed, thirty-six other positions were filled from candidates for enrollment in another new program designated "Ask." In the Ask program, the participants spend one week in a kashruth preceptorship program based at UOJCA headquarters. Thirty other applicants are on a waiting list, it was reported. Graduates and senior students of every major yeshivah are among the accepted and awaiting applicants.

Professor Kwestel further reported that, by 1996, the Ⓤ program had grown to include 150,000 products made in three thousand plants in fifty-four countries around the world. Further staff reorganizations were made, with a "team approach" for specialized product or processing areas.

~

A mark of the response of the Union's constituency to the vigorous current thrust of the Torah community central force is the fiscal status. Budgeting growth, with staff enlargement and operating expenses at a height undreamed of at one time, has required a major increase of income. Thanks to effective new departures in fundraising operations, together with further advances in established channels, the needed amounts have been successfully raised. Key figure in this accomplishment has been Sheldon Fliegelman, UOJCA director of development. With the full effort of the president and officers, as well as Rabbis Stolper and Butler, the program directed by Fliegelman and his associate, Steven M. Karp, produced notable results.

Accrued indebtedness of $750,000 was fully retired by the Ganchrow administration by early 1996. With the vigilant control of the Finance Committee headed by UOJCA treasurer Avi Blumenfeld, a well-balanced budget is being maintained.

~

In this setting of broad progress, certain objectives are seen by some as requisites for fulfillment of the Orthodox Union concept awaiting focused attention.

One need seen is for the clear-cut, comprehensive integration of the Union's program. The relationship of department to department, of function to function, of activity to activity belongs, in this view, in a fully conceived framework of defined program, as distinguished from a loosely linked miscellany.

Seen, too, is need for the thoroughgoing reconstruction of the UOJCA structure: a basic formulation of the composition and processes of the Union of Orthodox Jewish Congregations of America as the common arm and representative instrument of its Torah-community constituency, the collectivity of congregations functioning in common purpose.

Both of the foregoing point to a third requisite: a definitive exposition of the governing philosophy of the Union—its principles, its purpose, its standards, and its goals and the means to their attainment.

~

The notable vitality and forward pitch of the centenary-nearing Orthodox Union is manifestly reverberating through congregations across the land and in all channels of the Union's Torah community constituency. Amid an accrual of problems of continuing massiveness, Torah Jewry is making strong advances. The pace of progress has accelerated rather than slowed in the current period. The part played in this continuing renaissance by the Union of Orthodox Jewish Congregations of America is, as it has been throughout, pivotal.

CONCLUSION

Thus, with Jerusalem's call resounding, we bring to a close this account of the course of an organization bearing a noble mission. The reader has been offered a panorama of the manifold experience of Orthodox Jewry in America, as seen through the career of its unifying force. The experience has spanned changing times; change in the pattern of human life and in the makeup of the world's nations; change, profound and encompassing, in the conditions of Jewish life and the circumstances of the Jewish people.

We have seen how, in grappling through decades with epochal change, the Orthodox Union has held forth the Torah way, has spoken for the Torah Jew, and has worked to shape means for living the truly Jewish life amid the exigencies of a stormy era. The record is one of ups and downs in addressing particular objectives, but, seen in full view, there appears a vista of a great work for Jewish needs and the Torah ramparts of the House of Israel. There is ample reason to anticipate a continuing deep change on the human scene, and a continuing shift in world affairs. There may be foreseen continuing challenge to what the Union of Orthodox Jewish Congregations of America stands for and works to forward. These endeavors in resolution of historic dilemmas will surely be vital to Jewish needs through the coming years, as in past years.

May this Union's further course add to the work begun by the pioneers of a century ago, under the inspired leadership of Henry Pereira Mendes. May the endeavors of the Union of Orthodox Jewish Congregations of America be ever sustained by Heavenly guidance, ever onward bound in fulfillment of its high task.

Index

About the Author

Saul Bernstein was born in England, came to the United States at the age of 13, and is self-educated. In 1946, he was appointed as Associate Executive Director of the Orthodox Union and as Editor of *Jewish Life*. In 1948 he was named Administrator of UOJCA, where he headed its general operations. He continued with this responsibility until his retirement in 1975. He has been deeply involved with the Union of Orthodox Jewish Congregations of America for almost 50 years. Mr. Bernstein is the author of *The Renaissance of the Torah Jew, Jew and World, The Agenda of Change*, and numerous magazine and encyclopedia articles.